PERSPECTIVES ON COGNITIVE SCIENCE

Theories, Experiments and Foundations

edited by

Peter Slezak
University of New South Wales

Terry Caelli
University of Melbourne

Richard Clark
Flinders University

ABLEX PUBLISHING CORPORATION
NORWOOD, NEW JERSEY

Printed in the United States of America

Library of Congress Cataloging-in-Publication Data

Perspectives on cognitive science : theories, experiments, and foundations /
    edited by Peter Slezak, Terry Caelli, Richard Clark.
        p.   cm.
    Papers originally presented at the inaugural meeting of the Australasian
Society for Cognitive Science, held in Nov. 1990 at the University of
New South Wales.
    Includes bibliographical references and index.
    ISBN: 1-56750-105-2 (cl.).—ISBN: 1-56750-121-4 (ppk.)
    1. Cognitive Science—Congresses.   2. Human information processing—
Congresses.   3. Cognition—Congresses.   I. Slezak, Peter, 1947- .
Caelli, Terry. III. Clark, Richard. IV. Australasian Society for
Cognitive Science.

BF311.P355 1994
153—dc20   94-36549
                                                               CIP

Ablex Publishing Corporation
355 Chestnut Street
Norwood, New Jersey 07648

Contents

TECHNIQUES & APPLICATIONS

FOUNDATIONS

Introduction

Peter Slezak, Terry Caelli and Richard Clark

The papers collected here are representative of the leading work being done in Australia and New Zealand under the banner of 'cognitive science', and the appearance of the volume marks a significant occasion in the development of the interdisciplinary field in this region. Although the present volume has more than parochial value in view of the character and quality of the research reported here, nevertheless, its regional provenance is not without some interest. The papers have been selected from among those which were originally presented at the inaugural meeting of the Australasian Society for Cognitive Science held at the University of New South Wales in November 1990. Coming exactly ten years after the establishment of such a society in the United States in 1980, this conference might be seen, in one sense, as the 'coming of age' of cognitive science in the Australian region. This occasion was the first self-conscious gathering of researchers under the banner of 'cognitive science' in Australia and, in this sense at least, it was a significant step in the direction of a genuine dialogue between scholars in different fields — in a halting pidgin tongue, if not yet in a true interdisciplinary creole. Following the pattern elsewhere, in Australia and New Zealand there are now centers and programs in cognitive science emerging at several universities, and it is hoped that this dialogue will continue to flourish through such centers and through conferences like the one at which these papers were presented.

Of course, these institutional developments come a full 30 years after the establishment of the Center for Cognitive Studies at Harvard in 1960 by G.A. Miller and J. Bruner, and there are grounds for suspecting that the revolutionary developments which swept the United States in the 1960s and 1970s were somewhat attenuated by the time they reached the Antipodes. To take only one significant example, the extraordinary phenomenon of the Chomskian Revolution with its dramatic scientific and institutional impacts has been little in evidence Down Under (see Newmeyer 1986, Gardner 1987). The slower emergence of a truly interdisciplinary cognitive science can perhaps be explained in this way, confirming the remarks of one American psychologist who writes "The extraordinary and traumatic impact of the publication of *Syntactic Structures* by Noam Chomsky in 1957 can hardly be appreciated by one who did not live through this upheaval" (Maclay, 1971, p. 163).

Among the motivations for the landmark initiative of Miller and Bruner was their conviction that "psychology as too complicated a field to leave to the psychologists" (Bruner, 1988). In the spirit of Bruner's quip, the inaugural Australasian conference and papers collected here reveal the extent to which the fields of philosophy, linguistics, computer science and neuroscience have appropriated the subject matter of psychology, even if the traditional compartmentalization largely persists at an institutional level.

These institutional matters are not uninteresting and are not irrelevant to the intellectual questions at the heart of cognitive science, since ideas do not emerge in a vacuum. Rather, as histories of the 'cognitive revolution' amply reveal (Baars, 1986; Gardner, 1987; Hirst, 1988; Partee, Peters, & Thomason, 1985; Newmeyer, 1986), the appropriate social milieu is an essential ingredient for the multi-disciplinary mixture to gel. In the United States, a primary goal among leading scholars has been the fostering of special administrative and bureaucratic arrangements which are most conducive to innovative research in this field (see Partee et al., 1985). In particular, Donald Norman's 10-year retrospective analysis of the American Cognitive Science Society is especially pertinent: Reflecting on the decade since the founding of the American Society, Norman (1989) laments the persistence of a disciplinary compartmentalization and asks why a new society is necessary if the old territorial habits survive.

> All is not well within the Cognitive Science community. Despite much outward activity, the substantive issues under study by the society differ little from the topics under study within the individual, traditional scientific disciplines. If this is so, why do we need yet another discipline, another society? (1989, p. 1)

Norman points to both scientific and institutional reasons for this state of affairs and his reproaches have particular morals for the emerging developments in the Australian region.

Conferences, in particular, have had a catalytic role in the history of cognitive science, with the Hixon Symposium in 1948 and the MIT Symposium on Information Theory in 1956 being universally recognized as crucial turning points. The testimonies of George Miller and Jerome Bruner, for example, affirm the important role of the MIT meeting for the developments which have become characteristic of the 'cognitive revolution' (Miller quoted in Gardner 1987, p. 29). It may be hoped that the Kensington conference of 1990 serves as a similarly auspicious beginning for future developments in this part of the world. Thus, we offer this volume not only as evidence of the excellence and the vigor of cognitive science research in Australia and New Zealand, but also as a symbol of the first self-conscious interdisciplinary convocation – and as a hope for further such cognitive science 'corroborees'.[1]

REFERENCES

Baars, Bernard, J. (1986). *The cognitive revolution in psychology.* New York: The Guilford Press.

Bruner, J. (1988). 'Founding the Center for Cognitive Studies' in W. Hirst, (Ed.), *The making of cognitive science,* Cambridge: Cambridge University Press.

Gardner, H. (1987). *The mind's new science: A history of the cognitive revolution,* New York: Basic Books.

Hirst, W. (Ed.), (1988). *The making of cognitive science,* Cambridge: Cambridge University Press.

Maclay, H. (1971). Overview in D.D. Steinberg and L.A. Jakobovits (Eds.), *Semantics: An Interdisciplinary Reader in Philosophy, Linguistics and Psychology,* Cambridge: Cambridge University Press, 157-182.

Newmeyer, F. (1986). *Linguistic theory in American (Second Edition),* New York: Academic Press.

Norman, D. (1989). Four (more) issues in cognitive science, *Eleventh annual conference of the Cognitive Science Society,* August, Ann Arbor.

Partee, B.H., Peters, S., Thomason, R. (1985). *Report of Workshop on Information and Representation,* Washington, D.C.: National Science Foundation.

---

[1] Australian Aboriginal term meaning: 1. a native assembly of sacred, festive, or warlike character. 2. any noisy gathering. (Webster's English Dictionary)

CHAPTER 1

Implicit Learning in a Cued Reaction Time Task

R.A. Boakes, S. Roodenrys, and B.W. Barnes

Department of Psychology,
University of Sydney

Our world is a highly structured one in which many of the countless events we perceive are related in some way or other. Learning about such relationships goes on throughout our lives. Some of these relationships are ones we reflect upon, talk about, and act upon. The general question addressed by this research is whether — and how — we learn about relationships which we do not reflect upon, which we cannot talk about, but which nonetheless influence how we act. Put another way, are there unconscious processes of learning, so that what we do is affected by relationships we have not noticed, and, if so, do we learn about them in a different way from ones we do notice?

Very many cognitive scientists — and a great many other people besides — would answer 'yes' to such questions without hesitation. Yet very few have attempted to study such implicit learning. As is discussed later, there is not complete agreement among psychologists that such learning takes place. Consequently, much of the research on the topic has been devoted to demonstrating that implicit learning can occur under controlled conditions. Even fewer studies have gone on to inquire what its properties might be, and how such learning might differ from *explicit* learning, that is, learning which involves the conscious perception of relationships which may or may not result from intentional pattern-seeking effort and may or may not be based on linguistically encoded information.

At least there is general agreement that sufficiently early in a child's development most learning must be implicit (Krascum, 1990). The prime example is, of course, the set of processes underlying first language acquisition (Higginbotham, 1990; Pinker, 1990). It is in the general domain of language that much of the research on implicit learning in adults has been carried out. Following interest in people's ability to learn artificial grammars which arose in the context of early Chomskian psycholinguistics in the 1960s, Reber has reported a series of studies over the past two decades which he has recently summarized in a major review (Reber, 1989). These appear to show that, when given a number of strings of letters that are well-formed according to an arbitrary finite-state grammar, subjects acquire tacit knowedge of the structure of this grammar. This knowledge enables them to classify new strings as being grammatical or ungrammatical, or to show strong positive transfer when learning a new set of strings which follow the same generative rules, even when they are unable to report what these rules are.

Reber has also made a major contribution to a second line of approach to this topic, one based on learning about the probabilities with which events are likely to occur. Such experimental tasks range from ones involving learning about the simple frequencies of different events to tasks involving sequences of items whose probabilities change in cyclic fashion or are related to the occurrence of other items. Subjects can make accurate predictions about the occurrence of items in a way that reflects some knowledge of the statistical properties of the sequences they have been shown, even though they are unable to report these properties. The details of such studies are not of present concern. What is important to note is that learning about the frequencies of a set of events may provide the best example of a simple form of implicit learning, whether it is based on some form of automatic counting process occurring at the time an event is encoded, as argued, for example, by Hasher and Zacks (1984), or at the time of retrieval, as argued most recently by Begg, Maxwell, Mitterer, and Harris (1986).

The past few years have seen a flurry of papers reporting a variety of other experimental approaches to the study of implicit learning, or the related topic of procedural knowledge. One recent example is a study by Willingham, Nissen, and Bullemer (1989). In their task, subjects were required to press one of four buttons whenever a light appeared immediately above it. The measure of performance here was reaction time. The subjects were not informed that in fact the order in which the lights came on was a fixed sequence of ten trials which was simply repeated. Learning was indicated by a steady decrease in reaction times which was considerably greater than the decrease shown by control subjects given a random sequence. When questioned at the end, the answers subjects gave ranged from ones indicating fully explicit knowledge of the trial structure to a failure to notice any sequential pattern at all. Nonetheless, even the latter subjects showed evidence of learning, although the increase in their speeds of responding was much less than that shown by fully explicit subjects.

These general concerns have been shared by a separate research tradition within psychology which has used a different language and a different methodology. From Pavlov onward, students of conditioning have occasionally turned from their dogs, rats, or pigeons to investigate human conditioning. Usually such research has been guided by the belief both that processes of learning displayed by nonhuman animals operate to some degree in people and that there are different levels of learning, with conditioning operating at a relatively primitive level (e.g., Razran, 1971). Particularly during the

1950s and 1960s such research became concerned with the question of whether conditioning can take place without awareness. Many experiments yielded results which seemingly confirmed the then rarely questioned belief that it can. In an intriguing reversal of the recent trend within cognitive psychology, ever since a highly critical review of this research literature by Brewer in 1974 there has been increasing skepticism as to the existence of any good data indicating conditioning in the absence of conscious perception of the contingency between some stimulus or response and the reinforcing event that follows.

The most consistent body of experimental work to promote such skepticism has been that reported by Dawson and his colleagues (e.g. Dawson & Schell, 1987). In the typical paradigm he has used subjects who listen to a series of tones of different pitch and occasionally receive an electric shock. At the start of such an experiment, instructions are given to obscure its purpose. In fact, a shock is always preceded by, say, the highest tone. Conditioning is said to occur when the skin conductance response to this tone exceeds that to a control tone. Dawson and his colleagues have routinely found that no sign of conditioning is displayed by subjects who are unable to report the relationship between the high tone and the shock. It is important here to note that when such conscious perception does occur, it may easily be missed if questioning of the subjects about what they noticed during the experiment is careless or delayed. Such a result has been found by others who have used this approach. At the University of New South Wales a similar experimental procedure is used by Lovibond without the elaborate masking conditions that Dawson employs. Nevertheless, a good proportion of Lovibond's subjects fail to notice the simple relationship between one of a small set of stimuli and the shock which it always precedes (Lovibond, 1992). And such subjects fail to show any conditioning as measured by changes in their skin conductance response.

Such findings have served to increase the force of the two most general criticisms made of the earlier research by Brewer (1974). The first was that failure to detect awareness in subjects was not the same as showing that they were completely unaware of any of the relevant conditions of the experiment; as it appears happened in many of the early studies, casual questioning may well produce such a failure. The second was the point that is usually termed the problem of *correlated hypotheses*. In all but the simplest of tasks, subjects may well consciously perceive some aspect of the critical relationship or develop a hypothesis which, although incorrect, may well generate performance above chance level. Exactly these kinds of criticisms have been directed at the recent claims by cognitive psychologists to have demonstrated implicit learning. Thus, Peruchet and Pacteau (1990) have reported a replication of some of Reber's experiment on artificial grammar learning, in which they find that performance can be accounted for in terms of fragmentary explicit knowledge. Instead of learning the rules of such grammars, it seems that subjects in this kind of experiment acquire conscious knowledge of what bigrams — particular pairings of letters — are likely to occur in grammatical strings. Furthermore, in the reaction-time procedure used by Willingham et al. (1989), which was briefly described earlier, the increases in response speed shown by their subjects who did not notice the repeated 10-trial pattern may well have been based on noticing that the two central lights came on 50% more often than the two peripheral lights.

In a recent paper on implicit learning (Lewicki & Hill, 1989, p. 239) the complaint was made that, while unconscious learning should be treated as a bedrock of cognitive psychology, it is generally regarded at best as an "intriguing but peculiar property of human information processing, along with subliminal perception and hypnosis". It is our belief that this attitude is unlikely to change until a method is developed for studying implicit learning which is free of the problems we have briefly sketched. There is an additional consideration which is also important. The relationships which subjects have an opportunity to learn about in recent research are ones which are difficult to analyze and are unrelated to any theory of learning. Consequently in attempting to develop a suitable method for studying implicit learning, we chose to look at the formation of an association between two successive events. This has the potential for testing the applicability of the various theories of associative learning that have been developed over the past two decades on the basis of conditioning studies using animal subjects. Furthermore, there are now promising developments along the route of translating these noncomputational theories into network models (e.g., Kehoe, 1988).

In summary, the requirements of a satisfactory method for studying a particular kind of implicit learning are as follows:

1. The knowledge to be acquired should be simple, so as to exclude the possibility of improved performance based on correlated hypotheses or fragmentary knowledge involving explicit learning;
2. Items within the task should occur with equal frequency, so as to exclude the possibility of improved performance based on probability learning;
3. The measure of learning employed, and subsequent questioning, should be as immediate as possible, so as to exclude the possibility that explicit learning takes place, but is later poorly recalled and thus may come to appear to be implicit;
4. The incidence of aware subjects should be low, so that the study of learning without awareness is not confined to a low proportion of the subject population who may be aberrant in other ways, for example, unusually tired, hung over, or disinterested;
5. What is learned should be theoretically tractable, so that the processes by which subjects learn the task can be analyzed.

GENERAL PROCEDURES

With these considerations in mind, for the past few months we have been developing a reaction-time task (cf. Delamater, 1989; Dawson, Harper, & Dickinson, 1989) which takes advantage of the fact that reaction times to a signal are faster when some cue is provided that the signal is about to occur (Klemmer, 1956; Posner & Boies, 1971). Normally in such experiments, subjects are told at the outset that there is such a warning signal and what it is. In contrast, we wished to study how subjects might learn about such a warning signal, or cue, and its relationship to the target stimulus to which they reacted. It seemed possible that, under certain conditions, such cued reactions might become faster even when subjects were unaware of the relationship between cue and target. Since this relationship is a simple one, there is no question of any such effect being based on fragmentary knowledge or correlated hypotheses.

In the current version of the task, subjects watch a screen on which letters appear one at a time. Two of these letters are designated as targets: All subjects are instructed to press the left button whenever *L* appears and the right button whenever *R* appears. For half the subjects, *L* is preceded by a cue letter, while *R* remains uncued; for the remaining subjects this arrangement is reversed. Thus, a within-subject measure of learning is available, the difference between cued and uncued reaction times, which is relatively independent of the possible effect of general factors affecting reaction times, such as practice and fatigue. In addition to the single cue and the two target letters, there are a number of distractor letters. The subjects simply watch a continuous stream of letters in which an *L* or *R* sometimes occurs, whereupon they press the appropriate button. From the experimenters' point of view, this stream is made up of a series of trials, each ending with a target. Within a designated block of trials there are equal numbers of cued and uncued trials, and the overall frequency of the nontarget letters is equated.

A diagram showing the temporal characteristics of a trial is shown in Figure 1.1. As can be seen, all items appear on the screen for 0.5 sec and are followed by an interitem interval of 1.0 sec, except for a target letter, which is followed by a 1.5 sec interval. A response occurring before the onset of a target is classed as an anticipatory error. Another kind of error is pressing the wrong button. The final kind of error is one of omission: failing to respond within the 2.0-sec period following the onset of a target. As noted below, in some of the conditions subjects received feedback. For example, in Experiment 1 a correct response, that is pressing the appropriate button within the 2.0-sec interval, was followed by a 0.5-sec colored pattern filling the screen, while any form of error caused the screen to go blank for 0.5 sec with the word 'error' appearing in the center.

Subjects were tested within a single session. Immediately after they had completed the fixed number of trials, they were asked to complete a

CUED REACTION TIME TASK
e.g., J cues "Left"

Cued Trial: ... V D M J L
Uncued Trial: ... S D A R

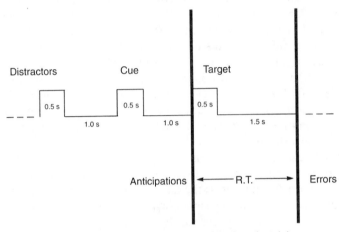

Figure 1.1. The temporal characteristics of a trial

questionnaire as accurately as possible. The first question was simply to establish whether they were right- or left-handed; the data from left-handed subjects have been completely excluded from our analysis so far. The next questions were designed to encourage a *report* of any relationship between the letters which they had noticed. Question 2 simply requested a comment on whether they felt at any time that they "had a better idea of when either of the target letters were about to appear." Question 3 was a little more directed: It asked whether they thought "that there was a relationship between any nontarget letter and when either of the target letters appeared" and, if so, to describe the relationship. Question 4 provided a *recognition* test in the form of two lists of all the nontarget letters and a request that subjects circle the letter they thought to have occurred most often before the *L* and, separately, to circle the letter they thought to have occurred most frequently before the *R*. (The order of these subquestions was randomized.) This fourth question also asked them to indicate their confidence about each of these two judgments using a visual analog scale: They marked what seemed to them the appropriate points on lines whose ends were labeled 'Very uncertain' and 'Certain.'

In the two experiments reported here, a low criterion was used for classifying a subject as having become 'aware' of the contingency between cue and target: either an answer to Questions 2 or 3 that reported the relationship, or in the recognition test of Question 4 identifying the letter that served as the cue, with an indication of some degree of certainty.

The instructions given to subjects were of an *incidental* kind. In other words, there was no indication that either of the targets was predictable. At the start subjects were simply told that it was an experiment on reaction times and asked to respond appropriately to *L* and *R*. Prior to the main part of the experiment, they received a block of training trials to get them used to the procedure. This allowed us to screen out subjects whose error rates were abnormally high. The criterion was that subjects had to complete a block of 30 training trials making fewer than two errors in the last 15 trials before proceeding to the main part of the experiment. If they failed to meet this criterion, the block of training trials was repeated. After three repeats without reaching this criterion, a subject was excluded. In fact, no subject was excluded on these grounds in Experiment 1 and only one subject was excluded in Experiment 2.

Three main aspects of the results are considered here: the proportion of subjects becoming aware; the difference in performance between these and nonaware subjects; and evidence for learning in the latter subjects. As detailed below, a large number of subjects were classified as aware in Experiment 1 and a much smaller proportion in Experiment 2. In both cases such subjects came to respond far more rapidly to the cued target than to the uncued target, and by the end of the session this difference was far greater than that shown by the nonaware subjects. Nonetheless, although for the latter the cued-uncued difference was much smaller in magnitude, it was consistent and thus provided evidence for implicit learning.

Experiment 1: J and Contingency

This experiment used *J* as the cue, so that for half the subjects this letter preceded *L* and for the other half it preceded *R*. Two contingencies were used: 100%, meaning that *J* was always followed by the target and the latter was never preceded by any other letter; and 67%, meaning that of the 12 trials containing the cued target in each block of 24, in only eight did *J* precede the target. Thus, a 2 x 2 design was used and the subjects, who were all students enrolled in a first-year psychology course, were arbitrarily allocated to one of the four conditions. Since our main interest was in nonaware subjects and since, as seen below, in some of the conditions there was a high proportion of aware subjects, we continued to assign subjects to conditions until a there were at least five unaware subjects per condition. This resulted in the assignment (discounting left-handers) of 23 subjects to the *J-L* 100% condition (5 unaware); 13 to the *J-L* 67% condition (7 unaware); 7 to the *J-R* 100% condition (7 unaware); and 9 to the *J-R* 67% condition (7 unaware).

Subjects were tested individually. After reaching criterion on the practice procedure, they were given 120 trials, consisting of five blocks of 24 trials constructed as follows. A trial was defined as the series of letters from the first letter after a target up to and including the next target letter. The trials varied in length between three and seven letters. The distractor letters were *A, D, G, M, S, V* and *Z*. Each was presented with a frequency equal to that of the cue, *J,* and in random sequence, with the constraints that no repetition of a letter occurred within a trial and that, over an experimental session, the distractors preceded the noncued target with equal frequency.

Within each block half of the trials ended with the *L* target and the other half with the *R* target. In the 100% conditions one target was always preceded by the cue *J,* and the other target was never preceded by the cue. For the 67% conditions, 4 of the 12 cued-target trials within each block were reconstructed by exchanging *J* with a distractor letter, in one case with one from within the same trial and in the three other cases with distractors from trials containing the noncued target. The *J* never preceded the noncued target. In all cases the order of trials within a block was randomized for each subject.

EXPERIMENT 1: J and CONTINGENCY

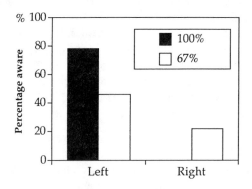

EXPERIMENT 2: V and FEEDBACK

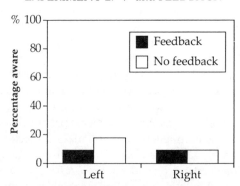

Figure 1.2. Top panel shows the percentage of subjects who were classified as aware in Experiment 1: J and contingency. Bottom panel shows the percentage of subjects who were classified as aware in Experiment 2: V and feedback.

The top panel of Figure 1.2 shows the percentage of subjects who were classified as aware at the end of the session. Only two of the subjects in the *J-R* conditions became aware, whereas a very high proportion of subjects in the *J-L* condition did so, particularly in the 100% condition (*chi sq* = 29.7; *p* <0.001). The differences in speeds of responding to cued and uncued targets between these two classes of subjects are shown in the top panel of Figure 1.3: This difference increased steadily in the aware subjects, but no such increase is apparent for the nonaware subjects on this scale.

Some explanation is needed at this point of the measures we have been using. In order to produce greater approximation to a normal distribution each individual reaction time is transformed into its reciprocal, giving a speed score (resp/sec). Within each 24-trial block the mean speed for cued trials and that for uncued trials is then calculated. To eliminate distortion by the occasional very slow reaction, separately for the 12-trial sets of cued and

EXPERIMENT 1: J and CONTINGENCY

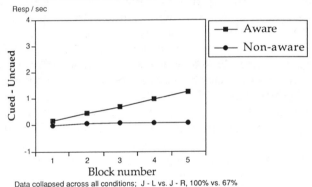

Data collapsed across all conditions; J - L vs. J - R, 100% vs. 67%

EXPERIMENT 2: V and FEEDBACK

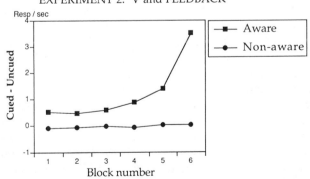

Collapsed across all conditions; V - L vs. V -R, Feedback vs. No feedback

Figure 1.3. The difference scores for aware and non-aware subjects in Experiment 1 (top panel) and Experiment 2 (bottom panel).

uncued trials within each block the slowest speed is dropped if it is more than three standard deviations below the mean for the set, whereupon the mean is recalculated. This trimming procedure results in the elimination of no more than 1% of the data. After this trimming has been carried out, a difference score for each 24-trial block is obtained by subtracting the mean uncued speed from the mean cued speed. The measure shown in Figure 1.3 is this difference score: Cued - Uncued. Since reaction time research traditionally deals in times rather than speed difference scores, some indication of their relationship might be helpful. A subject whose average reaction time to the uncued target was 0.5 sec and whose average time to the cued target was 0.33 sec, that is an RT difference of 170 msec, would have a difference score of 1.0 resp/sec. In the case where the cue allowed anticipatory responding to the extent that reaction time to the cued target was as low as 0.2 sec, then the speed difference score would be 3.0 resp/sec.

Since our main interest was in the question of whether unaware subjects showed any sign of learning, their data was examined in greater detail. The mean Diff scores for each of the four conditions are shown in the top panel of Figure 1.4, where some indication of an increase over successive blocks may be seen. The analysis of these data looked at two aspects: the consistency with which subjects showed an increase in Diff scores over blocks, and the magnitude of such a change. Consistency was measured by calculating the rank-order correlation for each subject between Diff scores and block number (Kendall's tau); a tau value between 0 and +1 indicated a tendency for the subject to respond more rapidly to cued than to noncued targets as the session progressed. The means for each condition of these correlational measures, transformed into z-scores, are shown in the top section of Figure 1.5. It may be seen that none are negative and that they are higher, and significantly above chance level, in the two *J-R* conditions. Thus, there was reliable evidence for learning in unaware subjects under these conditions. A comparison between the conditions using a 2 x 2 Anova failed to yield any significant difference. Since, however, the data shown here for the *J-L* conditions were obtained from the small proportion of subjects who failed to become aware and who, therefore, may have been generally poor performers, not much weight is to be attached to comparisons between conditions.

This note of caution also applies to the analysis carried out on the magnitude of the effect. This was measured in terms of improvement from first to final 24-trial block by subtracting the Diff score (cued speed - uncued speed) for the first block from the Diff score for the final block. The means for each of the four conditions are shown in the top half of Figure 1.6. The scores for the *J-R* conditions tend again to be higher, but no significant differences between the conditions were found. It can be seen that these scores are around 0.1 resp/sec, which corresponds approximately to the score that would be obtained by a subject who showed a reaction time to noncued targets of 0.5 sec and a reaction time to cued targets 25 msec less.

EXPERIMENT 1: J and CONTINGENCY

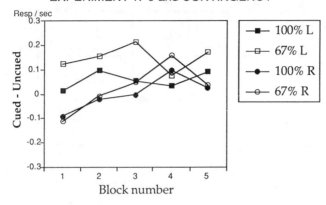

EXPERIMENT 2: V and FEEDBACK

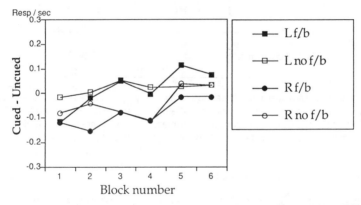

Figure 1.4. The difference scores for non-aware subjects in each condition for Experiment 1: hand by contingency (top panel) and Experiment 2: Hand by feedback (bottom panel).

In summary, the main findings to emerge from this experiment were:

1. that small variations in procedure — in this case whether *J* cued *L* or cued *R* — can produce large variations in the proportion of subjects who become aware of the contingency;

2. that the task is one in which implicit learning can be detected in that the speed of reacting to a cued target was greater than that to the uncued target even in subjects who were unaware, in terms of a stringent criterion, of the cue-target relationship; and

3. that, although consistent, the learning-based change in performance shown by unaware subjects was small in magnitude, particularly in comparison to that shown by aware subjects.

Exp 1: J and Contingency

	J - L	J - R
100%	+0.0	+1.12*
67%	+0.07	+0.70*

Exp 2: V and Feedback

	V - L	V - R
Feedback	+0.64	+0.71*
No feedback	+0.23	+0.53*

Figure 1.5. Consistency of implicit learning as measured by the z transformation of Kendall's Tau. The asterisk indicates significance at the 0.05 level using a one-tailed test. The top panel shows the scores for conditions in Experiment 1: hand by contingency, and the bottom panel shows the scores for the conditions in Experiment 2: hand by feedback.

Experiment 2: V and Feedback

The large proportion of subjects who noticed the *J-L* relationship suggested that the choice of *J* as cue had been an unfortunate one. Some subjects, for example, commented on their visual similarity, one being close to the mirror image of the other. Another possibility was that their relative positions in the alphabet might enable preexisting successive associations to play a role. Consequently, there was clearly a need to find out what might happen when another letter was employed as the cue; *V* was the letter chosen for this experiment. We also wished to test that implicit learning could also be obtained under more relaxed conditions than the one-to-one testing carried out in a small laboratory for Experiment 1. In Experiment 2, subjects were tested in groups of three to eight at a time in the undergraduate computer teaching laboratory in the psychology department at Sydney University. Although each subject worked at his or her own microcomputer (Apple Macintosh Plus), there was no form of visual or acoustic isolation of subjects.

The final factor of interest was the provision of immediate feedback for correct and incorrect responses, as had been included in Experiment 1.

There were a number of theoretical reasons for believing that this might be important. Thus, a 2 x 2 design was employed, with half the subjects given *L* as the cued target and half given *R*. Within these groups half were given feedback of a similar kind to that in Experiment 1. Four stars appeared toward the four corners of the screen whenever a response was made to a target within the critical time period. Whenever an error was made — either a response outside this period or a failure to respond within it — the screen went blank for 0.5 sec, except for the message "Error" in the center. The remaining subjects did not receive any form of feedback.

Further differences between this and the previous experiment were very minor. They consisted of an increase from 30 to 32 in the number of trials in the practice block, an increase from 120 to 144 in the total number of trials in the main part of the experiment (i.e., from five to six 24-trial blocks), and a reduction from 2.0 to 1.5 sec in the time from onset of a target in which a correct response could be made. In all four conditions a 100% contingency was used: The cue was always followed by one of the two targets and this target never occurred in the absence of the cue. The four groups were designated: *V-Lf* (*V* as cue for *L* and with feedback); *V-Lnf* (the same, but without feedback); *V-Rf;* and *V-Rnf*. The subjects were again students from a first-year psychology course. They were allocated arbitrarily to the four conditions until there were 10 subjects in each who were nonaware by the same criteria as in Experiment 1. This required a total of 58 subjects, not including left-handers, of whom 17 were classified as aware and one failed to meet the initial practice criterion by consistently making too many errors.

The percentage of aware subjects in each condition is shown in the bottom half of Figure 1.2. It may be seen that overall there were far fewer subjects in this category than in Experiment 1 and that there was no indication of any difference between the conditions in this respect. The Diff scores for the two categories of subjects are compared in the lower part of Figure 1.3. As in Experiment 1, aware subjects produced greater differences between speeds of responding to cued and uncued targets, while on the scale used in this figure nonaware subjects showed little sign of learning. Nonetheless, when examined in more detail, as shown in the lower part of Figure 1.4, some indication of learning may be seen.

The analysis carried out on the data from the ten nonaware subjects in each condition took the same form as in Experiment 1. The measure of consistency, the z-transform of Kendall's tau, is shown in the lower part of Figure 1.5. All four means are greater than zero and in the two *V-R* conditions they are significantly so. A two-way anova on this measure failed to reveal any main effect or interaction ($F < 1$). The magnitude of the effects in the four conditions is shown in the lower part of Figure 1.6. Although this suggests that the effect was greater for the *V-L* condition with feedback, a two-way anova on this second measure also failed to detect any significant main effect or interaction ($F < 1$).

Exp 1: J and Contingency

	J - L	J - R
100%	0.08	0.12
67%	0.05	0.15

Exp 2: V and Feedback

	V - L	V - R
Feedback	0.19	0.11
No feedback	0.05	0.11

Figure 1.6. Magnitude of implicit learning as measured by the difference score: Final block (cued - uncued) minus initial block (cued - uncued). The asterisk indicates significance at the 0.05 level using a one-tailed test. The top panel shows the scores for conditions in Experiment 1: hand by contingency, and the bottom panel shows the scores for the conditions in Experiment 2: hand by feedback.

To summarize the findings from this second experiment, consistent implicit learning was once again found and was again of small magnitude. There was no indication that either the provision of feedback or the choice of L or R as the target influenced the proportion of subjects who became aware or the degree of implicit learning shown by those who did not.

Experiment 3: *J* vs *V* as cue

The previous experiment met our expectation that, when the cue was changed from *J*, fewer subjects would become aware of the cue-target relationship than in Experiment 1. However, this change was confounded with other changes that accompanied the switch from the individual testing conditions used in Experiment 1 to the group testing used in Experiment 2. In case some of these changes were more important than they appeared — for example, subjects may be less motivated to perform well when being tested in a group — we needed to confirm that the particular cue used was the crucial factor. Experiment 3 again used a 2 x 2 design, in which the main factor was *J* vs.

V as the cue letter and the other was the standard counterbalancing for target, vs. *R*. The four conditions were designated: *J-L, J-R, V-L,* and *V-R.* The procedure was identical to that used in Experiment 2. Of the total of 58 subjects run in the experiment, two were excluded as they failed to reach criterion performance in two practice sessions and a further eight were excluded as they made more than seven errors. In this experiment, anticipatory responses, that is, responses made prior to the onset of the appropriate target, were not counted as errors as this may have excluded some of the aware subjects. The results were based on data from the remaining 12 subjects per group. The criterion for awareness was either an answer that correctly reported the relationship to the two 'recall' questions at the beginning of the postexperiment questionnaire or a correct identification of the cue in the following 'recognition' question, which was combined with some degree of certainty higher than that for the arbitrary forced choice concerning the uncued target.

There were large and significant differences in the proportion of subjects classified as aware in the four conditions, *chi sq* = 29.8, *p* < 0.001: with 75% in the *J-L* condition compared to only 8.3% in the *J-R* condition, and exactly a third of the subjects in each of the two conditions with *V* as cue. As for the reaction-time data learning, as measured by tau, was found only in aware subjects. In none of the groups did the unaware subjects show significant evidence for learning (*p* > .1). When effect size was analyzed, no difference between the groups was found for unaware subjects, while for aware subjects the effect was greater where *J* served as the cue.

In an attempt to find out whether aware subjects were able to report the factor that had enabled them to spot the cue-target relationship, a supplementary questionnaire was given to these subjects. On the basis of casual comments made by subjects in previous experiments, we asked whether the visual similarity between cue and target, their alphabetic sequence or "familiarity on the basis of past experience" had been of any importance. The answers were not enlightening. Three out of nine subjects in the *J-L* condition chose visual similarity, which added some support to our prior suspicion that the near mirror-image relationship of these two letters played some part. Although with hindsight such supplementary questioning could have been improved, these results suggested that subjects' reports are unlikely to provide insight into how they came to perceive the relationship.

In summary, the positive outcome from Experiment 3 was the demonstration that a particular choice of letter combinations can have a major effect on how subjects perform in this task, and the indication that the use of *V* generates an appropriately low incidence of aware subjects with no response bias. The disappointing aspect of Experiment 3 was that it failed to replicate the finding from Experiments 1 and 2 of significant learning in unaware subjects.

CONCLUDING REMARKS

The results we have reported here are encouraging, but very much of a preliminary nature. In the introductory discussion, we argued that a satisfactory method for studying implicit learning needs to meet the following requirements: a simple 'piece' of knowledge; exclusion of the possibility of probability learning; an immediate measure of learning; a low incidence of aware subjects; and theoretical tractability. The present task meets these requirements. What is needed now is to find out what combination of parameters will produce effects that are large and robust enough to allow us to explore the properties of this kind of learning.

At present we are optimistic about this. Nonetheless we have to face the possibility that implicit learning under such controlled conditions will remain barely detectable and, as such, remain a minor curiosity. What could one make of this outcome, in the face of the common belief that such learning is pervasive in everyday life? And in the face of the developmental case that early in childhood all learning is implicit? The skeptics, both in the learning tradition and among cognitive psychologists, have said little about this. One possibility is that, that although real, it is one of those phenomena that immediately crumbles in the face of controlled experimental scrutiny. Another is that present approaches have lacked some essential ingredient. Perhaps most interesting is the possibility that at some stage of human development essentially all learning of this kind has to become explicit; and our belief that this is not so are mistakenly based on the fact that we are amnesic for many of the brief conscious perceptions that enabled us to learn about the structure of our world.

As a final note, here is a quote from a recent subject who was classified as aware since, although unable to report the contingency in answer to the second and third questions on the questionnaire, when given the recognition test in the fourth question she chose the correct cue with great confidence. When asked why she had chosen that particular letter, her reply was "intuition."

REFERENCES

Begg, I., Maxwell, D., Mitterer, J.O., & Harris, G. (1986). Estimates of frequency: Attribute or attribution. *Journal of Experimental Psychology: Learning, Memory and Cognition, 12*, 496-508.

Brewer, W.F. (1974). There is no convincing evidence for conditioning in adult humans. In W.B. Weimer & D.S. Palermo (Eds.), *Cognition and the symbolic processes* (pp. 1-42). New York: Halsted.

Dawson, G., Harper, S.A., & Dickinson, A. (1989). *Associative processes in human performance: Conditioned inhibition.* Unpublished manuscript.

Dawson, M.E., & Schell, A.M. (1987). Human autonomic and skeletal classical conditioning: The role of conscious cognitive factors. In G. Davey (Ed.), *Cognitive processes and Pavlovian conditioning in humans* (pp.27-56). Chichester, UK: John Wiley & Sons.

Delamater, A.R. (1989). *Human Pavlovian conditioning: Associative influences on the speed of perceptual processing.* Unpublished doctoral dissertation, Dalhousie University, Halifax, Nova Scotia, Canada.

Hasher, L., & Zacks, R.T. (1984). Automatic processing of fundamental information: The case of frequency of occurrence. *American Psychologist, 39,* 1372-1388.

Higginbotham, J. (1990). Philosophical issues in the study of language. In D.N. Osherson & H. Lasnik (Eds.), *Language: An invitation to cognitive science, Vol.1.* Cambridge, MA: MIT Press.

Kehoe, E.J. (1988). A layered network model of associative learning: Learning to learn and configuration. *Psychological Review, 95,* 411-433.

Klemmer, E.T. (1956). Time uncertainty in simple reaction time. *Journal of Experimental Psychology, 95,* 179-184.

Krascum, R. (1990). *Representations and processes underlying categorisation in young children.* Unpublished doctoral dissertation, University of New South Wales, Kensington, NSW.

Lewicki, P., & Hill, T. (1989). On the status of nonconscious processes in human cognition: Comment on Reber. *Journal of Experimental Psychology: General, 118,* 239-241.

Lovibond, P.F. (1992). Tonic and phasic electrodermal measures of human aversive conditioning with long duration stimuli. *Psychophysiology, 29,* 621-632.

Perruchet, P., & Pacteau, C. (1990). Synthetic grammar learning: Implicit rule abstraction or explicit fragmentary knowledge? *Journal of Experimental Psychology: General, 119,* 264-275.

Pinker, S. (1990). Language acquisition. In D.N. Osherson & H. Lasnik (Eds.), *Language: An invitation to cognitive science, Vol.1.* Cambridge, MA: MIT Press.

Posner, M.I., & Boies, S.J. (1971). Components of attention. *Psychological Review, 78,* 391-408.

Razran, G. (1971). *Mind in evolution.* New York: Houghton Mifflin.

Reber, A.S. (1989). Implicit learning and tacit knowledge. *Journal of Experimental Psychology: General, 118,* 219-235.

Willingham, D.B., Nissen, M.I., & Bullemer, P. (1989). On the development of procedural knowledge. *Journal of Experimental Psychology: Learning, Memory and Cognition, 15,* 1047-1060.

CHAPTER 2

A Self-Modifying Production
System Model of Inference Strategies*

G.S. Halford, M.T. Maybery, S.B. Smith,
J.C. Dickson, and J.E.M. Stewart.

Department of Psychology
University of Queensland

Transitive inference (more generally, N-term series) problems consist of premises, each of which expresses a relation between a pair of terms, such as *aRb, bRc, cRd* and so on. The participant is expected to state the rank order of one or more terms. For example, given a set of premises such as "Tom is taller than Bill", and "Don is taller than Tom", the participant might be asked to say who is tallest, to say whether Don is taller than Bill, or to rank order all elements. Transitive inference tasks contain many of the basic features of reasoning processes: Prose comprehension is entailed in interpreting premises, then the information so obtained has to be mentally transformed and integrated. Consequently, transitivity has been the subject of much research in both the adult and child cognition literature. This chapter proposes a model of the way transitive inference strategies develop.

There are two contemporary models of N-term series reasoning that provide the starting point for our research. The first model (Sternberg, 1980) incorporates the main features of earlier models, and accounts for a high proportion of the variance in solution times. The essence of it is that premises are first processed to obtain the linguistic deep structural base strings that represent their meaning. These strings are then recoded as images of ordered pairs, such as (Tom, Bill), (Don, Tom). The pivot or common term (Tom) is then located, and the pairs are integrated into an ordered triple (Don, Tom, Bill). Sternberg's model can only produce solutions for three-term problems.

The second model (Foos, Smith, Sabol, & Mynatt, 1976) postulates that the ordered set of elements is progressively constructed in short term memory (STM). The first premise is stored in STM, then there is a set of constructive operators that can be used to combine later premises with those already stored. The Foos et al. model applies to problems with more than three terms.

---

* This work was supported by a grant from the Australian Research Grants Scheme.

The present model builds on earlier models, but there are several reasons why further theoretical work is necessary. One reason is that existing models deal only with relations between elements that are adjacent in the correct ordering, such as $a > b$, $b > c$, and so on. They do not deal with nonadjacent relations, such as $a > c$. This is necessary, however, for an ecologically valid model, because real-life ordering tasks entail nonadjacent relations. If we are rank ordering students with respect to grades, they do not come conveniently presorted into adjacent pairs. If we know Susie is better than Tom, it does not follow that Susie and Tom are adjacent. There might be someone else, Bill, who is better than Tom but poorer than Susie. N-term series models must be able to handle nonadjacent relations.

Both the Foos et al. and Sternberg models posit a single strategy, but there are several reasons for believing multistrategy models might be necessary. First, multiple strategies are used in a number of simple tasks (Greeno & Johnson, 1985; Greeno, Riley & Gelman, 1984; Siegler & Shrager, 1984). For example Greeno, Riley, and Gelman (1984) showed that even preschool children do not use a single strategy to count small sets, but used their understanding of counting to devise strategies for each task. Second, there is evidence for multiple strategies in some transitive inference and ordering tasks (Baylor & Gascon, 1974; Quinton & Fellows, 1975). Third, evidence from some of our experiments (Maybery, Halford, Bain & Kelly, 1988) is more consistent with a multistrategy model.

Perhaps the most important motivation for the present model is that we need to explain how strategies originate. Strategies themselves are not the explanation for cognitive processes, but themselves require to be explained, as Van Lehn and Brown (1980) have pointed out. The explanation for strategies forms an important part of our understanding of how thought develops.

THE DEVELOPMENT OF TRANSIVITY

In order to develop a multistrategy model, mechanisms for construction and selection of strategies are required. The planning net conception of Van Lehn and Brown (1980) has been used as the basis for the strategy development mechanism. Planning nets are directed graphs, in which the nodes represent plans for problem solving, and the links represent solution inferences. They search for a strategy that is consistent with task demands and the concept of the task. They have been used by Greeno et al. (1984) to model the development of counting strategies in children. In the Greeno et al. model the task concept (counting) was based on universally valid logical principles. In the present model the need for universal, abstract principles is avoided by using analogical mapping from concrete experiences that instantiate the relevant concept, the concept of order.

In the current model, when a transitive inference problem is presented, an attempt is made to retrieve an appropriate strategy. If no suitable strategy is available, a procedure for constructing a strategy is invoked. For any given set of task demands, an attempt is made to construct a strategy that is consistent with the way the task is understood.

Because transitive inference tasks are basically ordering tasks, understanding of the task is defined in terms of a concept of order. Some of the features that a psychologically realistic concept of order might be expected to contain are:

- understanding of one or more asymmetric binary relations (e.g., larger than, better than)
- each element occurs once and only once in a string
- end elements have the same relation to all other elements; for example, $a > b, a > c, a > d$ and so on
- the position of internal elements is defined by relations to elements on both sides of it; for example $b < a, b > c$
- the same relation must exist between all pairs, both adjacent and nonadjacent; for example, $a > b, b > c, .. a > c,$ and so on

The final feature really includes the transitivity property of ordered sets, but is wider because it includes the idea that one relation must be used consistently throughout the set; for example, you cannot order some elements according to height and some according to weight.

The representation of the concept of order could take many forms. Any ordered set of at least three elements can instantiate all five features of the concept of order. A psychologically realistic representation that could serve as a criterion for participants' own constructions would be a prototypical ordered set of at least three elements, acquired through play experiences such as sorting and stacking objects varying in size.

We postulate that the concept of order develops out of play experiences with ordered sets of objects. Suppose, for example, that a child has been given a set of blocks that vary in size. One type of play experience might entail making a "staircase" out of the blocks, by trial and error. A concept of order can be developed by progressively noticing the relevant relations in the ordered set. For example, the child might notice first that one block is bigger than all the rest, then that the second biggest block is smaller than the first one but larger than the third, and so on.

DEVELOPMENTAL SEQUENCE

We propose the following sequence of development in children. First, children learn to categorize objects with common features at approximately one year of age (Sugarman, 1982). They learn to encode and represent relations, at least by the age of 2 years 6 months (Bullock & Gelman, 1977; De Loache, 1987).

Primitive ordering strategies in which one premise is processed at a time are evident in 3-year-olds (Halford, 1984). For example, given the premises "Tom happier than John," "John happier than Bill," "Tom happier than Bill," the first step would be to produce "Tom John," then "Tom John Bill," then "Tom Bill John." The incorrect order "Tom Bill John" occurs because attention is paid only to the last premise, "Tom happier than Bill," ignoring the previous information that John is happier than Bill.

By about 5 years, children manage to integrate relations in a single decision. That is, they can reason that since $A > B$, $B > C$, and $A > C$, the correct order is ABC. This integration of two or more premises in a single decision imposes an information-processing load that exceeds the capacity of most children below 5 years (Halford, Maybery, & Bain, 1986). Development continues after age 5, but this point marks the beginning of effective ordering strategies.

This phase of our project is designed to model the transition from ineffective to effective ordering strategies. When feedback indicates an error, the confidence rating of the strategy is reduced. A new strategy will then be developed for subsequent problems.

The new strategy is developed under the dual constraints of task demands and the concept of order. The task demand is, given the premises such as "Tom is happier than John," "John is happier than Bill," to put Tom, John, and Bill in order of happiness. The concept of order is contained in previous experiences of ordered sets. The learning process entails using the concept of order to construct a strategy that conforms to task demands.

The problem is, of course, that the child has no strategy for producing the correct answer. The solution is to use the concept of order, based on previous experience with ordered sets, to generate the solution analogically. Once the solution is recognized, strategies for producing the solution are devised.

According to Gentner's (1983) theory, an analogy consists of a mapping from a base to a target. In this case, the concept of order is the base, and the correct order, "Tom, John, Bill," the target. The required mapping is shown in Figure 2.1.

Figure 2.1 shows how a known ordered set can be used to assess the correctness of the order "Tom, John, Bill." It is correct because it is the only order that would produce a valid structure mapping, where validity is defined by the criterion of consistency specified by Halford (1987). To see this, consider the incorrect order, "Tom, Bill, John," in Figure 2.2.

This produces an invalid, inconsistent mapping, because "larger than" corresponds to "happier than" on two occasions, and to "sadder than" on

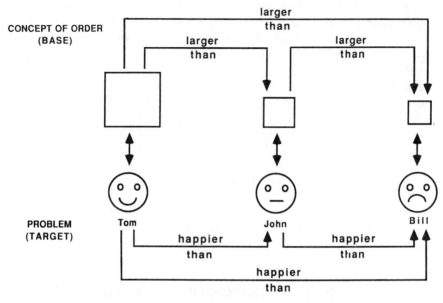

Figure 2.1. An ordered set of concrete objects used as an analog for the ordering required in a transitive inference task.

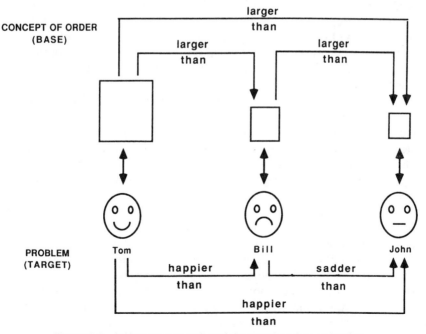

Figure 2.2. An incorrect mapping of the premises into an analog.

the third occasion. There is therefore no consistent mapping from concept of order to problem. The premise elements, Tom, Bill, John are not consistently ordered with respect to the "happier than" relation.

Analogical mapping from the concept of order to the current problem, as shown in Figure 2.1, provides a criterion for the correct answer to the problem. In effect, previously experienced ordered sets provide a kind of template for a task that entails putting new elements in order with respect to a new relation. This is important when we are considering the origin of reasoning strategies in young children. It may be self-evident to a sophisticated adult, with a vast array of problem-solving strategies at her disposal, that one order is correct and the other not. It is difficult therefore to envisage the problem of a child who has to develop these strategies. Analogy with previous, structurally similar situations can provide a useful guide for the construction of primitive strategies. The answer obtained by mapping the premises into an analogous situation is used to constrain development of a further strategy. A self-modifying production system has been developed to model this learning process. This model will be described in the next section.

IMPLEMENTATION OF THE MODEL

Our model of the transition from ineffective to effective ordering strategies is implemented in PRISM II, a production system language (Ohlsson & Langley, 1986). The production system consists of two memory types: procedural and declarative. Procedural memories consist of collections of condition-action rules called productions. The conditions of a production describe configurations of elements which may be in declarative memory. The actions of a production specify modifications to the content of procedural and declarative memories. Declarative memories consist of collections of symbolic data types. The two memory types interact through a simple recognition-act cycle. When the conditions of a production are met by elements in declarative memory, the actions of that production are carried out, that is, the production fires. If the conditions of more than one production are met on any processing cycle, the production with the greater strength will fire.

As stated earlier, strategy modification occurs under the dual constraints of task demands and the concept of order. Modification occurs when no existing strategies have a high enough confidence rating. In the production system, the confidence rating of a strategy is determined by the strength of the productions. Each production has a strength associated with it. The strength of a production is modified with feedback. So, if a strategy produces the correct answer, the strength of the productions that produced that answer will be increased; if a strategy produces the incorrect answer, the strength of the productions that produced that answer will be decreased.

When no production whose conditions are met by the contents of declarative memory has enough strength to fire, the system enters a modification phase. The modification process occurs in two steps. First, the premises are mapped to the concept of order. This mapping process returns a consistent order for the given premises. Second, given the result of the structure mapping process and the given premises, a production is built that will produce a result consistent with the order returned by the structure mapper. On subsequent problems of the same form, this new production will produce an answer without reference to the structure mapper. Through this process, effective strategies evolve.

Starting with a primitive strategy that pays attention to the most recent premise, we will illustrate how the system modifies itself to solve problems using an integration strategy. We will use the problem presented earlier in this example. The problem is, given the premises "Tom is happier than John," "John is happier than Bill," and "Tom is happier than Bill," to put Tom, John, and Bill in order of happiness. The example is given in a simplified form to focus on the major steps in the modification process. The productions presented are actually instantiations of productions for the specific problem. The actual productions use variables and will solve many different problems.

Figure 2.3 shows the productions that will fire when solving this problem using the primitive strategy.

```
(First__premise
  ((Tom happier than John))
  →
  ((add-to dm
    (Order (Tom John))]

(Add__premise__1
  ((John happier than Bill)
   (Order (Tom John)))
  →
  ((add-to dm
    (Order (Tom John Bill))]

(Add__premise__2
  ((Tom happier than Bill)
   (Order (Tom John Bill)))
  →
  ((add-to dm
    (Order (Tom Bill John))]
```

Figure 2.3. Productions fired for a sample problem.

When the first premise, "Tom is happier than John," is added to declarative memory, the production First_Premise will fire. This production has one condition and one action. Given a premise in declarative memory it adds an order to declarative memory. When the second premise, "John is happier than Bill," is added to declarative memory, the production Add_Premise_1 fires. This production has two conditions, a premise and an order, and one action, adding a new order to declarative memory. The new order is created by matching John in the premise with John in the order and appending Bill after John in the revised order.

When the third premise, "Tom is happier than Bill," is added to declarative memory, the production Add_Premise_2 fires. This production is similar to Add_Premise_1 in that it matches a premise and an order on the condition side and adds a revised order to declarative memory on its action side. The productions differ in the form of the conditions they match and the action they perform. In Add_Premise_2, Tom in the premise matches Tom in the order and Bill in the premise matches Bill in the order, so instead of appending an item (as in Add_Premise_1) the items John and Bill are switched in the revised order to make the order compatible with the most recent premise.

At this point, the system gives the order "Tom, Bill, John" as the result. This error has been found with relatively high frequency in both adult and child data from our laboratory using premise sets of this form. Because this order is incorrect, negative, external feedback will cause the strength of the production Add_Premise_2 to be decreased. The system will solve this problem (or problems of this form) in the same manner, until the strength of the Add_Premise_2 production is too low to allow it to fire. If the Add_Premise_2 production cannot fire and the contents of declarative memory do not match the conditions of any other production, the system will enter the modification phase.

As stated earlier, the strategy modification occurs in two steps. First, the current premises are mapped to the concept of order. Second, a new production is built. For this example, the structure mapper would take the premise "Tom is happier than Bill," and the order, "Tom, John, Bill," and would recognize that the order is consistent with the premise. In this problem, the order does not change with the integration of the new premise, "Tom is happier than Bill." Based on the structure mapper output and the current contents of declarative memory, the system builds a new production. This production is shown in Figure 2.4. The conditions of this production are identical to the conditions of Add_Premise_2, but the action differs. In Add_Premise_3 the order of the items does not change. The new production will fire when this problem is presented again, and will fire in place of the weakened production, Add_Premise_2.

Now let us consider another problem with the premises "Tom is happier than John," "Tom is happier than Bill." This problem is indeterminate

(Add__premise__3
    ((Tom happier than Bill)
    (Order (Tom John Bill)))
→
    ((add-to dm
        (Order (Tom John Bill)))]

Figure 2.4. New production developed by the model

because the premises are consistent with two orders, "Tom, John, Bill," and "Tom, Bill, John." This can be recognized through the structure mapping process because the premises can be mapped into the base in Figure 2.1 in two ways, and one of the relations is found to be missing. The metacognitive component of the model recognizes this, and devises strategies that deal with it. These strategies entail inserting an indeterminacy marker in the order stored in declarative memory. In the present example the order "Tom, (Bill * John)" would be stored, the character * indicating that the order of the terms within parentheses (Bill and John) is indeterminate.

This has two benefits. First, it permits indeterminate orders to be recognized. The model can be interrogated to see whether the problem is determinate. When the model has been run on a representative sample of problems and has developed strategies, it will recognize indeterminate problems. Second, the presence of an indeterminacy marker in the order stored in declarative memory is used to construct productions that deal with this situation. These productions integrate new premises with the partial order obtained from earlier premises. This is an important aspect of the premise integration process. To illustrate, consider the premise set $c > d, a > b, b > c$. After the second premise the order "$((cd) * (ab))$" will be stored in declarative memory. When $b > c$ is presented, it is recognized that the order of cd and ab is known, but the order of these pairs is not known. A production is then constructed which switches the pairs, yielding the order $abcd$. Earlier, more primitive strategies which do not mark indeterminacies would store the order cdab, then when $b > c$ is presented, will switch b only, yielding the order $bcda$, or will switch c only, yielding $bcda$. These are common errors for children and adults under high processing loads.

CONCLUSIONS

The model builds on earlier models by Sternberg (1980) and by Foos et al. (1976), but adds a number of new features. First, it is a multistrategy model, which constructs strategies consistent with task demands, and consistent with the concept of order that has been developed through experience.

Second, it is a model that includes a learning mechanism. It can make the transition from an inadequate to a more adequate strategy by making modifications that are consistent with task demands, and with its concept of task; that is, with the concept of order. One example of this is the transition from a strategy which takes account of the last premise only to a strategy that integrates the last premise with stored information from previous premises.

The model is able to "bootstrap" itself up to higher level strategies using information about ordered sets experienced in the past. This information is of a kind that could readily be acquired through play experiences with blocks and other objects that can be placed in order. Analogical structure mapping mechanisms are very important here, because they permit the child to recognize correspondences between old experiences and new tasks. Concrete experiences can be used as a kind of template for a new task because they have a structural correspondence to the new task. An abstract concept of order is not required. The model can be regarded as a prototype of the way thinking strategies develop, and has been incorporated into a general theory of cognitive development (Halford, 1993).

As our previous work has shown (Halford, 1984; Halford, Maybery, & Bain, 1986; Maybery, Bain, & Halford, 1986) structure mapping imposes a processing load. Because of this, children under 5 years of age have difficulty with mappings from one ordered set to another. This means they would be unable to develop strategies consistent with ordered sets in their experience. For example, they might recall a row of blocks stacked in order resembling a staircase, which is undoubtedly an example of an ordered set. However if they cannot recognize the correspondence between this ordered set and the premises of a problem, they will not be able to modify their strategies so as to be consistent with the ordered sets they have experienced. This means that children below age 5 have difficulty developing adequate strategies for N-term series — that is, transitive inference and ordering tasks — because of the processing loads that are imposed.

REFERENCES

Baylor, G.W., & Gascon, J. (1974). An information processing theory of aspects of the development of weight seriation in children. *Cognitive Psychology,* 1-40.

Bullock, M., & Gelman, R.(1977). Numerical reasoning in young children: The ordering principle. *Child Development, 48,* 427-434.

DeLoache, J.S. (1987). Rapid change in the symbolic functioning of very young children. *Science, 238,* 1556-1557.

Foos, P.W., Smith, K.H., Sabol, M.A., & Mynatt, B.T. (1976). Constructive processes in simple linear order problems. *Journal of Experimental Psychology: Human Learning and Memory, 2,* 759-766.

Gentner, D. (1983). Structure-mapping: A theoretical framework for analogy. *Cognitive Science, 7,* 155-170.

Greeno, J.G., & Johnson, W. (1985). Competence for solving and understanding problems. In G. d'Ydewalle (Ed.), *Cognition, information processing and motivation*. Amsterdam: Elsevier Science.

Greeno, J.G., Riley, M.S., & Gelman, R. (1984). Conceptual competence and children's counting. *Cognitive Psychology, 16,* 94-143.

Halford, G.S. (1984). Can young children integrate premises in transitivity and serial order tasks? *Cognitive Psychology, 16,* 65-93.

Halford, G.S. (1987). A structure-mapping definition of conceptual complexity: Implications for cognitive development. Unpublished manuscript.

Halford, G.S. (1993). *Children's understanding: The development of mental models.* Hillsdale, NJ: Erlbaum.

Halford, G.S., Maybery, M.T., & Bain, J.D. (1986). Capacity limitations in children's reasoning: A dual task approach. *Child Development, 57,* 616-627.

Maybery, M.T., Bain, J.D., & Halford, G.S. (1986). Information processing demands of transitive inference. *Journal of Experimental Psychology: Learning, Memory, and Cognition, 12,* 600-613.

Maybery, M.T., Halford, G.S., Bain, J.D., & Kelly, M.E. (1988). Children's solution processes with n-term series problems. Unpublished manuscript, University of Queensland, Brisbane, Queensland, Australia.

Ohlsson, S., & Langley, P. (1986). *PRISM tutorial and manual.* Irvine, CA: University of California.

Quinton, G., & Fellows, B.J. (1975) Perceptual strategies in the solving of three-term series problems. *British Journal of Psychology, 66,* 69-78.

Siegler, R.S., & Shrager, J. (1984). Strategy choices in addition and subtraction: How do children know what to do? In C. Sophian (Ed.), *Origins of cognitive skills* (pp. 229-293). Hillsdale, NJ: Erlbaum.

Sternberg, R.J. (1980). Representation and process in linear syllogistic reasoning. *Journal of Experimental Psychology: General, 109,* 119-159.

Sugarman, S. (1982). Developmental change in early representational intelligence: Evidence from spatial classification strategies and related verbal expressions. *Cognitive Psychology, 14,* 410-449.

VanLehn, K., & Brown, J.S. (1980). Planning nets: A representation for formalizing analogies and semantic models of procedural skills. In R.E. Snow, P.A. Federico, & W.E. Montague (Eds.), *Aptitude learning and instruction, Vol. 2: Cognitive process analyses of learning and problem solving* (pp. 95-137). Hillsdale, NJ: Erlbaum.

CHAPTER 3

A Nonlinear Associative Memory Model For the Storage and Retrieval of Complex Spatiotemporal Sequences

Richard A. Heath

Department of Psychology
University of Newcastle

INTRODUCTION

The associative memory model of Anderson, Silverstein, Ritz, and Jones (1977), which proposed that associations between items can be stored by superimposing matrices computed as the outer vector product of vector representations of the associated items, was the precursor of several different associative memory models devised by mathematical psychologists (Humphreys, Bain, & Pike, 1989; Murdock, 1982; Pike, 1984.). Although these models might account for a variety of empirically verifiable memory phenomena, they contain no mechanism which could allow learning and habituation to occur.

Subsequently, Murdock and Lamon (1988) proposed a modification to Murdock's original TODAM model so that the memory update depended on the discrepancy between the contents of the new input and what was currently stored in the memory. This type of model was elaborated in an adaptive filter model proposed by Heath and Fulham (1988) which employed a stochastic approximation algorithm to update the associative memory matrix by an increment that depended on the novelty contained in each new input stimulus. Provided that the subject is sensitive to this novelty, then the amount by which the associative memory matrix is updated depends on the discrepancy between what is currently stored in the memory and what is required to be memorized. Heath (1989) has shown that this model, which can be expressed more generally in terms of an adaptive Kalman filter, habituates when the input is invariant over time.

AN EXTENSION OF THE MATRIX MODEL
FOR HUMAN ASSOCIATIVE MEMORY

Heath (1991) has proposed an extension to the linear adaptive filter model for human associative memory (Heath & Fulham, 1988) so that it can account for nonlinear changes in the growth of the memory matching function. This function, which measures the covariance between the input to the memory system and its output, represents the familiarity of items stored in the memory.

The memory update equation for the adaptive filter model when the t-th input, represented by the vector $\mathbf{x}(t)$, is presented is given by:

$$\mathbf{M}(t) = \alpha\,\mathbf{M}(t-1) + \beta\,(t)[\mathbf{I} - \gamma\,\mathbf{M}(t-1)]\mathbf{x}(t)\mathbf{x}(t)', \tag{1}$$

where α, $0 \leqslant \alpha \leqslant 1$, is a memory parameter which allows for the decay of information in memory, and $\beta\,(t)$ is a sequence of scalar coefficients which weight the most recently presented inputs. For asymptotic convergence of the associative memory matrices, the $\beta\,(t)$ need to satisfy the convergence conditions:

$$\Sigma_{t=0}^{\infty}\,\beta\,(t) = \infty \text{ and } \Sigma_{t=0}^{\infty}\,\beta^{2}\,(t) < \infty.$$

γ is a novelty sensitivity parameter which controls the extent to which the associative memory is updated on the t-th trial.

This model is mathematically tractable and allows predictions of serial position effects in recognition memory tasks, for example. When the same input is presented repeatedly, the memory matching function for evaluating the familiarity of a probe input, $\mathbf{x}(t)$, $t < T$, after T learning trials is given by:

$$\mu\,(t, T) = \mathbf{x}'(t)\,\mathbf{M}(T)\,\mathbf{x}(t). \tag{2}$$

The difference equation for computing $\mu\,(t, T)$ from its value on the previous trial, $\mu\,(t, T-1)$, for a small constant β, is given by:

$$\mu\,(t, T) = (1-\beta\,)\mu\,(t, T-1) + \beta \tag{3}$$

As $T \rightarrow \infty$, $\mu\,(t, T)$ approaches 1 asymptotically, for all values of β, thus indicating the linearity of the model.

Heath (1991) proposed an Error Accumulation (EA) Model which assumes that the associative memory system accumulates the outer vector product of the discrepancy between the input to the memory and its corresponding output. This yields the memory update equation:

$$\mathbf{M}(t+1) = \alpha\,\mathbf{M}(t) + \beta(t)[\mathbf{x}(t) - \gamma_{1}\mathbf{M}(t)\mathbf{x}(t)][\mathbf{x}(t) - \gamma_{2}\mathbf{M}(t)\mathbf{x}(t)]', \tag{4}$$

where the γ_i, $i = 1,2$, are possibly unequal novelty sensitivity parameters. The adaptive filter model Equation 1 is a special case of the EA model when $\gamma_2 = 0$.

The nonlinear properties of the EA model can be studied by computing the scalar matching function for a probe stimulus equal to the t-th input stimulus which is given by the difference equation:

$$\mu(t, T+1) = \beta + [\alpha - \beta(\gamma_1 + \gamma_2)] \mu(t, T) + \beta \gamma_1 \gamma_2 (\mu(t, T))^2. \quad (5)$$

As $T \to \infty$, then the asymptotic memory matching function, μ_∞, satisfies:

$$\gamma_1 \gamma_2 \beta \mu_\infty^2 + [\alpha - \beta(\gamma_1 + \gamma_2) - 1] \mu_\infty + \beta = 0. \quad (6)$$

Hence

$$\mu_\infty = (a \pm \sqrt{b})/c$$

where

$$a = 1 - \alpha + \beta(\gamma_1 + \gamma_2)$$
$$b = (1 - \alpha)[1 - \alpha + 2\beta(\gamma_1 + \gamma_2)] + \beta^2 (\gamma_1 - \gamma_2)^2$$

and

$$c = 2\gamma_1 \gamma_2 \beta.$$

When $\alpha = 1$, μ_∞ equals $1/\gamma_1$ or $1/\gamma_2$ depending on the starting value of μ. The behavior of the system is complicated when the memory is leaky, that is, $\alpha < 1$. Chaotic behavior occurs when the rate of new stimulus input exceeds the processing capacity of the system, that is, when the ratio β/α is high. When $\alpha = 1$ the memory matching function becomes unstable for values of $\beta > 1.9$. This critical value of β increases when the novelty sensitivity parameters, γ_1 and γ_2, decrease. Thus, by altering the sensitivity of the error detection system, the memory update can be stabilized a little longer for relatively small increases in β. When the memory permanence parameter, α, is reduced, unstable memory performance occurs at smaller values of β (for example, instability occurs for $\beta > 1.5$ when $\alpha = 0.5$).

Figure 3.1 shows the regions of stability and instability for the EA model when $\gamma_1 = \gamma_2 = 1$. When $\alpha \leqslant 0.8$, the memory system passes from stability, through limit cycling to a region of chaotic behavior. Beyond the chaotic region, the memory system becomes quite unstable. For higher values of α the memory system passes from stability to instability without any discernible limit cycling or chaos.

Stability Regions
Error Accumulation Model

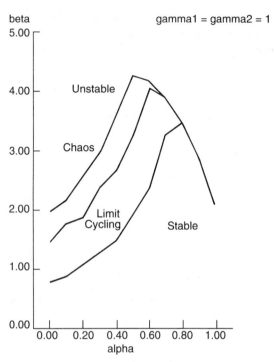

Figure 3.1. Stability and instability regions for the Error Accumulation (EA) Model as a function of the memory permanence (alpha) and incremental learning (beta) parameters

The EA model is a special case of a more general cascaded associative memory system containing N associative memories. The input to the $(i + 1)$-th associative memory is the residual input vector after it has been processed by the preceding i associative memories, M_k, $k = 1, i$. This input vector at time t is given by:

$$\left[\prod_{k=1}^{i} \mathbf{x}'(t)(\mathbf{I} - \gamma_k \mathbf{M}_k(t)) \mathbf{x}(t) \right] \mathbf{x}(t) = [1 - \mu_1(t)] [1 - \mu_2(t)] \cdots$$

$$[1 - \mu_i(t)] \mathbf{x} = P_i(t)\mathbf{x}(t),$$

where γ_k is the novelty sensitivity parameter for the k-th associative memory.

The update equation for the i-th associative memory at time $t + 1$ is given by:

$$\mathbf{M}_i(t + 1) = \alpha_i \mathbf{M}_i(t) + \beta_i(t) P_i(t) [\mathbf{I} - \gamma_i \mathbf{M}_i(t)] \mathbf{x}(t) \mathbf{x}'(t),$$

where the α_i and $\beta_i(t)$ are memory permanence and exponential averaging parameters, respectively. It can be shown that the memory matching functions, when the same stimulus is presented to the memory system, are given by the following sequence of coupled difference equations:

$$\mu_1(t + 1) = \alpha_1\mu_1(t) + \beta_1(t)[1 - \mu_1(t)],$$

$$\mu_2(t + 1) = \alpha_2\mu_2(t) + \beta_2(t)[1 - \mu_1(t)][1 - \mu_2(t)],$$

$$\mu_3(t + 1) = \alpha_3\mu_3(t) + \beta_3(t)[1 - \mu_1(t)][1 - \mu_2(t)][1 - \mu_3(t)],$$

$$\cdots$$

$$\mu_N(t+1) = \alpha_N\mu_N(t) + \beta_N(t)\prod_{i=1}^{N}[1 - \mu_i(t)].$$

This system contains nonlinearities of all orders up to the number of associative memories contained in the cascaded system and so provides a general information processing system. For a system with three associative memories, the residual output matching function at the third stage equals the difference between the memory matching function at this stage and the residual memory matching function at the previous stage. If the matching functions are all equal across stages then the difference equation for the third stage residual matching function is given by:

$$\mu(t + 1) = [1 - \mu(t)]^3 - p\{[1 - \mu(t)]^2 - q[1 - \mu(t)]\}$$

where p and q are arbitrary weighting constants. When $p = 2$, this equation has a similar structure to the difference equation for the real component of Gregson's Model Γ (Gregson, 1988), when the real gain parameter, a, equals 1 and the imaginary gain parameter, e, equals $\sqrt{(q - 1)}$.

A NONLINEAR MODEL FOR HUMAN ASSOCIATIVE MEMORY BASED ON SYSTEM IDENTIFICATION

An alternative framework for analyzing functional characteristics of the Human Information Processing (HIP) system is to use nonlinear system identification (NSI) techniques which are commonly used in control system engineering and which have achieved some success in the analysis of intact physiological systems (Marmarelis & Marmarelis, 1978). This technique views the HIP system as a "black box" which mediates the transformation of stimulus inputs into response sequences. For example, in complex skills such as musical performance, the "black box" is responsible for transforming the printed harmonic and melodic structure of written music into the controlled motor sequences required to play the music on a keyboard.

In discrete time we can represent the s-dimensional input vector sequences by $\mathbf{x}(\tau)$ and the t-dimensional output vector sequences by $\mathbf{y}(\tau)$, where the temporal index, τ, ranges over the set of positive integers. We also propose that the information processing system has a limited memory capacity equal to the number of input and output vectors occurring during the M previous time units.

One of the aims of NSI is to compute transfer functions which relate the spatiotemporal properties of stimulus sequences to their corresponding response sequences. These transfer functions represent the cognitive structure needed to produce the complex input-output mappings. They are input independent in the sense that the success of the NSI analysis can be evaluated by measuring how well novel inputs, which were not used in the study phase of an experimental sequence of input-output pairs, generate appropriate response output sequences. It is quite possible that these functions might serve as a procedural memory required for the future execution of a complex skill.

Once the learned skill has been stored in memory, system identification can be used to examine the spatiotemporal processing properties of the newly acquired information processing system. This is achieved by computing the correlation between random representative input signals and known output responses to infer the internal information processing mechanisms. If there is no relevant cognitive structure for the task, then all the input information will be transferred to the output, yielding a noisy output signal. If the input can be assimilated by the information processing system, then there will be significant spatiotemporal correlations between the input and output sequences.

The operations performed by a general nonlinear information processing system can be inferred by initially representing the response of the system by means of the Volterra expansion, which in discrete time is given by:

$$
y_t(\tau) = \sum_{s_1=1}^{S} a_{s_1 t} \sum_{m_1=1}^{M} h_{s_1 t}(m_1) x_{s_1}(\tau - m_1) +
$$

$$
\sum_{s_1=1}^{S} \sum_{s_2=1}^{S} a_{s_1 s_2 t} \sum_{m_1=1}^{M} \sum_{m_2=1}^{M} h_{s_1 s_2 t}(m_1, m_2) x_{s_1}(\tau - m_1) x_{s_2}(\tau - m_2) + \ldots +
$$

$$
\sum_{s_1=1}^{S} \ldots \sum_{s_p=1}^{S} a_{s_1 \ldots s_p t} \sum_{m_1=1}^{M} \ldots \sum_{m_p=1}^{M} h_{s_1 \ldots s_p t}(m_1, \ldots, m_p) \prod_{z=1}^{p} x_{s_z}(\tau - m_z) + e_t(\tau) \quad (7)
$$

where $a_{s_1 \ldots s_p t}$ is a weighting constant for the p-th order association between the input components; $h_{s_1 \ldots s_p t}(m_1, \ldots, m_p)$ is the processing characteristic, or transfer function, for the p-th order input associations; and $e_t(\tau)$ is the error obtained by truncation after p terms.

1. The linear transfer functions, $h_{s_1 t}(m_1)$, $s_1 = 1, S$; $t = 1, T$; $m_l = 0, M$ map the sth element, $x_s(\tau - m_1)$, of the input vector at time $\tau - m_1$, $\mathbf{x}(\tau - m_1)$, on to the tth element, $y_t(\tau)$, of the output vector at time τ, $\mathbf{y}(\tau)$, with a temporal lag of m_1 time units.

2. The second-order nonlinear transfer functions, $h_{s_1 s_2 t}(m_1, m_2)$, $s_i = 1, S$; $t = 1, T$; $m_i = 0, M$; $i = 1, 2$, map the s_1^{th} element, $x_{s_1}(\tau - m_1)$, of the input vector at time $\tau - m_1$, $\mathbf{x}(\tau - m_1)$, and the s_2^{th} element, $x_{s_2}(\tau - m_2)$, of the input vector at time $\tau - m_2$, $\mathbf{x}(\tau - m_2)$, on to the tth element of the output vector at time τ, $\mathbf{y}(\tau)$, $y_t(\tau)$, with temporal lags of m_1 and m_2 time units, respectively.

3. In general, the pth order nonlinear transfer functions, $h_{s_1 \ldots s_p t}$ $(m_1, \ldots, m_p)$, $s_i = 1, S$, $t = 1, T$, $m_i = 0, M$, $i = 1, p$, map the s_i^{th} element, $x_{s_i}(\tau - m_i)$, of the input vector at time $\tau - m_i$, $\mathbf{x}(\tau - m_i)$ on to the tth element, $y_t(\tau)$, of the output vector at time τ, $\mathbf{y}(\tau)$, with temporal lags of m_i time units, respectively, $i = 1, p$.

In this way the nonlinear system can accommodate very general spatiotemporal interactions within the memory system. In practical applications of the model, the working memory of the system, M, might be rather small, for example, $M = 4$, which is consistent with estimates of transient memory capacity (Grossberg, 1978). Also, the number of input and output dimensions could also be set to small values by the experimenter's choice of stimulus-response sequences in order to reduce the computational burden.

As suggested by Lee and Schetzen (1965) and applied to human information processing by Heath and Fulham (1985), the p processing characteristics can be estimated for an "unknown" information processing system by stimulating the system with white-noise inputs. The logic underlying this technique is that the cross-correlation function computed for the p-th order input product

$$\prod_{z=1}^{p} x_{s_z}(\tau - m_z)$$

and the residual output, derived from $y_t(\tau)$ when all the effects from i-th order processes, $0 < i < (p - 1)$, have been removed, should be nonzero if there is any p-th order information transmitted from the input sequences to the output sequences. Hence, any statistically reliable cross-correlation provides information on the processing characteristics of the HIP system. One possibility is to stimulate the system with exemplar patterns derived from fixed prototypes by adding zero mean Gaussian noise.

Equation 7 can be simplified by rewriting it in terms of matrix operations. For simplicity, we will set all the scalars $a_{s_1 s_2 \ldots s_i t}$, $i = 1, p$, equal to one. These multiplicative scaling constants can then be estimated using multiple linear regression (Heath & Fulham, 1985). The first term of Equation 7 can be expressed rather more succinctly for the input-output vectors as:

$$Lin\{\mathbf{y}(t)\} = \sum_{m_1=0}^{M} \mathbf{H}(m_1)\mathbf{x}(\tau - m_1)$$

where

$$\mathbf{H}(m_1) = \begin{pmatrix} h_{11}(m_1) & h_{21}(m_1) & \cdots & h_{S1}(m_1) \\ h_{12}(m_1) & h_{22}(m_1) & \cdots & h_{S2}(m_1) \\ \vdots & \vdots & \ddots & \vdots \\ h_{1T}(m_1) & h_{2T}(m_1) & \cdots & h_{ST}(m_1) \end{pmatrix}$$

This equation is a *temporal* convolution of the sequence of $M + 1$ input vectors and the same number of spatial linear transfer matrices.

In a similar fashion, the second term of Equation 7 can be written as:

$$Quad\{\mathbf{y}(t)\} = \sum_{m_1=0}^{M} \sum_{m_2=0}^{M} \mathbf{H}(m_1, m_2)\mathbf{x}(\tau - m_1) \otimes \mathbf{x}(\tau - m_2)$$

where

$$\mathbf{H}(m_1 m_2) = \begin{pmatrix} h_{111}(m_1, m_2) & h_{211}(m_1, m_2) & \cdots & h_{SS1}(m_1, m_2) \\ h_{112}(m_1, m_2) & h_{212}(m_1, m_2) & \cdots & h_{SS2}(m_1, m_2) \\ \vdots & \vdots & \ddots & \vdots \\ h_{11T}(m_1, m_2) & h_{21T}(m_1, m_2) & \cdots & h_{SST}(m_1, m_2) \end{pmatrix}$$

and $\mathbf{x}(\tau - m_1) \otimes \mathbf{x}(\tau - m_2)$ is the Kronecker product vector of the vectors $\mathbf{x}(\tau - m_1)$ and $\mathbf{x}(\tau - m_2)$. This vector has S^2 components, the $[S(i-1) + j]$th component, $i,j = 1, S$, being given by $x_i(\tau - m_1)x_j(\tau - m_2)$.

The Kronecker vector product is a generalized spatial convolution of two vectors which includes all possible products of the vector components. The spatial convolution operation reduces the information content of the Kronecker product by summing all terms which contain indices summing to the same constant. Whereas there are S^2 terms in the Kronecker product, there are only $2S - 1$ terms in the convolution vector. Hence the information contained in the Kronecker product vector is greater than that contained in the convolution vector.

Ignoring the scale constants, the complete vector representation of Equation 7 can be represented by:

$$y(\tau) = \sum_{m_1=0}^{M} H(m_1) x(\tau - m_1) + \sum_{m_1=0}^{M} \sum_{m_2=0}^{M} H(m_1, m_2) x(\tau - m_1) \otimes x(\tau - m_2) + \dots$$

$$+ \sum_{m_1=0}^{M} \sum_{m_2=0}^{M} \dots \sum_{m_p=0}^{M} H(m_1, m_2 \dots, m_p) x(\tau - m_1) \otimes x(\tau - m_2) \otimes \dots \otimes x(\tau - m_p) + e(\tau)$$

$$(8)$$

where $H(m_1, m_2, \dots, m_p)$ is a $t \times s^p$ matrix; $y(\tau)$ is a $t \times 1$ vector; each $x(\tau - m_i)$, $i = 1, p$, is an $s \times 1$ vector; and $e(\tau)$ is the p-dimensional prediction error vector at time τ. This model is an extension of the matrix model proposed by Humphreys, Bain, and Pike (1989).

LEARNING THE LINEAR AND NONLINEAR TRANSFER FUNCTIONS USING ARBITRARY INPUT SEQUENCES

The nonlinear model represented by Equation 8 describes the predicted performance at the completion of the learning phase of a skill. For example, in the case of learning to touch type, the input vectors are the visually transformed features of the text display and the output vectors are the set of signals to the muscle effectors which generate the appropriate key presses. The spatiotemporal procedural "knowledge" required to perform such a skilled activity is stored in the transfer matrices, $H(m_1, m_2, \dots, m_p)$. This suggests that, provided the subject's performance is not affected by environmental stressors or internal influences such as fatigue, the parameters describing relationships between the input and output sequences should be time invariant.

It is also important to be able to use the model to predict performance during the training phase of skill acquisition. This can be achieved by assuming that the subject attempts to minimize the sum of squared discrepancies between predicted and observed output sequences. This learning criterion is similar to that used in contemporary connectionist models which learn complex input-output mappings using techniques such as back-propagation (Rumelhart, Hinton, & Williams, 1986).

We define the error criterion in terms of the elements, $\hat{y}_t(\tau)$ and $y_t(\tau)$ of the predicted and observed output vectors, respectively, as:

$$E = \frac{1}{2} \sum_{t=1}^{T} (y_t(\tau) - \hat{y}_t(\tau))^2$$

We minimize E by differentiating it with respect to each of the possible h elements in the transfer matrices. For example, for the linear transfer function:

$$\frac{\partial E}{\partial h_{s_j,t}(m_i)} = \frac{\partial E}{\partial \hat{y}_t(\tau)} \frac{\partial \hat{y}_t(\tau)}{\partial h_{s_j,t}(m_i)} = -\delta_t(\tau) x_{s_j}(\tau - m_i),$$

where $\delta_t(\tau) = \hat{y}_t(\tau) - y_t(\tau)$. This equation measures the rate at which the total squared error between observed and predicted output vector components decreases with a change in the linear transfer function parameter. Hence the appropriate modification to the transfer function parameter should be proportional to this rate of change, but since we do not know the exact form of the error function, this change in transfer function parameter should be small so that the system tracks any smooth decrease in the error function. Hence the appropriate approximate learning equation for the parameters of a linear, or first-order, system is given by:

$$\Delta h_{s_j,t}(m_i;\tau) = \eta \delta_t(\tau) x_{s_j}(\tau - m_i) \tag{9}$$

In general, it can be shown that the learning equation for the parameters of the p-th order nonlinear system is given by:

$$\Delta h_{s_1 \ldots s_p,t}(m_1, \ldots, m_p;\tau) = \eta \delta_t(\tau) \prod_{i=1}^{p} x_{s_i^*}(\tau - m_i). \tag{10}$$

In Equation 10 the subscript s_i^* indexes a possible permutation of the set of indices $s_1, \ldots, s_p$ for the input vectors. Equations 9 and 10 are examples of the generalized delta learning rule. Their performance can be stabilized for stationary input vectors by letting η be a decreasing function of the number of learning trials as in stochastic approximation (Heath & Fulham, 1988).

A COMPUTER SIMULATION AND EXPERIMENTAL PARADIGM FOR EVALUATING THE PREDICTIONS OF THE NONLINEAR MODEL

A computer simulation of the learning phase of the NSI model employed unidimensional input and outputs, $x(t)$ and $y(t)$, respectively. In the first simulation the linear kernel was given by:

$$H_1(m_1) = (1.0 \quad 0.5 \quad 0.25)$$

and the second-order nonlinear kernel was given by:

$$H_2(m_1, m_2) = \begin{pmatrix} 0 & 0.5 & 0.25 \\ 0.5 & 0 & 0.5 \\ 0.25 & 0.5 & 0 \end{pmatrix}$$

The program first computed the predicted outputs corresponding to 1000 observations of the inputs using these kernels. It then estimated the kernels using the generalized delta rule yielding:

$$\hat{\mathbf{H}}_1 (m_1) = (\; 0.97 \quad 0.46 \quad 0.25 \;)$$

and

$$\hat{\mathbf{H}}_2 (m_1, m_2) = \begin{pmatrix} 0 & 0.5 & 0.22 \\ 0.5 & 0 & 0.48 \\ 0.25 & 0.48 & 0 \end{pmatrix}$$

which is very close to the actual kernels used in the generation of the simulation data, $MSE = 0.06$.

In a second simulation, a "hard" sequential exclusive-or function was generated using the function: $y(t + 1) = \text{XOR}[x(t), x(t - 1)]$, where both inputs and outputs assume values of ± 1. The predicted relationship using the generalized delta rule and 1000 samples was given by:

$$y(t + 1) = \text{sign}\{0.47x(t)[1 - 2x(t - 1)]\}$$

which provided a good fit to the output data, $MSE = 0.03$.

The nonlinear memory model can also be used for the storage of more complex sequences, such as the successive locations of a point in two dimensions during the execution of a learned skill such as handwriting. As an example of this application, the author drew two successive handwritten lower case as on a computer screen using a mouse. The first letter served as a teaching input for the writing of the second a. Hence both the input and outputs of the memory system were two-dimensional vectors.

A second-order nonlinear model was fit to these data using the generalized delta learning rule with a learning rate equal to 0.05 and a memory of 4 lags. The learning process terminated when the MSE was less than 0.01. Using multiple linear regression, it was shown that the nonlinear system identification model yielded a good fit to the output points with multiple correlation coefficients of 0.998 and 0.930 for the vertical and horizontal coordinates of the written letter, respectively. There were significant components for the linear cross-kernels indicating that control of movement in both the horizontal and vertical directions is needed. The statistically significant second-order kernels indicated that these temporal dependencies involved interactions between successive pairs of inputs, that is, the execution of the skill required the storage and subsequent use of temporal associations.

CONCLUSIONS

It has been shown that current matrix associative memory models can be generalized in several different ways to account for nonlinear aspects of cognitive processing. Firstly, by incorporating a more general error accumulation process, adaptive versions of the matrix model can be derived. These models generate nonlinear memory recognition functions which can exhibit chaotic behavior for suitable values of the memory permanence and incremental learning parameters. A cascaded version of the error accumulation model provides a physiologically realistic mechanism for generating all possible orders of nonlinear dynamic memory processing models.

A second, but complementary, approach involves the application of nonlinear system identification for the generation and use of a complex nonlinear information processing system, which stores and retrieves sequences of associated input-output vectors. During the learning phase, information is stored in the memory in terms of sets of linear and nonlinear kernels using a generalized delta rule. This information is stored in a distributed fashion within hierarchically organized multidimensional associative memory matrices which are specialized for the storage of higher-order spatiotemporal associations between the sequences of input and output vectors.

This model is a generalization of both the TODAM model of Murdock (1982) and the matrix model of Humphreys, Bain and Pike (1989) since the tensor calculus techniques for generating the higher order associative memory models are an extension of TODAM's convolution operator and the Humphreys et al. matrix memory scheme for storing triadic associations. The nonlinear model provides natural procedures for storing multiple associations whether they occur in time or between simultaneously presented items. The latter situation is handled by storing the associated items as subvectors within a single input vector which represents all the information presented at a given point in time (Heath, 1989).

The nonlinear model has many of the features of those connectionist models which learn by means of a generalized delta rule. Although quite general nonlinear mappings can be stored in the memory matrices, it is not clear how many mappings can be stored in the same hierarchical memory system. Hence, more research is needed to determine whether Ratcliff's (1990) criticism of connectionist models also applies to the nonlinear model.

The nonlinear model can also be used to represent changes in performance in the execution of complex motor skills. Once the skill has been learned and stable performance occurs, the nonlinear memory system can be used to detect a significant departure from normal performance. Hence it may be possible to use the system to detect performance deterioration in operator control applications.

REFERENCES

Anderson, J.A., Silverstein, J.W., Ritz, S.A., & Jones, R.S. (1977). Distinctive features, categorical perception, and probability learning: Some applications of a neural model. *Psychological Review, 84*, 413-451.

Gregson, R.A.M. (1988). *Nonlinear psychophysical dynamics.* Hillsdale, NJ: Erlbaum.

Grossberg, S. (1978). A theory of human memory: Self-organization and performance of sensory-motor codes, maps, and plans. In R. Rosen & F. Snell (Eds.), *Progress in Theoretical Biology, 5*, 233-374.

Heath, R.A. (1989). An autoassociative model for human memory based on an adaptive Kalman filter. In D. Vickers, & P. Smith, (Eds.), *Human information processing: Measures, mechanisms, and models* (pp. 411-434). Amsterdam: Elsevier Science.

Heath, R.A. (1991). A general adaptive model for human associative memory. In J.P. Doignon, & J.C. Falmagne, (Eds.), *Mathematical psychology: Current developments.* (pp. 415-436). New York: Springer-Verlag.

Heath, R.A., & Fulham, R. (1985). Applications of system identification and adaptive filtering techniques in human information processing. In G. d'Ydewalle (Ed.), *Cognition, information processing, and motivation* (pp. 117-147). Amsterdam: Elsevier Science.

Heath, R.A., & Fulham, R. (1988). An adaptive filter model for recognition memory. *British Journal of Mathematical and Statistical Psychology, 41*, 119-144.

Humphreys, M.S., Bain, J.D., & Pike, R. (1989). Different ways to cue a coherent memory system: A theory for episodic, semantic and procedural tasks. *Psychological Review, 96*, 208-233.

Lee, Y.W., & Schetzen, M. (1965). Measurement of the Wiener kernels of a nonlinear system by cross-correlation. *International Journal of Control, 2*, 237-254.

Marmarelis, P.Z., & Marmarelis, V.Z. (1978). *Analysis of physiological systems: The white-noise approach.* New York: Plenum Press.

Murdock, B.B., Jr. (1982). A theory for the storage and retrieval of item and associative information. *Psychological Review, 89*, 609-626.

Murdock, B., & Lamon, M. (1988). The replacement effect: Repeating some items while replacing others. *Memory & Cognition, 16*, 91-101.

Pike, R. (1984). Comparison of convolution and matrix distributed memory systems for associative recall and recognition. *Psychological Review, 91*, 281-294.

Ratcliff, R. (1990). Connectionist models of recognition memory: Constraints imposed by learning and forgetting functions. *Psychological Review, 97*, 285-308.

Rumelhart, D.E., Hinton, G.E., & Williams, R.J. (1986). Learning internal representations by error propagation. In D.E. Rumelhart, J.L. McClelland, and the PDP Research group (Eds.), *Parallel distributed processing: Explorations in the microstructure of cognition, Volume 1: Foundations.* Cambridge, MA: MIT Press.

CHAPTER 4

Computational Issues in Associative Learning*

E. James Kehoe

School of Psychology
University of New South Wales

Experimental research in associative learning grew out of 19th century intellectual concerns with empiricist philosophies and biological adaptation (Boakes, 1984; Boring, 1950; Kehoe, 1988a). Within modern cognitive science, research in artificial intelligence and machine learning has reinvigorated an interest in associative learning. This chapter will review key computational issues in learning and show how they are exemplified in the acquisition of conditioned reflexes, which are commonly regarded as a primitive type of associative learning. The key issues include the acquisition of predictive actions, credit assignment to reliable signals, and transfer in associative learning.

FUNDAMENTALS OF CLASSICAL CONDITIONING

Basic Procedure

Pavlov's (1927) method of conditioned reflexes is designated most commonly in the English-language literature as *classical conditioning* (Gormezano & Kehoe, 1975). In its basic form, classical conditioning entails the presentation of two stimulus inputs. First, there is the *conditioned stimulus* (CS), which is usually a relatively innocuous event, for example, the well-known ringing of a bell. Second, there is the *unconditioned stimulus* (US), which is an event usually of biological significance to the subject of the procedure, for example, the consumption of food. When presented in succession, the CS acts as a signal for the US. A wide variety of methods have been invented for measuring the associations formed by the CS-US pairing (Mackintosh, 1983). Traditional methods take advantage of the innate ability of the US to elicit a strong set of reactions, the *unconditioned* response (UR). Across

* This research was supported by Australian Research Council Grant AC89322441. The author extends his thanks to Renee Napier for her assistance in preparation of the manuscript.

repeated CS-US pairings, the CS itself comes to elicit a fragmentary form of the UR. This acquired response to the CS is designated as the *conditioned response* (CR).

Classical Conditioning as a Form of Supervised Learning

While the associative nature of classical conditioning has been long recognized (Lashley, 1916), computational considerations cast additional light on the problems that classical conditioning poses for its subjects. From the computational perspective, classical conditioning is a form of *supervised learning* in which the US and its elicited UR serve as a *teacher* that nominates the response to be attached to the CS. In this respect, classical conditioning resembles a category-learning task, in which the subject makes a guess as to the classification of an object and then, as instructive feedback, is told the correct classification. If the subject makes the correct choice, then the feedback confirms the subject's response. Alternatively, if the subject makes an incorrect response, then the feedback provides an explicit corrective. Likewise, in classical conditioning, if the subject responds to the CS with a CR, then the US-UR confirms the CR. If the subject responds in some other way or fails to respond, then the US-UR provides a corrective for the next presentation of the CS.

Classical Conditioning's Relationship to Instrumental Conditioning

The instructive nature of the US-UR provides a basis for distinguishing classical conditioning from another commonplace learning procedure, namely, instrumental conditioning, also called operant conditioning. Ordinarily, classical conditioning is distinguished from instrumental conditioning on the basis of its respective *response-reinforcer contingencies*. In classical conditioning, the reinforcer — that is, the US — follows the CS irrespective of the occurrence or nonoccurrence of the CR. In instrumental conditioning, however, the presentation of the reinforcer — for example, food reward — depends on the occurrence of a nominated response. From a computational perspective, the typical reinforcer used in instrumental conditioning provides no instruction as to the nominated response but acts only as a *critic*, indicating only the success or failure of the subject's actions (Kehoe, 1989; Sutton, 1984). Unlike the US in classical conditioning, the typical reward has no innate capacity to evoke most instrumental responses, for example, a lever press. On the basis of this difference in the role of the reinforcer, it can be seen that classical and instrumental conditioning place different computational demands on their subjects.

STIMULUS PREDICTION: THE ANTICIPATORY CR

A prevalent feature of learned behavior is its anticipatory nature. That is to say, it usually occurs during a warning period in advance of the reinforcer. In classical conditioning, there is no requirement that any behavior occurs during the CS, because it and the US are presented in an entirely preprogrammed fashion. Nevertheless, the CR typically emerges just before the US and gradually moves to an even earlier position about halfway along the interval between CS onset and US onset (Gormezano, Kehoe, & Marshall, 1983). From a computational perspective, the acquisition of the CR can be viewed as the subject's increasingly confident prediction that the CS will be followed by the US.

Computational Constraints on Anticipation

A fundamental computational conundrum for any adaptive organism concerns the timing of its response to signals for crucial events. On the one hand, early anticipation maximizes the amount of time available for planning and preparation. On the other hand, premature action can be wasteful and even deleterious to the organism. Take a basic protective response, namely eyelid closure. Closure in anticipation of a threat maximizes protection of the eye, but at the same time blinds the organism. Thus, the timing of such a response must be a compromise between protection of the eye and the need for current vision.

Contrary to the conception that a CR is a stereotyped replica of the UR, recent studies have revealed that the constraints on anticipatory responses are satisfied through a mechanism that finely grades the CR during the CS-US interval. While the CR's time of initiation moves away from the US, the maximal extent of the CR — the CR peak — remains near the time of US onset. For example, Figure 4.1 shows the time course for eyelid-closure CRs acquired by four groups of rabbits trained with different CS-US intervals, namely 125, 250, 500, and 1000 ms. As can be seen in Figure 4.1, closure of the eyelid was initiated shortly following the onset of the CS, but peak eyelid closure occurred around the time of US presentation at the end of the CS-US interval (Smith, 1968).

Although the eyelid CR is initiated and completed within a few hundred ms, it is highly adaptable. When the CS-US interval is altered, the CR peak near the original locus of the US disappears and reappears at the new locus of the US (Coleman & Gormezano, 1971). Moreover, when a single CS is paired with the US at two randomly mixed intervals, the CR develops two distinct peaks, one located at each locus of US delivery (Hoehler & Leonard, 1976; Millenson, Kehoe, & Gormezano, 1977). For example, Figure 4.2 shows the time course of an eyelid CR displayed by rabbits trained with a CS that randomly signaled the US after intervals of either 400 or 900 ms. Accordingly, the rabbits acquired a CR with two peaks at the appropriate locations.

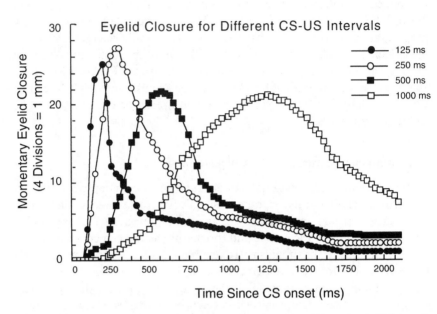

Figure 4.1. Time course of eyeblink conditioned responses in rabbits trained with intervals of 125, 250, 500, and 1000 ms between the onsets of the conditioned stimulus and unconditioned stimulus (Smith, 1968).

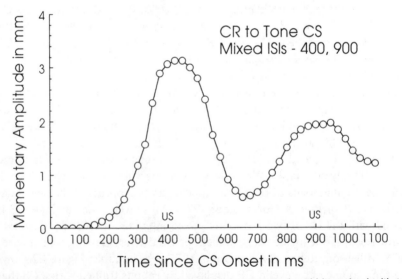

Figure 4.2. Time course of eyeblink conditioned responses in rabbits trained with two intermixed intervals of 400 and 900 ms between the onsets of the conditioned stimulus and unconditioned stimulus (Kehoe, Graham, & Schreurs, 1989).

Stimulus Trace Theories

The critical theoretical questions concerning generation of anticipatory CRs revolve around the representation of the CS, particularly the nature of its moment-by-moment control over the CR. Many theories originated in Pavlov's (1927, pp. 39-40) proposal that the CS leaves a "trace," that is, a perseverative representation in the central nervous system. Associative strength presumably accrues at the point of contiguity between the CS trace and the US-UR. Subsequently, anticipatory CRs are assumed to arise from generalization along time-related dimensions of the trace from its point of contiguity with the US to its earlier portions (Gormezano & Kehoe, 1981; Hull, 1937, 1943). More recently, the concept of the stimulus trace has reappeared as a central feature in "real-time" models of anticipatory CRs (Desmond & Moore, 1988; Grossberg & Schmajuk, 1989; Sutton & Barto, 1981).

STIMULUS INTEGRATION: CREDIT ASSIGNMENT

Reliable signals are usually embedded in a continuous and multifaceted stream of sensory events. An adaptive organism must possess mechanisms both for acquiring associations among reliable sequences of events and for rejecting spurious associations among accidental sequences. The identification of reliable sequences in classical conditioning is an example of the *credit assignment problem* (Sutton, 1984). The credit assignment problem was recognised during early attempts to write computer programs that would learn to play games such as draughts and chess (Minsky, 1961). In the context of game playing, the credit assignment problem was one of determining which single move or combination of moves during a game had been responsible for ultimately winning (or losing) a game. The key maneuvers for winning were to be assigned "credit" and used in future games. Similarly, in classical conditioning, stimuli that reliably signal the US receive credit in the form of associative strength.

Temporal Credit Assignment

CS-US contiguity. Temporal credit assignment involves both absolute and relative temporal relationships among potential CSs and the US. In its simplest form, temporal credit assignment has been examined by manipulating the interval between a single CS and US. As described above, the CS-US interval governs the time course of the CR. In addition, the CS-US interval governs the likelihood of a CR. Figure 4.3 shows the mean CR likelihood as a function of the CS-US interval across a number of groups from several studies of the rabbit eyelid response (Gormezano et al., 1983). As can be seen, the highest level of conditioning occurs when the CS precedes the US by a brief but appreciable interval of approximately 250 ms. CS-US intervals less than 100 ms produce virtually no CR acquisition, and intervals longer than 250 ms produce progressively lower levels of responding.

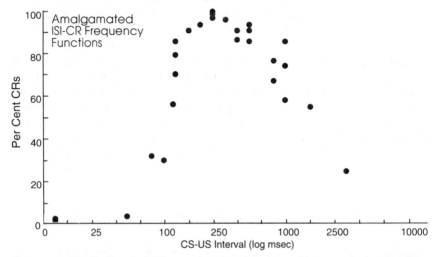

Figure 4.3. The likelihood of CRs as a function of the interval between the onsets of the conditioned stimulus and unconditioned stimulus (Gormezano, Kehoe, & Marshall, 1983).

As the fundamental heuristic for temporal credit assignment, traditional conditioning theory adopted the contiguity principle from the 19th century associationist philosophies (Gormezano & Kehoe, 1981; Lashley, 1916; Robinson, 1932). In brief, CSs that occur just before the US appear to gain associative strength, whereas CSs that occur too far in advance of the US apparently gain no associative strength. To provide a mechanism for the contiguity principle, stimulus trace theories have postulated that the trace possesses a time-related intensity dimension. For example, Hull (1937, 1943) postulated that CS onset initiates a trace that quickly rises in intensity to a maximum value some time after CS onset and then decays, eventually returning to a null value. Furthermore, the rate of association presumably depends on the intensity of the CS trace at its point of contiguity with the US. Thus, as the CS trace decays with time, the rate of CR acquisition also declines. While modern real-time models of conditioning have elaborated Hull's version of trace theory, they have retained the central assumption that the rate of conditioning depends in some fashion on time-related features of the CS's representation (Desmond & Moore, 1988; Grossberg & Schmajuk, 1989; Sutton & Barto, 1981).

Temporal primacy. Temporal credit assignment has been examined using a sequence of CSs prior to the US, for example, CSA-CSX-US (Egger & Miller, 1962; Kehoe, 1979). According to a simple application of the contiguity principle, the stimulus closer to the US, namely CSX, should gain greater associative strength than the more remote stimulus, CSA. However, under certain circumstances, CSA gains more associative strength than CSX by depressing the acquisition of associative strength to CSX. This depressive effect of CSA on CSX depends on the contiguity of CSA and CSX.

The effect of CSA's temporal primacy as a function of the CSA-CSX interval is illustrated in Figure 4.4. Four groups of rabbits were trained with a sequence in which the gap between the offset of CSA and onset of CSX was manipulated over values of 0, 500, 1000, and 2000 ms. The contiguity between CSX and the US was constant at a near-optimal interval of 400 ms. The figure shows the mean likelihood of eyelid CRs to the CSA-CSX-US compound as a whole and to its separate components, CSA and CSX, for the four different CSA-CSX gaps (Kehoe et al., 1979).

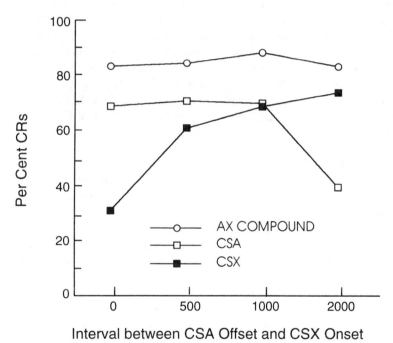

Interval between CSA Offset and CSX Onset

Figure 4.4. The likelihood of CRs in a serial compound (AX), the first stimulus (CSA), and the second stimulus (CSX) as a function of the interval between the offset of CSA and the onset of CSX (Kehoe, Gibbs, Garcia, & Gormezano, 1979).

Inspection of Figure 4.4 reveals a tradeoff in the level of responding to CSA and CSX. In agreement with a contiguity principle, responding to CSA declined as the gap between CSA and CSX-US increased. Contrary to the contiguity principle, the level of responding to CSX varied in a reciprocal fashion despite its fixed, highly contiguous relationship with the US.

Thus, for the shorter gaps between CSA and CSX, CSA's temporal primacy in the sequence overrode CSX's contiguity with the US.

A variety of hypotheses have attempted to reconcile the temporal primacy effect in serial CSs with the contiguity principle. Among these hypotheses, Sutton and Barto (1981) have proposed a real-time connectionist account of the temporal primacy effect. At the center of their general account of classical conditioning is a competitive learning rule (Rescorla & Wagner, 1972), now known widely as the delta rule. According to that rule, CSA and CSX compete directly for access to the associative strength that can be maintained by the US at any one moment. Whereas the basic implementation of the delta rule assumes that associative strengths are altered only at the time of the US, the Sutton-Barto model assumes that the animal is continuously updating associative strengths by comparing recent values with current values. Thus, changes in the associative strength of a CS occur whenever there is a discrepancy between the associative strength at one moment and the associative strength at the next moment. Such a discrepancy could arise through presentation of either another CS or the US. Hence, in the cases of serial CSs, CSA's associative strength would gain increments from any associative strength previously gained by CSX. Thus, as quickly as CSX gains associative strength, it would be transmitted to CSA. In this way, CSA not only competes with CSX but also could be said to steal CSX's associative strength (Kehoe, Schreurs, & Graham, 1987).

Intermittent reinforcement. The contiguity principle is usually supplemented by a frequency principle. In computational terms, the frequency principle dictates that the association between two events grows gradually over successive pairings. In this way, the subject acquires an association only where there is consistent contiguity between events, rather than an accidental conjunction. Empirically, something like a frequency principle does prevail. Although some associations can be established in one pairing, for example, between a novel taste and subsequent nausea (Garcia, McGowan, & Green, 1972), CR acquisition in most cases grows slowly over successive CS-US pairings (Hilgard & Marquis, 1940; Gormezano et al., 1983).

Although consistent contiguity produces the most rapid CR acquisition, inconsistent contiguity produces the most sustained responding to a CS when US presentations are suspended altogether. More specifically, the strength of an association is often tested by submitting the CS to extinction, a procedure in which the CS is presented repeatedly without the US. In extinction, responding disappears quickly when the subject has been trained previously with *continuous reinforcement,* in which every CS was followed by the US. Responding disappears more slowly when the CS was trained with a *partial reinforcement* schedule, in which the CS was followed intermittently by the US, for example, on only 50 percent of all occasions (e.g., Gibbs, Latham, & Gormezano, 1978).

Computational models of associative learning, even connectionist models, have not addressed the positive effect of partial reinforcement on the persistence of responding in extinction. However, there is a large store of research and theory in the conventional conditioning literature that provides insight into how the associative system incorporates less-than-perfect statistical relationships between a CS and US. For example, sequential memory theory contends that the effective conditioned stimulus consists of a compound of the nominal, discrete CS plus a hypothetical lingering trace of the previous trial, something akin to a short-term memory (e.g., Capaldi, 1966; Sheffield, 1949). In continuous reinforcement, the CR becomes conditioned to a compound stimulus consisting of (a) the CS, and (b) the memory of the US that occurred on the preceding trial. Subsequently, when the US is no longer presented in extinction, half the compound stimulus is lost, leaving the nominal CS by itself to activate the association necessary to generate the CR. However, in partial reinforcement, the CR becomes conditioned to two compound stimuli, that is to say, the CS plus a memory of the preceding CS-alone trial as well as the nominal CS plus a memory of the preceding US. In extinction, CRs would persist because they are already conditioned to the prevailing compound, namely, the CS plus a memory of preceding CS-alone presentations.

Structural Credit Assignment

In addition to temporal credit assignment, there is a second credit assignment problem that arises when multiple events are equally contiguous with the reinforcer. In classical conditioning, the study of structural credit assignment has involved *simultaneous compounds,* which contain two or more concurrent CSs (e.g., Kehoe, 1987; Kehoe & Gormezano, 1980). Manipulations that influence credit assignment in simultaneous compounds involve, for example, the previous training of CSs, their relative physical intensity, and whether the compound or an individual CS is a better predictor of the US.

Selective association. Even when two CSs are equally contiguous with the US, the subject often acquires one of the potential associations but not the other. For example, in the phenomenon of overshadowing, the subject will tend to show acquisition to the more physically salient of two CSs to the detriment of the other CS (Pavlov, 1927, pp. 110-113). This latter CS need not be a weak stimulus but can itself be very salient. Figure 4.5 shows just such a case, in which acquisition of an eyelid CR to a salient visual CS was progressively overshadowed as the physical intensity of a simultaneous tone CS was raised across values of 85, 89, and 93 dB in three different groups. As can be seen in the figure, the likelihood of the CR to the compound of the light plus tone hovered around 90% CRs. As for the tone, its level of responding was generally high but showed a small rise as the tone intensity was increased. In contrast, the level of responding to the fixed light CS was as high as that of the 85 dB tone but dropped precipitously when trained in compound with the 89 and 93 dB tones.

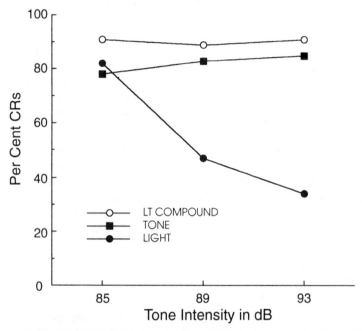

Figure 4.5. The likelihood of CRs in a compound (LT), the tone stimulus (T), and the light stimulus (L) as a function of the tone intensity (Kehoe, 1982).

Another prominent example of selective association is blocking. In blocking, one CS (A) is given initial training until a strong CR is established. Then, training is conducted in which the established CSA is compounded with a novel CS (X). Even after considerable training with the AX compound, tests with CSX reveal that it acquires little or no ability to evoke the CR (Kamin, 1968; Kehoe, Schreurs, & Amodei, 1981; Marchant & Moore, 1973; Schreurs & Gormezano, 1982). Although it might seem that a novel stimulus should engage the subject's attention, the blocking phenomenon suggests that the subject will continue to use an established CSA in predicting the US and not learn anything further about a novel but redundant CSX.

Among the theories that have been proposed to account for selective association, most assume that there is a competition among compounded CSs for attention (Sutherland & Mackintosh, 1971, p. 122) or associative strength (Rescorla & Wagner, 1972). Recent versions of these theories have relaxed the assumption that there is a direct competition for a fixed resource, but they still assume that there is a tradeoff among CSs in gaining access to the associative apparatus (e.g., Mackintosh, 1975; Moore & Stickney, 1980; Pearce & Hall, 1980; Schmajuk & Moore, 1985, 1988). Following Sutton and Barto's (1981) landmark article, competitive learning rules have been a common feature in connectionist models of learning (e.g., Gluck & Bower, 1988; Rumelhart & McClelland, 1986).

Configural Learning

In order to maximize flexibility in structural credit assignment, there is need for a Gestalt-like mechanism that permits a compound to be represented as a unit distinct from all of its elements. Learning tasks requiring Gestalt-like representations can be created with just two stimulus inputs. In particular, the exclusive-OR (XOR) problem requires a response to each of two inputs separately but not to their joint occurrence (Barto, 1985, p. 35; Kehoe, 1988b; Rumelhart, Hinton, & Williams, 1986, p. 319). The XOR problem demands a distinctive representation of the compound, because suppression of responding to the compounded inputs cannot possibly reflect a summation of the positive responses to the separate inputs (Minsky & Papert, 1969; Rumelhart et al., 1986, p. 319).

In both classical and instrumental conditioning, a clear exemplar of the XOR problem is found in the phenomenon of *negative patterning*. In the negative patterning schedule, the subject is trained with three types of trials: (a) one CS that is paired with the US (A +), (b) another CS that is also paired with the US (B +), and (c) a compound of A and B that is always presented alone (AB-). When all three trials are intermixed, subjects learn to respond on A + and B + trials but to suppress responding on AB- trials (Pavlov, 1927, p. 144; see Bellingham, Gillette-Bellingham, & Kehoe, 1985; Kehoe & Graham, 1988; Rescorla, 1972, 1973). For example, Figure 4.6 shows the development of negative patterning as it appears in rabbit eyelid conditioning (Bellingham et al., 1985). Early in training, the subjects tend to respond on AB- trials slightly more than on A + or B + trials, thus revealing an initial tendency to treat the AB compound as a sum of A and B. However, with extended training, configural learning emerges in that responding on AB- trials drops below that on A + and B + trials. Complete suppression of responding to AB- is not always achieved, but 75% of the subjects do show evidence of representing AB in a configural fashion.

To explain configural learning, there have been a variety of descriptive hypotheses which have tended to beg the question as to how the representation of any arbitrary compound is established without an explosive proliferation of special hardwired compound representations (Barto, 1985, pp.15-19; Kehoe & Gormezano, 1980, p. 375; Schlimmer & Granger, 1986). In connectionist modeling, the problem of compound representation has been addressed through the development of layered networks of adaptive elements, in which the intermediate "hidden" layers can become "tuned" to significant

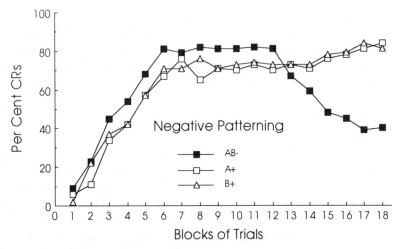

Figure 4.6. The likelihood of CRs in a negative patterning schedule, in which two stimuli were paired with the US (A +, B +) but their compounded presentation was not followed by the US (AB-) (Kehoe, 1988b).

combinations of stimuli through alterations in the connection weights, thus effectively synthesizing configural stimuli as they are needed (e.g., Anderson, 1973, 1977; Barto, Anderson, & Sutton, 1982; Rumelhart & McClelland, 1986). For a small number of stimuli, the whole range of configural learning phenomena, including negative patterning, can be explained in a coherent fashion by a small feed-forward network composed of three adaptive units that operate according to the delta rule (Kehoe, 1988b, 1989).

STIMULUS TRANSFER

No situation ever repeats itself exactly, even in the most tightly controlled laboratory (Hilgard & Marquis, 1940, pp. 176-177; Pavlov, 1927, p. 111). Thus, a key requirement for the success of any adaptive organism is its ability to transfer what has been learned in one situation to another situation. Transfer of learning not only permits the organism to tolerate random variation across recurring situations but also permits the organism to capitalize on previous experience to deal productively with novel situations as they arise. Transfer can appear in one of two ways, either immediately upon first presentation of a new situation or gradually in the course of training in the new situation.

Immediate Transfer

The common laboratory example of immediate transfer is *stimulus generalization*. This type of transfer is based on the similarity between a trained stimulus and a new stimulus along their common sensory dimensions. For example, suppose a subject is trained to respond to a tone of a fixed frequency. If the subject is tested with a tone of a different frequency, the initial level of responding to the new tone will vary as a direct function of the difference between its frequency and the frequency of the previously trained stimulus (Moore, 1972).

Gradual Transfer

The gradual emergence of transfer occurs when initial training with stimulus A does not alter the initial response to the new stimulus B but rather alters the rate of learning with stimulus B. A clear example of such transfer is *learning to learn*, which denotes a progressive acceleration in the rate of learning across a series of tasks that are similar in structure but differ dramatically in their superficial stimuli (Ellis, 1965, p. 32). In both classical and instrumental conditioning, learning to learn has been repeatedly demonstrated using stimuli in Task A and Task B that differ in their sensory modalities (e.g., Holt & Kehoe, 1985; Thomas, Miller, & Svinicki, 1971).

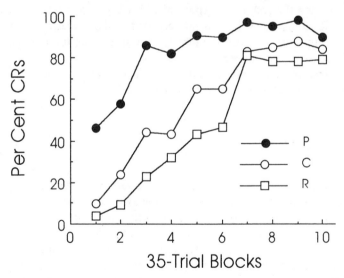

Figure 4.7. Learning to learn. CR acquisition to a novel stimulus after either (P) previous training with another CS closely paired with the US, (C) control training with unpaired presentations of another CS and the US, and (R) no previous exposure to either a CS or US (Kehoe & Holt, 1984).

Figure 4.7 shows the results that typify learning to learn in classical conditioning. The figure shows the learning curves for three different groups during Stage 2 of a transfer experiment. In Stage 1, one group of rabbits (P) was trained with either a tone or light CS that was paired with an electrotactile US. Two other groups served as "no learning" controls. One control group (C) was given exposure to the CS and US but separated by a wide interval. The other control group (R) was a rest control that did not receive presentations of either the CS or US in Stage 1. In Stage 2, all groups received pairings of a new CS with the US. As can be seen in Figure 4.7, the pretrained group (P) showed extremely rapid CR acquisition to the new CS. For example, Group P achieved a mean CR likelihood of 46% CRs within the first block of CS-US trials. In comparison, the control groups, C and R, achieved a mean CR likelihood less than 10% CRs within the first block of trials.

Learning to learn has long resisted rigorous theoretical explanation. However, layered networks have considerable potential for explaining learning to learn (Kehoe, 1988b; Schreurs & Kehoe, 1987). In brief, virtually all layered network models assume that connections from stimulus inputs converge on the intermediate, "hidden" units. In turn these hidden units have connections with response output units. Thus, in a layered network, initial establishment of a mapping between a CS input and CR output will be a relatively slow affair, because it will be necessary to establish a sequence of two connections, one from the CS to the hidden unit and one between the hidden unit and the response output unit. However, for a new CS, the rate of overt CR acquisition will be faster because it will be necessary to establish only the connection between the new CS input and the hidden unit. Once that connection is established, it can be used to trigger the hidden unit. The previously-established connection between the hidden unit and the response unit will then immediately generate a CR.

DISCUSSION

One consequence of the "cognitive revolution" has been a loss of interest in the research and theory connected with conditioning, usually thought to be the heartland of stimulus-response behaviorism. However, from the contemporary computational perspective, conditioning offers many phenomena that exemplify issues fundamental to understanding learning. The recent spread in connectionist modeling techniques has helped to identify the shared issues in what have been otherwise disparate areas of research. It can now be seen that the general issues of prediction, credit assignment, and transfer are common to animal conditioning, human learning, and machine learning.

The particular contribution by animal conditioning arises from its simplicity. As has been described above, uncluttered manipulations involving two or three stimuli can capture the essential features of the key issues. For example, the manipulation of the CS-US interval poses a prototypic problem in temporal credit assignment, and the negative patterning schedule poses a prototypic problem in structural credit assignment. Moreover, the abilities of nonhuman animals, sometimes as simple as insects or sea slugs (e.g., Alkon & Farley, 1984), to solve such computational problems suggests that these abilities are fundamental to understanding biological survival as well as cognition. It would be premature to assert that all animals, including humans, solve these problems in the same way. However, it can be said more safely that the ability to solve computational problems at a very simple level of neural and behavioral organization does suggest a continuity rather than an impenetrable barrier between what is considered "cognitive" and what are considered more primitive neural and behavioral processes.

REFERENCES

Alkon, D. L., & Farley, J. (Eds.). (1984). *Primary neural substrates of learning and behavioral change*. Sydney: Cambridge University Press.

Anderson, J. A. (1973). A theory for the recognition of items from short memorized lists. *Psychological Review, 80,* 417-438.

Anderson, J. A. (1977). Neural models with cognitive implications. In D. LaBerge & S. J. Samuels (Eds.), *Basic processes in reading: Perception and comprehension* (pp. 27-90). Hillsdale, NJ: Erlbaum.

Barto, A. G. (1985). Learning by statistical cooperation of self-interested neuron-like computing elements. *Human Neurobiology, 4,* 229-256.

Barto, A. G., Anderson, C. W., & Sutton, R. S. (1982). Synthesis of nonlinear control surfaces by a layered associative search network. *Biological Cybernetics, 42,* 1-8.

Bellingham, W. P., Gillette-Bellingham, K., & Kehoe, E. J. (1985). Summation and configuration in patterning schedules with the rat and rabbit. *Animal Learning & Behavior, 13,* 152-164.

Boakes, R. (1984). *From Darwin to behaviourism*. Cambridge, UK: Cambridge University Press.

Boring, E. G. (1950). *A history of experimental psychology*. New York: Appleton-Century-Crofts.

Capaldi, E. J. (1966). Partial reinforcement: An hypothesis of sequential effects. *Psychological Review, 73,* 459-477.

Coleman, S. R., & Gormezano, I. (1971). Classical conditioning of the rabbit's (*Oryctolagus cuniculus*) nictitating membrane response under symmetrical CS-US interval shifts. *Journal of Comparative and Physiological Psychology, 29,* 587-612.

Desmond, J. E., & Moore, J. W. (1988). Adaptive timing in neural networks: The conditioned response. *Biological Cybernetics, 58,* 405-415.

Egger, D. M., & Miller, N. E. (1962). Secondary reinforcement in rats as a function of information value and reliability of the stimulus. *Journal of Experimental Psychology, 64,* 97-104.

Ellis, H. C. (1965). *The transfer of learning*. New York: MacMillan.

Garcia, J., McGowan, B. K., & Green, K. F. (1972). Biological constraints on conditioning. In A. H. Black & W. F. Prokasy (Eds.), *Classical conditioning II: Current research and theory* (pp. 3-27). New York: Appleton-Century-Crofts.

Gibbs, C. M., Latham, S. B., & Gormezano, I. (1978). Classical conditioning of the rabbit nictitating membrane response: Effects of reinforcement schedule on response maintenance and resistance to extinction. *Animal Learning & Behavior, 6,* 209-215.

Gluck, M. A., & Bower, G. H. (1988). Evaluating an adaptive network model of human learning. *Journal of Memory & Language, 27,* 166-195.

Gormezano, I. (1972). Investigations of defense and reward conditioning in the rabbit. In A. H. Black & W. F. Prokasy (Eds.), *Classical conditioning II: Current research and theory,* (pp. 151-181). New York: Appleton-Century-Crofts.)

Gormezano, I., & Kehoe, E. J. (1975) Classical conditioning: Some methodological-conceptual issues. In W. K. Estes (Ed.), *Handbook of learning and cognitive processes, Vol. 2: Conditioning and behavior theory.* New York: Erlbaum.

Gormezano, I., & Kehoe, E. J. (1981). Classical conditioning and the law of contiguity. In P. Harzem & M. D. Zeiler (Eds.), *Advances in analysis of behavior, Vol. 2: Predictability, correlation, and contiguity* (pp. 1-45). Sussex, England: Wiley.

Gormezano, I., Kehoe, E. J., & Marshall, B. S. (1983). Twenty years of classical conditioning research with the rabbit. In J. M. Sprague & A. N. Epstein (Eds.), *Progress in psychobiology and physiological psychology, Vol. 10* (pp. 197-275). New York: Academic Press.

Grossberg, S., & Schmajuk, N. A. (1989). Neural dynamics of adaptive timing and temporal discrimination during associative learning. *Neural Networks, 2,* 79-102.

Hilgard, E. R., & Marquis, D. G. (1940). *Conditioning and learning.* New York: Appleton-Century-Crofts.

Holt, P. E., & Kehoe, E. J. (1985). Cross-modal transfer as a function of similarities between training tasks in classical conditioning of the rabbit. *Animal Learning & Behavior, 13,* 51-59.

Hoehler, F. K., & Leonard, D. W. (1976). Double responding in classical nictitating membrane conditioning with single-CS dual-ISI pairing. *Pavlovian Journal of Biological Science, 11,* 180-190.

Hull, C. L. (1937). Mind, mechanism and adaptive behaviors. *Psychological Review, 44,* 1-32.

Hull, C. L. (1943). *Principles of behavior.* New York: Appleton-Century-Crofts.

Kamin, L. J. (1968). Attention-like processes in classical conditioning. In M. R. Jones (Ed.), *Miami symposium on the prediction of behavior: Aversive stimulation.* Miami, FL: University of Miami Press.

Kehoe, E. J. (1979). The role of CS-US contiguity in classical conditioning of the rabbit's nictitating membrane response to serial stimuli. *Learning and Motivation, 10,* 23-38.

Kehoe, E. J. (1982). Overshadowing and summation in compound stimulus conditioning of the rabbit's nictitating membrane response. *Journal of Experimental Psychology: Animal Behavior Processes, 8,* 313-328.

Kehoe, E. J. (1983). CS-US contiguity and CS intensity in conditioning of the rabbit's nictitating membrane response to serial and simultaneous compound stimuli. *Journal of Experimental Psychology: Animal Behavior Processes, 9,* 307-319.

Kehoe, E. J. (1987). "Selective association" in compound stimulus conditioning with the rabbit. In I. Gormezano, W. F. Prokasy, & R. F. Thompson (Eds.), *Classical conditioning* (3rd ed., pp. 161-196). Hillsdale, NJ: Erlbaum.

Kehoe, E. J. (1988a). Behaviourism as an intellectual icon: Behavioural psychology's role in cognitive science. In R. H. Albury & P. Slezak (Eds.), *Dimensions of cognitive science* (pp. 43-59). Sydney: Centre for Cognitive Science, University of New South Wales.

Kehoe, E. J. (1988b). A layered network model of associative learning: Learning-to-learn and configuration. *Psychological Review, 95,* 411-433.

Kehoe, E. J. (1989). Connectionist models of conditioning: A tutorial. *Journal of the Experimental Analysis of Behavior, 52,* 427-440.

Kehoe, E.J., Gibbs, C.M., Garcia, E., & Gormezano, I. (1979). Associative transfer and stimulus selection in classical conditioning of the rabbit's nictitating membrane response to serial compound CSs *Journal of Experimental Psychology: Animal Behavior Processes, 5,* 1-18.

Kehoe, E. J., & Gormezano, I. (1980). Configuration and combination laws in conditioning with compound stimuli. *Psychological Bulletin, 87,* 351-378.

Kehoe, E. J., & Graham, P. (1988). Summation and configuration in negative patterning of the rabbit's conditioned nictitating membrane response. *Journal of Experimental Psychology: Animal Behavior Processes, 14,* 320-333.

Kehoe, E. J., & Holt, P. E. (1984). Transfer across CS-US intervals and sensory modalities in classical conditioning of the rabbit. *Animal Learning & Behavior, 12,* 122-128.

Kehoe, E. J., Schreurs, B. G., & Amodei, N. (1981). Blocking acquisition of the rabbit's nictitating membrane response to serial conditioned stimuli. *Learning and Motivation, 12,* 92-108.

Kehoe, E. J., Schreurs, B. G., & Graham, P. (1987). Temporal primacy overrides prior training in serial compound conditioning of the rabbit's nictitating membrane response. *Animal Learning & Behavior, 15,* 455-464.

Kehoe, E. J., Graham, P., & Schreurs, B. G. (1989). Temporal patterns of the rabbit's nictitating membrane response to compound and component stimuli under mixed CS-US intervals. *Behavioral Neuroscience, 103,* 283-295.

Lashley, K. S. (1916). The human salivary reflex and its use in psychology. *Psychological Review, 23,* 446-464.

Mackintosh, N. J. (1975). A theory of attention: Variations in the associability of stimuli with reinforcement. *Psychological Review, 31,* 519-526.

Mackintosh, N.J. (1983) *Conditioning and associative learning.* Oxford: Clarendon Press.

Marchant, H. G., III, & Moore, J. W. (1973). Blocking of the rabbit's conditioned nictitating membrane response in Kamin's two-stage paradigm. *Journal of Experimental Psychology, 108,* 155-158.

Minsky, M. L. (1961). Steps toward artifical intelligence. *Proceedings of the Institute of Radio Engineers, 49,* 8-30. Reprinted in E. A. Feigenbaum & J. Feldman (Eds.), (1963). *Computers and thought* (pp. 406-450). New York: McGraw-Hill.

Minsky, M. L., & Papert, S. (1969). *Perceptrons: An introduction to computational geometry.* Cambridge, MA: MIT Press.

Millenson, J. R., Kehoe, E. J., & Gormezano, I. (1977). Classical conditioning of the rabbit's nictitating membrane response under fixed and mixed CS-US intervals. *Learning and Motivation, 8,* 351-366.

Moore, J. W. (1972). Stimulus control: Studies of auditory generalization in rabbits. In A. H. Black & W. F. Prokasy (Eds.), *Classical conditioning II: Current research and theory,* (pp. 206-230). New York: Appleton-Century-Crofts.

Moore, J. W., & Stickney, K. J. (1980). Formation of attentional-associative networks in real time: Role of the hippocampus and implications for conditioning. *Physiological Psychology, 8,* 207-217.

Pavlov, I. P. (1927). *Conditioned reflexes.* (trans. by G. V. Anrep) London: Oxford University Press.

Pearce, J. M., & Hall, G. (1980). A model for Pavlovian learning: Variations in the effectiveness of conditioned but not of unconditioned stimuli. *Psychological Review, 87,* 532-552.

Rescorla, R. A. (1972). Informational variables in Pavlovian conditioning. In G. Bower (Ed.), *The psychology of learning and motivation, Vol. 6.* New York: Academic Press.

Rescorla, R. A. (1973). Second-order conditioning: Implications for theories of learning. In F. J. McGuigan & D. B. Lumsden (Eds.), *Contemporary approaches to conditioning and learning* (pp. 127-150). Washington, DC: Winston.

Rescorla, R. A., & Wagner, A. R. (1972). A theory of Pavlovian conditioning: Variations in the effectiveness of reinforcement and nonreinforcement. In A. H. Black & W. F. Prokasy (Eds.), *Classical Conditioning II* (pp. 64-99). New York: Appleton-Century-Crofts.

Revusky, S. H. (1971). The role of interference in association over a delay. In W. K. Honig & P. H. R. James (Eds.), *Animal memory* (pp. 155-213). New York: Academic Press.

Robinson, E. S. (1932). *Association theory today.* New York: Century.

Rumelhart, D. E., Hinton, G. E., & Williams, R. J. (1986). Learning internal representations by error propagation. In J. L. McClelland & D. E. Rumelhart (Eds.), *Parallel distrubuted processing: Explorations in the microstructure of cognition, Vol 1: Foundations* (pp. 318-362). Cambridge, MA: MIT Press.

Rumelhart, D. E., & McClelland, J. L. (1986). *Parallel distributed processing, Vol. 1. Foundations.* Cambridge, MA: MIT Press.

Schlimmer, J. C., & Granger, R. H., Jr. (1986). Simultaneous configural classical conditioning. In C. Clifton (Ed.), *Proceedings of the eighth annual conference of the cognitive science society* (pp. 141-153). Hillsdale, NJ: Erlbaum.

Schmajuk, N. A., & Moore, J. W. (1985). Real-time attentional models for classical conditioning and the hippocampus. *Physiological Psychology, 13,* 278-290.

Schmajuk, N. A., & Moore, J. W. (1988). The hippocampus and the classically conditioned nictitating membrane response: A real-time attentional-associative network. *Psychobiology, 46,* 20-35.

Schneiderman, N. (1966). Interstimulus interval function of the nictitating membrane response in the rabbit under delay versus trace conditioning. *Journal of Comparative and Physiological Psychology, 62,* 397-402.

Schreurs, B. G., & Gormezano, I. (1982). Classical conditioning of the rabbit's nictitating membrane response to CS compounds: Effects of prior single-stimulus conditioning. *Bulletin of the Psychonomic Society, 19,* 365-368.

Schreurs, B. G., & Kehoe, E. J. (1987). Cross-modal transfer as a function of initial training level in classical conditioning with the rabbit. *Animal Learning & Behavior, 15,* 47-54.

Sheffield, V. F. (1949). Extinction as a function of partial reinforcement and distribution of practice. *Journal of Experimental Psychology, 39,* 511-526.

Smith, M. C. (1968). CS-US interval and US intensity in classical conditioning of the rabbit's nictitating membrane response. *Journal of Comparative and Physiological Psychology, 66,* 679-687.

Sutherland, N. S., & Mackintosh, N. J. (1971). *Mechanisms of animal discrimination learning.* New York: Academic Press.

Sutton, R. S. (1984). *Temporal credit assignment in reinforcement learning.* Unpublished doctoral dissertation, University of Massachusetts, Amherst, MA.

Sutton, R. S., & Barto, A. G. (1981). Toward a modern theory of adaptive networks: Expectation and prediction. *Psychological Review, 88,* 135-170.

Thomas, D. R., Miller, J. T., & Svinicki, J. G. (1971). Nonspecific transfer effects of discrimination training in the rat. *Journal of Comparative and Physiological Psychology, 74,* 96-101.

CHAPTER 5

Metacognitive Processes and Learning with Intelligent Educational Systems

Kathryn Crawford and Judy Kay

Faculty of Education
and Department of Computer Science
University of Sydney

INTRODUCTION

There is a growing belief among educators that it is important to give students opportunities to review their learning and to reflect about how the learning occurred. That is, students need to know both *what* they know and to know *how* to learn. These metacognitive processes are thought to be particularly important when students need to learn abstract and generalized information from experience in such a way that they can apply the knowledge in new situations.

The perceived importance of metacognitive processes is a direct result of a paradigm shift in learning theory and a resulting change in the beliefs about learning that are used as a rationale for educational practice. There is now consensus among cognitive scientists that knowledge is not transmitted from teacher to learner but rather constructed by learners through reflection on their experience.

We believe that a computer system's model of a learner's knowledge and related learning characteristics can provide an invaluable tool for encouraging learners to reflect about these. Wahlster and Kobsa (1986) describe a system's set of beliefs about the user as a *user model*, and a *user modeling component* as programs that create, update, and maintain a user model. In this chapter we will use the term *learner model* to describe individual models of individual learners. Learner models are an important part of individualized interfaces, especially those in teaching systems.

Intelligent Educational Systems (IESs) differ from human teachers in an important way. It is possible for the learners to understand the explicit and completely deterministic control mechanism of a computer system. Further, the learner model can be displayed externally (on a monitor screen) which provides ideal conditions for conscious reflection, discussion and review.

In contrast, the learner models used by human teachers are often intuitive and implicit. Teachers frequently have difficulty making explicit the underlying beliefs about the learner and the learning process that determine their teaching practice and assessment decisions. Moreover, studies like those of Nisbett and DeCamp Wilson (1977) suggest that there are many situations where teachers may not have access to such understanding. In such conditions of interaction, communication difficulties often arise between teachers and learners. These are caused by erroneous assumptions about "mutual knowledge" (Sperber & Wilson, 1986) or "shared understanding" (Edwards & Mercer, 1987). These assumptions are often a result of the widely held transmission model of learning in which knowledge is believed to be communicated to learners by teachers. Learners often misinterpret the clues human teachers give about a range of critical aspects: the teachers' learner models; the consensual knowledge in the curriculum; and criteria for assessment. As a result, many approach learning tasks in dysfunctional ways and develop idiosyncratic and personal beliefs about knowledge domains.

In this chapter we explore the implications of the changing models of learning and the function of metacognitive processes in the construction of knowledge under various conditions. The potential of intelligent educational systems to provide a learning context that enhances the use of metacognitive processes will be discussed with particular reference to one form of a learner model.

CHANGING MODELS OF LEARNING:
THE IMPORTANCE OF LEARNER ACTIVITY IN REVIEW
AND REFLECTION ABOUT LEARNING

The communication difficulties described above are exacerbated by the tensions and inconsistencies (see Cobb, 1988) that exist between traditional teaching practice (including the structure and organization of educational institutions) and theories of learning based on more recent psychological research. A critical aspect of the traditional transmission model is its basis of an expert teacher passing knowledge to an essentially passive, receptive learner. By contrast, more recent theories of learning and human development (for example, Brown & Deloach, 1986; DiSessa, 1979; Duckworth, 1986; Resnick, 1985, 1988; Sternberg, 1984; von Glasersfeld, 1987) stress the importance of the *active* and *purposeful participation* of the learner in the construction of knowledge, and of experience in interpreting and reasoning on the basis of new knowledge. Flavell (1979), Lawson (1984), and Yussen (1985) have also suggested that students need to reflect about their learning and review new knowledge (metacognitive processes) and also to be aware of how they came to know (metacognitive knowledge).

Research suggests (Crawford, 1986; 1988; Resnick, 1988) that in traditional situations knowledge is constructed through memorizing and practicing until skills, procedures, and information are well established. In such cases metacognitive processes, if they are used consciously, are directed to facilitate the memorization of techniques and procedures. Knowledge that has been acquired in such a way is generally not available for critical review. Further, there is evidence (Crawford, 1984; 1986; 1990; Hiebert, Carpenter, & Moser, 1983; Luria, 1982) that such cognitive behavior is counterproductive. Research data suggests that such an approach to learning inhibits students from developing concepts along with the metacognitive knowledge and cognitive processes that are an essential prerequisite for the application of knowledge in novel situations. There is now consensus among researchers such as Cobb (1988), Resnick (1985; 1988), and Davydov, Zinchenko, and Talysina (1983) that concepts, knowledge about the relationships between them, metacognitive processes, and metacognitive knowledge are developed by each individual through reflection upon and interaction with the social and physical environments.

An alternative and detailed interactionist perspective is provided by Leont'ev (1981) and Davydov, Zinchenko, and Talysina (1983) gives a detailed theoretical framework for the analysis of the relationships between needs, goals, and conscious reasoning activity. These authors suggest that learners perceive the goals of any task in an individual and subjective way. According to Leont'ev (1981), these subjective perceptions of goals and the needs of the individual delimit cognitive activity. Davydov et al. (1983, p. 33) emphasize the difference between the above process and stimulus-response theories in which the state of the subject is determined directly by objects. They describe the interaction between an individual and their subjective representation of a context for intellectual or physical activity as involving the following:

- A need that impels a subject to search for an object or goal.
- The discovery of an object or goal. Once the object is discovered, intellectual activity is no longer guided by the characteristics of the object itself but by its (subjective) image.
- The generation of an "image" is seen as a bilateral process between subject and object.
- The conversion of activity into objective results.

For the above theorists, the social context of thinking is seen as a critical factor in cognitive development and learning. In particular, Leont'ev values the achievement of consensus between the teacher and the learner about the goals of any task and the meaning of culturally important objects. Indeed, they see this as a major aim of public education. Traditionally, teachers have commonly assumed their own goals are shared by their students.

Leont'ev (1981) describes object-related information processing in a social context as "activity." He stresses the inseparability of human mental reflection from those aspects of human activity that engender it. He uses the term *activity* to describe intellectual and other behavior that is stimulated by a motive and subordinated to a conscious goal. Leont'ev (1981, p. 61) gives a microanalysis of activity and describes actions and operations as the basic components. He distinguishes between actions and operations as follows:

- An action involves conscious behavior that is subordinated to a goal.
- An operation is an action that has been transformed as a means of achieving a result under given conditions.

Leont'ev (1981, p. 64) suggests that "It is generally the fate of operations that, sooner or later they become the function of a machine."

In Leont'ev's terms, one impact of information technology on human enterprise has been an increased emphasis on involvement in *actions* rather than *operations*. This change is already evident in most adult work places but has yet to be seen in institutional forms of education. This may be due to the social organization of schools.

The research of Mugney & Doise (1978) suggests that hierarchical relationships between teacher and learner are counter-productive for the kind of reflective learning described above. Decision making, introspection, and review are appropriate cognitive activities in self-directed learning or creative purposeful activities, but are generally perceived as less appropriate for students who see their role as subordinate.

THEORIES OF LEARNING AND IESs

Theories of learning are implicit in the design of all IESs. Very often, these theories are covert and the interactions with learners are structured to reflect the software designer's experience of education. Far too infrequently, the IES is designed to optimize the quality of learning intended. IESs have a particular potential to avoid the debilitating effects of hierarchical relationships that we have discussed above. In human-computer interactions, this change is socially appropriate.

In such a context, the learner has the right to be in control. Even more, because they are dealing with a machine, a controlling role for the learner also changes the quality of the learning in desirable ways. That is, learners who are in control of a machine perceive themselves as responsible for the outcomes of the interaction. In such a case they perceive their needs and goals in terms of overall decision making about interpretation of the task, strategy selection and review of solutions obtained. Being accountable for the outcomes, metacognitive processes are perceived as appropriate cognitive activity and are more likely to occur.

Bodker (1989) used Leont'ev's activity theory as a framework for data analysis in her research on the role of the user interface in purposeful human work. She concluded that the user interface cannot be seen independently of the human perceptions of the purpose or meaning of work. That is, human interactions with a user interface are delimited by subjective perceptions of the goal of such interaction (and personal needs) as well as the characteristics of the interface.

For example, secretarial staff using an interface to prepare documents under pressure of time are most likely to develop a rather simple and entirely functional model of the system they are using. A computer scientist using the same system for different, more generalizable purposes would be expected to construct quite a different mental representation of the system.

Educators now agree about the fact that knowledge is constructed through active engagement in practical experience. Accordingly, active, hands-on learning processes are increasingly used for education in abstract fields such as mathematics, science and computing. However, some difficulties have become evident in processes associated with generalization and abstraction from such experiences. For these to occur, review and reflection on the experience are also important.

Research (Olsen, 1987; Crawford, 1988; Ivanova, 1980) suggests that metacognitive processes are enhanced by the use of externalized representation of ideas and information. An interactive IES learner model has the potential to provide these conditions with a graphic representation of the learner's knowledge on a monitor screen. This form of representation could be available as a focus for review, analysis, reflection, and modification.

In sum, learning models in the shape of IESs have the potential to provide a learning environment with important characteristics that are likely to facilitate the process of reflecting about experience and becoming conscious of the resultant learning.

First, it is possible and desirable for the learner to be in control of a machine. A controlling role is likely to enhance the use of metacognitive processes and concept development. In addition the user interface of an IES can be designed to encourage active interaction between learner and machine. Reflection and review are possible. They may be explicitly required by the interface design.

Second, an IES has the potential to provide an explicit visual display of the learner model or a representation of the consensual knowledge that is the goal of the learning activity. Such a display is known to facilitate the effective use of metacognitive processes.

Third, reflection and review about the task at hand may be the explicit goal of interaction with an IES. School socialization gives most students a highly instrumental approach to learning tasks. This socialization means that it is often difficult to construct a learning context in which reflection and review occur. An IES may provide a context where the use of metacognitive processes is perceived by students as relevant to interaction with a learner model.

Finally, an IES has the potential to make details of its learner model explicit and available for review and possibly argument.

HOW MIGHT WE ENCOURAGE REFLECTION AND METACOGNITION IN AN IES?

Given the desirability of metacognitive learning, how might we nurture it? One approach is to encourage the learner to reflect. We can encourage this by creating contexts where they need to reflect about what they know and how they know it. There are many ways one may do this. The manner that we recommend is to take advantage of the *learner model* that is the basis for individualization of any IES. It captures the conclusions and teaching goals of the IES and it summarizes the system's assessment of the student's achievements and progress.

For the remainder of the chapter, it will be helpful to have an example that can serve to illustrate the general discussion. We now introduce an example of a learner model that might be part of an IES concerned with children's learning of arithmetic. Figure 5.1 shows a list of the components of an individual learner model (where a component is the primitive element of such models). The first component indicates this learner's knowledge of how to add any pair of single digit numbers. Figure 5.1 shows that this student partially knows these. The second component concerns ability to multiply any pair of single-digit numbers. The third and fourth components are misconceptions this student has and the model indicates that this student sometimes gives two different (both incorrect) results when adding zero to a number. The last three components are an indication of this learner's liking of mathematics, their sex and age.

Description of component	Value
1. student knows number facts for addition	partially
2. student knows number facts for multiplication	some
3. student believes that adding 0 increases by 1	partially
4. student believes that adding 0 gives a 0 result	partially
5. student likes arithmetic	yes
6. student's sex	male
7. student's age	6

Figure 5.1. Example of a learner model

Although the actual representation of the learner model differs greatly between different systems, essentially most have a good deal in common with this one in the ways discussed below.

First, the learner model is generally a list of components (often referred to by various terms) with some indication of the value. Many components have a truth value. Common representations for this are numeric, possibly with one value indicating how true the component is and another for the confidence in that value. Regardless of the actual representation, these could be interpreted in a form like that shown in the value column of Figure 5.1. Other components, like the student's sex and age, have arbitrary values. Although Figure 5.1 gives a simple list of components, it is not unusual to have some structure in the learner model of an IES. Goldstein (1982) has described a relatively sophisticated structure used in his system. This uses several classes of relationships between the components to structure them into what he calls a genetic graph. Even in Figure 5.1, we can see relationships between some components. For example, we represent knowledge of addition number facts and separately deal with a particular instance of one number fact, the addition of zero. A learner who knows all the number facts must also know about addition of zero. So the components (3 and 4) concerned with the latter are related to component 1. It is reasonable that an IES would be designed to maintain consistency in the model by relating these components and ensuring that it could not represent a learner as always knowing all the number facts and yet sometimes believing that addition of zero alters the number.

Implementation of an Accessible Learner Model

Now we consider the implications of accessible learner models for the implementation of that learner model. First we review some of the existing approaches to implementing learner models and then we introduce an approach that has been driven by a concern for making the model accessible to the learner.

Learner Models in Existing IESs

The learner model is the basis of individualization in any IES, so there is one as part of each IES. Typically, the learner model and the processes that define it are deeply embedded within the IES. This is because the design of the learner model is driven exclusively by the overall needs of the IES.

Because of this, the learner model needs only to be useful to the IES and to the programmer who created and maintains it. It should be noted that this does not necessarily mean that it is inaccessible. After all, the programmer needs good displays of the model as they develop the IES. Commonly, there are debugging tools which provide displays of the learner model.

One might imagine that these displays are the learner model that we advocate making available to the learner. Unfortunately, this would not usually be the case. As we have observed, the learner model typically is designed and implemented for the creator's eyes alone. This means that it may be inappropriate for viewing by the learner or even a human teacher working with the learner. Problems include the choice of terms, which may be technical and closely related to the details of the implementation. Worse still, they may be offensive or, at the very least conceived without thought to the framework within which the learner is operating. Like Kobsa (1990), we emphasize that where a program maintains long-term models of a person, privacy issues must be taken into account. Indeed, a cornerstone of such models should be that individuals should have access to the model of them kept by the machine. Moreover, that model should be accessible, not just in the strict sense, but they should be able to understand it and effect changes where they believe the model to be wrong.

There are difficulties in taking existing learner models and using them as the basis for reflection by the learner, but we now discuss how small adjustments to the programmer's view of the learner model can permit it to serve the needs of the IES and, at the same time, to be useful for the learner as a basis for reflection on a learning experience.

Structure and Representation

We believe that it is desirable (and not difficult) to design the representation of the learner model so that it is directly accessible to the learner. This permits the learner to use the normal utilities for viewing data on the computer to display the learner model. Provided it is directly accessible and in a form that is reasonably natural, the learner can then see that there is no magic involved. They can see exactly the same information that the IES uses in dealing with them.

Now let us examine the implications of this accessibility. The long-term learner's model constituting the information that must exist between each session with the IES needs to be stored in a file. We argue that there is little difficulty in making this an ordinary text file that is formatted in a manner that is comprehensible. We consider it desirable that the casual reader should be able to easily see the correspondence between this external form and a form that is presented by a display program.

The learner model is also more meaningful if it is structured. This means that related model components are stored together. This reduces the likelihood of drowning the reader in a large and unstructured mass of modeling components.

In addition, the learner model should enable the learner to get access to the reasoning processes that defined it. This means there need to be links to the domain knowledge and the teaching strategies that interact with the learner model.

In all this, it is most likely that the best way to view a learner model is with the aid of a utility which we call a *viewer*. This can give a helpful interface to the learner model, presenting related components a few at a time, with the option to select ones reflecting misunderstandings, or recent achievements or the like. The viewer can then take the tedium out of following the links to the reasons for conclusions in the model. In addition to the viewer, it is natural to have an an *editor* that allows the learner to correct the learner model or explore the effect of various changes. Such a utility needs an undo facility so that a learner can return to earlier versions of the model. Of course, the amendments that a learner makes are an important part of the model. How an IES can deal with these types of changes is discussed in a later section on reasoning about the model.

One implementation of the guidelines above is described in Kay (1990a). It keeps the learner models as ASCII file in a tree hierarchy. This organizes the model into a collection of partial models with related ones grouped together. The facility for editing or altering the model is described in Cook and Kay (1993).

Distinctions between Different Component Classes

From the learner's point of view, there are a number of different classes of components in a learner model:

- knowledge — the abstract notions for the domain (e.g., understanding 1:1 correspondence between numbers and objects when counting) as well as the ways to do a particular task in a domain (e.g., knowing how to add two numbers)
- characteristics — the learner's characteristics (e.g., sex and age)
- preferences — the things the learner likes or dislikes (e.g., arithmetic)

These appear to be useful distinctions between components, the way that they are used, and the reasoning that may apply to them. For the first, there is a further distinction that is useful. This is whether the component relates to *consensual* (knowledge the IES 'believes' to be true) or nonconsensual knowledge which reflects a *misconception* that the learner may have. As the example below indicates, this reflects whether the IES 'believes' this component or not and that a particular learner may or may not believe it. For an IES this distinction is important as it frequently needs to deal with malknowledge or incorrect beliefs held by the the learner.

System 'believes' that the learner believes this	System 'believes' that this component is true	false
true	true, consensual	true, 'misconception'
false	false, consensual	false, 'misconception'

Similar distinctions between classes of knowledge and beliefs have been suggested by others, for example Abelson (1979), and Benyon, Innocent, and Murray (1987).

Bases for reasoning about components. There are two main forms of reasoning about the learner. The first is evidence available from various sources, including the various interactions between the learner and the IES and other information provided to the system. The second form of reasoning is the method used for *conflict resolution*, where this means the way that the IES deals with conflicting evidence about the same components. For example, the students may have been observed to use a method but in a test they could not indicate any understanding of that method. If the system draws any conclusion from these sets of evidence, the process that underlies that conclusion is one of the bases of the IES's reasoning. Although there are many ways that conflicts might be resolved, we argue that the IES constructor should be able to provide a simple explanation of how such conflicts are resolved.

Now let us return to the evidence that is the basis for conclusions about the learner. We have found it useful to distinguish between the various sources of information about the learner. These are:

1. *given:* covers information the system is provided as fact, where this includes aspects like the learner's age, sex, and levels of educational attainment.

2. *knowledge-based inference:* based on the structure of knowledge in the domain as captured in the IES. So, for example, this includes the IES model of *prerequisite* knowledge so that evidence that the learner really knows some concept X can be used to conclude that they also know the concepts that are prerequisites for X. Other structures in the knowledge may also be used, as for example in the cases of genetic graphs (Goldstein, 1982).

3. *obtrusive observations:* observations of the learner's behavior at times when they knew that this was being assessed. So, for example, they may have been doing a diagnostic task or answering a questionnaire.

4. *unobtrusive observations:* those where the learner may have been unaware that the system was collecting data on their interaction with the system.

5. *covered:* aspects that the learner has been told or that the IES may have covered with this learner. Although this is not necessarily very strong evidence that the learner has learnt from it, it does give some support for this conclusion.

6. *stereotypes:* statistically based forms of default reasoning like those of Rich (1983). Here, the system uses information that has statistical validity but may well not apply to this learner. For example, it may

be that a very high proportion of students with a particular educational background have not learned certain concepts. The IES may use this to create an initial default model for the learner until it has more information. Clearly, this type of information must be used carefully and it should not be confused with the knowledge-based inference described above.

We have found the above distinctions are sufficient to usefully categorize different sources of information about the learner. In addition, they have inherently different levels of credibility. In one system (Kay, 1990a), there is one conflict-resolution strategy that is partially based on the above distinctions, with the order above corresponding to decreasing degree of validity.

It should be noted that there is no need to limit the IESs to a single conflict-resolution strategy. For example, our current implementation uses two very simple strategies, both based on the entrenchments of Gardenfors (1988). The first treats the six sources listed above as being in decreasing order of reliability. So, for example, unobtrusive observations suggesting that the learner does not know something would be overriden by a knowledge-based inference that they did know it. Where there is conflicting information from sources of equal reliability, the time at which the source provided the information is used, with more recent information deemed more reliable.

The difference between the two strategies relates to the handling of given information. Since the model contains an identification of who gave the information, it is possible to deal with the varying reliability of the sources of the given information. Our second strategy treats information given by the individual about themselves as less reliable than the next three levels listed above. This corresponds to an interpretation of the information in the model by an agent which does not regard the learner as being the most reliable source of information. This might correspond to the view of a skeptical teacher. In our system, it enables us to compare the effect of this difference in conflict resolution strategy.

Accessibility of the model has a benefit in addition to being a basis for nurturing metacognitive learning. It increases the *accountability* of the authors of the IES as they know that learners and their human teachers can study the bases for the system's conclusions. This seems especially important in the case of the stereotype-based reasoning that is sixth on our list.

Motivating Learners to Reflect on Their Learner Model

Making the learner model accessible is only useful if learners actually look at it. It is clear that at least some learners are incorrigibly curious and with any opportunity will explore their learner model.

However, even the curious learner may not react on the basis of their learner model. For this, we need systematic activities based on the learner studying their own learner model. These will be critical to facilitating the sort of reflective activity we have been discussing. Indeed, they will be all the more important if the less curious learner is even to be coaxed to look at their learner model at all.

There are many possible activities that could be based on the the analysis of the learner model. At the simplest level, the student can be called to define areas which they need to revise. More interesting is a case like this: They are asked to reflect on their own perceptions of their understanding of selected high-level aspects in the domain and then be required to consult their user model. Here they can compare their own assessment of learning with the machine's model. In particular aspects of interest, like those where there is a mismatch between the learner's own and the machine's assessment of learning, the learner should delve into the bases of the machine's reasoning. Then they can analyze the reasons for the differences between their own assessment and the machine's.

Another approach to encouraging the student to reflect can involve sessions with the human teacher managing the learning activities that include the IES. The teacher and learner could sit together analyzing the assessment embodied in the learner model.

A quite different possibility is to integrate the processes of assessing learning, maintaining learner models, and giving learners access to the bases for the conclusions in the learner model. This has been done in a system (Kay, 1990b; 1991). This uses the technique of concept mapping (Novak & Gowin, 1984) as an explicit means of assessing a student's knowledge. Because this was designed in association with an accessible learner model, the system supports quite detailed information about why it concludes that a student knows something (or not).

In all this, one of the most obvious learner responses involves disagreeing with the IES assessment as seen in the learner model. This can itself be used as a powerful tool for reflection. The learner can record a disagreement with particular aspects of the learner model and the system (or human teacher) can challenge them to find the precise point in the machine's reasoning where the student considers that the machine drew the wrong conclusion about them. So, for example, it may be that a particular problem-solving task indicated the student's failure to learn some concept. On analysis, the student may recall that they were not feeling well at that time and did not do the task properly. At that point, it may be possible to allow the student to redo that task. The new entry in that part of the learner's model would override the earlier one. It is also probably desirable to study other ways of amending the learner model. One obvious approach would be to mark that part of the model as *contested*, and another is to *undo* the effects of the student's performance on that particular task.

Another benefit of allowing the student to disagree with the IES, learner model, or its underlying reasoning, is that it may be a valuable basis for improving the IES. This can apply in at least two different ways. Firstly, it may be that the IES has a bug in this particular aspect. Whoever maintains the IES could use logs of learner's disagreements to identify these. A second possibility is that the IES is indeed correct but significant numbers of students complete a learning experience with incorrect assessments of what they have learned. In this case, the record of disagreements could be the basis for revising the teaching.

CONCLUSION

Changing theories of human learning and development indicate the importance of active revision and reflection by learners. Using such metacognitive processes to *learn how to learn* and to review what has been learned is an important aspect of the educational process. The central argument of this chapter is that the learner model that is essential to the individualization of interaction by an IES is a valuable learning tool. In particular, as it captures the goals and assessments of the IES, it is a useful basis for the learner's reflection, and this can be the basis for encouraging metacognitive learning.

We have examined the reasons that the learner model is not currently used in this way in IESs. We have described the requirement of the learner model in terms of

- its structure and representation;
- its primitive components;
- the major distinctions we see between different sources of reasoning about the learner model; and
- the utilities needed.

It appears that learners' reflection about their learning is an invaluable means of acquiring metacognitive knowledge and a conceptual frame of reference as a basis for intellectual activity. Making the learner model accessible to the student requires externalizing the conclusions and reasoning processes of the IES. As we have discussed, the fact that the IES can make this available is an important and inherent difference between an IES and a human teacher. This chapter has discussed one means of exploiting this difference between human and machine teaching as a basis for nurturing metacognitive learning. This approach seems likely to realize the educational potential of IESs in a most useful way.

REFERENCES

Abelson, R.P. (1979). Differences between belief and knowledge systems. *Cognitive Science, 3,* 355-266.

Benyon, D., Innocent, P., & Murray, D. (1987). System adaptivity and the modelling of stereotypes. Human computer interaction - INTERACT '87. Elsevier Science Publishers B.V.

Bodker, S. (1989). A human activity approach to uder interfaces. *Human Computer Interaction, 4* (3), 171-195.

Brown, A., & deLoach, J. (1978). Skills, plans and self-regulation. In R.S. Seigler, (Ed.), *Children's thinking: What develops?* Hillsdale, NJ: Erlbaum.

Cobb, P. (1988). The tension between theories of learning and instruction in mathematics. *Educational Psychologist, 23* (2), 2-7.

Cook, R., & Kay, J. (forthcoming). Tools for viewing the justified user model. Forthcoming SSRG Report, Dept of Computer Science, University of Sydney.

Crawford, K.P. (1984). Some cognitive abilities and problem solving behaviour: The role of the generalised images and/or simultaneous processing. *Proceedings of the Eighth Conference of the International Group for the Psychology of Mathematical Education* 269-274, Math. Assoc. of NSW, Sydney.

Crawford, K.P. (1986). Cognitive and social factors in problem solving. *Proceedings of the 10th Conference of the International Group for Psychology of Education,* 415-421. University of London, Institute of Education, London.

Crawford, K.P. (1988). New contexts for learning mathematics. *Proceedings of 11th Conference of the International Group for the Psychology of Education,* 239-246. Ferne Genzwen, Vesprew, Hungary.

Crawford, K.P. (1990). School definitions of work: Their impact on the use of technology in mathematics education. *Proceedings of the Conference on the Political Dimensions of Mathematics Education.* London: London Institute of Education.

Crawford, K.P., Groundwater-Smith, S., & Milan, M. (1989). *Gender and the evolution of computer literacy.* Report for the NSW Ministry of Education, Australian Government Printer, Sydney.

Davydov, V., Zinchenko, V., & Talysina, N.F. (1983). The problem of activity in the works of A.N. Leont'ev, *Soviet Psychology, 21,* 4.

di Sessa, A.A. (1979). On learnable representations of knowledge: A meaning for the computational metaphor. In J. Clement (Ed.), *Cognitive process instruction.* Philadelphia, PA: Franklin Institute Press.

Duckworth, E. (1986). Teaching as research. *Harvard Educational Review, 56* (4), 481-495.

Edwards, D., & Mercer, N. (1987). *Common knowledge.* London: Methuen.

Flavell, J. (1979). Metacognition and monitoring: A new area of psychological enquiry. *American Psychologist, 34* (4), 906-911.

Gardenfors, P. (1988). *Knowledge in flux.* Cambridge, MA: MIT Press.

Glasersfeld, E. von, (1987). Learning as constructive activity. In C. Janvier (Ed), *Problems of representation in the teaching and learning of mathematics.* Hillsdale, N.J.: L. Erlbaum Associates.

Goldstein, I.P. (1982). The genetic graph: A representation for the evolution of procedural knowledge. in J.S. Brown (Ed.), *Intelligent tutoring systems.* New York: Academic Press.

Hiebert, J.T., Carpenter, P., & Moser, J. (1983). The effect of instruction on children's solutions to addition and subtraction word problems. *Educational Studies in Mathematics, 14* (1), 55-72.

Ivanova, L.G. (1980). The acquisition of generalized images and their use by pupils in problem solving situations, *Voprosi Psiklology, 1,* trans by L. Kouzman. Australian National University, Canberra.

Kay, J. (1990a). Um: A toolkit for user modelling. *Second International Workshop on User Modelling,* Honolulu, Hawaii, March 30-April 1.

Kay, J. (1990b). *Exploratory experiment in the use of concept mapping for eliciting models of users' conceptual knowledge,* Technical Report 380, Basser Department of Computer Science, University of Sydney.

Kay, J. (1991). An explicit approach to acquiring models of student knowledge. In S. Otsuki (Ed.), *Advanced research on computers and education* (pp. 263-268). North Holland: Elsevier.

Kobsa, A. (1990). User modeling in dialog systems: Potentials and hazards. *SFB- 314: AI knowledge based systems.* Dept. of Computer Science, Univ. of Saarbrucken, West Germany.

Lawson, M.J. (1984). Being executive about meta-cognition. *Cognitive strategies and educational performance.* Orlando, FL: Academic Press.

Leont'ev, A. (1981). The problem of activity in psychology. In J. Wertsch (Ed.), *The concept of activity in Soviet psychology.* Armonk, NY: Sharpe.

Luria, A.R. (1982) Language and Cognition (trans J. Wortche) US, Wiley.

Mugney, G., & Doise, W. (1978). Sociocognitive conflict and the structure of individual and collective performances. *European Journal of Social Psychology, 8* (2), 181-192.

Nisbett, R., & Wilson, C. (1977). Telling more than we can know: Verbal reports on mental processes. *Psychological Review, 84* (3) 231-259.

Novak, J. D., & Gowin, D.B. (1984). *Learning how to learn.* Cambridge, UK: Cambridge University Press.

Olsen, S.E. (1987). Catool: A computer-based tool for investigations of categorical information in mental models. *Human computer interaction - INTERACT '87.* Amsterdam: Elsevier Science Publishers B.V.

Resnick, L.B. (1985). Cognition and instruction: Recent theories in human competence. In B.L. Hammonds (Ed.), *Master Lecture Series, Vol. 4, Psychology and learning.* Washington, DC: American Psychological Association.

Resnick, L.B. (1988). Constructing knowledge in school. In D.H. Feldman (Ed.), *Development of Learning: Conflict or congruence?,* Hillsdale, NJ: Embaum.

Rich, E. (1983). Users are individuals: Individualising user models. *International Journal of Man-Machine Studies, 18,* 199-214.

Sperber, M. & Wilson, D. (1986). *Relevance: Cognition and communication.* Blackwell, London, UK.

Sternberg, R. (1983). Components of human intelligence. *Cognition, 15* (I), 1-48.

Wahlster, W. & Kobsa, A. (1986 July). Dialogue-based user models. *Proceedings of the IEEE, 74* (7), 948-960.

Yussen, S. (1985). The role of metacognition in contemporary theories of cognitive development. In D. Forrest-Pressley (Ed.), *Metacognition, cognition and human performance, Vol. I.* Orlando, FL: Academic Press.

CHAPTER 6

The Shape of Learning Functions During Transfer

Craig P. Speelman

Department of Psychology
University of Western Australia

Anderson's (1982, 1983) ACT* theory of skill acquisition proposes that skills develop through a process of interpretation of declarative knowledge which, with practice, leads to productions, the embodiment of procedural skill. The initial interpretative stage is slow and error-prone because declarative knowledge must be kept in working memory. With practice comes proceduralization and composition which lead to productions. These can be considered condition-action statements that have the effect of the initial interpretive processes but which are faster and more efficient. Productions contain task-specific information that eliminate the necessity of maintaining declarative information in working memory. With further practice these productions become automatic in the sense that satisfaction of their conditions will automatically initiate their actions.

The ACT* theory provides an account of the speed up in performance that comes with practice. Composition leads to efficient productions that do the work of a series of separate productions in one step. Proceduralization enables productions to fire without the constant need to check the contents of working memory. In addition, productions are strengthened with practice which speeds up their firing. The reduction in performance time that comes as a result of these three processes has been shown by Anderson (1982) to account for the ubiquitous power law of learning (Newell & Rosenbloom, 1981). This basically says that with practice time to perform a task will decrease by diminishing amounts. This law can be described by the following equation:

$$T = NP^c \qquad (1)$$

where T is the time to perform the task, N is a parameter related to the number of processing steps involved in performing the task, P is the amount of practice, and c is the learning rate ($c < 0$).

Recently Anderson has extended the ACT* theory to encompass the transfer of procedural skill (Anderson, 1987; Singley & Anderson, 1989). The ACT* theory of transfer is described by Anderson as a modern version of Thorndike's identical elements theory (Thorndike & Woodworth, 1901). In the original theory, transfer between tasks was determined by the extent to which they shared identical elements, where these elements were stimulus-response pairs. The modern version proposes that these elements are instead productions, which are more abstract stimulus-response rules. Thus the amount of transfer from one task to another will be determined by the number of productions underlying performance in one task that can be applied in the performance of the other task. Singley and Anderson (1985, 1989) have recently reported considerable evidence in support of this theory of transfer.

The issue examined in this chapter is the effect of transfer on learning functions. The ACT* account of the power law of learning (i.e., Equation 1) assumes that the more productions executed in the performance of a task, the longer will be the performance time. This suggests a number of effects on learning functions depending on the degree of transfer between tasks. For instance, if the same productions developed with one task are applied to perform another task, complete transfer will result. Performance with the new task will involve further improvement of the productions developed in the first task. Thus the learning function observed with the new task should be predicted by extrapolating the learning function observed with the first task. However, the situation is more complex if the new task requires that new productions be developed in addition to the old productions. In this case, it is obvious that extrapolating a learning function that describes improvement only in the old productions will not provide a good description of performance with the new task. The aim of the present study was to examine the changes in learning functions in such a transfer situation. Experiment 1 examined the initial effect on performance time of switching tasks to one that requires the execution of both old and new productions. Experiment 2 examined practice with a new task that involves both old and new productions and the learning function that results.

EXPERIMENT 1

A task was devised whereby particular features could be manipulated which would encourage subjects to adopt strategies involving either more or fewer productions. The task involved solving syllogisms of the sort displayed in Table 6.1. There were two types of these syllogisms presented in this study. These differed only in the order of the premises. Thus the ABBC type (this label corresponds to the order of the elements in the premise pairs presented in Table 6.1 — A for 'acrobat', B for 'butcher' etc.) is equivalent in meaning to the BCAB type but has the reverse order of premises. The valid conclusions for these two types of syllogism are the same (see Table 6.1).

Premises

ABBC	**BCAB**

All of the acrobats are BUTCHERS.   All of the BUTCHERS are cricketers.
All of the BUTCHERS are cricketers.   All of the acrobats are BUTCHERS.

response   →   *READY*

Conclusion

(True)   All of the acrobats are cricketers.
(False)   All of the cricketers are acrobats.

response   →   *TRUE or FALSE*

Table 6.1: Sample syllogism presented to the experimental group during the Training phase of Experiment 1. Illustrated are the two forms of premise pairs (ABBC and BCAB), the two forms of conclusions (TRUE and FALSE), and the appropriate responses to each part of the syllogism.

During the training phase of Experiment 1, subjects were given extensive practice at solving the syllogisms. On each trial, the premise pairs were presented for study. Subjects indicated when they had processed these, and then a conclusion was presented. The subjects were to indicate whether the presented conclusion was 'true' or 'false' with respect to the premises presented earlier.

There is good reason to predict that subjects will develop a perceptual strategy with the syllogism task as opposed to a reasoning strategy (Quinton & Fellows, 1975). Speelman (1990) has demonstrated that subjects appear to adopt a strategy that involves locating the common elements in the premise pairs and then using this information to locate the elements that will comprise the true conclusion (i.e., the uncommon elements). Speelman (1990) also reported evidence that subjects locate common elements by processing and matching each of the elements in the premise pairs. This suggests that if the process of matching elements could be circumvented then this would reduce the need to develop the skill of matching elements to locate common ones. One way of cirumventing this process is to highlight the common elements in relation to the rest of the premise pairs. This is illustrated in Table 6.1 where the common elements of each syllogism have been capitalized.

Two groups of subjects were used in this experiment. During training, the experimental group was presented with the two types of syllogism in a random order with the common elements highlighted. The control group was presented with the same items but without this highlighting. During the transfer phase, both groups solved the same new syllogisms without highlighting. The assumption underlying the highlighting manipulation was that the experimental group would rely on this feature to solve the syllogisms, whereas the control group would learn to locate common elements the hard way. Thus the experimental group should perform the task with less productions than the control group, and therefore should perform faster during the training phase. However, during the transfer phase, the experimental group would be forced to solve problems without the highlighting, upon which they previously relied. As a result these subjects would need to develop new productions that perform the location of common elements, in addition to applying their old productions that perform the rest of the task. In contrast, the control group would have developed productions in the context of no highlighting and so would be well-equipped for this situation.

If the experimental group is required to develop and execute new productions in addition to old productions during transfer, then this suggests that performance would be slowed substantially. This slowing should be evident by two indicators. The first concerns the transfer performance of the control group. This group will have developed productions during training that can perform the task efficiently. For these subjects the task does not change with the transition to the transfer phase. As a result the old productions will execute and so produce efficient performance during this phase also. In contrast, the experimental group will be required to execute new productions during transfer and so should be substantially slower than the control group during this phase. In addition, the experimental group should also be slower than the performance predicted by extrapolating the learning function observed with this group during training. That function only describes the improvement of the old productions and so will not account for the development and execution of additional productions.

The highlighting manipulation should have no effect on the processing of conclusions. After the premises of a syllogism have been processed, subjects press a button which results in the premise pairs disappearing and a test conclusion appearing in their place. Thus subjects would be required to solve the syllogism prior to the presentation of the test conclusion. As a result, subjects in both groups should process test conclusions in similar ways, attempting to match them with the solutions to the premise pairs. This implies that, with respect to processing conclusions, complete transfer should be observed in both conditions.

METHOD

Subjects

Seventy-four students from the University of Western Australia Department of Psychology first-year course volunteered to participate in the experiment for course credit. Ten subjects failed to reach the learning criterion of an error rate not exceeding 25% in the last half of the training phase. The data from these subjects were not further analyzed, leaving 64 subjects, 32 in each condition.

Materials

Three hundred eighty-four syllogisms were constructed. They were all of a categorical form (see Table 6.1). The premises were constructed so that one term denoted an occupation and two terms denoted preoccupations or interests. This constraint minimized semantic relations within premise pairs without sacrificing plausibility for them or their corresponding conclusions, valid or invalid (Johnson-Laird & Steedman,1978). Premise pairs were avoided that led to contradictory or confusing conclusions (e.g., "All of the fathers are aunties.").

The first 96 syllogisms were constructed using 288 different terms. The following 96 items were constructed on the basis of the first set by using a different permutation of terms across items. The next 96 items were also a different permutation of the set of terms. These three sets of 96 items were used as training items. Thus each of the 288 terms was presented three times during training, with different terms each time, and also in a different position of the syllogism each time. An additional set of 96 items was constructed by deriving another permutation of the first 96 items. These additional items were used as transfer items. A further two syllogisms were constructed and presented as practice items.

Half of the syllogisms were always presented in ABBC form, the other half were always in BCAB form (see Table 6.1). Across subjects each item was presented half the time with a true conclusion and half with a false conclusion (see Table 6.1).

Design

Two groups were used in this experiment. During training the experimental group was presented with syllogisms with capitalized common elements (see Table 6.1). The control group was trained with the same items except the common elements were presented in lower case. During the transfer phase, both groups were presented with syllogisms without the highlighting feature.

Apparatus and Procedure

The experiment was controlled by a PDP 11/73 computer. All experimental sessions were conducted in soundproof booths. Syllogisms were presented on a CRT and subjects made responses on a keyboard.

Subjects were tested in one one-hour session. They were instructed that they would be presented with a number of small problems to solve. Each problem would consist of three statements. The first two statements (premises) would describe particular types of people. The third statement (conclusion) could be a conclusion based on what the first two statements said. The subjects' task was to decide whether the third statement was true or false of what the first two statements described.

Each item was presented as follows (see Table 6.1). The premises were presented on the screen. Subjects were instructed to press the 'READY' button (space bar of the keyboard) when they had read the premises. Premises were visible for a maximum of ten seconds. When a subject pressed "READY" or did not respond within ten seconds, the premises disappeared. The conclusion then appeared on the screen below where the premises had been. Subjects were then to press "TRUE" (the 'z' key of the keyboard) or "FALSE" (the '/' key of the keyboard) dependent on how they felt the statement corresponded to the preceding premise pair. Again subjects were given a maximum time of ten seconds to respond. When a subject pressed "TRUE" or "FALSE" or did not respond within ten seconds, the conclusion disappeared. Following this subjects were provided with feedback on the screen for two seconds. This consisted of a sentence of the form: "Correct/Incorrect, conclusion was True/False," dependent on the subjects' response. No feedback was provided if subjects did not press "TRUE" or "FALSE." After the feedback disappeared from the screen the next item was presented automatically.

Subjects were given two practice trials at the beginning of the experiment. They were presented in the same fashion as the experimental trials and were both of the ABBC form. The first one was presented with a true conclusion, the second with a false conclusion, and subjects were provided with feedback after each trial. Following these practice trials subjects were presented with the 288 training trials. At the end of the training phase, subjects were given a one-minute rest during which they were instructed on the screen that the next phase of the experiment (transfer phase) would be similar to the previous phase though much shorter. Subjects in the experimental group were not forewarned that training and transfer conditions were different. After the rest period, the computer automatically presented the 96 trials in the transfer phase.

RESULTS AND DISCUSSION

Mean premise and conclusion RTs for both groups during the training and transfer phases are displayed in Figure 6.1. As is obvious from this figure, both groups improved substantially in both measures throughout training. Overall, the subject's premise RTs improved from 5751.65 ms during the first block of training to 2120.46 ms in the last block ($F(5,310)$ = 158.661, $p < 0.05$). Conclusion RTs were reduced from 1923.18 ms to 788.79 ms ($F(5,310)$ = 81.847, $p < 0.05$) and accuracy improved from 76.25% to 97.27% ($F(5,310)$ = 49.305, $p < 0.05$).

Analyses of variance indicated that there were no overall differences in premise RTs between the two groups in training (Exp = 3171.95 ms vs. Cont = 3224.22 ms, $F(1,62) < 1$). However, there was an interaction between training block and condition ($F(5,310)$ = 8.307, $p < 0.05$). Inspection of Figure 6.1 reveals that this interaction involves the two groups studying premises for similar amounts of time during the early blocks of training, but in the latter half of this phase, the experimental group seems to perform this part of the task in less time than the control group. A post-hoc comparison using Tukey's WSD procedure (Maxwell & Delaney, 1990) was made between the premise RTs of the two groups during the final block of training. This comparison indicated that the experimental group (1751.17 ms) was faster than the control group (2489.75 ms) during this block ($F(1,62)$ = 5.691, $p < 0.05$). This result supports the assumption that the experimental group would process premises with less productions than the control group, at least toward the end of training.

There was no difference during training between the two groups in conclusion RTs (Exp = 1124.94 ms vs. Cont = 1078.89 ms, $F(1,62) < 1$). This result supports the assumption that both groups would process conclusions in similar ways, that is, with similar productions. In contrast the two groups did differ in accuracy, with the experimental group performing, on the whole, less accurately than the control group (Exp = 89.48 ms vs. Cont = 94.21, $F(1,62)$ = 7.253, $p < 0.05$). It is not clear what this result indicates about the assumptions concerning strategy.

The transfer results show a clear effect of the different training conditions. Figure 6.1 indicates that the experimental group were slowed markedly with the transition from premises with highlighted elements to premises without this highlighting. However, this slowing was only apparent with the processing of premises. The conclusion RTs of this group did not appear to be affected by the highlighting manipulation.

Two forms of analysis were used to investigate the transfer effects apparent in Figure 6.1. The first involved direct comparisons between the transfer performance of the two groups. Over the two blocks of the transfer phase there were no differences between the two groups in premise RTs (Exp = 2557.97 ms vs. Cont = 2168.90 ms, $F(1,62)$ = 1.878, $p < 0.05$), conclusion

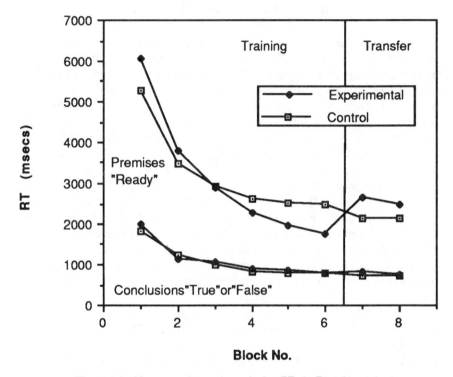

Figure 6.1: Mean premise and conclusion RTs in Experiment 1.

RTs (Exp = 795.29 ms vs. Cont = 720.42 ms, $F(1,62) < 1$) or accuracy (Exp = 95.51% vs. Cont = 97.67%, $F(1,62) < 1$). However, a one-tailed comparison of the premise RTs in the first block of transfer, the most obvious difference between the groups in Figure 6.1, revealed that the experimental group was slower than the control group, at least in the initial stages of transfer (Exp = 2638.37 ms vs. 2142.36 ms, $F(1,62) = 3.171$, $p < 0.05$, one-tailed). This difference is consistent with the prediction that the experimental group would bring to the transfer phase a set of productions that were not as well-equipped as the productions of the control group for processing premises without highlighting. As a result the experimental group needed to develop new productions to fill the gap between what the old productions could achieve and what was required in the new task. The execution of the new productions would mean that, overall, the experimental group would be slower than the control group whose productions are all well-practiced.

The second form of analysis used to examine the transfer effects evident in Figure 6.1 involved comparing each group's transfer performance with that predicted on the basis of their training performance. Power functions were fit to the learning functions observed during training and then extrapolated into the transfer phase. Any difference between the observed and predicted transfer performances will indicate the extent to which transfer performance relies on the application of the same productions developed during training. Figure 6.2 displays the results of this analysis for the control group. It is obvious from this figure that, in both premise and conclusion RTs, transfer performance is consistent with that predicted on the basis of training performance. These results are further support that the control group applied the same set of productions developed during training to the problems presented during transfer.

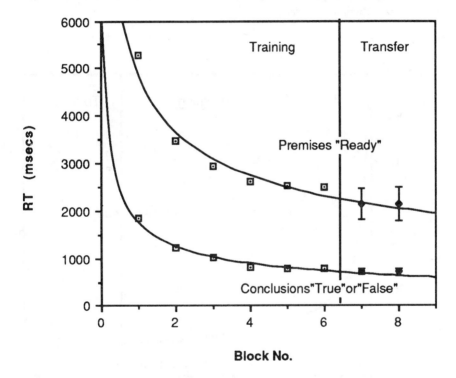

Block No.

Figure 6.2 Mean premise and conclusion RTs of control group during training and transfer phases of Experiment 1. Error bars are confidence limits (alpha = 0.05). Lines are power functions fit to training data and extrapolated into the transfer phase, with the following equations:

Premises: RT = 4947.2 Block $^{(-0.43)}$, r^2 = 0.956;
Conclusions: RT = 1774.1 Block $^{(-0.50)}$, r^2 = 0.971.

Figure 6.3 displays the results of the second form of transfer analysis to the experimental group data. The pattern of results during transfer is very different from that observed with the control group. In premise RTs the

experimental group was markedly slower during transfer than is predicted
on the basis of their training performance. In contrast, the conclusion RTs
of this group are entirely consistent with the predictions from training. Thus,
as predicted, the removal of the highlighting of common elements during
transfer only affected the processing of premises. The removal of the highlighting feature meant that the experimental group lacked productions for
locating common elements and so were required to develop these during the
transfer phase. This resulted in a slowing of performance, but only as
indicated by premise RTs. The presentation of conclusions during transfer
was identical to their presentation during training. Hence the experimental
group possessed a set of productions that were suitable for processing
conclusions during transfer.

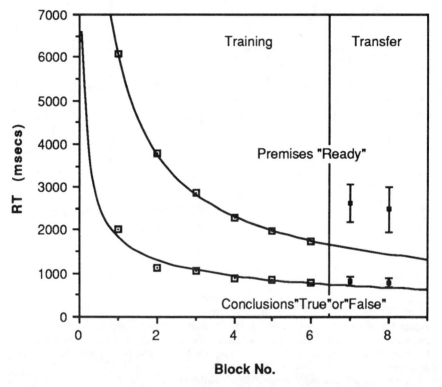

Figure 6.3: Mean premise and conclusion RTs of experimental group during training and
transfer phases of Experiment 1. Error bars are confidence limits (alpha = 0.05). Lines are
power functions fit to training data and extrapolated into the transfer phase, with the following
equations:

Premises: RT = 6105.1 Block $^{(-0.70)}$, r^2 = 0.999;

Conclusions: RT = 1831.8 Block $^{(-0.49)}$, r^2 = 0.941

In conclusion, the results of Experiment 1 provide further support for the role of productions in transfer. Where task situations were predicted to rely on identical productions, complete transfer was observed. Partial transfer was observed when the development of new productions to complement old productions was predicted. The slowing effect of executing both old and new productions on performance time was clear. Thus partial transfer was shown to result in a change in the relationship between amount of practice and performance time. In particular, the learning functions observed during training were not capable of predicting performance with partial transfer, but were entirely adequate with complete transfer.

The performance examined in Experiment 1 involved only a small amount of practice following transfer. In order to examine the longer term effects of partial transfer on learning functions, more practice during transfer is necessary. The amount of practice during transfer was increased in Experiment 2 to investigate further the shape of learning functions during this phase.

EXPERIMENT 2

The previous experiment demonstrated that the combination of old and new productions in a transfer task will result in slower performance than if performance relies on the execution of old productions only. It is obvious, though, that given sufficient practice with the new task, performance will improve. This raises the interesting question of how improvement with the transfer task will compare with the improvement observed with the training task. A number of possible scenarios exist. One that will be examined in this study is based on the assumption that all new skills are learned at the same rate. In other words, all things being equal, each person has a constant learning rate at which completely new skills are learned. This assumption is implicit in Anderson's (1982) explication of the power law of learning (see Speelman, 1990).

The assumption of a constant learning rate for new skills can be used as the basis for a model of the effect of partial transfer on performance time. In a simple situation where a task involves only new productions, a power function like Equation 1 is usually adequate to describe improvement with practice. In this type of function initial time to perform the task is a function of the number of productions involved in the task. However, if a task involves the combination of old and new productions, then functions of the form described by Equation 1 will not be adequate. The simple reason is that in this situation the components underlying performance will not have had equal amounts of practice. As a result, a power function with one term that describes amount of practice is not sufficient. This then raises the question of how varying amounts of practice can be incorporated into a function that describes improvement on a task with old and new productions.

One possibility is suggested by Anderson, Conrad and Corbett (1989) who propose that "acquisition of ... skill can be predicted by composing simple learning functions for (the) units" underlying tasks (p. 503). One interpretation of this proposal is that it is suggesting that components underlying performance of a task have their own learning functions and that the learning function for the task as a whole is a combination of these separate functions. This would suggest that old and new components improve with practice according to their own learning functions. These separate functions would then include the fact that the components have had unequal amounts of practice. The learning function for the task would then be a combination of these "old" and "new" learning functions.

The form of this combination needs to be considered before the implications of this suggestion can be examined. Underlying a great deal of the research into skill acquisition is the assumption that the more steps involved in a task the longer it takes to perform (e.g., Anderson, 1982; Staszewski, 1988; Carlson, Sullivan, & Schneider, 1989). This assumption also was the basis of the predictions examined in Experiment 1. The assumption implies a serial process where each step contributes a particular amount of time to the whole performance time. Following this logic with the combination of old and new skills requires the combination to be a serial one. That is, the processing of one set of components should not impinge upon the processing of the other set except to provide input information. If this is the case then the learning function for the whole task should be a simple linear combination of power functions describing improvement in each of the underlying components. If the components can be separated into old and new then this function will have the following form:

$$T_{\text{task}} = T_{\text{old}} + T_{\text{new}}$$
$$= N_o P_o{}^c + N_n P_n{}^c. \qquad (2)$$

This equation represents the linear combination of two power functions of the form described in Equation 1. Terms with the subscript "o" represent parameters of the old components of the task, and terms with the subscript "n" represent parameters of the new components.

There are a number of implications of Equation 2 that should be made explicit. The first is that the contribution of each set of components to the overall task time is weighted by the number of productions involved in each set. That is, the greater the number of productions in a set of components, the greater will be the contribution of this set. The second implication is that this weighted combination will be qualified by the amount of practice that the sets of components have had prior to the combination. This qualification has two forms: (a) the more practice a set of components have had, the faster they will be; and (b) as the amount of practice of a set of components increases, the room for improvement decreases. Both of these factors serve to reduce the contribution of a set of components to the overall performance time of a task.

The most important implication of Equation 2 concerns the rate at which improvement will occur in the whole task. In this equation the learning rate of the two separate power functions (c) is the same in each function. This represents the assumption described above that the learning of all components of a task for any one person is a constant. Incorporating this assumption into the equation results in a power function describing improvement in the overall task that has a different learning rate to that of each of the components. This difference is always in the direction of a reduction: The learning rate of the whole task will be slower than the learning rate of its underlying components. The amount by which the learning rate will be reduced is a function of the relative number of steps in the old and new components, and of the relative amount of practice each set of components had prior to combination.

For example, consider the case of a subject who has practiced a task for 6 sessions. Let the task have 100 productions ($N = 100$) and the learning rate be -0.8 ($c = -0.8$). The improvement in the time to perform the task can now be described by the equation $T = 100P^{-0.8}$ (this is only a loose description as N in Equation 1 is only proportional to the number of productions, not equal to this number). Now suppose the subject is given a new task to practice that includes all of the productions in the old task plus a new set of productions that number 20. The subject will be able to execute the old productions quickly but will be starting from scratch with the new productions. The time to perform such a task that includes old and new components can be described by the combination of the power functions that would describe improvement on the separate components. Thus,

$$T = T_{old} + T_{new}$$

$$= 100\ P_{old}^{-0.8} + 20\ P_{new}^{-0.8}$$

$$\text{where } P_{old} = P_{new} + 6$$

This function now has an overall learning rate of $c = -0.44$ (i.e., plot T against P_{new} on log-log axes and the gradient of the resulting straight line is -0.44). Therefore, learning rate has been attenuated as a result of combining two skills that differ in the amount of practice they have had and the number of productions involved with their execution. The rate of improvement in the overall task is slower than in the components underlying performance in the task. However, the attenuation will not always be as dramatic as in this example. Speelman (1990) has demonstrated that the amount of attenuation is moderated by two factors: (a) the relative number of steps between old and new components of the task, and (b) the amount of practice that the old skills had prior to learning the new task. Some evidence exists in the research literature to support these predictions (see Speelman, 1990).

Experiment 2 was designed as an explicit test of the main prediction that can be derived from Equation 2, that the combination of old and new productions will result in an attenuation of learning rate. The design of this experiment was similar to that of Experiment 1. Two groups were given extensive practice with the syllogism task. Both the experimental group and the control group were presented with syllogisms during training with the common elements of the premises highlighted. During transfer, the control group again solved syllogisms with the highlighting feature. In contrast, the experimental group was presented with items without this feature. The transfer phase of this experiment was longer than in Experiment 1, with the same number of trials as in the training phase.

The purpose of the highlighting manipulation in this experiment was the same as in the previous experiment. The experimental group was assumed to rely on the highlighting feature during training and so be ill-equipped for the transfer situation where this cue was no longer present. As a result this group should develop new productions during transfer to complement their old productions. According to Equation 2, the learning function of this group during transfer should be at a slower rate than was observed during training. However, this effect should only be evident with premise RTs. The productions developed to process conclusions during training are assumed to be adequate for this task during transfer. Therefore, conclusion RTs should continue to improve according to the learning function observed during training. For similar reasons, the premise and conclusion RTs of the control group during transfer should be described by extrapolating the learning function observed with these measures during training.

An important methodological point should be made at this stage. This point concerns determining whether transfer performance reveals a learning rate attenuation or the continuation of a previously observed learning function. The latter situation will be observed as a learning function, during transfer, that also has a slower learning rate than that observed during training. However, this attenuation is simply a result of using an inappropriate point to represent 'session one' in plotting the learning function and then determining learning rate. Figure 6.4 illustrates that in this situation a practice function with a 'slow' learning rate is in fact the tail end of a learning function with a faster learning rate. This phenomenon can result in inaccurate measures of learning rate when prior experience with a task is not taken into account. Newell and Rosenbloom (1981) suggest that using a more general form of the power function that incorporates the amount of prior practice can improve the accuracy of power function descriptions of practice data. Such a function would have the following form:

$$T = N (P + E)^c \tag{3}$$

This equation is the same as Equation 1, except that the term which represents the amount of practice on a task is now divided between practice that is observed (*P*) and practice prior to observation (*E*). This form of the power function has been shown to provide a better fit to some practice data but is also no better than simpler functions (Equation 1) with other data (Singley & Anderson, 1985). It appears that the reason why Equation 3 is no better than Equation 1 for some practice data is that the assumption of prior experience with a task is too general an assumption. As demonstrated above, prior experience may only apply to some components of a task. Other components will not have had any practice. Hence Equation 2 should be a more accurate depiction of some situations.

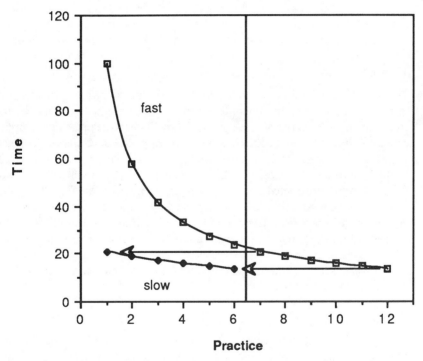

Figure 6.4: Demonstration that a practice function with a 'slow' learning rate may be the tail end of a function with a faster rate. The last six data points of the fast curve (learning rate = -0.80) have been displaced 6 practice units. The new curve now has the slower learning rate of -0.239.

In summary, if transfer performance relies on the combination of old and new productions or further improvement of old productions, then learning rate will appear to be slower than is observed during training. However, Speelman (1990) has demonstrated that the learning rate attenuation that results from the combination of old and new productions is in fact less than that which is associated with further continuation of old productions. Despite this though, because both of these situations result in an attenuation of learning rate, a reduction in learning rate was not considered sufficient support for the model of transfer described by Equation 2. Therefore the degree to which transfer performance can be accounted for by the various equations was also considered.

METHOD

Subjects

Forty-two subjects from the same subject pool as Experiment 1 participated in this experiment for course credit. Ten subjects failed to reach the learning criterion and so their data were eliminated from further analysis. The remaining 32 subjects were divided evenly between the two conditions.

Materials

The items used in this experiment during the training phase were identical to those used in the experimental condition in Experiment 1. That is, the common elements in the premise pairs of these items were presented in upper case to highlight them in comparison to the lower case uncommon elements.

In the transfer phase of this experiment, the first 96 items were identical to those used during transfer in Experiment 1. An additional 192 items of this form were constructed by recombining the elements in the first 96 training items. The new combinations of elements followed the same constraints described in Experiment 1 concerning the plausibility and implications of the resulting syllogisms. In the experimental condition of this experiment, all of the elements in the premise pairs of these transfer items were presented in lower case. In the control condition the common elements of these items were presented in upper case.

Design

Two groups of subjects were used in this experiment. In the experimental condition, subjects were presented with training items that contained capitalized common elements and then transfer items with all elements in lower case. In the control condition, subjects were presented with items that contained capitalized common elements during both the training and transfer phases. For both conditions, the order of presentation of ABBC and BCAB problems during the training and transfer phases was random.

Apparatus and Procedure

These were identical to those in Experiment 1 except in two respects: (a) Subjects in this experiment were presented with 288 transfer items instead of 96 and so experimental sessions often lasted for longer than 60 minutes; and (b) As a result of the greater number of trials, more rest periods were considered necessary. In this experiment the computer automatically signaled a one-minute rest period every 48 trials, and when the minute had elapsed, it automatically presented the next trial. The message that was presented by the computer to signal the rest period was the same in each period. Thus the transition from the training phase to the transfer phase of the experiment was not announced.

RESULTS AND DISCUSSION

Mean premise and conclusion RTs of both groups during training and transfer are displayed in Figure 6.5. It is clear from this figure that when stimulus conditions were equivalent for the two groups (i.e., during training), performance did not differ appreciably between the two groups in either premise or conclusion RTs. However, when the highlighting feature was removed from the premises during transfer, the experimental group exhibited a marked slowing in premise RTs, but not in conclusion RTs. In contrast, the control group continued to improve during transfer as if nothing had changed from the training phase, as indeed nothing had for this group.

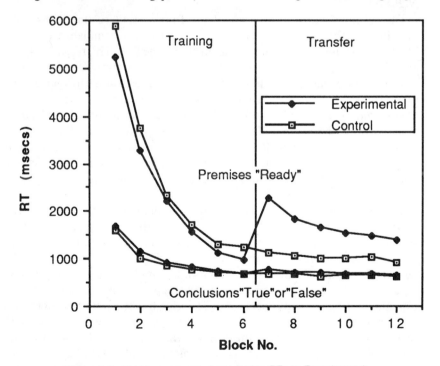

Figure 6.5. Mean premise and conclusion RTs in Experiment 2.

Power functions were fit to the reaction time data in order to evaluate the prediction based on Equation 2. The results of this curve-fitting are displayed in Figures 6.6 and 6.7. The equations for all curves and information concerning their goodness of fit to the observed data are presented in Table 6.2. Two important features should be noted of the functions fit to the data of this experiment. The first is that these functions include nonzero asymptotes (e.g., $T = X + NP^c$, where X = performance time at asymptote). According to Anderson (1982), the value of X is usually very small relative to $X + N$ (i.e., performance on Trial 1). In addition power functions approach asymptote slowly. Anderson suggests that it is for these reasons that power functions with zero asymptote (i.e., $X = 0$) can provide very good fits to practice data. The practice data in Experiment 1 were fit very well by power functions with zero asymptotes. Furthermore, the degree of fit was not improved significantly by incorporating nonzero asymptotes. However, Anderson makes the point that when practice involves a sufficient number of trials, careful analysis of data will reveal evidence of nonzero asymptotes. It was considered likely that nonzero asymptotes would be evident in this experiment because of the extra practice included in the transfer phase. Thus the functions described in Table 6.2 all include asymptotic values, and the form of Equation 2 tested in this experiment is: $T = X + N_o P_o^c + N_n P_n^c$.

The second feature to note about the functions fit to the data in this experiment is that performance time was plotted against cumulative accuracy, instead of against block number, as in Experiment 1. The reason for this modification is related to the ACT* account of the power law of learning. This account proposes that most of the improvement in performance time that results from practice is related to the strengthening of productions (Anderson, 1982). In ACT* productions are only strengthened in response to successful application. Therefore plotting performance time against amount of successful practice (i.e., cumulative accuracy as a proportion of number of blocks of practice) was considered to provide a more accurate test of the predictions based on Equation 2, which is itself based on the ACT* account of skill acquisition.

The control group experienced the same stimulus conditions in both phases of the experiment. Therefore it was assumed that during transfer these subjects would apply the same productions executed during training. This was predicted to result in improvement during transfer that would be described by extrapolating the learning function observed during training. Figure 6.6 shows that this prediction was supported by the results of this experiment. Premise and conclusion RTs during transfer were consistent with performance predicted on the basis of training performance. Table 6.2 shows that fitting power functions to the observed transfer data and to performance predicted by extrapolating training performance results in similar functions. These functions are similar in terms of their equations and therefore the degree to which they can account for the data. Note that in both premise and conclusion RTs, the learning rate observed during transfer is slower than observed during training, but is at least of similar magnitude to that predicted by extrapolating training performance. Therefore, as predicted, when transfer performance is assumed to rely on continued improvement of old productions, this performance will be described by extrapolating the learning functions that describe the initial learning of these old productions.

The experimental group was assumed to perform during transfer with a combination of old and new productions. The old productions are those developed during training and the new productions are those developed during transfer to cope with the new stimulus conditions during this phase. Therefore transfer performance was predicted to be described by application of Equation 2, rather than by extrapolating training performance. This prediction only applied to premise RTs, however. Conclusion RTs were predicted to be described by extrapolating training performance. Figure 6.7 shows that conclusion RTs during transfer were accounted for well by extrapolating the power function fit to the training conclusion RTs. In contrast, the transfer premise RTs were far removed from the reaction times predicted by extrapolating the power function fit to the training premise RTs.

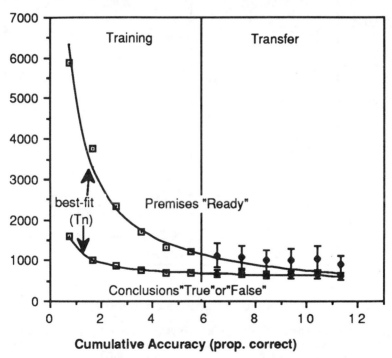

Figure 6.6: Mean premise and conclusion RTs of the control group (Experiment 2). Lines are power functions fit to training data and extrapolated into the transfer phase (see Table 6.2 for equations). Error bars are confidence intervals (alpha = 0.05).

A version of Equation 2 was derived for this data set and compared with
the observed transfer data (see Appendix A for details of the derivation of
this particular version). It is clear from Figure 6.7 that although this function
accounts for the initial slowing in the first block of transfer, it accounts for
little more of the data in the remaining blocks of transfer. Despite this result,
though, some support is provided by the data for the model represented by
Equation 2. As can be seen from the results in Table 6.2, the learning rate
of the power function fit to the transfer premise RTs (-0.408) is slower than
the learning rate observed during training (-0.877). On the other hand, it is
faster than the learning rate predicted by extrapolating training performance
(-0.273). This result supports the *general* learning rate prediction of Equation
2. However, the specific learning rate prediction of Equation 2 for this data
(-0.585) was somewhat faster than observed. The version of Equation 2
displayed in Figure 6.7 predicted reaction times that did not match the
observed values very closely, as is evident in this figure, and by the large
rmsd value (434.764 ms).

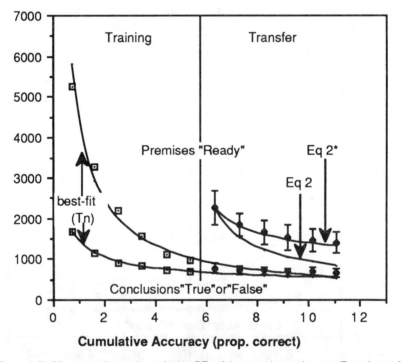

Figure 6.7: Mean premise and conclusion RTs of the experimental group (Experiment 2).
Lines labeled "best-fit (*Tn*)" are power functions fit to training data and extrapolated into the
transfer phase (see Table 6.2 for equations). Line labeled "Eq 2" is a function of the form
described by Equation 2 (see Table 6.2 for equation). Line labeled "Eq 2*" is a modified
version of Equation 2 that incorporates a change in asymptote (see text for details and Table
6.2 for Equation). Error bars are confidence intervals (alpha = 0.05).

In conclusion, the model of transfer represented by Equation 2 appears to provide a fair approximation to what occurs when old and new productions are combined to perform a task. However, this equation does not fully capture the pattern of improvement that follows the initial slow performance. Learning rate appears to be attenuated even more than is predicted by Equation 2. Thus Equation 2 requires some refinement in order to provide a more accurate account of improvement following partial transfer.

| | Parameters | | | Goodness of Fit | |
	X	N	c	r^2	rmsd
Control Group					
Training					
Premises	0	5009.50	-0.835	0.979	267.335
Conclusions	535	790.14	-0.993	0.999	12.315
Transfer					
Premises					
Observed	0	1128.20	-0.093	0.700	37.193
Training-Extrapolated	0	1083.10	-0.260	0.707	212.357
Conclusions					
Observed	0	675.62	-0.033	0.286	20.005
Training-Extrapolated	0	660.36	-0.047	0.309	31.940
Experimental Group					
Training					
Premises	0	4475.70	-0.877	0.976	288.657
Conclusions	255	1189.60	-0.602	0.999	10.842
Transfer					
Premises					
Observed	600	1624.40	-0.408	1.000	6.885
Training-Extrapolated	0	908.40	-0.273	0.951	1016.981
Equation 2	60	2150.30	-0.585	0.999	434.764
Equation 2*	290	1934.90	-0.370	1.000	64.934
Conclusions					
Observed	75	696.85	-0.093	0.952	8.166
Training-Extrapolated	30	622.23	-0.112	0.926	123.824

Table 6.2: Parameters of power functions fit to premise and conclusion RTs during training and transfer phases of Experiment 2. Functions labeled "Observed" were fit directly to the data. Functions labeled "Training-Extrapolated" were fit to values extrapolated from training performance. The function labeled "Equation 2" was fit to values predicted by a version of Equation 2 (see text for details). The function labeled "Equation 2*" was fit to values predicted by a modified version of Equation 2. r^2 = proportion of variance in the observed reaction time values accounted for by the predicted values. rmsd = root mean squared deviation between predicted and observed reaction time values.

A tentative begining to the refinement process is possible. The first step is to consider the observation that not only learning rate is affected by partial transfer. Table 6.2 shows that in premise RTs, the power function fit to the transfer data not only has a smaller learning rate than observed during training, but it also has a larger asymptote. This observation has been noted in a number of other experiments as well (Speelman, 1990). There are at least two possible explanations for this observation. One is that the amount of practice provided during training was not sufficient to enable an accurate estimation of the experimental group's asymptote. This could have resulted in an underestimation of the asymptote during training and so affected the accuracy of the power function fit to the Training data. In turn, this would have affected the ability of Equation 2 to account for the Transfer data because the derivation of this equation is based on the training data. This possibility is currently being investigated with longer training sessions.

An alternate explanation is to assume that the observed asymptote increase is not an artifact of too few training trials and that it is in fact a result of the combination of old and new productions. The process whereby the combination of productions leads to changes in asymptotic performance is not clear at this stage, although the data does reveal some support for such a relationship. A new version of Equation 2 that incorporates a change in asymptote (see Appendix B for details of the derivation of this version) is plotted in Figure 6.7 (labeled Equation 2*). It is obvious that this new version of Equation 2 accounts for more of the improvement pattern during transfer than the original version. It also predicts a learning rate that is much closer to the observed rate than was predicted by the original version (see Table 6.2). However, the derivation of this new version of Equation 2 is not entirely satisfactory from a prediction perspective. As is obvious from Appendix B, the derivation relied to a large extent on parameters observed in the transfer data. A more satisfactory approach would rely on performance information gathered prior to observing transfer. Furthermore, in the absence of a process theory concerning changes in asymptotic performance, this new equation functions only as a convenient descriptor of the data rather than providing any insight to the processes underlying transfer. Therefore the utility of this new version of Equation 2 will also need to be evaluated by further experimentation. However, the impressive degree of fit provided by this new function is encouraging. In fact, the results of this study suggest that combining separate functions for the various components underlying performance is a promising step toward accounting for learning following transfer.

REFERENCES

Anderson, J.R. (1982). Acquisition of cognitive skill. *Psychological Review, 89,* 339-406.
Anderson, J.R. (1983). *The architecture of cognition.* Cambridge, MA: Harvard University Press.

Anderson, J.R. (1987). Skill acquisition: Compilation of weak-method problem solutions. *Psychological Review, 94,* 192-210.

Anderson, J.R., Conrad, F.G., & Corbett, A.T. (1989). Skill acquisition and the LISP tutor. *Cognitive Science, 13,* 467-505.

Carlson, R.A., Sullivan, M.A., & Schneider, W. (1989). Practice and working memory effects in building procedural skill. *Journal of Experimental Psychology: Learning, Memory, and Cognition, 15,* 517-526.

Johnson-Laird, P.N., & Steedman, M. (1978). The psychology of syllogisms. *Cognitive Psychology, 10,* 64-99.

Maxwell, S.E., & Delaney, H.D. (1990). *Designing experiments and analyzing data.* Belmont, CA: Wadsworth.

Newell, A., & Rosenbloom, P.S. (1981). Mechanisms of skill acquisition and the law of practice. In J.R.Anderson (Ed.), *Cognitive skills and their acquisition.* Hillsdale, NJ: Erlbaum.

Quinton, G., & Fellows, B.J. (1975). 'Perceptual' strategies in the solving of three-term series problems. *British Journal of Psychology, 66,* 69-78.

Singley, M.K., & Anderson, J.R. (1985). The transfer of text-editing skill. *International Journal of Man-Machine Studies, 22,* 403-423.

Singley, M.K., & Anderson, J.R. (1989). *The transfer of cognitive skill.* Cambridge, MA: Harvard University Press.

Speelman, C.P. (1990). *Transfer of training and skill acquisition.* Unpublished PhD. thesis, University of Western Australia, Nedlands, Western Australia.

Staszewski, J.J. (1988). Skilled memory and expert mental calculation. In M.T.H. Chi, R. Glaser, & M.J. Farr (Eds.), *The nature of expertise.* Hillsdale, NJ: Erlbaum.

Thorndike, E.L., & Woodworth, R.S. (1901). The influence of improvement in one mental function upon the efficiency of other functions. *Psychological Review, 8,* 247-261.

Appendix A: DERIVATION OF A VERSION OF EQUATION 2 TO DESCRIBE THE TRANSFER PREMISE RTs OF THE EXPERIMENTAL GROUP IN EXPERIMENT 2.

Equation 2 is supposed to account for improvement with practice in a situation where new productions are developed to fill the gap between a repertoire of old skills and those skills necessary to perform a task. Underlying part of the improvement with the new task will be continued improvement with the old skills. This improvement is described by extrapolating the training function. In addition to this improvement is improvement of the new skills. Description of this improvement will require a new power function. As discussed in the text, this new power function will have a learning rate that is the same as the learning rate of the training function. This new function will also have an intercept that reflects the number of new productions involved in the new task. In practice, this intercept will reflect the time that the extra productions add to the initial overall performance time. This suggests that the intercept of this new power function can be approximated by subtracting the performance time for the first block of transfer that is expected on the basis of training (i.e., execution of old productions) from the observed performance time in Block 1 of the transfer phase. Unfortunately the practice of fitting curves to data plotted against cumulative accuracy complicates this estimation procedure. In Experiment 2, the expected premise RT of the experimental group in the first block of transfer was 889.01 ms. This was calculated by extrapolating the training function of this group ($T = 4475.7$ $P^{-0.877}$) one block from the end of training (i.e., $P = 6.314 =$ cumulative accuracy up to Block 7). The observed RT for this group in the first block of transfer was 2263.75 ms. Therefore the intercept value for the new power function (N_n) can be estimated by the following application of Equation 2:

$$T = X + N_o P_o{}^c + N_n P_n{}^c \quad \text{where } P = \text{cumulative accuracy}$$

$$\Rightarrow \quad 2263.75 = 0 + 4475.7 \, (6.314)^{-0.87711} + N_n \, (0.953)^{-0.87711}$$

$$\Rightarrow \quad \frac{2263.75 - 889.01}{1.043128} = N_n$$

$$\Rightarrow \quad 1317.90 = N_n$$

Therefore $T = 4475.7 \, P_o{}^{-0.8711} + 1317.90 \, P_n{}^{-0.8711}$

Appendix B. DERIVATION OF A MODIFIED VERSION OF EQUATION 2 TO DESCRIBE THE TRANSFER PREMISE RTs OF THE EXPERIMENTAL GROUP IN EXPERIMENT 2 (LABELLED EQUATION 2* IN TABLE 2).

If the combination of old and new productions during transfer results in an increase in asymptotic performance time, then this can be included into Equation 2 by subtracting the asymptote observed during training (in this experiment, $X_o = 0$ ms) from the asymptote observed during transfer (600 ms). The result is then included in Equation 2 as a new asymptote (X_n). This will then result in a smaller estimate for N_n.

$$T = X_o + N_o P_o{}^c + X_n + N_n P_n{}^c \quad \text{where } X_n = \text{asymptote observed}$$
$$\text{during transfer}$$

$$\text{and} \quad P = \text{cumulative accuracy}$$

$$\Rightarrow \quad 2263.75 = 0 + 4475.7(6.314)^{-0.8711} + 600 + N_n(0.953)^{-0.8711}$$

$$\Rightarrow \quad \frac{2263.75 - 889.01 - 600}{1.043128} = N_n$$

$$\Rightarrow \quad 742.71 = N_n$$

Therefore $T = 4475.7 \, P_o{}^{-0.8711} + 600 + 742.71 \, P_n{}^{-0.8711}$

Neurocognitive Pattern Classification of Distributed Brain Electrical Activity *

C.R. Clark, D.E. Pomeroy, and J. Tizard

School of Psychology and Cognitive Neuroscience Laboratory
Flinders University

The most useful source of information from brain electrical activity about mental events in the human is the event-related potential (ERP) that can be derived from the much larger electroencephalogram (EEG). ERPs are small-amplitude ($\pm$ $20\mu v$) brain field electrical potentials that are time-locked to a designated event such as the onset of a stimulus, its expectancy, or an overt response. Usually, electrical activity is amplified, filtered, and digitized and signal averaging techniques are used to extract the ERP signal from the EEG. The resulting averaged waveform consists of a series of positive and negative components whose shape, size, and latency are determined partly by the physical nature of the event to which they are time-locked, and partly by cognitive processes associated with the event. Further, the distribution and temporal appearance of many such components over the scalp surface is quite distinctive and reflects the different origins of the underlying neural generators. Primary examples of averaged ERP components that reflect cognitive operations are the centroparietally distributed P300 which occurs 300-700 ms following a stimulus and reflects the timing and capacity involved in the evaluation of stimulus significance (e.g. Isreal, Wickens, Chesney, & Donchin, 1980) and the centrally located contingent negative variation (CNV) which reflects anticipation of an impending stimulus (e.g. Rohrbaugh, 1983).

The conventional use of signal averaging to extract ERPs from the ongoing EEG requires that stimuli be repetitively presented over many trials under the same task conditions. However, intrinsic to this approach is the loss of the potential information relating to cerebral patterns of neurocognitive activity within single-trial records. Further, the use of the averaging technique introduces its own set of difficulties, such as uncertainty about variability over trials in the timing, energy, and nature of mental operations and the

* The work reported in this study was funded in part by a grant made to the first author (C.R. Clark) by the Julia Farr Research Foundation, Adelaide, South Australia.

effects of factors such as fatigue, practice, strategy, attention, and arousal on mental operations and their electrophysiological analogs.

As a result, a few researchers have in recent years begun to study the characteristics of ERPs within single-trial EEG records (e.g. Childers, 1986; Farwell & Donchin, 1988; Gevins et al., 1989a; 1989b; Gratton, Coles & Donchin, 1989; Horst & Donchin, 1980; Squires & Donchin, 1976; Sutter, 1984). This has placed emphasis on pattern recognition techniques examining both the temporal and spatial (i.e., multielectrode) domains of single-trial ERPs, and on investigating data and noise-reduction strategies that permit reliable feature selection or extraction. One technique that has been used is stepwise discriminant analysis (SWDA). This proceeds by defining a number that is a weighted combination of the best n features of the data, with the weighting function specific to a class of patterns (see Childers, 1986). The value derived then permits allocation of a given pattern to a particular class when its value falls within the range associated with that class. In this way, sampled data can be conceptualized as points in an n-dimensional feature-vector space, with point clusters according to pattern class.

Recent studies, however, have suggested that the dynamic properties of the EEG are due in part to a nonlinear interaction of different cognitive subsystems (Basar, 1988a; Pockberger, Rappelsberger, & Petsche, 1988). Thus, nonlinear analysis may provide a better understanding of dynamic EEG patterns of activity (Freeman, 1988). Artificial neural networks (ANNs) of the type described by Rumelhart and McClelland (1986), for example, have the ability to represent nonlinear relationships between categories, and thus may be able to exploit nonlinearities in the EEG in a manner unavailable to SWDA (see Gevins, 1984; Gevins et al., 1989a). However, whilst ANNs represent a different class of algorithm to SWDA, the principle of classification by identification of pattern clusters is common to both techniques.

The detection of neurocognitive patterns in brain electrical activity is particularly topical at this time. Credence is now being widely given to conceptualizations of cognitive function in terms of cortical networks in which parallel distributed activity integrates in temporal patterns of focal activity (see Goldman-Rakic, 1988; Mesulam, 1981; Posner & Peterson, 1990). This chapter reports exploratory work associated with the use of nonlinear techniques for the recognition and classification of spatiotemporal, neurocognitive patterns in brain electrical activity derived from multiple scalp sites. The experimental paradigm employed in this study focuses on the correct classification of single-trial ERPs according to whether a sequence of mental operations has occurred (GO trials) or not (NOGO trials) following an auditory cue. Results from single-subject data are reported which evaluate the comparative utility of ANNs and SWDA as methods for classifying single-trial ERPs on the basis of a priori grouping variables and which consider the significance of the spatiotemporal patterns obtained for cognitive modeling.

METHOD

Subjects

One normal 19-year-old female acted as the subject for this study. She had no self-reported history of major medical or neurological abnormality. Audiometric tests revealed no hearing abnormalities.

Task

The task was based on the GO/NOGO paradigm (Rugg et al., 1989). Each trial consisted of the presentation of two tones, the cue stimulus and the imperative stimulus IS, separated by 1100 ms and presented through a speaker attached to a PC-AT microcomputer. The cue was always 1000 Hz and consisted of either two tones of 50 ms duration and 100 ms apart (the GO cue), or a single tone of 200 ms duration (the NOGO cue).

The IS was a 100 ms tone with a randomly selected frequency of either 1000 Hz or 2000 Hz. If presented with a GO cue, the subject was required to make a push-button response with her right index finger following the IS. Following a NOGO cue, the subject was required to ignore the IS. Speed and accuracy of response were equally emphasized in the task instructions. Trials were presented automatically under computer control with an intertrial interval (ITI) randomly between one to two seconds.

Procedure

The subject completed one experimental session in which six blocks of 50 trials were completed with a short rest between each block. The first two blocks were for practice only. GO and NOGO cues were equiprobable and randomly ordered within each block.

The subject was seated in a comfortable chair in a darkened room. She was requested to keep as still as possible during each trial, and to fixate on a centrally located point at eye level to minimize eye movements. Recording apparatus was in an adjacent room, from which the experimenter observed responses on a closed-circuit television system and communicated via intercom equipment.

ERP Recording

EEG was recorded using an electrode cap from eight scalp sites according to the 10/20 system: left and right frontal (F3, F4), central (C3, C4), and parietal (P3, P4), midline anterocentral (aCz, midway between Fz and Cz), and midline anteroparietal (aPz, midway between Cz and Pz).

Eye movements (EOG) were monitored via 8mm tin electrodes placed on the supraorbital ridge and on the outer canthus of the eye. Interelectrode impedances were kept below 4kΩ. EEG and EOG were amplified 20,000 times and 10,000 times respectively using Grass RPS7C8B preamplifiers. Analog filtering was set to bandpasses of 0.01-30 Hz and 0.1-30 Hz respectively, down 3dB attenuation points of 6dB per octave roll-off rate. All channels were also filtered with a 50 Hz notch filter. The signals were derived using a DT2821-16SE analog-to-digital converter connected to the microcomputer which also presented the tones.

EEG and EOG were sampled at 333 Hz from 100 ms prior to cue onset to 1100 ms post-IS (total sample time of 2300 ms). Trials with extensive changes in the amplitude of EEG ($\pm$ 85μv) or EOG ($\pm$ 65μv) activity were automatically excluded from data collection. The first trial in each block and trials with significant alpha activity were also excluded from subsequent data analysis. Single-trial EEG and averaged ERPs were digitally filtered (low pass 11 Hz, filter gain 0.707 at 6 dB) to remove high-frequency activity (see Ruchkin & Glaser, 1978).

Data Analysis

The first step was to compute averaged GO and NOGO ERPs for each scalp site from acceptable trials obtained during the four experimental blocks. Data analysis was then completed in four stages.

Latency analysis. This involved a priori identification of a limited number (L) of time points in the averaged ERPs that marked deflections optimally differentiating the GO and NOGO conditions. This was achieved by visual inspection of superimposed plots of the averaged GO and NOGO waveforms for each electrode site. Each deflection identified in this way was noted as either positive-going or negative-going according to the voltage direction (vector) of the waveform immediately preceding the deflection.

Measurement of single-trial data. This stage involved measurement of single-trial waveform amplitudes at latencies corresponding to each of the L deflections. The single-trial measurement procedure for each deflection latency was carried out automatically by computer program according to the following rules: Define a search window of 140ms centered on the deflection latency value; measure the maximum amplitude of the single-trial waveform within that window: choose the maximum positive value if the vector of the averaged ERP deflection is positive, otherwise choose the maximum negative value. A 140ms search window was chosen to accommodate variability in the temporal location of the deflections in single-trial waveforms and to meet the assumption that the cycle frequency of any components contributing to such a deflection would be less than 7 Hz.

Creation of training and test data sets. This involved division of the trials into training and test data sets, with approximately equal numbers of GO and NOGO trials in each set. The allocation of trials to sets was carried out by random selection without replacement. Training set data was subjected to univariate and multivariate outlier analysis using the methods recommended by Tabachnick and Fidell (1989). Any trial containing an outlier value (> 3sd from the mean) was removed from the training set.

Classification analysis. Training set data was subjected to classification analysis using both stepwise discriminant function analysis (SPSS-X DISCRIMINANT) and supervised nonlinear network analysis employing the back-propagation learning technique described by Rumelhart, Hinton, and Williams (1986). The reliability or generalizability of the classification formulae obtained by these methods were then assessed by their application to the test set data.

RESULTS

The averaged ERPs at each scalp site for the GO and NOGO conditions over the four experimental blocks are shown in Figure 7.1. These averages were constructed from 86 GO and 78 NOGO trials that met the acceptance criteria outlined above.

Latency Analysis

An examination of the waveforms in Figure 7.1 identified a number of latencies at which the GO and NOGO conditions were clearly separated. From these, the following were selected as the basis for single-trial measurement:

1. A positive deflection at about 500ms post-cue and best seen at centroparietal sites. This deflection corresponds to the post-cue P300 deflection associated with the evaluation of relevant stimuli (see Donchin & Coles, 1988). This component is hereafter termed 'P3.'
2. The slow negative shift leading up to and measured at stimulus onset. It is best seen in Figure 7.1 at centroparietal sites and corresponds to the contingent negative variation (CNV) associated with expectancy for impending events (e.g., Rohrbaugh, 1983). As one might expect, therefore, it is evident for GO but not NOGO trials. It is hereafter termed 'SO.'
3. The negative deflection at about 275ms poststimulus which corresponds to the N200 component. The N200 has been associated with attention to and classification of relevant stimulus information (see Naatanen, 1990; Sams, Alho, & Naatanen, 1985). In Figure 7.1, this deflection is best seen frontocentrally. Hereafter, it will be termed 'N2.'

4. The positive shift peaking at about 645ms following the stimulus and best seen in Figure 7.1 at parietal sites. This deflection corresponds to the Slow Wave (see Ruchkin & Sutton, 1983) which may be associated with processes subsequent to stimulus evaluation (see Gevins & Cutillo, 1987). This component is termed 'SW'.

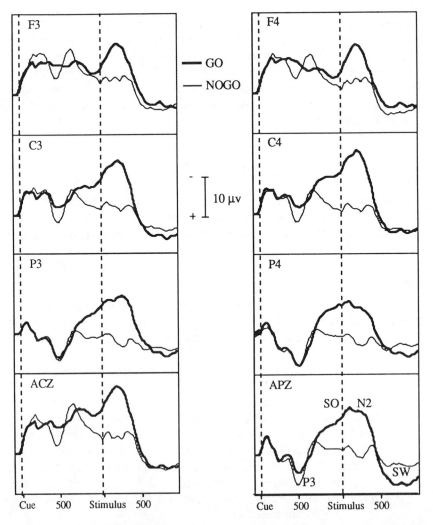

Figure 7.1 Averaged GO and NOGO event-related potentials (ERPs) obtained from eight scalp sites. GO and NOGO trials are superimposed for each site with waveforms aligned on a 100ms pre-cue baseline. The latencies of the four temporal components selected for SWDA and ANN classification analysis that best separate GO and NOGO trials are labelled P3, SO, N2, and SW. These represent, respectively, the post-cue P300 component, the contingent negative variation at stimulus onset, and the N200 and Slow Wave components that follow the imperative stimulus. Their latencies are indicated on the APZ plot.

Measurement of Single-Trial Data.

The mean amplitudes (and standard deviations) for P3, SO, N2, and SW obtained after measurement of these components from single-trial waveforms are shown in Table 7.1. Differences between GO and NOGO means for each of these four dependent measures were tested using two-way (Site x Condition) repeated measures analyses of variance (SPSS-X MANOVA). This was done to establish that the component latencies selected by visual inspection of the averaged ERP waveforms did in fact represent points that reliably differentiated the GO and NOGO task conditions. The Geisser-Greenhouse correction was used for violations of symmetry. Significant Site x Condition interactions were obtained for P3 ($F[3,461] = 3.48$, $p \leqslant 0.05$), SO ($F[3,536] = 4.12$, $p \leqslant 0.01$), N2 ($F[3,465] = 3.72$, $p \leqslant 0.05$) and SW ($F[3,528] = 2.65$, $p \leqslant 0.05$). Analysis (Scheffé) of the differences between means showed that for P3, GO and NOGO means differed significantly at sites aCz, F3, F4 and C3 ($p < 0.05$). For SO, significant differences were found at sites aPz, aCz, C3, C4, F4, P3 and P4 ($p < 0.001$). Differences for N2 were obtained at all sites ($p < 0.001$) and for SW at site aPz only ($p < 0.001$).

Table 7.1 Mean (μ volts) and standard deviation of the measured amplitude from each GO (n, 86) and NOGO (n,78) single trial at each scalp site within the P3, SO, N2 and SW latency windows. The four windows were centered ($\pm$70ms) around the latencies which best separated the GO and NOGO task conditions in the averaged ERP waveforms. Single trials were obtained from one subject over four blocks of trials.

COMPONENT X CONDITION			F3	F4	C3	C4	P3	P4	aCz	aPz
	GO	mean	3	2	7	7	14	15	5	14
P3		sd	15	15	14	14	13	13	17	15
	NOGO	mean	7	7	12	11	16	16	10	17
		sd	15	14	14	14	13	13	17	15
	GO	mean	-13	-12	-15	-17	-13	-14	-19	-17
SO		sd	14	14	14	14	14	14	17	15
	NOGO	mean	-10	-9	-9	-9	-8	-9	-12	-10
		sd	15	14	14	14	14	14	17	15
	GO	mean	-17	-16	-19	-20	-16	-13	-22	-18
N2		sd	15	16	16	15	15	14	18	16
	NOGO	mean	-11	-10	-9	-9	-6	-6	-13	-9
		sd	16	15	15	14	15	14	17	14
	GO	mean	12	13	14	14	13	13	15	17
SW		sd	14	15	12	14	12	13	16	14
	NOGO	mean	9	11	9	10	10	10	11	10
		sd	14	14	13	13	13	13	14	13

ELECTRODE SITE

Creation of Training and Test Data Sets

Single-trial data were split randomly into two parts to provide training and test sets of comparable size. The test data set consisted of 33 GO and 40 NOGO trials. After outlier analysis, the training set contained 48 GO and 35 NOGO trials.

Stepwise Discriminant Function Analysis (SWDA)

SWDA carried out on the training data set selected four components which together resulted in a classification accuracy of 81%. These were the SO components at sites F3 and C4, the N2 component at site C4 and the SW component at site aPz. The C4[SO] and aPz[SW] components accounted for most of the variance. The signing of the SWDA coefficients for these four components indicated that the two C4 components were weighted in favor of NOGO trials and the F3 and aPz components in favor of GO trials. The classification formula proved to be quite reliable, yielding a classification accuracy of 81% when applied to the test data set.

A second SWDA was then completed using as much of the single trial data for training as possible. Nine randomly selected trials were retained as a test data set. All 32 predictor variables were used. The analysis yielded a classification accuracy of 85% during training and 100% on the test set. Six components were incorporated in the classification function. These were the SO component at site C4, the N2 component at sites F4 and C4, and the SW component at sites F3, C3 and aPz. The component SO at site F3 was not selected as in the first analysis.

Artificial Neural Network Analysis (ANN)

Training set data was fed into a number of three-layer networks consisting of 17 input nodes, between 3 and 5 hidden nodes, and a single output node. Each layer was fully connected to all nodes in the subsequent layer. The training algorithm used the back-propagation method of Rumelhart et al. (1986) with the expected value (E) from the network set to 1 for NOGO and 0 for GO trials. Connection weights were initialized randomly in the range ± 0.3. The number of network nodes was restricted to provide a ratio between training trials and input layer predictor variables that would permit generalizability of the training algorithm. Thus, it was necessary to run a number of networks using different subsets of input variables and different numbers of hidden nodes in order to optimize the classification result.

Network training proceeded with a weight decay factor of 0.9. Connection weights were updated after each pass through the training set. Training was terminated when 95% of trials generated an output value within 0.5 of the expected value (E). A higher level of classification could be obtained, but a limit of 95% was set to limit overtraining on the data set and a loss of generalizability. When applied to the test data set, the most successful network configuration yielded a classification accuracy of 82%. As for SWDA, this result indicated the good reliability of the technique for classifying single trials according to task condition.

As for the SWDA analysis, the reliability obtained prompted a second analysis using an expanded training set to provide as much data as possible for development of the classification algorithm. The same nine randomly selected trials were used as the test data set. All 32 predictor variables were used in a three-layered design with 32 input nodes and up to 5 hidden nodes. As before, network training was terminated when 95% of trials were correctly classified. Application to the test data yielded a classification accuracy of 89%.

Figure 7.2a presents in graphical form the pattern of weights obtained from a network containing three hidden nodes. An inspection of these weights shows that only two of the three hidden nodes contributed to single-trial classification. Other networks that were run with different numbers of hidden nodes presented similar patterns of activity over two dominant nodes. This suggests that ANN analysis discerned two, discrete, spatiotemporal patterns of activity from the data set provided. Examination of weight size suggested that about two-thirds of the 32 components (4 latencies x 8 electrodes) input to the 2 active hidden nodes played a significant role in classification.

It is clearly of interest to identify the relative contribution of each of the 32 component connections to each hidden node during single-trial classification. This should provide some insight into the timing and distribution of the neuroelectric activity critical to the associated cognitive judgements. However, it is not possible to do this from the pattern of weights alone, since classification depends on the sum of the signed products of these connection weights with input voltage values. Thus, to assess those input nodes relevant to GO classification, the 32 component values from the averaged GO ERP were fed into the network. Similarly, to identify those relevant to NOGO classification, component values from the averaged NOGO ERP were fed into the network. The rationale for this approach is that the averaged waveforms represent the closest approximation available to the actual event-related brain activity associated with the processing of GO and NOGO trials.

Figures 7.2b and 7.2c represent the GO and NOGO component input (i.e., weight x averaged ERP component voltage) to the hidden nodes from each input node, and the summed and weighted output after sigmoid transformation (see Rumelhart et al., 1986) from each hidden node to the output node. It can be seen from these figures that there are differentiated patterns of activity for the averaged GO and NOGO ERPs for each of the two active hidden nodes. In addition, a number of component inputs from the averaged GO and NOGO ERPs make similar contributions to both ERP patterns. No formal analysis of these spatiotemporal patterns is attempted here since the components involved only represent a limited proportion of the waveform

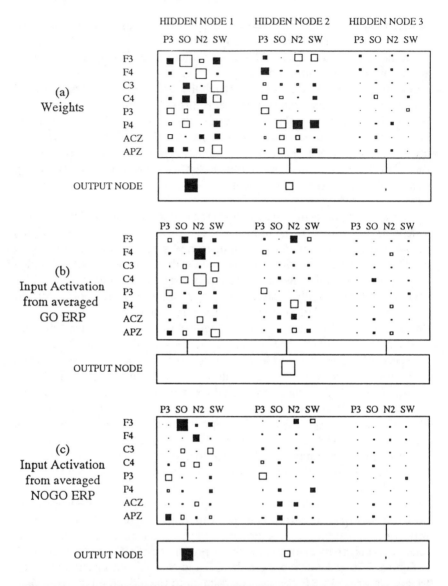

Figure 7.2. (a) the pattern of weights obtained after training in a 3-layer network with 32 input, 3 hidden, and 1 output node. Each layer was fully connected to all nodes in the subsequent layer. The input layer received single-trial amplitude measurements from 4 component latencies at each of 8 electrode sites located symmetrically over the scalp. These represented points of good separation between the averaged ERPs from GO and NOGO trials. Filled squares represent negative weights and open squares positive weights, with symbol size proportional to weight; (b) the pattern of input node activation obtained when component values from the *averaged* ERP for GO trials were fed into the trained network; (c) the pattern of input node activation when component values from the *averaged* ERP for NOGO trials were fed into the trained network.

activity associated with GO and NOGO trial discrimination: Though adequate for single-trial classification, it could not be assumed that the components selected contained all of the critical neuroelectric activity. The more exhaustive analysis is beyond the scope of this exploratory study.

In an attempt to assess the replicability of the network classification algorithms obtained, the training pass on one of the networks was rerun. This produced a classification algorithm with a weight pattern very similar to that obtained in the original run. Another run was then completed in which the GO or NOGO status of each trial was masked by randomly assigning an expected value (E) of 0 or 1 to each training and test set trial. This was done to see if a high classification accuracy could be serendipitously obtained with random a priori groupings. Poor classification accuracy was obtained for both the training set (68%) and test set (40%) even though the network was allowed to run for a considerable length of time. These results indicated that the classification algorithms obtained on the previous runs recognized patterns of neurocognitive rather than coincidental significance in the training data.

Comparison of SWDA and ANN Classifications

Table 7.2 shows the proportional distribution of classification scores for correctly classified trials in terms of their distance from the GO/NOGO classification boundary. For SWDA analysis, classification scores ranged between ± 1 and for ANN analysis between 0 and 1, with the classification boundary located at the midpoint in each case. For SWDA classification, more trials were classified closer to the boundary, with 51% of trials classified within three deciles of the boundary and only 9% in the last three deciles of the score range. For ANN classification, however, no trials were within six deciles of the classification boundary, 96% in the three most distant deciles, and 88% in the 10th decile. This difference between the methods in the dispersion of classification scores suggests that the nonlinear classification algorithm provided a more robust discrimination.

A comparison of those trials in the test data set that were misclassified by either method showed a high degree of overlap (69%). Further, all but two of the trials misclassified by ANN, and all of those misclassified in common by SWDA, were strongly misclassified into the alternate category. These results indicate that most misclassification was related to some crucial variation in the pattern of neurocognitive processing of such trials by the subject rather than some spurious failure in the classification algorithms. Such variations could occur when cognitive misjudgment "almost" results in error; such as when the subject erroneously plans to respond following a NOGO cue but pulls back in just in time. Clearly, the pattern characteristics of such trials could not be identified a priori. However, once recognized by virtue of strong misclassification, a rerun of the training algorithm with such trials reclassified could proceed. For this to be successful, though, the new categories would need to be adequately represented in the data set. In the present study, this was not the case so the idea could not be tested.

Table 7.2. Proportional distribution of classification scores for correctly classified trials by decile distance from the GO/NOGO classification boundary. Data shown are from the application of trained, linear (SWDA) and nonlinear (ANN) classification algorithms to the test data set of 33 GO and 40 NOGO trials. For SWDA analysis, classification scores ranged between ± 1 and for ANN analysis between 0 and 1, with the classification boundary located at the midpoint in each case.

		Distance from classification boundary by decile									
		10	9	8	7	6	5	4	3	2	1
NOGO trials	SWDA	.04	.00	.04	.07	.04	.19	.11	.22	.11	.19
	ANN	.87	.03	.10	.00	.00	.00	.00	.00	.00	.00
GO trials	SWDA	.00	.09	.00	.03	.19	.13	.06	.31	.13	.06
	ANN	.90	.03	.00	.07	.00	.00	.00	.00	.00	.00
All trials	SWDA	.02	.05	.02	.05	.12	.15	.08	.27	.12	.12
	ANN	.88	.03	.05	.03	.00	.00	.00	.00	.00	.00

A comparison of components contributing to the most successful classifications by each method indicated a degree of overlap. In the first analysis, the four components selected by SWDA (C4[SO], C4[N2], aPz[SW] and F3[SO]) also made strongly weighted connections to ANN hidden nodes (see Figure 7.2). However, a number of other components (e.g., P3 at sites F3, F4, and P3; SO at sites C3 and P4; N2 at sites F3, F4, and P4; and SW at sites F3, C3, C4, and P4) also contributed strongly to ANN classification. In the second analysis, a similar result held: all of the components contributing to the SWDA classification algorithm established strong network weights but a number of components with strong network weightings (e.g., F3[SO], P4[SO]) did not contribute at all to SWDA classification. This suggests that much of the network weighting information is redundant for the purpose of single-trial classification.

DISCUSSION

The results of this study indicate that both the SWDA and ANN procedures described can be used reliably to classify multichannel, single-trial ERPs differentiated by neurocognitive factors. Both procedures involved development of classification algorithms on training data sets and an evaluation of the reliability of these algorithms on independent test data sets. SWDA was able to correctly classify up to 90% of trials during training and up to 100%

on evaluation data using no more than six scalp measurements derived from eight electrode sites. The ANN procedure had the potential for 100% classification of trials during training but this was restricted to 95% to prevent the generation of algorithms with limited generalizability to independent data sets. The classification algorithms obtained were then able to classify reliability evaluation data with up to 89% accuracy. The ANN procedure used 32 measures from eight scalp sites for classification.

This study explores two issues associated with the analysis of human neurocognitive activity: the classification of single-trial ERP waveforms and the patterns of neuroelectric activity expressed in the classification algorithms. For the purpose of single-trial classification in this study, stepwise discriminant function analysis appeared to be superior to nonlinear analysis: SWDA classification accuracy was better and fewer measures were required to obtain the classification result. The SWDA results also match those reported in previous work (Horst & Donchin, 1980; Squires & Donchin, 1976). One important point of difference, however, is the choice of SWDA technique used for classification training. The work cited used the Jackknife technique (see Dixon, 1975) in which the data from each case to be classified is left out when the classification coefficients are computed. Thus each case has a separate set of classification coefficients developed from all other cases.

The ANN technique employed in the present study generates a single classification algorithm which can be used to classify new data. In principle, this should permit real-time classification of cognitive state from single-trial ERPs. Ongoing work is developing this potential by adapting the GO/NOGO task described to provide a basis for binary (Yes/No) communication with patients with severe to total loss of muscular function. The medical reasons for this sort of condition may be temporary such as in stroke patients, or may be permanent such as in cerebral palsy, motor neurone disease, amyotrophic lateral sclerosis or severe trauma. A number of devices have been developed which allow disabled individuals to communicate by computer but in all cases these employ the use of spared motor systems (e.g. Downing, 1985). Similarly, a few studies have reported the successful use of single-trial ERPs as aids in communication (e.g. Farwell & Donchin, 1988) but in each case use of the oculomotor system was a necessary corequisite. Whilst the present study required a physical response to auditory GO stimuli, it is well-established that each of the ERP components (P300, CNV, N200, and Slow Wave) which formed the basis of single-trial analysis can be elicited equally well in the absence of overt behavior (e.g., Gevins & Cutillo, 1987; Hillyard & Kutas, 1983; Regan, 1989).

In relation to the second issue outlined above, it is proposed that the patterns expressed by the coefficients of the classification algorithms obtained bear relevance to current expressions of cognition as a parallel and distributed brain activity (e.g., Goldman-Rakic, 1988; Posner and Peterson, 1990). This view is held for two reasons. Firstly, the spatiotemporal, single-trial ERP data contributing to the analyses reflect amongst other things processes or activity associated with such brain activity. Secondly, the coefficient patterns successfully discriminated between single trials that were implicitly differentiated by cognitive factors. It might be argued that differences in the physical characteristics of the GO and NOGO cues could account for the success of classification. However, each of the component latencies selected for classification analysis are well-known from averaged ERP studies to reflect endogenous rather than exogenous brain processing (see Regan, 1989). Thus, it would seem reasonable to conclude that the coefficient patterns obtained reflect the timing and distribution of underlying cognitive activity in the brain.

Of the two analysis methods used, ANN provided the more interesting representation. In contrast to SWDA, the patterns of activity revealed by ANN analysis incorporated the contributions of all input components. These patterns provide information not available from traditional measurement of the surface components in averaged ERP activity since they additionally quantify the degree and extent of the spatiotemporal association between such components. Further, as shown in Figure 7.2, ANN analysis was able to discern more than one pattern of activity relevant to the processing of GO and NOGO trials. While the independence of these patterns has not been established, it is conceivable that they may represent components of parallel, though presumably coupled, processing streams. If established, this would bear directly upon current theory in cognitive electrophysiology concerned with such issues (see Donchin & Coles, 1988). As indicated earlier, however, no formal analysis of these patterns was attempted in this exploratory study since the components from which they were derived represented only a subset of the neuroelectric activity associated with GO and NOGO trial discrimination. It remains to extend the method employed to incorporate a more complete representation of this activity.

A number of studies have attempted to identify the underlying event-related component activity in the brain (e.g., Gratton et al., 1989; see also Donchin & Heffley, 1978) and their spatiotemporal pattern of activity (e.g. Gevins, 1990) from the timing and distribution of ERP surface deflections. In all of these studies it is recognized that the measure of a surface deflection at any time may represent the composite activity of more than one underlying source component and that the timing and energy of such components may vary over repeated trials. Clearly the relationships between these factors may not be linear though the critical methods of analysis employed in these studies (multiple regression, principle components, and covariance analysis, respectively) depend upon the assumption of linearity. As indicated earlier, a number of studies have suggested that the dynamic properties of surface electrophysiological activity may be due in part to a nonlinear interaction of different cognitive subsystems (Basar, 1988b; Pockberger, Rappelsberger, & Petsche, 1988). Thus, the use of nonlinear analysis techniques, such as that employed in the present study, may be necessary for the identification of underlying components and their relationships. To validate the results of such work, however, it will be necessary to assess the likelihood of an isomorphic relationship between the component patterns obtained by ANN analysis and those within the brain mediating the surface neuroelectric activity. For this purpose, computational modeling of simulated component activity perhaps offers the best prospect.

REFERENCES

Basar, E. (1988a). Dynamics and evoked potentials in sensory and cognitive processing by the brain. In E. Basar (Ed.), *Dynamics of sensory and cognitive processing by the brain* (pp. 30-55). Berlin: Springer-Verlag.

Basar, E. (1988b). Brain waves, chaos, learning, and memory. In E. Basar (Ed.), *Dynamics of sensory and cognitive processing by the brain* (pp. 395-406). Berlin: Springer-Verlag.

Childers, D.G. (1986). Single-trial event-related potentials: Statistical classification and topography. In F. H. Duffy (Ed.), *Topographic mapping of brain electrical activity* (pp. 255-294). MA: Butterworths.

Dixon, W.J. (1975). *BMD-Biomedical computer programs.* Los Angeles, CA: University of California Press.

Donchin, E., & Heffley, E.F. (1978). Multivariate analysis of event-related potential data: A tutorial review. In *Proceedings of the Fourth International Congress on Event-related slow Potentials of the Brain: Multi-disciplinary Perspectives in Event-related Potential Research* (pp. 555-572) Washington, DC: U.S. Government Printing Office.

Donchin, E. & Coles, M.G.H. (1988). Is the P300 component a manifestation of context updating? (Precommentary). *Brain and Behavioural Sciences, 11,* 357-374.

Downing, A.R. (1985). Eye controlled and other fast communicators for speech impaired and physically handicapped persons. *Australasian Physical & Engineering Sciences in Medicine, 8,* 17-21.

Farwell, L. A., & Donchin, E. (1988). Talking off the top of your head: Towards a mental prosthesis utilizing event-related potentials. *Electroencephalography and Clinical Neurophysiology, 70,* 510-523.

Freeman, W. J. (1988). In E. Basar (Ed.), *Dynamics of sensory and cognitive processing by the brain* (pp. 378-380). Berlin: Springer-Verlag.

Gevins, A.S. (1984). Analysis of the electromagnetic signals of the human brain: Milestones, obstacles, and goals. *IEEE Transactions on Biomedical Engineering, BME-31,* 833-850.

Gevins, A.S. (1990). Dynamic patterns in multiple lead data. In J.W. Rohrbaugh, R. Parasuraman, R. Johnson, Jr (Eds.) *Event-related brain potentials: Basic issues and applications.* New York: Oxford University Press.

Gevins, A.S., & Cutillo, B.A. (1987). Signals of cognition. In F.H.L. da Silva, W.S. van Leuwen, A. Remond (Eds.) *Handbook of electroencephalography and clinical neurophysiology* (pp. 335-381). Amsterdam: Elsevier.

Gevins, A. S., Bressler, S. L., Morgan, N. H., Cutillo, B. A., White, R. M., Greer, D. S., & Illes, J. (1989a). Event-related covariances during a bimanual visuomotor task. I. Methods and analysis of stimulus- and response-locked data. *Electroencephalography and Clinical Neurophysiology, 74,* 58-75.

Gevins, A. S., Cutillo, B. A., Bressler, S. L., Morgan, N. H., White, R. M., Illes, J., & Greer, D. S. (1989b). Event-related covariances during a bimanual visuomotor task. II. Preparation and feedback. *Electroencephalography and Clinical Neurophysiology, 74,* 147-160.

Goldman-Rakic, R.S. (1988). Topography of cognition: Parallel distributed networks in primate association cortex. *Annual Review of Neuroscience, 11,* 137-156.

Gratton, G., Coles, M.G.H., & Donchin, E. (1989). A procedure for using multi-electrode information in the analysis of components of the event-related potential: Vector filter. *Psychophysiology, 26,* 222-232.

Hillyard, S.A., & Kutas, M. (1983). Electrophysiology of cognitive processing. *Annual Review of Psychology, 34,* 33-61.

Horst, R. L., & Donchin, E. (1980). Beyond averaging. II. Single-trial classification of exogeneous event-related potentials using stepwise discriminant analysis. *Electroencephalography and Clinical Neurophysiology, 48,* 113-126.

Isreal, K. B., Wickens, C. D., Chesney, G. L., & Donchin, E. (1980). Human factors. *Electroencephalography and Clinical Neurophysiology, 17,* 259-273.

Mesulam, M. (1981). A cortical network for directed attention and unilateral neglect. *Annals of Neurology, 10,* 309-325.

Naatanen, R. (in press). The role of attention in auditory information processing as revealed by event-related potentials and other brain measures of cognitive function. *Behavioural and Brain Sciences.*

Pockberger, H., Rappelsberger, P., & Petsche, H. (1988). In E. Basar (Ed.), *Dynamics of sensory and cognitive processing by the brain* (pp. 266-274). Berlin: Springer-Verlag.

Posner, M.I., & Petersen, S.E. (1990). The attention system of the human brain. *Annual Review of Neuroscience, 13,* 25-42.

Regan, D. (1989). Human brain electrophysiology: Evoked potentials and evoked magnetic fields in science and medicine. New York: Elsevier.

Rohrbaugh, J.W. (1983). Sensory and motor aspects of the contingent negative variation. In A.W.K. Gaillard & J.M. Ritter (Eds.), *Tutorials in ERP research: Endogenous components* (pp. 269-310). Amsterdam: North-Holland.

Ruchkin, D. S., & Glaser, E.M. (1978). Simple digital filters for examining CNV and P300 on a single-trial basis. In D. A. Otto (Ed.), *Proceedings of the Fourth International Congress on Event-related Slow Potentials of the Brain: Multi-disciplinary Perspectives in Event-related Potential Research* (pp. 579-581). Chapel Hill, NC: U. S. Environmental Protection Agency, Office of Research and Development.

Ruchkin, D.S., & Sutton, S. (1983). Positive slow wave and P300: Association and dissassociation. In A.W.K. Gaillard, & J.M. Ritter (Eds.), *Tutorials in ERP research: Endogenous components* (pp. 233-250). Amsterdam: North Holland.

Rumelhart, D.E., Hinton, G.E., & Williams, R.J. (1986). Learning representations by back-propagating errors. *Nature, 323,* 533-536.

Rugg, M.D., Cowan, C.P, Nagy, M.E, Milner, A.D. Jacobson, I., & Brooks, D.N. (1989). *Brain, 112,* 489-506.

Sams, M., Alho, K., & Naatanen, R. (1985). The mismatch negativity and information processing. In F. Klix, R. Naatanen and K. Zimmer (Eds.), *Psychophysical approaches to human information processing* (pp. 161-176). Elsevier: North-Holland.

Squires, K. C., & Donchin, E. (1976). Beyond averaging: The use of discriminant functions to recognize event related potentials elicited by single auditory stimuli. *Electroencephalography and Clinical Neurophysiology, 41,* 449-459.

Tabachnick, B. G., & Fidell, L. S. (1989) *Using multivariate statistics* (2nd ed.). New York: Harper & Row.

CHAPTER 8

The Simon then Garfunkel Effect: Priming and the Modularity of Mind *

Gillian Rhodes & Tanya Tremewan

Department of Psychology
Canterbury University

One of the fundamental aims of cognitive science is to map out the functional architecture of the mind, and central to any account of this "cognitive architecture" is a specification of the constraints that exist on information flow between components of the system (see Fodor, 1983). In fact, such constraints form the core of information-processing models which attempt to describe "the flow of information through the mind" (Anderson, 1990).

Many cognitive scientists have proposed highly interactive architectures, with relatively unconstrained information flow between components (e.g., Anderson, 1983; Marslen-Wilson & Tyler, 1980; McClelland & Rumelhart, 1981; Newell & Simon, 1972; Reddy & Newell, 1974; Schank, 1972). For example in Reddy and Newell's model of speech understanding, various processors (phonetic, phonological, lexical, semantic, syntactic, and strategic) operate on the input in parallel and communicate with each other via a "blackboard," on which hypotheses about the input are written, to which they all have access.

Recently, however, Fodor (1983) has challenged the interactive view, arguing instead for a modular architecture with much tighter restrictions on information flow. Specifically he claims that perceptual input analyzers are *informationally encapsulated* from the central, semantic system. To use more familiar terminology, top-down influences on perception are minimal. Fodor cites several advantages for this kind of architecture. For example, he argues that it facilitates the delivery of accurate descriptions of the external world to the central system, and that it allows the perceptual modules to be fast and reflex-like (i.e., obligatory).

* This research was supported by a grant from the University Grants Committee of New Zealand. This manuscript is based on a talk given at the first annual conference of the Australasian Society for Cognitive Science, held in Sydney, Nov. 4-7, 1990. We thank Alan Parkin for helpful discussions about this work. Experiments 1 and 2 are reported in more detail in Rhodes and Tremewan (1993).

In this modular system, top-down influences from the central system, such as the beliefs, knowledge, and goals of the individual, cannot penetrate the perceptual input analyzers, and hence cannot affect perceptual encoding processes. To use Fodor's example, knowing that the lines in the Muller-Lyer illusion are not equal in length should not (and does not) make them appear so. The input analyzers themselves may be computationally complex, and interactions between levels within a module are allowed, but influences from the central system or from other modules are prohibited.

One of the features of nonmodular, interactive architectures is that processes such as attention are uniform and general purpose. Recently Farah (1989) has argued that the attentional mechanisms underlying different kinds of contextual facilitation (priming) are not uniform, a claim that challenges interactive models, but which is consistent with a modular architecture. Her argument against the uniformity of attentional processes is based on two premises: first, that perceptual priming affects sensitivity, the signal detection measure of encoding efficiency, and second, that semantic priming does not. By perceptual priming, Farah means the facilitation of perceptual judgments by advance perceptual information, such as when a location cue facilitates detection. By semantic priming she means the facilitation of semantic judgments by prior information about semantic properties, such as when a related word facilitates lexical decision. The term "semantic" is used generically, and is not intended to distinguish "semantic" from "associative" priming.

It is uncontroversial that perceptual priming affects sensitivity (see for example, Downing, 1988). Farah's argument against the uniformity of attention therefore hinges on the claim that semantic priming does not affect sensitivity. The failure of semantic priming to affect sensitivity would be consistent with modularity on two counts. First, by showing that the mechanisms of perceptual and semantic priming are different, it would favor the existence of modular attentional processes that operate differently in different parts of the system over a general-purpose attentional system. Second, the absence of sensitivity effects would be consistent with encapsulation of the input analyzers. This is because sensitivity measures perceptual efficiency (Sekuler & Blake, 1990), so that the absence of a sensitivity effect means that semantic information has not penetrated the perceptual modules. The question of whether semantic priming affects sensitivity is therefore of considerable relevance to the modularity debate.

Farah's claim that semantic priming does not affect sensitivity is based on a review of five semantic priming studies. We have argued elsewhere that these studies do not provide strong support for this claim (Rhodes, Parkin, & Tremewan, 1993). In brief, two of the studies did not measure sensitivity (Norris, 1984; O'Connor & Forster, 1981). Of the three that failed to find a sensitivity effect, one was unpublished (Hale & Johnston, 1983, cited in Farah, 1989), another reported the sensitivity results in a footnote with no details provided (Schvaneveldt & McDonald, 1981) and the third (Samuel, 1981) actually reported higher sensitivity in related than unrelated contexts (for discriminating between words with and without a noise burst). Farah argues that this sensitivity result is due to an effect of context on post-perceptual decision processes because it only occurred when subjects responded at the end of the sentence and not when they responded immediately after the target word. However, sensitivity is a measure of perceptual efficiency, not of post-perceptual decision processes. Furthermore, if one makes the reasonable assumption that a full sentence provides a more meaningful context than a partial sentence then context effects might well be restricted to the full-sentence condition.

Given the potential theoretical importance of the sensitivity issue, Alan Parkin and I decided to test measure sensitivity and bias for semantic priming in a lexical decision task. We found that sensitivity was significantly greater for words following related primes than for those following unrelated primes (Rhodes, Parkin & Tremewan, 1993). (The bias to say "word" was also larger for words following related than unrelated primes). The sensitivity effect obtained further undermines Farah's conclusion that semantic priming does not affect sensitivity.

In the experiments reported here, Tanya Tremewan and I sought to extend the evidence for sensitivity effects in semantic priming beyond the lexical domain, by measuring sensitivity and bias effects for judgments about faces in a face-priming paradigm. Our paradigm was modeled on that used by Bruce and Valentine (1986). Target faces were preceded by famous prime faces that were either closely associated with the target face (related primes), not associated with it (unrelated primes), or else were unfamiliar (neutral primes). For example, a related pair would be Simon-Garfunkel (in random order), an unrelated pair would be Reagan-Garfunkel and a neutral pair would be NobodySpecial-Garfunkel.

Three experiments were carried out. In Experiment 1 subjects decided whether or not each target face was famous, a task that is analogous to lexical decision (Bruce & Valentine, 1986). Sensitivity and bias were measured as a function of semantic context (type of prime face). In Experiment 2 subjects were asked to decided which of two target faces was famous. A forced-choice task such as this eliminates criterion bias effects (Sekuler & Blake, 1990), so that any context effects are likely to reflect a sensitivity change. In Experiment 3 we asked subjects to decide whether each target face was an accurate or an inaccurate version of a famous face. This third experiment was exploratory in nature and was included to determine whether or not any context effects found for the famous/nonfamous judgments would extend to the more subtle discrimination required in the accurate/inaccurate task.

FACE-PRIMING EXPERIMENTS

General Procedure

Thirty-two subjects participated in each experiment. The same subjects participated in Experiments 2 and 3. The basic trial sequence was the same in all three experiments. Subjects initiated each trial by pressing a key on the computer keyboard. A fixation point appeared on the screen for 750 ms, followed by a prime face (for 250 ms in Experiment 1 and 1000 ms in Experiments 2 and 3), followed by a fixation point for 750 ms, followed by a target face (or faces) for 150 ms. Subjects were instructed to pay close attention to the first face as it might sometimes be related to the second face, but to respond only to the second face.

In Experiment 1 there were 20 related, 20 unrelated, and 20 neutral pairs on famous target trials. Nonfamous trials were created by replacing each famous target with a comparable nonfamous face (same sex, similar age and hair). Primes were shown in the center of the screen with targets to the left or right of center. The nonparametric signal detection measures A' and B" (MacMillan & Creelman, 1990) were used to measure sensitivity and bias, respectively, in Experiment 1. A' ranges from .5 to 1, with higher values indicating greater sensitivity. B" ranges from -1 to + 1, with values below 0 indicating a bias to say "famous" and values above 0 indicating a bias to say "non-famous."

In Experiment 2 subjects decided which of two faces (shown one above the other) was famous. The stimuli were the same as in Experiment 1 except that the famous and nonfamous targets were presented simultaneously, one above the other. Proportion correct was used as a measure of the effect of context on perceptual processing.

In Experiment 3 subjects decided whether a centrally presented target face was an accurate or an inaccurate version of a famous face, in which the lower part of the face (mouth and chin) had been switched with that from another face. A' and B" were used to measure sensitivity and bias. Otherwise the procedure was the same as for Experiment 1.

Results

For each experiment one-way ANOVAs were carried out on each dependent variable with prime type as a within subject factor. Planned comparisons were carried out to test the hypothesis that sensitivity and bias would be higher in the related than in the neutral and unrelated conditions. The results are summarized in Table 8.1.

In Experiment 1 there was a significant main effect of prime type for both sensitivity and bias, $F(2,62) = 3.97, p < .03$, and $F(2,58) = 8.43, p < .0006$, respectively. (Data from two subjects were excluded from the bias analysis due to missing data). Planned comparisons showed that A' was significantly higher for faces following related rather than neutral or unrelated primes (p's $<$ .025, one-tailed). The same was true for bias (p's $<$ .005, one-tailed). In neither case did the unrelated and neutral conditions differ significantly.

In Experiment 2 there was a significant effect of prime type, $F(2,62) = 3.76, p < .03$. Planned comparisons showed that the proportion correct was significantly higher for faces following related rather than neutral or unrelated primes (p's $<$ .025, one-tailed). The latter two did not differ.

In Experiment 3 there was a significant effect of prime type for bias, $F(2,62) = 4.20, p < .02$, but not for sensitivity, $F < 1$. Planned comparisons showed that the bias to say "accurate" was significantly greater for faces following related rather than for faces following neutral or unrelated primes (p's $<$ .025, one-tailed). The latter two did not differ.

Table 8.1. Summary of sensitivity and bias effects in Experiments 1-3.

Dependent Variable	Neutral	Prime type Related	Unrelated
Experiment 1 - "famous/non-famous" judgments			
Sensitivity (A') *	.80 (.01)	.82 (.01)	.81 (.01)
Bias (B") ***	.25 (.04)	.16 (.04)	.29 (.05)
Experiment 2 - "top or bottom face famous" judgments			
Proportion Correct (Sensitivity) *	.67 (.03)	.75 (.02)	.68 (.03)
Experiment 3 - "accurate/inaccurate famous face" judgments			
Sensitivity (A')	.79 (.03)	.80 (.02)	.79 (.02)
Bias (B") *	-.23 (.05)	-.36 (.04)	-.21 (.05)

Notes: Significance levels for the main effect of prime type: *$p < .05$; ** $p < .01$; ***$p < .001$. Standard errors are given in parentheses. All significant priming effects have Related $>$ Unrelated = Neutral (significant by planned comparisons).

Discussion

The effect of semantic priming on sensitivity found in Experiments 1 and 2 indicates that the perceptual encoding of famous faces is facilitated by the immediately prior presentation of a closely associated (but not necessarily visually similar) face. These results extend the evidence for sensitivity effects in semantic priming beyond the lexical domain (Rhodes, et al., 1993) into the face-recognition domain. Context did not affect sensitivity when subjects were required to discriminate between two visually similar versions of a famous face. Thus the perceptual facilitation provided by a related semantic context appears to be limited to discriminating between famous and nonfamous faces and does not extend to subtler discriminations about whether a famous face is exactly correct or not.

Our data are relevant to the modularity debate on two counts. First, the sensitivity results suggest that the attentional processes underlying perceptual and semantic priming effects are similar, in that both facilitate perceptual encoding. Although uniform attentional processes are not inconsistent with a modular architecture (which could have similar perceptual and semantic attentional priming mechanisms), they are certainly not predicted by such an architecture. Alternatively, uniform attentional processes are a feature of nonmodular, interactive architectures. Therefore, although a result in favor of a uniform attentional system cannot discriminate decisively between modular and nonmodular architectures, it is more consistent with nonmodular architectures.

Second, our data are relevant to the encapsulation issue. As we have already argued, the facilitation of perceptual encoding by advance semantic information, indicated by sensitivity effects, is prima facie evidence against the encapsulation of perceptual input analyzers. Therefore the sensitivity effects found in both the present experiments and in our previous lexical decision study (Rhodes, et al., 1993) appear to be problematic for modularity.

The semantic context in which a face appeared affected bias as well as sensitivity in both the famous/nonfamous judgments and the accurate/inaccurate judgments. Bias effects are difficult to interpret because they can arise from either perceptual or post-perceptual decision processes (Massaro, 1989). On the more usual post-perceptual decision interpretation a bias effect would be consistent with encapsulated input analyzers. Alternatively, if bias effects are perceptual, then our bias results would provide further evidence against encapsulation.

One possible interpretation of perceptual effects in semantic priming is that they are due to top-down influences from the central semantic system onto the perceptual input analyzers. On this view, our results are contrary to encapsulation. However, Fodor has proposed an alternative interpretation of such effects. The alternative view is that the semantic priming effects are mediated by connections between units within a perceptual module. In the case of words, these connections are assumed to be direct associative links between lexical items that co-occur. In the case of faces, the links might exist between face recognition units (structural descriptions of faces that are hypothesized to mediate judgments of familiarity, Bruce & Young, 1986) for faces that are typically seen together. The within-module interpretation would reconcile our sensitivity results with encapsulation because the priming information does not come from outside the perceptual module, hence there is no penetration of the module.

There is little direct support for the within-module interpretation, although Fodor does present some suggestive arguments in its favor (Fodor, 1983, pp. 79-80). We are currently attempting to determine whether cross-domain priming between semantically related *names* can prime fame judgments about *faces*, a result that would be difficult to account for by within-module links.[1]

---

[1]Since this article went to press we have found evidence for cross-domain priming (see Rhodes & Tremewan, 1993).

REFERENCES

Anderson, J. R. (1983). *The architecture of cognition*. Cambridge, MA: Harvard University Press.

Anderson, J. R. (1990). *Cognitive psychology and its implications (3rd ed.)*. New York: Freeman.

Bruce, V., & Valentine, T. (1986). Semantic priming of familiar faces. *Quarterly Journal of Experimental Psychology, 38A,* 125-150.

Bruce, V., & Young, A. (1986). Understanding face recognition. *British Journal of Psychology, 77,* 305-327.

Downing, C. J. (1988). Expectancy and visual-spatial attention: Effects on perceptual quality. *Journal of Experimental Psychology: Human Perception & Performance, 14,* 188-202.

Farah, M. J. (1989). Semantic and perceptual priming: How similar are the underlying mechanisms? *Journal of Experimental Psychology: Human Perception & Performance, 15,* 188-194.

Fodor, J. A. (1983). *The modularity of mind*. Cambridge, MA: MIT Press.

MacMillan, N.A., & Creelman, C. D. (1990). Response bias: Characteristics of detection theory, threshold theory and "nonparametric" indices. *Psychological Bulletin, 107,* 401-413.

Marslen-Wilson, W., & Tyler, L. K. (1980). The temporal structure of spoken language understanding. *Cognition, 8,* 1-71.

Massaro, D. W. (1989). *Experimental psychology: An information processing approach*. San Diego CA, Harcourt Brace Janovich.

McClelland, J. L., & Rumelhart, D. E. (1981). An interactive model of context effects in letter perception: 1. An account of basic findings. *Psychological Review, 88,* 375-407.

Newell, A., & Simon, H. A. (1972). *Human problem solving*. Englewood Cliffs, NJ: Prentice-Hall.

Norris, D. (1984). The mispriming effect: Evidence of an orthographic check in the lexical decision task. *Memory & Cognition, 12,* 470-476.

O'Connor, R.E., & Forster, K.I. (1981). Criterion bias and search sequence bias in word recognition. *Memory & Cognition, 9,* 78-92.

Reddy, D. R., & Newell, A. (1974). Knowledge and its representation in a speech understanding system. In L. W. Gregg (Ed.), *Knowledge and cognition*. Baltimore, MD: Erlbaum.

Rhodes, G., Parkin, A. J. & Tremewan, T. (1993). Semantic priming and sensitivity in lexical decision. *Journal of Experimental Psychology: Human Perception & Performance, 19,* 154-165.

Rhodes, G., & Tremewan, T. (1993). The Simon then Garfunkel effect: Semantic priming, sensitivity and the modularity of face recognition. *Cognitive Psychology, 25,* 147-187.

Samuel, A.G. (1981). Phonemic restoration: Insights from a new methodology, *Journal of Experimental Psychology: General, 110,* 474-497.

Schank, R. C. (1972). Conceptual dependence: A theory of natural language understanding. *Cognitive Psychology, 3,* 552-631.

Schvaneveldt, R.W., & McDonald, J.E. (1981). Semantic context and the encoding of words: Evidence for two modes of stimulus analysis. *Journal of Experimental Psychology: Human Perception & Performance, 7,* 673-687.

Sekuler, R., & Blake, R. (1990). *Perception* (2nd ed.). New York: McGraw-Hill.

CHAPTER 9

Determining Light-Source Direction from Images of Shading

D. Gibbins

Discipline of Computer Science
Flinders University of South Australia

M. Brooks, W. Chojnacki

Department of Computer Science,
University of Adelaide

INTRODUCTION

A black-and-white photograph of a smooth object will typically exhibit brightness variation, or *shading*. Of interest to researchers in computer vision has been the inverse problem of how object shape may be extracted from image shading. This *shape-from-shading* problem has been shown by Horn (1975) to correspond to that of solving a first-order partial differential equation. Specifically, a function $u(x,y)$ is sought, representing surface depth in the direction of the z-axis, satisfying the equation

$$R(\partial u/\partial x, \partial u/\partial y) = E(x,y)$$

over the image. Here R is a known function (the so-called *reflectance map*) capturing the illumination and surface reflecting conditions, and E is an image formed by (orthographic) projection of light along the z-axis onto a plane parallel to the xy-plane. The above *image irradiance equation* essentially constrains any hypothesized solution shape to generate an image identical to that which is given. Note that provision of the reflectance map may be regarded as being equivalent to knowledge of an image of a sphere generated under conditions similar to those under which the given image has been created.

A commonly adopted (and relatively tractable) reflectance map has been that which pertains to a Lambertian surface illuminated by a point source. A small portion of such a surface acts as a perfect diffuser, appearing equally bright from all directions. Images of Lambertian surfaces tend to yield shading patterns conveying a strong sense of three-dimensionality.

Boundary conditions are often critical in the solving of the shading problem. Usually, they take the form of the prescribing of surface normals at perhaps one or two (singular) points inside the domain, as well as perhaps at points around the periphery. The presence of an *occluding boundary* is a particularly constraining property. Suppose that light exitant from a smooth rock is projected orthographically onto the image. Then, because the object disappears smoothly from view, we may compute normals at those points on the object that correspond to points on the boundary of the object's image. Indeed, given a point on such a boundary, the corresponding normal on the object must be perpendicular to the boundary contour, and must lie in a plane parallel to the image-plane. It is important that any computational shape-from-shading technique be able to incorporate bounding normals of this kind.

Many methods have been devised for the recovery of shape from images of brightness variation. Most of the recent iterative techniques have been parallel in nature. Typically, a normal is sought for each image point so that the resulting vector field corresponds to the projection of the required surface's normals. Recovery of relative depth from the vector field of normals can then be straightforwardly determined.

An elegant example of a shape-from-shading method is that due to Brooks and Horn (1985). This method which seeks normals $\mathbf{n}(x,y)$ defined over the image. A minimization technique is used in the derivation, leading to the scheme

$$\mathbf{n}_{i,j}^{k+1} = \bar{\mathbf{n}}_{i,j}^{k} + k(E_{i,j} - R(\mathbf{n}_{i,j})) R_{\mathbf{n}}(\mathbf{n}_{i,j}),$$

where $\bar{\mathbf{n}}_{i,j}$ is a local average of $\mathbf{n}_{i,j}$, R is the reflectance map parameterized *on* $\mathbf{n}$, $R_{\mathbf{n}}$ is the derivative of R in direction $\mathbf{n}$, and k is a particular constant. Thus at a each image point a new normal is computed from neighboring normals, the image at that point, and the reflectance map. The method works reasonably well given an image E, a reflectance map R, and some prescribed normals. However, a criticism of this approach (amongst others) is the need for considerable prerequisite information in the form of the reflectance map R. Even if we assume that our depicted object is a Lambertian surface illuminated by a point source, we still require knowledge of the precise direction of the light source.

However, it is clear that people are often able to perceive shape from shading in a photograph without prior knowledge of any scene conditions. There is therefore a need to consider whether the light-source direction can be recovered automatically prior to shape analysis. Of course, it may be that people perform no such preprocess, instead recovering surface shape and source direction simultaneously. We shall consider these issues later in this work. First, however, we analyze the performance of computational techniques that determine the source direction.

TESTING OF AUTOMATED TECHNIQUES

Methods Considered

The factors involved in the formation of an image include illumination configuration and strength, surface reflecting properties, and image projection. Recovery of the direction of the source is therefore a highly ill-posed problem if many factors involved in image formation are unknown. Such a highly ill-posed problem requires strong assumptions to be made in order for an estimate of source direction to be obtained. A typical assumption is that a point source illuminates a Lambertian surface that is either spherical or has isotropically distributed change in normals.

Computational approaches tested in this study are the methods of Pentland (1982), Lee and Rosenfeld (1985), Zheng and Chellappa (1990) (Voting and Contour techniques), along with the Disc method and the Shadow method (Gibbins, Brooks, & Chojnacki 1991). An analysis and rationalization of all of these methods may be found in a companion paper to this one (Gibbins et al., 1991).

Implementation Aspects

All of the methods tested seek the slant and tilt of the source direction, as defined in Figure 9.1. Each of the above methods was tested on a number of images of simple smooth surfaces. The shapes employed were a sphere, ellipsoids of various eccentricities, an ellipsoid with protrusion, a crater, and a stretched Gaussian solid of revolution. Figure 9.2 displays the various shapes, with the exception of the sphere.

First-difference approximations were used to compute derivatives of image intensity needed by most of the methods. Expectations were computed by summing values over the appropriate region and dividing by the number of points sampled (see Gibbins et al., 1991). Four image directions were used in applying Pentland's tilt estimator, one in each of the directions of the x and y axes, and two others at $45°$ to these. It is worth noting that only two directions are actually required here, and if only two are used, then the method is equivalent to the tilt estimator of Lee and Rosenfeld.

Estimating Tilt

We now examine results achieved by the methods of Pentland, Lee and Rosenfeld, and Zheng and Chellappa in determining the tilt component of the source direction.

Response profiles for sphere and ellipsoids. In these tests, each method was applied to an image of a sphere, as well as to images of three ellipsoids. The principal x, y, z axes of the ellipsoids were in the ratios 2:3:3, 1:2:2, and

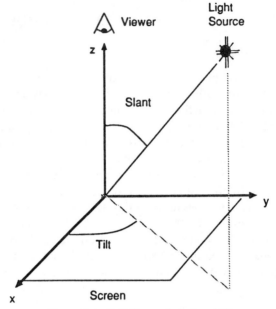

Figure 9.1. Definitions of slant and tilt

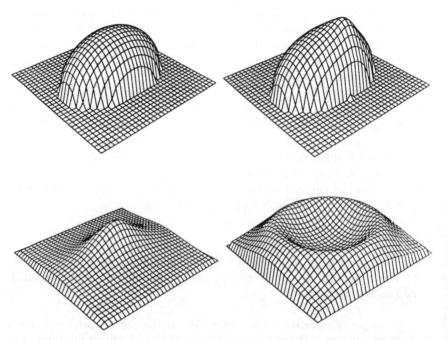

Figure 9.2. Shape used in the performance analysis: Ellipsoid, Ellipsoid with lump, Stretched Gaussian, and Crater

1:3:3. (Of course, the sphere may in these terms be regarded as having axis ratios of 1:1:1.) Slant was fixed at 45° and the angle of tilt was varied from 0° to 360°. Graphs are shown in Figure 9.3 of actual tilt against error in the estimate of tilt for each of the surface shapes and methods mentioned above. As is to be expected, all methods performed well on the image of the sphere. However, in all cases the estimate of the tilt worsened as the ellipsoid eccentricity increased. The estimators of Pentland, and Lee and Rosenfeld produced errors of up to 40°. Both of the Zheng and Chellappa methods worked relatively well, with the Contour method being least affected by variation in eccentricity.

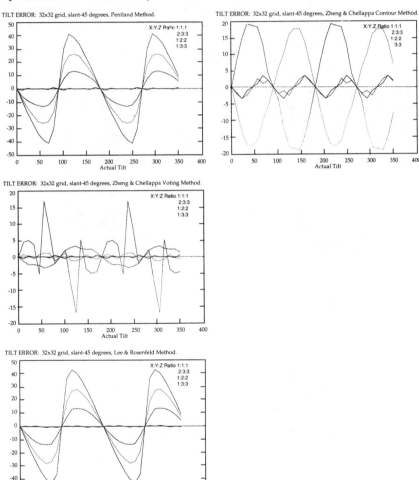

Figure 9.3 Tilt error against actual tilt for ellipsoids of varying eccentricity; slant is fixed at 45 degrees, errors are shown in degrees.

Error surfaces for an ellipsoid. Attention was then turned to an image of an ellipsoid with axes in the ratios 5:8:7. Results for this test are given in Figure 9.4. Here, error surfaces are displayed, each having a circular (unit-disc) domain. A light-source direction is associated with each point in the domain. This direction coincides with that of the surface normal of the unit-hemisphere corresponding to the given point in the domain. Each height value of the error surface specifies the error in estimated tilt. The error surface thus arises out of tests on hundreds of images, each generated with a different light-source direction. It should of course be noted that the ideal error surface is a flat disc in the zero height plane. Note that height is scaled so that an error surface corresponding to a unit hemisphere would have a maximum error of 1 radian (approximately 57°). Note also that when the slant is zero, the tilt angle is undefined. An interpolated artificial value has been given at each of surface centers. A spike nevertheless appears in some diagrams due to a tendency for the error to increase markedly as the center is approached. As can be seen from the diagrams, the methods of Pentland and Lee and Rosenfeld performed poorly at certain light-source tilts, independently of slant; nevertheless, the error did not exceed 20°. Once again, the two methods of Zheng and Chellappa were reasonably well-behaved.

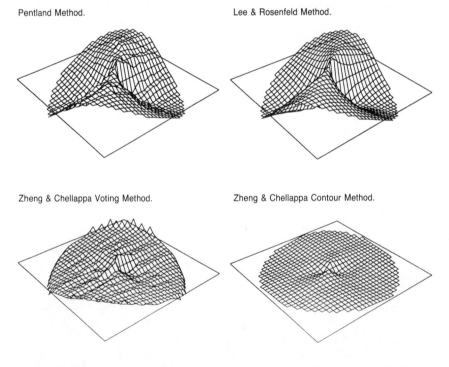

Pentland Method.

Lee & Rosenfeld Method.

Zheng & Chellappa Voting Method.

Zheng & Chellappa Contour Method.

Figure 9.4 Tilt error surfaces describing the performance of various methods when confronted by images of an ellipsoid.

Lumpy ellipsoid. Here the previous test was repeated with the only difference being the nature of the imaged surface shape. This time a smooth "lump" was added to the ellipsoid (refer to Figure 9.2). The lump was placed away from the center so as to add to the asymmetry of the surface. The aim here was to see how performance might be affected by additional surface undulation and asymmetry. The results illustrated in Figure 9.5 are not dissimilar to those of the previous test, with the exception of the Zheng and Chellappa Voting method whose performance deteriorates.

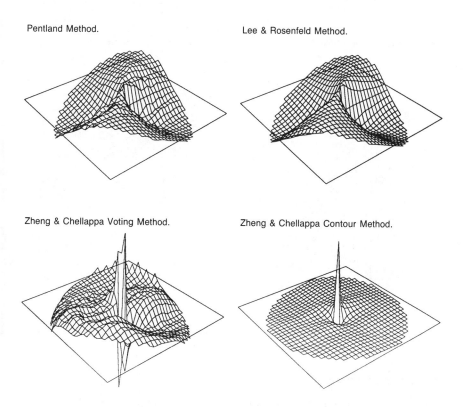

Figure 9.5 Tilt error surfaces describing the performance of various methods when confronted by images of an ellipsoid with lump.

Stretched Gaussian and crater. The two shapes adopted in these tests were a Gaussianlike solid of revolution, stretched in the direction of the y-axis, and a moonlike crater. These surfaces differ from previous examples in that they are smoothly connected to a surrounding, horizontal, planar region. The methods gave almost ideal results for the crater surface (not illustrated), and quite good results for the Stretched Gaussian (see Figure 9.6), with the notable exception of the Voting method, which performed very poorly.

Pentland Method.

Lee & Rosenfeld Method.

Zheng & Chellappa Voting Method.

Zheng & Chellappa Contour Method.

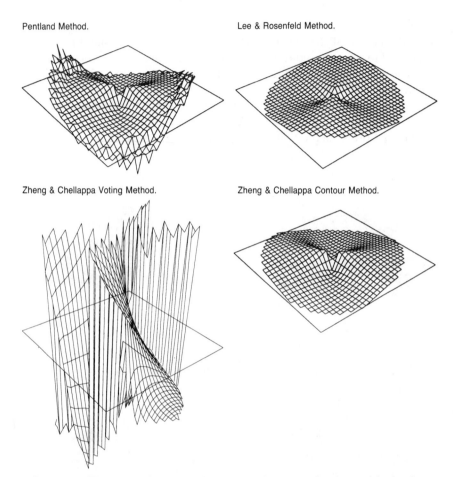

Figure 9.6 Tilt error surfaces describing the performance of various methods when confronted by images of a stretched Gaussian surface.

Local Slant Estimation

The tests carried out on slant estimation were analogous to those for tilt estimation. One difference, however, was that the ellipsoids were produced by stretching a sphere in the direction of the z-axis instead of the x-axis. We compare the methods of Pentland, Lee and Rosenfeld, and Zheng and Chellappa (which is an improved Lee and Rosenfeld technique), along with the Disc method and the Shadow method. The last of these methods is extremely naive and is intended to give a lower bound on performance that other techniques ought to better.

Response profiles for sphere and ellipsoids. Slant error against actual slant is displayed in Figure 9.7 for a variety of ellipsoids as well as the sphere.

The various estimation techniques exhibited responses with varying characteristics even when confronted with the simple sphere. Thus, for example, results of the Pentland estimator deteriorated as light-source slant was increased up to 40°, while results of the Lee and Rosenfeld estimator deteriorated as slant decreased. The Disc estimator performed best of all, except in the case of large slant when there were insufficient illuminated points in the domain for the estimates of image derivatives to be reliable. The Shadow estimator performed very well, but with some instabilities when few shadow points existed in the image, this occurring with small slant.

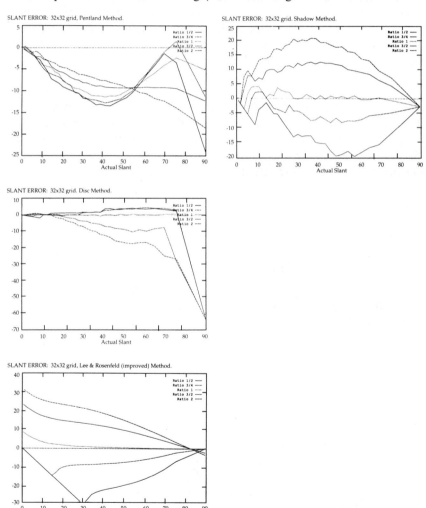

Figure 9.7 Slant error against actual slant for ellipsoids of varying eccentricity; tilt is fixed at 0 degrees, errors are shown in degrees.

Figure 9.7 also shows responses to ellipsoids of various kinds. Pentland's method remained relatively stable over the range of eccentricities, with errors not worsening much over those recorded for the sphere. On the other hand, both the original and improved Lee and Rosenfeld methods were very sensitive to the changes in eccentricity. Note that only the improved version is illustrated, this yielding small errors for high values of slant. However, with an ellipsoid of eccentricity 2, the error exceeded 25° for any slant of less than 15°. The Disc method showed deterioration as slant was increased, with the rate of degradation being dependent on the eccentricity.

The Shadow estimator did not perform as well over midrange slant values (20° - 60°) as at the extremities of slant. Interestingly, however, the errors exhibited were comparable with those obtained for the improved Lee and Rosenfeld method; indeed, the Shadow method gave less significant errors in the case of ellipsoids with larger eccentricity.

Error surfaces for an ellipsoid. Here we again examine the performance of the methods when applied to images of an ellipsoid generated under a range of source directions. Figure 9.8 clearly illustrates the poor performance of the Lee and Rosenfeld estimator as compared to the improved version. Performance of the other estimators was quite good.

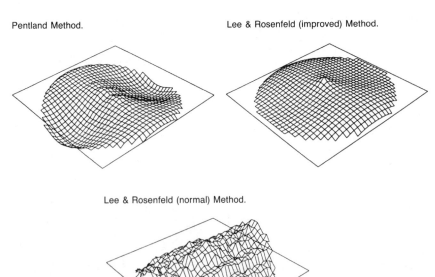

Pentland Method.

Lee & Rosenfeld (improved) Method.

Lee & Rosenfeld (normal) Method.

Figure 9.8a

Disk Method.   Shadow Method.

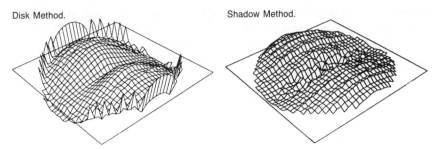

Figure 9.8b Slant error surfaces describing the performance of various methods when confronted by images of an ellipsoid.

Lumpy ellipsoid. When confronted with an image of an ellipsoid with protuberance, all of the methods suffered some degradation in performance (see Figure 9.9). Pentland's method gave poor estimates of steeper light-source slants. The improved Lee and Rosenfeld method performed somewhat better. The Disc method struggled severely in this test, producing highly unreliable estimates for steeper slants. Perhaps surprisingly, the Shadow method coped well with images of the test surface, again performing much like the improved Lee and Rosenfeld method.

Pentland Method.   Lee & Rosenfeld (improved) Method.

Disk Method.   Shadow Method.

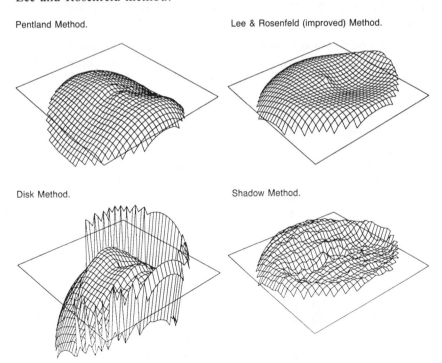

Figure 9.9 Slant error surfaces describing the performance of various methods when confronted by images of an ellipsoid with lump.

Stretched Gaussian and crater. Here, the Gaussian and crater images were used, and all of the methods failed to produce remotely tolerable results (consequently no figures are presented). It would appear that the assumptions implicit in the derivations of all methods are violated in the case of these surface shapes.

Comments

It is evident from the testing that each method has domains in which it works well, and domains in which it performs badly. Most of the methods are based either on the assumption that the depicted surface is spherical, or has an isotropic distribution of some property of the normals. As mentioned previously, these strong assumptions are made in order to render tractable a highly ill-posed problem. Accordingly, when the assumptions are violated by a given surface, then, not surprisingly, estimates of source direction will tend to be poor. Moreover, estimates will be similarly unreliable when a surface satisfies the assumptions made, but is partially occluded from view by other objects, or is only partly visible due to image clipping. Note also that determination of slant appears to be a much more difficult problem than determination of tilt.

Comparison of Lee and Rosenfeld's method with the Zheng and Chellappa improvement shows clearly that the latter is more stable and accurate. This is due to the incorporation of the shadowed region in the estimator, which may be considered a further source of information.

It is interesting to reflect on the performance of the Shadow slant estimator. Although it is simpler and more naive than methods such as those of Pentland, and Lee and Rosenfeld, it nevertheless produces comparable results. This is despite the fact that it uses considerably less data than its counterparts, being simply based on the portion of the object's image which is in shadow. That a naive method performs comparably to more sophisticated techniques raises obvious concerns. The Shadow method is, of course, invariant under change in albedo.

It is possible that further improvement in estimates might be obtained by judicious combination of various techniques. Nevertheless, it is hard to envisage an automated technique having true versatility, with good responses across a wide range of surface types. For example, none of the techniques considered is tuned to the situation in which an essentially planar landscape exhibits undulations. This is commonly found in aerial photographs of terrain. (Horn has suggested in a private communication that a useful estimator here might be the inverse cosine of irradiance averaged over the image.)

TESTING HUMAN PERFORMANCE

The Environment

Informal tests were carried out on the ability of people to estimate light-source direction from various images of a sphere and an ellipsoid. Results were obtained from sessions conducted with 24 individuals. Subjects were asked to examine a given synthetic image, and to gauge the direction of the sun. They were trained to express their results in terms of slant and tilt, and were provided with diagrams useful for estimating angles. Each subject examined

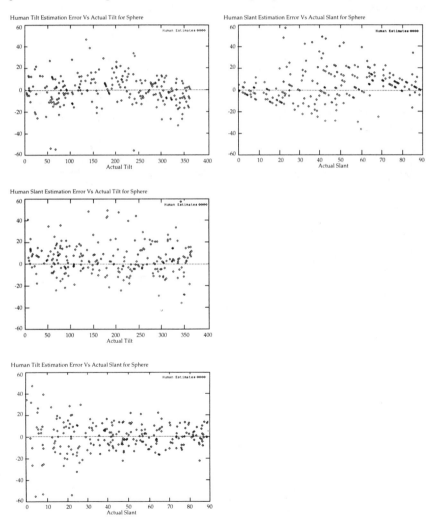

Figure 9.10 Human performance analysis for images of a sphere. Result show: Tilt error vs tilt, tilt error vs slant, slant error vs tilt, and slant error vs slant.

20 images of Lambertian surfaces presented in random order (10 spheres and 10 ellipsoids). In all, therefore, 480 human estimates of source direction were obtained. The images used in the tests were influenced by a minor ambient contribution that improved depth perception. The ellipsoid used in the tests was the same as that used previously to test the automated methods.

Performance Analysis

Various results were obtained in response to an image of a sphere, and these are shown in Figure 9.10. The following observations are made in relation to the various plots:

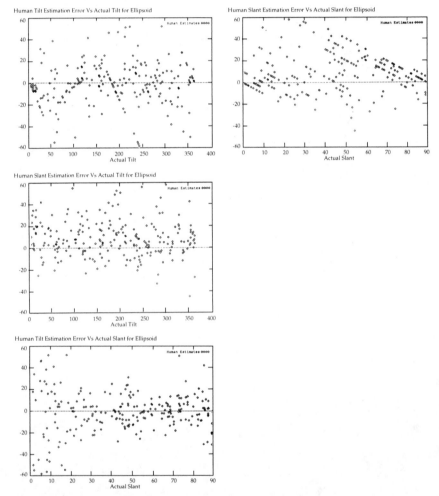

Figure 9.11 Human performance analysis for image of an ellipsoid. Result show: Tilt error vs tilt, tilt error vs slant, slant error vs tilt, and slant error vs slant.

- Tilt estimation error against correct tilt: The graph suggests that estimation of tilt is unaffected by rotation of the image.
- Tilt error against correct slant: As the "sun goes down" tilt error seems to decrease. Of course, it should be recalled that tilt is undefined at zero slant.
- Slant error against tilt: Here it appears that slant estimation is invariant under image rotation.
- Slant error against correct slant: In this test, the variance of the estimates appears to decrease for small or large slants. There would also seem to be a tendency to underestimate small slant values, and to overestimate large slant values.

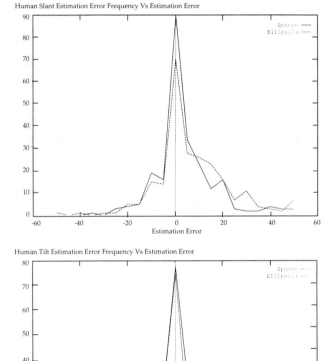

Figure 9.12 Histogramlike plots of error frequency against estimation error in slant and tilt, respectively.

Tests were also carried out on images of the ellipsoid, with similar results (see Figure 9.11).

Finally, histogram-type graphs were plotted of estimation error against the frequency of making that error (5° ranges were used). One diagram deals with slant error, the other with tilt error (see Figure 9.12). Each diagram plots a graph for the sphere and the ellipsoid. A mean estimation error of close to zero is indicated in each case. The variance remains reasonably small, increasing somewhat in the case of the ellipsoid.

Other informal tests not recorded here suggest that people respond reasonably well in a wide variety of situations, including, for example, aerially-viewed terrain.

CONCLUSIONS

We now return to the main question posed earlier: Might a prior determination of source direction be a useful approach to reducing the prerequisite needs of computational schemes, and might this also be the strategy employed by the human visual system? First we turn to some psychological studies on shading analysis.

Ramachandran (1988) suggests that shading is perhaps one of the most primitive cues for depth, having been developed early in the evolution of animal life. Thus it may be that some animals and fish exhibit "counter-shading" in order to neutralize depth-perception and, presumably, to reduce the risk of falling prey. It also appears that shape information obtained from shading can be used as input to the processing of motion data, and the determination of figure-ground relations. Contours are shown to be an important influence on the perception of shape from shading. Also, as is well-known, the human visual system appears to have a predilection for a single overhead source. Shape interpretations of multiple objects in a scene are generally kept consistent with an assumption of a single sun in a given direction.

Berbaum, Bever, & Chung (1983) consider the influence of an image of a well-known object (such as a human hand) on the perception of a possibly ambiguous image of an unknown object. Again, it appears that humans generally achieve consistency by having the perception of the familiar surface affect the interpretation of the unknown object. Note that the image of the human hand might be considered similar in information content to the reflectance map. Further studies are conducted on the memorizing of source direction and its preconditioning effect on the interpretation of a sequence of images.

It is in the work of Mingolla and Todd (1986) that contributions most relevant to our concerns may be found. Here, it is suggested that subjects tend to show low correlation between the quality of their source-direction estimates, and the quality of their shape estimates. That is, on a given test, a good estimate may be obtained for source direction, yet shape is estimated poorly. Alternatively, shape may be well estimated, but the source direction is substantially in error. This, the authors claim, is contrary to the nature of automated techniques. Mingolla and Todd further suggest that the human visual system does not act to partially invert the image-forming process. Thus the isoluminance contour work of Koenderink and Van Doorn (1980) is cited as an example of an approach that is perhaps more consistent with human performance. Finally, the claim is made that Lambertianness is not a default assumption in human perception given that people are equally able to interpret images depicting a range of materials, including shiny surfaces.

An obvious caveat needs to be registered here in relation to psychological studies in which the subject is asked to report on such as perceived light-source direction. Perhaps it is the case that humans determine source direction prior to shape. Alternatively, recovery of source direction and shape might be a coupled activity, with an intermingling of processing. Either way, it may well be that the subject has no conscious access to either of these processes. If this is correct, a subject confronted with questions on source direction or shape will be basing answers on the outcome of the complete process of shape and source recovery. It is therefore essential that results of psychological tests are interpreted with this in mind.

Returning to the low correlation observed between the quality of estimates of source direction and shape, it is the view of the authors that this is weak information on which to base the conclusion that present shape-from-shading techniques are wholly inappropriate models of cognition. (What is clear, however, is that their performance is poor in comparison with human perception, but this is a separate point since we are essentially dealing with a methodological issue.) It is useful at this stage to consider the Brooks and Horn method (1985) which is the only approach to date that seeks to determine in a coupled manner both shape and source direction from shading information. In this technique, a point light source is assumed to illuminate a smooth Lambertian surface. By modifying the minimization technique mentioned in the Introduction, a dual scheme is obtained in which, repeatedly, shape is computed using an estimate of source direction, and then a new source direction is computed from the revised shape. It turns out that the search space for this scheme is not entirely convex, and so the technique is susceptible to falling into local minima. A difference in the quality of estimates for source direction and shape is then entirely plausible. Of course, there will also be many cases where both estimates are poor (as is presumably the case with humans). Note that the intention here is not to suggest that the Brooks-Horn method is a possible model of cognition. Rather, it suggests that the conclusion drawn by Todd and Mingolla is stronger than the evidence will bear.

On the basis of data before us, early indications are that automated techniques for determining source direction are unlikely to be able to deliver reasonably accurate results over images of a wide range of surface types. This is because the necessary strong assumptions that need to be made in the derivation of these techniques are likely to be very different for varying surface types. If a robust preprocess for determination of source direction turns out to be infeasible, it might well be that the relatively versatile skills of the human subject are due to a coupled approach to recovery. Further psychological work is clearly needed to help resolve this problem.

REFERENCES

Berbaum, K., Bever, T., & Chung, C.S. (1983). Light source position in the perception of object shape. *Perception, 12,* 411-416.

Brooks, M.J., & Horn, B.K.P. (1985). Shape and source from shading. *Proceedings of the International Joint Conference in Artificial Intelligence* (pp. 932-936). Los Angeles, CA: Morgan Kaufmann Publishers, Los Altos, CA.

Gibbins, D., Brooks, M.J., & Chojnacki, W. (1991). Determining light source direction from a single image. *Technical Report TR91-26.* School of Information Science and Technology, Flinders University, Adelaide, South Australia.

Horn, B.K.P. (1975). Obtaining shape from shading information. In P.H. Winston (Ed.), *The psychology of computer vision* (pp. 115-155). New York: McGraw-Hill.

Koenderink, J.J., & van Doorn, A.J. (1980). Photometric invariants related to solid shape. *Optica Acta, 27,* (7), 981-996.

Lee, C.H., & Rosenfeld, A. (1985). Improved methods of estimating shape from shading using the light source coordinate system. *Artificial Intelligence, 26,* (2), 125-143.

Mingolla, E., & Todd, J.T. (1986). Perception of solid shape from shading. *Biological Cybernetics, 53,* 137-151.

Pentland, A.P. (1982). Finding the illuminant direction. *Journal of the Optical Society of America, 72,* (4), 448-455.

Ramachandran, V.S. (1988). Perceiving shape from shading. *Scientific American, 259,* (2), 76-83.

Zheng, Q., & Chellappa, R. (1991). Estimation of illuminant direction, albedo, and shape from shading. IEEE Transactions on Pattern Analysis and Machine Intelligence, 13, (7), 680-782.

CHAPTER 10

Goal Inference in
Information-Seeking Environments *

Bhavani Raskutti and Ingrid Zukerman

Department of Computer Science
Monash University

INTRODUCTION

In this chapter, we present a mechanism which infers the plans and goals of a user from his/her statements by generating the possible interpretations of these statements, evaluating them, and then selecting the more likely interpretations. The inference is done using several strategies that constrain the number of possible interpretations of a user's statements. Our mechanism has been implemented in a task oriented consultation domain, and it is part of a system which also contains a Natural Language Interface (NLI) and a planner. However, in this chapter, we focus on the inference mechanism, and the only references that we make to the NLI and the planner concern our assumptions about them.

Our mechanism infers the plans of a user by generating the possible interpretations of his/her statements. An interpretation of a user's statements consists of a set of plans that the user proposes to carry out, and a plan consists of an action with a number of parameters defining the action. For instance, in the travel domain, the proposal to fly from Melbourne to Sydney on December 1, 1990, is a plan, where *flying* is the action, and the parameters *origin, destination,* and *departure date* are instantiated.

A number of researchers have used plan recognition as a means to response generation during consultation (Allen & Perrault, 1980; Carberry, 1983; Grosz, 1977; Litman & Allen, 1987; Pollack, 1989; Sidner & Israel, 1981). However, the models of plan recognition developed by these researchers cope only with a single interpretation of a user's actions or utterances, whereas

* This research was supported in part by grant Y90/03/22 from the Australian Telecommunications and Electronics Research Board. We thank Prof. J. Roach and D. Sanford from the Virginia Polytechnic Institute and State University for allowing us to use their transcripts of telephone conversations at travel agencies. We also thank Wilson Wen from Telecom Research Laboratories for his advice on probability theory.

our mechanism is concerned with the problem of selecting a likely interpretation from among multiple possible interpretations.

The inference process in our mechanism can be divided into three stages: (a) direct inference, (b) indirect inference, and (c) evaluation of interpretations. Direct inferences are those that are drawn on the basis of the user's statements, the definition of domain actions, and the discourse coherence. Indirect inferences are those that are based on domain knowledge and common sense and world knowledge, and are less certain than direct inferences. Direct and indirect inferences yield a set of possible interpretations, which are evaluated prior to selecting a likely interpretation. During the course of the inference process, a number of strategies are used to guide this process toward likely interpretations of a user's statements.

During direct inference, we apply *guiding principles* to constrain the number of plans which may be valid interpretations of a single statement. In addition, *metapredicates,* such as CAN and MUST, which are directly derived from a user's statements, are used to bias our preference toward the more suitable interpretations. *Coherence relations* are then used to choose the more promising interpretations of multiple statements, where the likelihood of an interpretation is calculated by means of Bayesian theory of probability.

Indirect inferences are applied to infer information that has not been explicitly stated by the user. The strength of these inferences is assessed on the basis of their source of information. For instance, the desired mode of transport between Sydney and Hawaii may be inferred by taking into consideration typical assumptions about the domain. This type of inference is stronger than a default inference based on general 'world knowledge', but weaker than a direct inference from the user's statements.

After the inference process, the set of interpretations is pruned by using a measure of the *information content* of the interpretations. The information content of an interpretation is a measure of how well-defined an interpretation is in terms of the actions to be performed on the basis of this interpretation. In the cooperative interactions that we are exploring, we have observed that in general, the user communicates enough information so that his/her plans may be understood by the listener. Hence, the better defined the plans in an interpretation, the more likely it is that this is the interpretation intended by the user. This tenet is valid only in intended plan recognition, such as the one occurring in cooperative interactions. In *keyhole* recognition of plans and goals by unobtrusively observing an agent (Schmidt, Sridharan & Goodson, 1978), we cannot assume the same strong desire for communication and hence cannot use the information content of an interpretation to assess its likelihood.

In the subsequent sections, we discuss two approaches for plan inference, and describe our mechanism with particular reference to the travel domain.

To illustrate our ideas, we make use of the following dialogue excerpt:

Traveler: "I want to be in Sydney the day after tomorrow.
                 I am going to Hawaii on the 11:00 am flight.
                 By the way, I'll be leaving from Adelaide."

Travel Agent: "What about your transport to Adelaide?"

Traveler: "That's OK. I am flying there this afternoon."

APPROACHES TO THE INFERENCE PROCESS

We distinguish between two main approaches to plan inference in cooperative communications on the basis of the timing of indirect inferences. Indirect inferences may be performed on each statement as it is uttered, or deferred until all the direct inferences are drawn. Thus, the two approaches are as follows:

1. The *cognitive* approach occurs when the system makes a large number of inferences from each statement as it is uttered. For instance, upon receiving the first statement in our sample text, the system, after making all the direct inferences, will go on to make the indirect inference that the speaker is probably leaving from the place where the conversation is being conducted, say Melbourne. However, some of the indirect inferences drawn by the system may have to be retracted due to information given by the speaker in later statements, as when the traveler says "By the way, I'll be leaving from Adelaide," in our sample text. We believe that this approach models human cognition, but it is computationally expensive.

2. The *implementational* approach occurs when the system first draws all the direct inferences from an initial chunk of discourse, and then draws the indirect inferences using the interpretations generated by the direct inferences. In this context, a chunk of statements is a set of statements that are uttered together, after which the user pauses for some response from the system. For instance, the first three statements in the dialogue excerpt presented earlier constitute a chunk. This approach offers less chance of early unwarranted inferences, and hence, from the point of view of implementation, it is more attractive. However, this approach alone cannot cope with follow-up statements issued after the main chunk of discourse has been delivered.

We propose a hybrid approach, where the implementational approach is applied to the first chunk of statements issued by the speaker, and the cognitive approach is applied to relate follow-up statements to the previous discourse. We believe that the order in which the inferences are drawn should not affect the final inference drawn, and hence the initial use of the implementational approach is justified. Thus, the hybrid approach is capable of handling follow-up statements, while partially retaining the efficiency of the implementational approach.

THE MAIN MECHANISM

In this section, we present the main algorithms used by the two approaches to plan inference and then describe the three stages of the inference process in the two approaches. The algorithms for the cognitive and implementational approach are embodied in the procedures *Cognitive-Infer* and *Implementational-Infer,* respectively.

Procedure *Cognitive-Infer(S)*
1   Set *InterpretationSet* to *nil*
2   For each statement *s* in the discourse *S*
3   Generate a set of interpretations *I(s)* using guiding principles and metapredicates
4   Infer the set *R* of possible discourse relations between *I(s)* and *InterpretationSet*, and order them according to the coherence measure
5   Combine *I(s)* and *InterpretationSet* using *R* to create a new *InterpretationSet,* and determine the likelihoods of the interpretations in the new set
6   Use these likelihoods to prune unlikely interpretations from *InterpretationSet*

7   For each interpretation *I* that is left in *InterpretationSet*
8   Repeat until [interpretation *I* is fully defined] or [the information content of *I* cannot be increased]
9   Use inter-plan relationships and indirect inference rules to infer the values of all the necessary parameters in all the plans in *I*
10   Update the parameter values so that weaker inferences do not refute the results of earlier stronger inferences
11   EndRepeat
12   EndFor
13 EndFor

14 For each interpretation *I* in *InterpretationSet*
15   Use the information content of *I* to revise its likelihood
16 EndFor
17 Prune unlikely interpretations from *InterpretationSet*
18 Check *InterpretationSet* to see whether the user is to be queried or a valid interpretation can be passed to the planner

Procedure *Implementational-Infer(S)*
1 Set *InterpretationSet* to *nil*
2 For each statement *s* in the discourse *S*
3   Perform direct inferences as in lines 3-6 in procedure *Cognitive-Infer*
4 EndFor

5 Prune *InterpretationSet* using information content as in lines 14-17 in
     procedure *Cognitive-Infer*

6 For each interpretation *I* that is left in *InterpretationSet*
7   Repeat until [interpretation *I* is fully defined] or
               [the information content of *I* cannot be increased]
8   Use interplan relationships and indirect inference rules to
               infer the values of the undefined necessary parameters
               in all the plans in *I*
9   EndRepeat
10 EndFor

11 Prune *InterpretationSet* using information content as in line 5
12 Check *InterpretationSet* to see whether the user is to be queried or a
     valid interpretation can be passed to the planner

Direct Inference

The direct inference stage (lines 3-6 in procedure *Cognitive-Infer* and line 3 in procedure *Implementational-Infer*) consists of: (a) inferring a set of interpretations from each of the user's statements (line 3 in procedure *Cognitive-Infer*); (b) inferring a set of relations between each interpretation of a user's statement and the previous discourse (line 4); and (c) generating a set of new interpretations, where each new interpretation consists of an interpretation of the new statement, an inferred relation, and an interpretation of the previous discourse (line 5). In this process, the likelihood of each interpretation is determined, and the less likely interpretations are not pursued.

The inference of interpretations from one statement issued by a user consists of inferring a set of possible actions which match this statement, and computing their likelihoods. This inference is done by using a STRIPS-like operator library (Fikes & Nilsson, 1971) and plan inference rules (Allen & Perrault, 1980). Since the number of interpretations based on just one statement and the operator library can be quite large in a realistic domain, we control the activation of the plan inference rules by means of guiding principles, so that only a few of the many possible interpretations are chosen. In addition, metapredicates are used during this stage to modify the strength of the plan inference rules.

The inference of the discourse relations between the interpretations of one statement and the interpretations of the previous discourse is done so that the coherence of the discourse is increased. Our approach here is similar to that of Litman and Allen (1987), but it differs from theirs in that initially we maintain all the possible interpretations, whereas they maintained only one interpretation.

The inference of a new interpretation based on an interpretation of a new statement, an interpretation of the previous discourse, and one of the inferred discourse relations, is done by updating the interpretation of the previous discourse using the discourse relation and the information in the interpretation of the new statement. The likelihoods of the new interpretations are determined using Bayesian theory, and interpretations with likelihoods that are lower than an acceptable threshold are dropped (Raskutti & Zukerman, 1991).

Indirect Inference

The indirect inference stage (lines 7-12 in procedure *Cognitive-Infer,* and lines 6-10 in procedure *Implementational-Infer*) is used to infer information that has not been explicitly stated by the user. In the cognitive approach, it is performed after direct inference of each statement. In the implementational approach, it is performed after direct inference of a chunk of statements. The strength of indirect inferences is assessed on the basis of their source of information. Hence, the ranking and categorization of inferences according to their information source play a crucial part during this stage.

Indirect inferences are applied to infer each of the parameters that are necessary for plan definition. The indirect inference process is performed until a complete interpretation is inferred or no more inferences can be drawn on the basis of the existing information. In the implementational approach, only the parameters that remain undefined after direct inference are inferred by means of indirect inference. In the cognitive approach, on the other hand, all the necessary parameters have to be inferred, and inferences may be refuted or corroborated in light of new inferences which are as strong or stronger than earlier inferences (line 10 in procedure *Cognitive-Infer*). In addition, in the implementational approach, indirect inference is performed after pruning according to both coherence and information content measures, whereas in the cognitive approach, it is performed after pruning according to the coherence measure alone.

A parameter can be inferred either by using plan relationships, such as Enable, Constrain, After and Before, or by using indirect inference rules (line 9 in procedure *Cognitive-Infer* and line 8 in procedure *Implementational-Infer*). The plan relationships can be either inferred or explicitly stated. The use of plan relationships for the inference of parameters, and the inference of such relationships when they are not explicitly stated is discussed in Raskutti and Zukerman (1991).

Evaluation of Interpretations

After a chunk of statements is processed, the generated interpretations are evaluated using a measure of information content, and the interpretations that are better defined according to this measure are retained. This evaluation is performed twice in the implementational approach, first after all the direct inferences have been drawn, and then again after the completion of the indirect inferences (lines 5 and 11 in procedure *Implementational-Infer*). In the cognitive approach, on the other hand, the evaluation is deferred until all the statements in a chunk are fully processed (lines 14-17 in procedure *Cognitive-Infer*).

STRATEGIES IN DETAIL

In this section, we describe the strategies used during the course of the inference process to reduce the number of possible interpretations of a user's statements.

Guiding Principles

Guiding principles restrict the number of interpretations that match a single statement of a user by controlling the search through an operator library that defines the basic actions in the domain. Each operator definition in the library consists of the preconditions, effects and body of an action, where the body defines the composition of an operator. These definitions are in terms of domain predicates. In addition, our operator definition includes a plan schema which holds the various parameters that have to be filled to complete the definition of an action. For example, the plan schema of the operator TAKE-PLANE is TAKE-PLANE (origin = ?loc1, departure_date = ?date1, departure_time = ?time1, destination = ?loc2, arrival_date = ?date2, arrival_time = ?time2).

During the inference of interpretations of a single statement of a user, all those operators that have the input predicate in the definition of their precondition, effect or body are chosen as possible matches. This can lead to the selection of a large number of operators as possible interpretations of a user's statement. Hence, we use the following guiding principles to constrain the number of operators that are chosen.

> 1. *Minimal Cover* requires that the operator that minimally covers the action mentioned by the user be selected. In practice, this means that primitive operators are searched before composite operators. For instance, when a user says "I want to go to Sydney," then while both one-way and two-way travel are possibilities, one-way travel is chosen. The common-sense notion that people return to their place

of residence would later postulate a plan for returning, if it is not mentioned in subsequent statements. However, since this is a weak inference, the system will require confirmation from the user.

2. *Least Commitment* requires that the operator that needs the least number of additional assumptions be chosen (Sacerdoti, 1977). In practice, this means that the more general operators are chosen unless there is an explicit reference to a specific operator. For instance, when a user says "I want to go to Sydney," then while it is possible to go to Sydney by plane, train, and so on, the selected operator is simply GO, without specifying any particular means of transport.

MetaPredicates

Metapredicates, such as CAN, MUST and WANT, are returned by the NLI when they are mentioned by the user. They modify the predicate that the NLI returns on the basis of the user's statement, and are used to update the strength of the inferences drawn using the plan inference rules.

As mentioned earlier, the plan inference rules choose as possibilities all those operators that have the input predicate in the definition of their precondition, effect or body. This may lead to ambiguity, since the same predicate can be used in the definition of many operators. For instance, all of the operators that define transportation have "BE" in their precondition and effect. The precondition is that the user should "BE" at the departure location at the required time, and the effect is that the user arrives at the destination and "IS" at the destination. Hence, if a user's request about BEing at a place is expressed as "I want to be ... " or "I can be ... ," but the NLI returns it as BE(...), this predicate can refer either to the precondition or the effect of an operator with equal likelihood. By taking into consideration the presence of a metapredicate, we increase the bias toward the appropriate inference rule. For example, if the user had said "I can be ... " then the likelihood of the precondition rule would have been increased. Thus, the presence of metapredicates enables us to retain information that may otherwise be lost when parsing from natural language into predicates.

Discourse Coherence

Discourse coherence considerations are used during direct inference to bias the inference process toward interpretations that make the discourse more coherent. To this effect, the inferred relations are assigned likelihoods that reflect normal patterns of discourse. For example, the elaboration of the last referenced plan is preferred to the elaboration of older plans; the likelihood of an introduction is reduced if elaboration is possible; and if there are cue words to indicate that one relation is preferable to another, then these are used during the inference of discourse relations (Raskutti & Zukerman, 1991).

A new statement of the user can either *elaborate* on an earlier topic, *introduce* a new topic, *digress* from the last topic, or *correct* some information specified earlier. The different possible relations coupled with the different topics that may be corrected or elaborated give rise to a number of different interpretations. The likelihoods of these interpretations depend on the likelihoods of the inferred relations, which, in turn, depend on whether the NLI has recognized a discourse-statement relationship and/or the topic that is being referenced. Thus, there are four possibilities:

1. If there is an explicit reference to an earlier topic, and a discourse relation is specified, then the system has no uncertainty regarding the referenced topic or the relation.

2. If only a topic is specified, then we assume an elaboration relation, for example, "*About the Hawaii trip,* I'll be flying Qantas."

3. If only a discourse-statement relation is specified, for example, "*On second thought,* make it 10:00 a.m." (correction), the system needs to determine which of the earlier topics is being referred to. Notice, however, that the only possible discourse relations pertaining to previous topics are elaboration and correction. This is due to the fact that in introduction, the introduced topic is unrelated to previous topics, and digression is considered as a special case of elaboration, where the likelihood of elaborating on the latest topic is substantially reduced. The determination of the topics which are elaborated or corrected is performed by following common patterns of discourse where the elaboration or correction of topics referenced later in the discourse is preferred to that of topics mentioned earlier.

4. If neither a topic nor a discourse relation is specified, then the inference of discourse relations is performed by first determining which relations are possible and then calculating the likelihood of each postulated relation. We do not postulate that the new domain predicate is a correction or a digression unless there is an explicit indication from the NLI. Hence, the only possible relations are elaboration of each topic in the interpretation of the earlier discourse, and introduction of a new topic. Like above, the elaboration of topics referenced later in the discourse is preferred to that of topics mentioned earlier. Introduction of a new topic is always considered a possibility. However, its likelihood is reduced if elaboration is possible.

Ranking of Inferences According to Their Information Source

The certainty of an inference depends on the reliability of the information source that is used as the basis for this inference. Hence, we categorize different information sources and rank them according to their reliability. The certainty of a parameter is then determined by the ranking of the information source used to obtain it. We consider the following sources of information and list them in decreasing order of reliability.

1. *User's Statements* yield direct inferences that follow directly from what is explicitly stated. While these inferences can be presumed correct, there is still a degree of uncertainty in relating a new statement to the previous statements due to the different discourse relations possible.
2. *Domain Knowledge* yields indirect inferences that are derived by using the system's beliefs about the user's domain knowledge. A typical example is the inference of the arrival time at the destination once the departure time is known. Such an inference is useful when there are multiple legs in a proposed journey, requiring that departure times at subsequent locations be inferred.
3. *Domain Assumptions* yield indirect inferences that are derived by assuming what is normal in the domain. For example, when no details about the mode of travel are specified, it is possible to derive this information from the usual mode of transport between two places.
4. *User Model* yields indirect inferences that are made on the basis of the system's model of the user. The user model may be a stereotypical model describing a typical user, or it may be more specific. In the context of a travel agency, we have adopted a stereotypical model based on the assumption that normally, in a travel agency, the information provider cannot form an extensive user model.
5. *Common Sense* yields indirect inferences that are derived by assuming normal behavior or common notions outside the domain of interest. Typically, such notions are used when we postulate return journeys based on the assumption that people usually do not move from their residence. These are default inferences in the sense that they are accepted when there is nothing contradicting them.

The inference types are assigned a ranking in the (0,1) range. This ranking is directly used as the certainty component during the computation of the information content of a parameter. The inferences derived directly from the user's statements have a ranking of 1, and all other inference types have a progressively decreasing ranking according to the reliability of their source of information. The undefined parameters are assigned a minimum ranking. This assignment enables us to distinguish between parameters that are defined inexactly by the user and parameters that are left undefined, and assign less information content to undefined parameters.

During the process of inferring the value of a parameter, we emulate one aspect of human behavior whereby once a conclusion is accepted with a particular degree of confidence, people consider it to be certain when drawing subsequent conclusions (Gettys, Kelly & Peterson, 1982). To this effect, each parameter in the plans in each interpretation is tagged with the type of inference that gave rise to the value of the parameter, without taking into consideration the inference types of other parameters that were used for computing the parameter in question. Thus, like Carberry (1990), we do not compound the uncertainty in chains of inferences.

The ranking of the inference type in a parameter's tag is used in the cognitive approach to determine whether a particular parameter should be revised by a new inference. If the ranking of the new inference is the same or higher than the ranking of the inference type in the tag, the new inference replaces the old one. Otherwise, the old inference is retained. In this manner, a weaker inference is prevented from refuting the results obtained from a stronger inference.

Information Content

We define the information content of an interpretation as the sum of the information content of all the plans in the interpretation, and the information content of a plan as the sum of the information content of all the parameters that are necessary for the definition of the plan. The information content of a parameter, in turn, depends on two factors: (a) its specificity, which is defined as the reciprocal of the number of possible values assigned to this parameter; and (b) its certainty, which depends on the source of information from which this parameter was obtained, and is the ranking defined in the previous section. Thus, both a parameter with multiple values assigned to it and a parameter derived from an unreliable source of information are deemed to have a low information content.

The information content measure is used to update the likelihood of each interpretation in the set of interpretations, and the new likelihoods are normalized. The set of interpretations is then pruned by dropping those interpretations whose likelihoods fall below a relative rejection threshold. In this manner, the interpretations with more information content are chosen.

CONCLUSION

We have offered a mechanism which directs inferences toward more likely interpretations of a user's statements by applying Bayesian methods and coherence and information content considerations. In particular, we have used the extent to which the plans in an interpretation are defined to assess the likelihood that this interpretation is the one intended by a speaker. To this end, we have ranked inferences according to the information source on which they are based.

Currently, the algorithm for the implementational approach and the algorithm for the cognitive approach are fully operational, with the indirect inferences restricted to a few rules from each category. Our experiments with a few discourse samples have indicated that our algorithms choose the same interpretation that people choose. For instance, in the example presented in the Introduction, our mechanism considers four possible itineraries, and then chooses the obvious one, that is, Melbourne — Adelaide — Sydney — Hawaii — Melbourne, as the best interpretation.

REFERENCES

Allen, J.F., & Perrault, C.R. (1980). Analyzing intention in utterances. *Artificial Intelligence, 15,* 143-178.

Carberry, S. (1983). Tracking user goals in an information-seeking environment. In *Proceedings of the Third National Conference on Artificial Intelligence* (pp. 59-63). Washington, DC.

Carberry, S. (1990). Incorporating default inferences into plan recognition. In *Proceedings of the Eighth National Conference on Artificial Intelligence* (pp. 471-478). Boston, MA.

Fikes, R.E., & Nilsson, N.J. (1971). STRIPS: A new approach to the application of theorem proving to problem solving. *Artificial Intelligence, 2,* 189-208.

Gettys, C.F., Kelly, C., III, & Peterson, C.R. (1982). The best-guess hypothesis in multistage inference. In D. Kahneman, P. Slovic, & A. Tversky, (Eds.), *Judgment under uncertainty: Heuristics and biases* (pp. 370-377). Cambridge University Press, New York.

Grosz, B.J. (1977). The representation and use of focus in dialogue understanding (Tech. Note 151), Menlo Park, CA: SRI International.

Litman, D., & Allen, J.F. (1987). A plan recognition model for subdialogues in conversation. *Cognitive Science, 11,* 163-200.

Pollack, M. (1989). Plans as complex mental attitudes. In P. Cohen, J. Morgan, & M. Pollack (Eds.), *Intentions in communications,* Cambridge, MA: MIT Press.

Raskutti, B., & Zukerman, I. (1991). Generation and selection of likely interpretations during plan recognition in task oriented consultation systems. *User Modeling and User Adapted Interaction 1 (2),* 323-353.

Sacerdoti, E. D. (1977). *A structure for plans and behavior.* New York: American Elsevier.

Schmidt, C.F., Sridharan, N.S., & Goodson, J.L. (1978). The plan recognition problem: An intersection of artificial intelligence and psychology. *Artificial Intelligence, 10,* 45-83.

Sidner, C.L., & Israel, D.J. (1981). Recognizing intended meaning and speakers' plans. In *Proceedings of the Seventh International Joint Conference on Artificial Intelligence,* (pp. 203-208). Vancouver, Canada.

CHAPTER 11

Two Data Structures in Cognition

Paul L. Roberts and Colin MacLeod

Department of Psychology
University of Western Australia

INTRODUCTION

Currently in cognitive science there is considerable debate about whether the connectionist paradigm can legitimately supplant the traditional classical paradigm as a description and explanation of human cognition. To a large extent the argument revolves around the question of whether connectionist architectures can guarantee certain crucial properties of cognition, namely systematicity and compositionality.

Systematicity in language and thought refers to the fact that the ability to think some thoughts necessarily implies the ability to think certain others. Being able to think "John loves the girl" implies the ability to think "The girl loves John." Compositionality refers to the fact that "the girl," "John," and "loves" play the same semantic role in both the sentences although the sentences are structurally different.

Fodor and Pylyshyn (1988) have argued that these features of language and thought are easy to explain if the architecture of cognition is classical. In a classical architecture, representations are constituted by structurally atomic parts. These parts (symbols) can be combined to form complex representations. Critically, in complex representations the atomic parts retain their identity. So the representation of concept X with defining features P and Q entails the representation [$P\&Q$]. This allows the operation of processes which are sensitive to the structure of representations. Roughly, symbols can be concatenated and representations decomposed at will provided that the symbols exist to begin with. Hence the representation of X can be decomposed into its constituents P and Q.

Fodor and Pylyshyn note that in connectionist architectures, however, because the only mechanism is association, all representations are structurally atomic. Constituents do not retain their identity in complex representations. States of affairs can be associated but not structurally related representationally. So representation of a concept X with defining features

P and Q does *not* entail the representation [$P\&Q$]. Hence X is undecomposable — unless of course X is fortuitously associated (in a probabilistic sense) with the appropriate constituents. Consequently, Fodor and Pylyshyn are able to point out that such features of human cognition as systematicity and compositionality would be a mystery if the architecture of cognition was like this, so they assume that it is not.

This kind of argument has been vigorously opposed by connectionists. Some of the most convincing refutations have come from connectionists who claim to have demonstrated how connectionist models might embody these crucial properties without merely implementing a classical architecture (e.g., Chalmers, 1990; Smolensky, 1987). However, Fodor remains unconvinced, at least by Smolensky's arguments (Fodor & Maclaughlan, 1990). Other more pragmatic arguments against connectionism have also been raised (Hadley, 1990).

We do not attempt to do justice to the numerous facets of the debate here. The point to be made is simply that it is far from being resolved. The debate as formulated above is extremely important as it forces confrontation with fundamental questions about the nature of the mind. However, an alternative approach to the questions at issue seems to have been neglected. It is this approach and the results of its application that we will explore here.

Obviously even if Fodor and Pylyshyn's argument is absolutely correct it does not demonstrate that *none* of human cognition is connectionist. Fodor and Pylyshyn (1988) acknowledge this fact (p. 68) but are skeptical that much of human cognition will be found to be so. The theory and evidence presented here suggest that, potentially, a lot of human cognition could be nonclassical.

A number of existing findings in cognitive psychology demonstrate that there are often two qualitatively different modes that can be engaged when performing cognitive tasks. Examples include s-mode and u-mode learning (Hayes & Broadbent, 1988), analytic and holistic processing (Smith & Shapiro, 1989), and explicit vs. implicit learning (Reber, 1989). U-mode learning, holistic processing, and implicit learning all have a similar nonclassical flavor. Of course on its own this does not establish that these processes are tied to an independent nonclassical architecture.

We suggest that an appropriate methodological strategy would be to try to establish experimentally the architectural basis of these known processing distinctions. This would consist mainly of attempting to ascertain whether the representations involved preserve classical properties. That is, is the evidence for compositionality equivalent for both modes of processing? We should also attempt to provide a theoretical account of how, why, and when these architectures operate and interact. This could be quite a productive strategy and we believe that it is shown to be so in what follows where we apply it to s-mode and u-mode learning.

In what follows, we suggest that a recent distinction made by Hayes and Broadbent (1988) between s-mode and u-mode learning may be explained by postulating the existence of both classical and nonclassical architectures. It is suggested that something like the model of Norman and Shallice (1986) can explain how the features of s-mode and u-mode learning could be related to the existence of these two architectures. Next, some empirical evidence for the existence of these two architectures is presented. Finally, the implications of the kind of model we propose are discussed.

DEVELOPING THE THEORY

S-Mode and U-Mode Learning

In a recent paper, Hayes and Broadbent (1988) make an argument that there are two functionally independent systems that can be involved in knowledge acquisition. The two systems are characterized by two modes of learning.

S-mode, or selective learning is selective, effortful, and reportable and requires working memory capacity. It proceeds by forming hypotheses about the relations between a small number of variables in working memory, in a typical problem solving fashion.

U-mode, or unselective learning, proceeds by unselective, passive aggregation of environmental events. It occurs when the s-mode strategy fails. This failure can occur when the number of relevent variables exceeds the capacity of working memory to manipulate them, when the relevent variables are not salient, or when working memory capacity is consumed by other activities. According to Hayes and Broadbent, anything that precludes the contribution of what they call abstract working memory to encoding should result in u-mode learning. This includes the concurrent load manipulation employed in the experiments to be mentioned here.

Hayes and Broadbent report an experiment in which equivalent initial learning in the two modes results in differential transfer to a second task where the relations between the relevent variables is reversed. These results can be interpreted as suggesting that subjects learning in u-mode are not able to utilize structural knowledge about the task, essentially having to relearn the whole task.

A possible explanation for this failure to utilize structural knowledge could be that it is not recoverable. Knowledge acquired under u-mode conditions may result in undecomposable representations.

Two architectures. While Hayes and Broadbent talk about the difference between s-mode and u-mode learning being an architectural one, they do not go into much detail about precisely what this difference might be, save mentioning that u-mode learning may be represented as multiple instances, in the manner described by Brooks (1978).

While s-mode learning looks like the operation of a classical architecture, we suggest that u-mode learning has a decidedly nonclassical look about it. More specifically, the characteristics of the u-mode system closely resemble the characteristics of the class of connectionist models that Kaplan, Weaver, and French (1990) call feed-forward pattern associators (FFPA). This class of models is exemplified by the pattern associator program in the McClelland and Rumelhart (1988) package.

As with all connectionist architectures, FFPAs are associationistic and hence suffer from the problem that all data structures are atomic, as noted above. However unlike Fodor and Pylyshyn, Kaplan et al. do not believe that this is a terminal disadvantage. Models such as that of Chalmers (1990) suggest that they could be correct in this view. More problematic they believe is the stimulus-driven nature of such models. That is, the output is always fully determined by the input. In this respect FFPAs are like the old S-R models — with the addition of a powerful generalization ability. Consequently they are always a product of their history. So although they can learn to negotiate their way around a particular domain, if the contingencies within that domain change — even if they do so in a *systematic* way — they will be stuck with learning the new input-output mapping from scratch rather than modifying existing knowledge in a systematic way.

But this is exactly what u-mode learning is like. It is this stimulus drivenness, plus the atomic nature of the data structures involved that we suggest is the basis of u-mode learning.

A Rogue Model

Given that the above appears to be a sensible hypothesis, the question arises as to how and why the factors producing the two modes of learning could recruit different architectures. A model proposed by Norman and Shallice (1986) to explain willed and automatic control of action appears to go a long way toward providing answers to these questions.

The model consists of two processing structures, horizontal threads and vertical threads. Horizontal threads consist of schemas which are run off automatically under the appropriate stimulus triggering conditions. The schemas are also highly interactive, facilitating, and inhibiting other related and unrelated schemas, respectively.

Schemas may also be selected by the action of the supervisory attentional system (SAS) which operates via the vertical threads. It acts indirectly by activating or inhibiting individual schemas in a controlled fashion to influence the outcome of processing.

We propose that the horizontal thread processors are FFPAs that engage in u-mode learning. Working memory capacity is some resource that determines the amount of "downward" activation or inhibition available for vertical thread processes. The vertical threads enable s-mode learning by providing added and direct activation or inhibition of input and output patterns of the FFPAs. Thus when this downward activation is not, or cannot be supplied, the system is by default in u-mode and utilizing data structures which do not preserve compositionality.

Of course for the direct activation s-mode strategy to succeed, the vertical thread structure must be capable of testing hypotheses about, and representing (to some extent), the structure of the environment. It must be, in short, a classical architecture (or something like it that preserves compositionality)[1].

Thus we are proposing a general model of cognition that has both connectionist and classical competence. Clark (1990) refers to such models as rogue models.

EMPIRICAL EVIDENCE

The experiments discussed here (Roberts & MacLeod, submitted) were designed to address the question of whether the evidence for the classicality of s-mode and u-mode representations is equivalent. If u-mode learning employs a nonclassical architecture there should be less evidence for the decomposability of u-mode representations than there is for s-mode representations.

In these experiments u-mode learning is induced with a secondary task manipulation (simultaneous rehearsal of a string of digits) in the first phase of the experiment. Phase 2 is always load free. Recall that in Hayes and Broadbent's model a simultaneous load should preclude s-mode processing of the primary task and ensure u-mode processing, while the absence of a simultaneous load should allow full application of the s-mode system.

Both experiments employ a traditional concept learning task. Two kinds of concept are employed. Conjunctions of defining features ([a&b]) and disjunctions (exclusive or, XOR) of the defining features ([aVb]). Defining features are color and geometrical shape. These are embedded in a display that consists of two shapes in various colors. Features can be distributed across items. So an example of a conjunctive category employed would be "red & triangle" and an exemplar would be a display with a blue triangle and a red square. Likewise, an exemplar of a disjunctive category with the same defining features ("red or triangle") would be a display with a blue triangle and a yellow square.

In the training procedure subjects are presented with a display and asked to say whether it is an exemplar or not. They begin by guessing and immediately recieve feedback about the correctness of their response. This

---

[1] Note that there is no requirement that every node or feature or schema in the horizontal threads have a counterpart in the vertical thread structure. It is interesting to speculate that there could be horizontal thread content driving behavior for which we have no concepts represented in the vertical thread architecture.

procedure is repeated on each trial and subjects are asked to try to use the feedback to improve their responding.

Importantly, the ratio of examples to nonexamples is such that, for a conjunctive category {a&b}, it is just as likely that a display with "a" in it is a nonexample as it is that it is an example. That is, P(example | a) = P(non example | a) and similarly for b. This is important for our purposes as it means that there can be no (spurious) association between {a&b} and {a} that would allow a nonclassical associationistic architecture to behave as if it knows about the constituents of its representation of {a&b}. The same state of affairs holds for the disjunctive category.

Experiment 1

In this experiment subjects were trained on the conjunction, with load (u-mode) or without load (s-mode), and then transfered to a disjunction (or vice versa) where the defining features for the conjunction and the disjunction were the same, for example, red, triangle (or different).

What we might expect here is that under s-mode conditions, if the SAS manages to extract the salient features in the training phase it will be able to utilize them in the transfer phase where they are also salient, albeit in a different way. So having learned to respond to displays with "red and triangle" in them should facilitate learning to respond to "red or triangle" displays.

But consider what would be predicted under u-mode conditions. Hypothetically the representation of the phase 1 concept will be undecomposable. Consequently in phase 2 the vertical thread processors will have nothing to go on. This may make it difficult to override interference from horizontal thread processes. Having learned to make a positive response to "red and triangle" and a negative response to nonexamples, including those which satisfy "red *or* triangle," the horizontal thread processors would then be required to invert their previous input-output mapping in order to learn the transfer phase concept. In the transfer phase they are required to make a positive response to "red or triangle" and a negative response to nonexamples including "red and triangle." This suggests that if the horizontal thread processors can dominate responding there may be negative transfer from u-mode knowledge. Minimally, there should be less transfer effect from u-mode knowledge than from s-mode knowledge.

	U-mode		S-mode	
	Same	Different	Same	Different
r	-0.51	-0.14	0.45	0.10

Table 11.1 Experiment 1, correlations between training and transfer performance

As can be seen from Table 11.1, consistent with predictions, the results show a positive correlation between training and transfer performance under s-mode conditions, $r = 0.45$, but a negative correlation between training and transfer performance under u-mode conditions, $r = -0.51$. The difference between these correlations was significant. These effects were not apparent in control conditions where the defining features of the training concept and the transfer concept were different.

It appears that in complex s-mode representations the constituents are available and hence can facilitate transfer, while in u-mode representations this is not the case. In addition it appears that there is an interference effect due to the stimulus driven nature of the u-mode process.

Experiment 2

A potential problem with Experiment 1 is that u-mode subjects just may not have utilized their knowledge from the training phase appropriately in the transfer phase for some reason. The effect may be cognitively penetrable (see Pylyshyn, 1984) and hence not attributable to an *architectural* difference. In this experiment, instead of transfering to another concept-learning task, we use a task which necessitates subjects using knowledge from the training phase in order to succeed. It is aimed at a more direct test of the relative decomposability of s-mode and u-mode representations.

In the first phase of the experiment, subjects learned two conjunctions simultaneously, one under s-mode conditions and one under u-mode conditions. In the second phase they were required to make an inference about the constituent structure of the concept. The display was rendered monochrome and subjects were asked to identify potential examples of the concept they had just learned. This required them to know what the shape feature was in order to succeed. In the third phase subjects were given a retest which contained 50% new examples.

As can be seen from Figure 11.1, despite equivalent initial learning and recall for s-mode and u-mode concepts, the ability to make an inference about the constituent structure of the u-mode concept was impaired relative to the s-mode concept. This interaction is highly significant. There was no difference between the modes in ability to generalize to the new examples and there was no difference for either mode in identifying new vs. old examples.

These results appear to be in accord with the kind of model we have postulated. In the training environment provided, the representations in an associationistic, stimulus-driven (nonclassical) architecture should be incapable of yielding information about the constituent structure of the concept, essentially because the data structures involved do not preserve compositionality. There seems to be some evidence that u-mode knowledge is like this.

However when the vertical thread (classical) processes have been involved

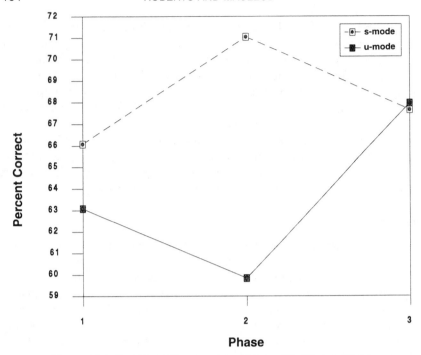

Figure 11.1 Experiment 2, percentage of items identified correctly

in learning the concept, this information should be readily available, complex representations should be decomposable by appropriate processes. S-mode knowledge appears to be like this.

CONCLUSIONS AND IMPLICATIONS

In this chapter, we have suggested that the debate about the validity of connectionist models can be fruitfully addressed in a rather different way to that which has been typical so far. The debate as currently formulated is extremely valuable as it has focused attention on the question of the fundamental architectural nature of the mind. Importantly it has also provoked analysis of what potential candidates for a cognitive architecture are capable of.

It is uncertain to what extent connectionist architectures can exhibit classical properties while computing in a nonclassical way. However what is certain and interesting is that a class of connectionist models, (those that Kaplan et al. call FFPAs), which seem to fail to exhibit classical properties, have their psychological counterpart in a number of findings in cognitive psychology.

We have recomended a strategy of trying to establish the architectural basis of these processing distinctions. Some preliminary results of pursuing that strategy have been mentioned. They are consistent with a theory that postulates both classical and nonclassical architectures subserving cognition.

If the model we have proposed is correct then it has a number of important implications.

Firstly, it suggests that a lot of cognition could be nonclassical. Any knowledge which has been acquired in the absence of the s-mode strategy will be, according to this model, represented in a nonclassical architecture. Since a number of paradigms in the experimental literature deal with unselective "u-mode" processing and much of everyday cognition appears to be like this, it seems likely that much of everyday cognition is nonclassical.

This conclusion is in contrast with that of Fodor and Pylyshyn (1988). While they admit that some cognitive processes could be connectionist, they see no reason to believe that many are. The link between mode of learning and architecture of representation provides such a reason.

Secondly, it suggests that real-world cognition is going to be complexly determined by contributions from both these architectures. Attempting to understand the interaction between these architectures will be a critical area of study. We suggest that the development of expertise may be one area where this interaction is important.

The moral of this story is that if you think that there is sufficient reason for believing classical theory to be true then you should also believe that connectionism is nontrivially true.

REFERENCES

Brooks, L.R. (1978). Nonanalytic concept formation and memory for instances. In E. Rosch & B.B. Lloyd (Eds.), *Cognition and categorization.* New York: Wiley.

Chalmers, D.J. (1990). Syntactic transformations on distributed representations. *Connection Science, 2,* 53-62.

Clark, A. (1990). Connectionism, competence, and explanation. *British Journal for the Philosophy of Science, 41,* 195-222.

Fodor, J., & McLaughlin, B. (1990). Connectionism and the problem of systematicity: Why Smolensky's solution doesn't work. *Cognition, 35,* 183-204.

Fodor, J.A., & Pylyshyn, Z.W. (1988). Connectionism and cognitive architecture: A critical analysis. *Cognition, 28,* 3-71.

Hadley, R.F. (1990). Connectionism, rule following, and symbolic manipulation. *Proceedings of the American Association for Artificial Intelligence,* August. Boston, MA.

Hayes, N.A., & Broadbent, D.E. (1988). Two modes of learning for interactive tasks. *Cognition, 28,* 249-276.

Kaplan, S., Weaver, M., & French, R. (1990). Active symbols and internal models: Towards a cognitive connectionism. *AI and Society, 4* (1), 51-73.

McClelland, J.L., & Rumelhart, D.E. (1988). *Explorations in parallel distributed processing.* Cambridge, MA: MIT.

Norman, D.A., & Shallice, T. (1986). Attention to action — Willed and automatic control of behaviour. In R.J. Davidson, G.E. Schwartz, & D. Shapiro (Eds.), *Consciousness and self-regulation,* (Vol.4, pp. 1-18). New York: Plenum.

Pylyshyn, Z. (1984). *Computation and cognition.* Cambridge, MA: MIT.

Reber, A.S. (1989). Implicit learning and tacit knowledge. *Journal of Experimental Psychology: General, 118,* (3), 219-235.

Roberts, P.L., & MacLeod, C. (submitted). *Representational consequences of automatic learning.*

Smith, J.D., & Shapiro, J.H. (1989). The occurrence of holistic categorization. *Journal of Memory and Language, 28,* 386-399.

Smolensky, P. (1987). The constituent structure of mental states: A reply to Fodor and Pylyshyn. *Southern Journal of Philosophy, 26,* 137-160.

CHAPTER 12

Connectionist, Rule-Based and Bayesian Decision Aids: An Empirical Comparison *

Steven Schwartz, Janet Wiles, and Steven Phillips

Departments of Psychology and Computer Science
The University of Queensland

INTRODUCTION

Diagnosis is one of the doctor's central tasks. As an intellectual activity, it is a variant of the more general skill of classification — assigning entities to different classes or categories. Classification is easy when each category (or, in the present case, each disease) has a specific, reliably detected, sign. Unfortunately, such "pathognomonic" signs are rare. The common signs of illness (such as fever or pain) are shared by many different diseases and most laboratory test results have more than one possible cause. This nonspecific relationship between signs and diseases ensures that there will always be an element of uncertainty in medical diagnosis. This uncertainty can be reduced by the discovery of more sensitive clinical signs, but it can never be eliminated. No test is perfectly accurate, signs can be misleading, and even the best treatments do not always succeed (see Schwartz & Griffin, 1986, for more on the probabilistic nature of medical decision making.)

Complicating matters even further is the frequent lack of any specific causal theory relating diagnostic signs to underlying pathophysiology. Consider, for example, patients who present at hospital casualty rooms complaining of acute abdominal pain. There are many possible causes: appendicitis, perforated ulcer, urinary tract infection, and so on. Doctors use a pattern of signs to discriminate among these conditions. For example, it is most common for appendicitis to occur in males, to begin with a central pain that moves to the right lower abdominal quadrant and to be accompanied by vomiting,

---

* Preparation of this paper was assisted by grants from the Australian Research Council and the NHMRC Public Health and Development Committee to the first author. The authors are also grateful to ICI Limited for access to the MEDICL program and to Dr. U. Gough for access to his patient database. An earlier version of this paper appeared in D.Z. Hand (Ed.) (1993) *Artificial Intelligence Frontiers in Statistics: AI and Statistics* III. London: Chapman and Hall, pp. 246-277.

loss of appetite, and so on. However, this is not always the case. Females also get appendicitis and sometimes it begins with pain in the lower right quadrant. Some patients mimic the complete appendicitis pattern but turn out to have some other illness. Because there is no clear physiological theory to explain why appendicitis should produce a particular pattern of signs, we are left with purely empirical correlations — correlations with values distinctly less than 1.0 (de Dombal, 1984).

Given the uncertain relationship between signs and illnesses, it is often difficult for doctors to decide whether a patient's abdominal pain requires an immediate operation or whether it is safe to merely "watch and wait." There are risks either way. An infected appendix allowed to fester may perforate, creating a potentially lethal peritonitis. This situation can be avoided by an early operation. On the other hand, removing a healthy appendix needlessly exposes the patient to the risks of surgery. Because the risks of perforation are greater than those of an operation, all surgeons support the philosophy of "when it doubt, cut it out." An unavoidable result of this decision rule is that 25 percent or more of all appendix operations result in the removal of perfectly healthy organs (Adams et al., 1986). Clearly, there would be considerable savings in money, time, and surgical morbidity if these unnecessary operations could be avoided (and if diseased appendixes could be removed as quickly as possible). It has often been suggested that computerized decision aids might be able to help doctors make better diagnoses. However, obtaining the necessary expertise in a form suitable for computer coding is often a major problem. System designers consult medical experts but, in many cases, these experts have considerable difficulty explaining how they go about diagnosing patients. In recent years, it has been suggested that this "knowledge elicitation bottleneck" can be broken by using the machine learning techniques developed by cognitive scientists (Gallant, 1988; Schwartz, 1989; Schwartz, et al., 1989).

Connectionist Networks

One increasingly popular approach uses connectionist networks to produce diagnostic advisors (Bounds et al., 1988; Gallant, 1988; Hart & Wyatt, 1989). The argument in favor of connectionist networks derives from extensive research showing that much human expertise resides in complex pattern recognition. Chess grand masters, for example, excel because they have a large memory store of game patterns (de Groot, 1965). Similarly, in the medical domain, expert radiologists appear to differ from newly trained doctors mainly in their ability to recognize abnormal patterns quickly (Hillard et al., 1985). Because connectionist networks can learn to recognize ill-defined patterns, they should — in principle at least — be able to learn to make difficult diagnoses even in the absence of a causal theory relating signs to diseases.

It should be kept in mind that the term "connectionist" is a generic one that refers to many different types of networks. Thus, although several attempts to use connectionist networks for diagnostic tasks have been published (Bounds et al., 1988; Gallant, 1988; Hart & Wyatt, 1989), no two have used exactly the same structure or learning rules. Not surprisingly, therefore, the results have been equivocal. In general, studies using simple networks and artificial laboratory data find connectionist networks to work well (Gallant, 1988; Hunt, 1989) while those using actual patient data have found them to perform rather poorly (Hart & Wyatt, 1989). The reason for this difference is not entirely clear. It may result from differences in the specification of the various networks or, possibly, in the relative completeness of the respective training sets. (Real patient data are never as complete, or "clean," as artificial data.) In the present research, we used a network with one hidden layer which learned to classify patients using "backpropagation" (Rumelhart & McClelland, 1986).

Rule Induction

Connectionist networks are not the only way that cognitive scientists have modeled learning from experience. Ross Quinlan's ID3 algorithm (1983, 1986, 1988) tackles classification by breaking down the overall problem into a series of subclassifications. Specifically, ID3 constructs a decision tree. Each tree node represents the influence of the most diagnostic sign at that point in the sequence. At each node, the value of the sign is used to partition the cases into separate groups. The algorithm is then invoked recursively on the separate groups. The process continues until all the cases at a node fall into the same partition. When that happens a "leaf node" is created and given a unique label.

   ID3 is a particularly attractive alternative to a connectionist network because it is "rule-based." To convert the decision tree into a collection of conjunctive rules one simply traces each path from the root to a leaf (Quinlan, 1987). The rules generated by ID3 may produce new insights into the relationship between signs and diseases. In contrast, connectionist networks represent knowledge mathematically and are difficult to interpret in terms specific to a problem domain. ID3's "divide and conquer" strategy is also consistent with the way doctors are actually taught to make diagnoses (Schwartz & Griffin, 1986). Indeed, branching algorithms, in the form of flow charts, are common in medical textbooks (Komaroff, 1982). In the present research, we directly compared ID3 and connectionist networks by applying both to the same set of patient data.

Bayesian Probability Revision

A third approach to diagnosis, one that has been used extensively in designing decision aids in the domain of acute abdominal pain, is based on the probabilistic relationship between signs and diseases. Specifically, the conditional probabilities of the signs given the various diseases are combined using Bayes' formula to yield the posterior probability of the disease given a specific patterns of signs (see Sox et al., 1988). This approach does not claim to model human learning or cognition. Nevertheless, it was included in our research because of the normative status of Bayesian probability revision and its widespread use in medicine.

Research Aims

This research project was conceived as an attempt to apply cognitive science techniques to a domain in which categorization carries "life-and-death" implications. Specifically, the aims of the present research were:

1. To compare the effectiveness of a backpropagation network, ID3, and Bayesian probability revision in classifying acute abdominal pain patients using a set of real patient data.
2. To examine the "practical value" of the three techniques by comparing their performance with the performance of trained doctors.
3. Can the various techniques produce new insights concerning the relationships between signs and diseases?

METHOD

Problem Domain: Differential Diagnosis of Acute Abdominal Pain

The data used in this study were collected prospectively from 276 patients over the age of 12 who presented to the casualty room at the Royal Brisbane Hospital complaining of acute abdominal pain (see Gough, 1988, for details). For our present purpose, the most important aspects of the data were the signs gathered for each patient, the doctor's initial diagnostic impression and the final diagnosis which served as the definitive criterion of accuracy or the "gold standard."

Although there were 41 diagnostic signs, each could take on at least two, and sometimes more, values. For example, there were two values for the sign "Sex" (male and female) and six values for the sign "aggravating factors" (movement, coughing, food, etc.). We coded each value of a sign as either present or absent. Thus, the total number of inputs available for classification purposes was not 41 but 159. As is often the case with real patient data, some signs were not available for some patients. We assumed that such absent signs were distributed randomly across patients and diagnostic groups. For analytic purposes, we made the arbitrary decision to treat such signs as "absent."

As noted earlier, there are many possible causes of acute abdominal pain, but from the point of view of the casualty room doctor there are really only two important categories: either the patient needs an operation or the patient does not need an operation. Because most patients who need an operation are suffering from acute appendicitis, the differential diagnosis often boils down to whether the patient has appendicitis, some other serious illness or, for want of a better term, nonspecific abdominal pain. These were the three diagnostic categories used in the present research.

Designation of Training and Testing Sets

The holdout method (Weiss & Kapouleas, 1989) was used to partition the cases into a training set (which included approximately 90% of the cases) and a testing set of about 10% of the cases. A potential problem with this approach is that the test cases may, by chance, not be a fair representation of the problem domain. This would not affect comparisons across different algorithms, because all would be trained and tested on the same cases. Nevertheless, we were reassured by an examination of the respective sets which showed that the percentages of cases falling in the three categories were approximately the same in both the training and testing sets.

Backpropagation Procedures

The network consisted of three layers (input, hidden, output). Each input unit was completely connected to each hidden unit and each hidden unit was completely connected to each output unit. There were no lateral connections among the units. The input layer consisted of one unit for each value of a sign. (For example, sex had two input units: 1 0 encoding a male and 0 1 encoding female.) On the output side, we had a similar coding for appendicitis, nonspecific abdominal pain and, other illness. This method minimized the amount of decoding required and maximized the separation (or dissimilarity) between different inputs. It did mean, however, that there were a great number of weights to be updated. The approach taken was to use only a few diagnostic signs (a small, fast network) as a starting point. We then added inputs checking performance at each stage. This allowed us to determine whether some subset of inputs produces optimum classification (or whether all diagnostic signs are necessary).

Using the implementation provided by McClelland and Rumelhart (1988), training involved repeated epochs (one forward and one backward pass through the network for all cases). For the purpose of calculating errors, the output with the highest weight was selected as the system's "conclusion." Processing continued until the network error (sum of the squares of the difference between the desired output minus the actual output for each output unit) was minimized.

To optimize the network's classification performance, the number of hidden units was progressively varied. Also varied were the network parameters: lgrain, lrate, and weights. Lgrain was set to either pattern (weights were adjusted after each pattern was presented), or epoch (errors were accumulated and the weights adjusted after all patterns have been presented). Lrate is the fraction of the error used when updating the weights. Weights were initialized randomly. After finding the best combination of factors and parameters, the data set was repartitioned and backpropagation rerun over the new training set using the new parameters.

ID3 Procedures

ID3 has various parameters with which to "fine tune" performance. The parameters used in the present research included:

1. Confidence Factor (CF). Under certain circumstances, ID3 may "overfit" the training data. That is, the trees generated are specific to the particular training set and may not generalize well to the test set. Overfitting is usually caused by rules formulated to explain "noise" in the data. The CF attempts to suppress noise by pruning unnecessary parts of the tree. To ensure that only noise, not relevant information, is eliminated, ID3 was run over a range of CFs.
2. Gain Criterion versus Gain Ratio Criterion. These are two methods of choosing which feature to place at the root of each decision tree (and subtree). The gain criterion tends to favor signs with large numbers of values while the gain ratio is either neutral or slightly biased toward signs with few values.
3. Windowing versus No Windowing. If windowing is specified, then a tree is constructed from a subset of the training data called a "window." The process, called a "cycle," of generating a tree from a window is repeated until all items not in the current window have been classified correctly. The size of the initial window and the window increment rate — the maximum number of items that can be added to a window at each cycle — may be specified by the researcher. If windowing is not specified then a single tree is constructed from the entire training set.
4. Subsetting versus No Subsetting. Subsetting partitions the set of items into two subsets. Thus, decision trees constructed using this option are binary trees. Subsetting, like the CF, is an attempt to improve generalization by restricting the tree's sensitivity to the specifics of the training set.

Bayesian Procedures

The conditional probability of the signs given each of the three classifications was calculated for the training set cases making the unrealistic, but nevertheless common, assumption that the signs were conditionally independent (the probability of a sign given a classification is not affected by the presence or absence of other signs). These probabilities were then used to classify the test set cases. We also had available a more reliable set of conditional probabilities collected from more than 6,000 cases by the Organisation Mondiale de Gastro-Enterologie (OMDG) and coded in a commercial computer program called MEDICL. For comparison purposes, we also used MEDICL to classify our patients.

RESULTS

Backpropagation

Varying the network parameters produced dramatic performance effects. We also found considerable differences in performance depending on the criterion used to define a "correct" classification. Table 12.1 summarizes system performance under a number of different conditions, using a relatively lenient criterion of "correct." A classification was considered to be correct if the output unit with the maximum activation corresponded to the patient's final diagnosis (the present "gold standard"). Stricter criteria, using various thresholds for counting a classification as correct, significantly reduced performance.

Table 12.1 Effects of Varying the Number of Hidden Units, 1grain and 1rate on Classification Performance. The net has 159 input units.

Hidden Units	Lgrain	Lrate	Epochs	Error (Sums of Squares)	No. of Correct Test Case Classifications (out of 30)
30	epoch	0.5	100	246	0
30	pattern	0.5	100	246	0
30	epoch	0.1	100	194	16
30	pattern	0.02	100	13	15
30	pattern	0.02	400	10	15
30	pattern	0.02	1000	8	15
125	epoch	0.5	100	194	16
125	pattern	0.5	100	194	16
125	pattern	0.01	100	14	17
125	pattern	0.01	500	7	18
220	epoch	0.5	100	194	16
220	pattern	0.5	100	296	0
220	epoch	0.02	100	194	16
220	pattern	0.02	100	194	16

All other things being equal, setting lgrain equal to epoch produced better performance than lgrain set to pattern, and slow learning rates were better than high rates (although these required many epochs to reach convergence). The optimal number of hidden units was somewhat less than the number of input units, but not much less (125). Although it might be expected that at least some of the signs were redundant, reducing the number of inputs always resulted in degraded performance. This suggests that the network was learning fairly specific features of the training cases rather than generalizable rules. From a practical viewpoint, it also means that backpropagation was not able to suggest any way in which the amount of data collected for each case could be reduced. Table 12.2 summarizes the performance of the most successful network. It used all 159 input units and 125 hidden units, had lgrain set to epoch and lrate set to 0.01.

Table 12.2 Performance on the Training and Test Sets at Selected Stages of Learning. The net has 159 input units and 125 hidden units.

		Number of Correctly Classified Cases	
Epochs	Error (Sums of Squares)	Training Set (N = 246)	Testing Set (N = 30)
100	71.3	204	16
300	37.8	232	19
500	22.0	237	18
700	15.7	240	17
1000	9.8	242	17
1500	5.9	244	17
2000	4.8	244	18
3000	4.4	244	18

As may be seen, after 300 epochs, this network correctly classified 232 of the 246 training cases and 19 of the 30 test cases. After 3,000 epochs, the network had reduced its error considerably and was able to classify more than 99% of the training cases correctly, but this did not lead to any improvement on the test cases. In fact, test-case performance was actually a little worse. Thus, it appears that there is some tradeoff between the modeling of the training set and generalization to the testing set. It should be noted that the optimal network learned fairly slowly, taking 72.5 hours to converge running continuously on the Sun 3/50.

Rule Induction

Table 12.3 summarizes the effects of changing various parameters on ID3's classification performance. The values in the table are the number of correctly classified test cases out of 30 averaged over 10 trees and rounded to the nearest whole number. Each cell in Table 12.3 represents the performance using a specific combination of parameters. For example, the first row of the table shows that with a CF of 10% and windowing, ID3 was correct on 16 cases using the gain criterion but only classified 15 cases correctly using the gain ratio criterion. Looking at the table as a whole, it is apparent that, unlike backpropagation, ID3's performance was not greatly affected by changes to its parameters. The only exception was the gain criterion which was consistently better than the gain ratio criterion — a rather unusual finding (Quinlan, 1986)

Table 12.3 Classification Performance of ID3 Under Varying Conditions (using all inputs)

Pruning Confidence Factor (%)	Gain Criterion			Gain Ratio Criterion		
	Windows	No Window (Single Tree)		Windows	No Window (Single Tree)	
		No Subset	Subset		No Subset	Subset
10	16	16	16	15	15	15
20	15	15	15	14	14	11
30	16	16	15	13	13	11
40	16	16	16	13	11	11
50	15	15	16	12	11	11
60	15	15	16	12	11	11
70	14	15	16	12	11	11
80	14	15	16	13	11	11
90	14	15	16	12	11	11
100	14	15	16	11	11	11

Why should the gain criterion outperform the gain ratio criterion? The answer undoubtedly lies in the specific characteristics of the abdominal pain domain. The gain criterion resulted in smaller and "shallower" trees than the gain ratio criterion. In addition, signs with many values such as "pain onset site" (13 values), and age (8 values) tended to be used first (they were closer to the tree root) when trees were constructed using the gain criterion, whereas signs with relatively few values were closer to the root in trees constructed using the gain ratio criterion. In the present domain, signs with only a few values tend to be less diagnostic than those with many values. For example, "severity of pain" could take on only two values: "moderate" or "severe." This highly subjective distinction does not differentiate well among classifications. Because the gain ratio criterion favors such signs it may have focused excessively on less diagnostic information.

An important exception to this argument is the two-valued clinical sign, "rebound tenderness" versus "no rebound tenderness," which was regarded as the most important sign and chosen as the root of the tree under both the gain and the gain ratio criteria. This ability to provide new insight into the data — in this case, the identification of the most important sign — is one of the benefits ID3 has over backpropagation.

Neither the gain nor the gain ratio are inherently superior (both need to be tested to determine which is best for a particular domain). The same is true of the remaining parameters. For example, windowing (using various initial window sizes) made little difference because the number of training cases from which trees were constructed with windowing (an average of 220) was almost the same as without windowing (246). Also, because tree generation required up to 10 cycles, it was actually slower than building a single tree from the total number of items. The finding that windowing is slower than no windowing is not typical (See Quinlan, 1986); it emphasizes the differences among problem domains.

Although the data used here were undoubtedly noisy, there is little evidence that ID3 was seriously overfitting the data. Pruning the tree using the CF and subsetting produced only small improvements in performance. Nevertheless, it is possible that some of the signs were redundant to ID3's diagnostic process. To find out, we examined ID3s performance with reduced numbers of inputs. In contrast to backpropagation, ID3's performance actually improved when the number of inputs was reduced. ID3's best performance — 18 cases correctly classified out of 30 — was recorded using the only 11 inputs, the gain criterion, subsetting, and a CF of 20 percent. Cross validation was conducted by repartitioning the set into a new training, and a new test set produced the same results.

ID3, then, was slightly less accurate than backpropagation (18 versus 19 correct) but it was more robust; it correctly classified 15 of 16 cases regardless of the parameters used. It was also of more practical value because it was able to identify the most important signs. Finally, ID3 had a great advantage in speed. In single window mode, a complete run required only a few minutes.

Conditional Probabilities

Conditional probabilities were calculated from the training set for each sign given each classification. Using Bayes' formula, these probabilities were used to calculate the posterior probability of each of the three classifications given the particular pattern of signs presented by a case. Using a lenient criterion, each case was assigned to the category with the highest posterior probability. This method corectly classified 16 of the 30 test cases. The MEDICL program (which uses the conditional probabilities derived from the OMDG survey of 6,000 cases) classified 19 of the 30 cases correctly, but its results are not strictly comparable to those obtained in the present study because of a different definition of categories.

The sign with the highest conditional probability for appendicitis was "tenderness migrating to the right lower quadrant." This was related to, but not the same as, the "rebound tenderness" sign designated most important by ID3.

Physicians

The doctors' initial diagnoses correctly classified 21 of the 30 cases in the test set. Thus, their performance was better than any of the other procedures. This is to be expected, given their far greater experience with the domain and the strong possibility that some of the information they gained from their examination of the patients was not coded in the 159 signs.

The doctors' "hit" rate of 70% compares well with their hit rate in the larger training (76%). This suggests that the partitioning of cases into the training and test sets was fair; the test set cases were no more difficult than the training set.

Sensitivity and Specificity

The raw performance of the various classification algorithms is summarized in Table 12.4. As may be seen, the differences among the various classification procedures are too small to justify statistical analysis. No diagnostician reaches the level of the doctors, although backpropagation comes close. However, pure accuracy measures tell only part of the story. As noted earlier, different types of errors can have different costs. For example, it is less costly to misdiagnose a nonspecific pain patient as having appendicitis than to misdiagnose an appendicitis patient as nonspecific pain. In the first instance, the patient will have an unnecessary operation. In the second case, the patient may die. Looked at in this way, pure accuracy becomes less important than sensitivity (true positive rate) and specificity (true negative rate). These are summarized in Table 12.5 for appendicitis versus the other two categories.

Table 12.4 Summary of the Best Performances

Diagnostician	Appendicitis	Other Serious Illness	Non-Specific Pain	Total Cases
Back Prop.	14	2	3	19
ID3	15	0	3	18
Bayesian	11	1	4	16
Doctors	14	2	5	21
Total Cases	16	5	9	30

As may be seen, all three diagnosticians have a relatively high sensitivity for appendicitis, with ID3 performing best. However, ID3's specificity is low. This means that its success in diagnosing appendicitis is achieved by overusing the diagnosis. Because of their large number of false-positives, the predictive value (true-positives/all positives) of ID3, backpropagation, and Bayesian probability revision are all relatively low. Overall, the doctors probably perform best. They miss only 2 cases of appendicitis and have the lowest number of false positives. Another way of looking at this question is to examine the specific cases correctly and incorrectly diagnosed by the various diagnosticians. We looked at this question by correlating the performance of the various procedures. Actually, we used the contingency coefficient (Siegal, 1956). We found that these correlations were remarkably low. For example, the correlations between the classifications reached by the Bayesian and ID3 procedures was only .29 and no correlation exceeded .55. Clearly, the various procedures are attacking the classification problem in rather different ways.

Table 12.5 Sensitivity, Specificity and Predictive Value of Diagnosticians for Diagnosing Appendicitis

Diagnostician	Sensitivity (True-Positive Rate) %	Specificity (True Negative Rate) %
Backprop.	88	36
Bayesian	69	36
ID3	94	21
Doctors	88	50

DISCUSSION

This research compared ID3, backpropagation, Bayesian probability revision, and doctors' performance on a diagnostic task. The doctors, who were 70% accurate, outperformed all other techniques. Backpropagation, with 63% correct classifications using the entire set of input signs, was slightly more accurate than ID3, which achieved its best performance of 60% using only 11 signs. Both backpropagation and ID3 performed better than a Bayesian analysis based on the relationship between signs and classifications in the training set, which only achieved 53% accuracy. (Conditional probabilities derived from a much larger training set were able to match the performance of backpropagation.) Given the relatively small training set, all of the techniques, but especially backpropagation and ID3, performed remarkably well. Nevertheless, none of the techniques were able to match the doctors and all had unacceptably high false positive rates. Thus, there is little in these data to recommend these as practical decision aids for to clinical practitioners. Still, there are various aspects of the results that are worth noting. First, ID3 was generally more robust than backpropagation. For most runs, it achieved 15 or 16 correct classifications. Its worst performance was 11 out of 30. Backpropagation, on the other hand, was highly susceptible to the lrate parameter. If not set low enough, the algorithm would not converge at all. Backpropagation was also a much slower process than either ID3 or Bayesian probability revision (it takes days as compared with minutes running on the same machine.) The workings of ID3 are more accessible than backpropagation; its trees can easily be stated as rules. It was able to give new insights into the data emphasizing the importance of a particular sign and identifying the 11 most important signs. Backpropagation, in contrast, appeared to be learning-pattern specific to the training set and provided no new insights into the data. The present results are limited by the small number of training and test cases. It has been suggested that a training set should contain at least five cases per item of input data per classification (Wasson et al., 1985). In the present case, this would mean a set of 2,400 cases. Few medical databases are anywhere near this size. We should also note that the Bayesian analysis may perform better when signs are not all considered conditionally independent (Seroussi et al., 1986).

REFERENCES

Adams, I.D., Chan, M., Clifford, P.C., Cooke, W.M., Dallos, V., de Dombal, F.T., Edwards, M.H., Hancock, D.M., Hewett, D.J., McIntyre, M., Somerville, P.G., Spiegelhalter, D.J., Wellwood, J., & Wilson, D.H. (1986). Computer aided diagnosis of acute abdominal pain: A multicentre study. *British Medical Journal, 298,* 800-804.

Bounds, D. G., Lloyd, P.J., Matthew, B., & Waddell, G. (1988). A multilayer perceptron network for the diagnosis of low back pain. *Proceedings of the San Diego Conference on Neural Networks, 2,* 481-489.

de Dombal, F. T. (1984). Computer-based assistance for medical decision making. Gastroenterology and Clinical Biology, 8, 135-137.

de Groot, A.D. (1965). *Thought and choice in chess.* The Hague, Netherlands: Mouton.

Dietterich, T.G., Hild, H., & Bakiri, G. (1990). A comparative study of ID3 and backpropagation for English text-to-speech mapping. *Proceedings of the International Workshop on Machine Learning.* (June). Austin, TX.

Gallant, S. I. (1988). Connectionist expert systems. *Communications of the ACM, 31,* 152-169.

Gough, I. (1988). A study of diagnostic accuracy in suspected acute appendicitis. *Australia and New Zealand Journal of Surgery, 58,* 555-589.

Hart, A., & Wyatt, J. (1989). Connectionist models in medicine: An investigation of their potential. In J. Hunter, J. Cookson & J. Wyatt (Eds.), *AIME89: Proceedings of the Second European Conference on Artificial Intelligence in Medicine* (Lecture notes in Medical Informatics, pp. 115-124). Heidelberg, Germany: Springer-Verlag.

Hillard, A., Myles-Worsley, M., Johnston, W., & Baxter, B. (1985). The development of radiological schemata through training and experience: A preliminary communication. *Investigative Radiology, 18,* 422-425.

Hunt, E. B. (1989). Connectionist and rule-based representations of expert knowledge. *Behavior Research Methods, Instruments and Computers, 21,* 88-95.

Komaroff, A.L. (1982). Algorithms and the "art" of medicine. *American Journal of Public Health, 72,* 10-12.

McClelland, J.L., & Rumelhart, D. (1988). *Explorations in parallel distributed processing.* Cambridge, MA: MIT Press.

Quinlan, J.R. (1983). Learning efficient classification procedures and their application to chess endgames. In R.S. Michalski, et al., (Eds.), *Machine learning: An artificial intelligence approach* (Vol 1, pp. 149-166). Palo Alto, CA: Tioga Press.

Quinlan, J.R. (1986). Induction of decision trees. *Machine Learning, 1,* 81-106.

Quinlan, J.R. (1987). Simplifying decision trees. *International Journal of Man-Machine Studies, 27,* 221-234.

Quinlan, J.R. (1988). An empirical comparison of genetic and decision-tree classifiers. *Proceedings of the Fifth International Conference on Machine Learning.* Ann Arbor, MI June 1988.

Rumelhart, D. E., & McClelland, J.L. (1986). *Parallel distributed processing: Explorations in the microstructure of cognition: Vol. 1: Foundations.* Cambridge, MA: MIT Press.

Schwartz, S. (1989). Computer consultants in the clinic. In P. Lovibond & P. Wilson, (Eds.), *Proceedings of the XXIV International Congress of Psychology: Vol. 9. Clinical and Abnormal Psychology.* Amsterdam: North-Holland.

Schwartz, S., & Griffin, T. (1986). *Medical thinking: The psychology of medical judgment and decision making.* New York: Springer-Verlag.

Schwartz, S., Griffin, T., & Fox, J. (1989). Clinical expert systems versus linear models: Do we really have to choose? *Behavioral Science, 34,* 305-311.

Seroussi, B., ARC & AURC Cooperation Group. (1986). Computer-aided diagnosis of acute abdominal pain when taking into account interactions. *Methods of Information in Medicine, 25,* 194-198.

Siegal, S. (1956). *Non-parametric statistics.* New York: McGraw-Hill.

Sox, H. C., Biah, M.A., Higgins, M.C., & Marton, K.I. (1988). *Medical decision making.* Boston, MA: Butterworths.

Wasson, J.H., Sox, H.C., Neff, R.K., & Goldman, L. (1985). Clinical prediction rules: applications and methodological standards. *New England Journal of Medicine, 313,* 793-799.

Weiss, S. M., & Kapouleas, I. (1989). *An empirical comparison of pattern recognition, neural nets and machine learning classification.* Paper delivered at the Eleventh International Joint Conference on Artificial Intelligence. August, 1989, Detroit, USA.

CHAPTER 13

A Cognitive Approach to Autonomous Mobile Robot Development *

A. Sowmya

Department of Computer Science
University of New South Wales, Kensington

INTRODUCTION

Autonomous Mobile Robots (AMRs) belong to the class of intelligent robots, and are distinguished by their planned motion capability. The origin of their complexity lies in the dynamic event-driven nature of their environment interactions, the need to conceptualize the components of motion, and the demands of autonomy. These features turn the AMR development task into a difficult one, since any development methodology must first decompose the problem to make the complexity manageable.

Current trends in AMR development tend to concentrate on building tools and developing programming techniques which would ease the task at hand. These tools and programs are centered upon the existing capabilities of an AMR, and build more sophisticated capabilities out of them. However, the basic capabilities themselves are often put together in an ad-hoc fashion. In this chapter, I shall discuss the role of cognitive science in formulating the underlying cognitive processes of motion. I shall also discuss briefly a methodology for AMR development proposed by me and others earlier (Sowmya, Ramesh, & Isaac, 1990a), which attempts to emulate the spirit of the processes underlying motion. Specifically, the actual motion of an AMR could be produced in any number of ways; however, my hypothesis is that the cognitive functions must be realized, and the appropriate responses produced when demanded by events, by the AMR. This paper collates some studies on the semantics of motion and hypothesizes their application in a practical problem: the development of an AMR. The paper is organized as follows. The next section reviews the current trends in AMR development.

---

* My sincere thanks to Professor J.R. Isaac, formerly of Department of Computer Science, I.I.T., Bombay, for turning my attention to cognitive science, and for many stimulating discussions on the subject.

In the following section, the cognitive view of autonomy and motion are discussed. Another section presents an analysis of motion based on existing studies. A development methodology for AMRs, drawing upon these studies, is presented in a following section. Concluding remarks appear in the final section.

TRENDS IN AMR DEVELOPMENT

Many existing AMR designs utilize a traditional decomposition of control based on AMR functions. The components of such designs include perception, world modeling, planning, task execution, and motor control (Brooks, 1986). In these models, the perceived sensory data is converted into a world model and planning for problem solving is based on this model.

In contrast to this approach, Brooks (1986) proposes a vertical decomposition of AMR control, based on its desired external manifestations, which he calls its *behaviors*. A level of competence of the AMR defines a class of *behaviors*, and a number of such concurrent levels are defined. In Brooks' example, the lowest level of competence, called level 0, is that of avoiding collision with obstacles in the environment. Higher levels of competence include all the lower ones, and a higher level could examine and modify data from lower levels, thus *interfering* with the normal flow. Control, however, is distributed over all the levels. In the example, level 1 is the ability to wander, which requires the lower level capability to avoid collisions. Brooks calls his scheme the subsumption architecture, since higher levels subsume lower levels. On evaluation, Brooks' scheme appears to be a model of control, not a theory of representation of autonomous motion. Likewise, the research reported by Smithers and Malcolm (1987) and Georgeff and Lansky (1987) are also based on behaviors. However, in the first, it is the robot task which is decomposed into behaviors. In the second, robot reasoning is based on behaviors, but not robot development.

In conclusion, one could say that robot development has received no systematic treatment, and there has been very little effort expended on basing development on a sound theory. It is my contention that the insights gained by cognitive science on autonomy and mobility could well form the basis of a theory, which robot development could rely on. A good way to get the problem in perspective is to break up the development effort into the design of formalisms, tools and programs (Colins & Smith, 1988). Formalisms are standard models for representing and implementing cognitive processes, while tools build upon the formalisms to enable the development of programs or systems. The aim of this paper is to demonstrate that a formalism to aid AMR development may be based on the results from cognitive science studies.

THE COGNITIVE VIEW

An AMR must make the intelligent connection from perception to action (Brady, 1984). Any formalism which attempts to model the cognitive processes of an AMR must model this connection. This task demands an understanding of the cognitive processes underlying autonomy and mobility. Thring's (1983) model of the human brain divides the brain into three functional components: the *physical or body brain* dealing with the knowledge of reality through observations and manipulations, the *intellectual brain* dealing with logic, analysis and abstraction, and the *emotional brain* dealing with judgments, conscience, motives, and emotions. Based on this model, one could hypothesize autonomy as a function of the intellectual brain, and mobility as a function of both the intellectual and the body brain. Since autonomy subsumes decision making, problem solving, and goal-achieving behaviors, the analytical and logical powers of the intellectual brain are put to use. For mobility, what is required is an understanding of the dynamic real-time interactions of the moving artifact with its environment, the interpretation of sensorimotor input, decision making based on the input, and the transmission of the decision to the sensorimotor level (Rasmussen, 1986). These are issues which are an interplay between the intellectual and physical brains. Artificial intelligence is studying and proposing formalisms for many of the aspects dealing with autonomy. This chapter focuses on the issue of mobility.

THE ANALYSIS OF MOTION

As described earlier, the components of motion include the structuring of available information at a higher level, the choice of an alternative at that level, and the planning of a sequence of acts which fulfill the higher level intention of motion. The structuring of information could be interpreted as pattern recognition at a higher level. The description and analysis of such motion patterns have been studied in the semantic approach to representation of motion concepts. In this approach, *action* rather than *motion* is studied. One might define a discrete action as a momentary intentional or causal description of motion. Thus, an action may have many underlying motions. A review of semantics-based action specification may be found in Sowmya (1990).

The classical study in this area is the conceptual dependency of Schank (1975). Conceptual dependency is a theory of the representation of sentence meanings. The meaning propositions underlying natural language are called conceptualizations. Four primitive conceptual categories are defined, namely, objects, actions, modifiers of objects, and modifiers of actions. Further, actions themselves may be any one of eleven primitive categories; a set of allowable dependencies between the conceptualizations are also defined. Admittedly, it is not the eleven primitive actions one is interested in; subsequent studies have shown that the number is very simplistic, to say the least. Nonetheless, it is the idea of dividing the world into objects and actions, and decomposing actions into simpler ones, that is appealing.

Miller and Johnson-Laird (1976) describe a conceptual representation of actions based on logico-linguistic analysis. Every action definition comprises three parts: the proposition defining the action, its presuppositions, and its entailments. The most primitive action in their system is TRAVEL which is defined as follows:

TRAVEL(x): *Something x "travels" from time t_0 to time t_m if,* $\forall$ t *such that* $t_0 \leqslant t_i \leqslant t_m$, $\exists$ *a place y_i such that* R_{t_i} (AT(x, y_i)) *and* $R_{t_{i+1}}$ (notAT(x, y_i)).

Here, t is the conventional time indicator and R a statement forming operator where R_t corresponds to "this statement is recognized as true at time t." Actions of greater complexity are built of Boolean predications from the primitive actions. Thus a taxonomic system for actions may be built up from these definitions.

Miller and Johnson-Laird's conceptual specifications of actions is said to be superior to Schank's (Thibadeau, 1986), since it specifies the presuppositions and entailments additionally. It utilizes the hierarchical nature of actions, and is a top-down method of specifying conceptual activity. Thus an action could be specified as a higher level descriptor of the underlying motions.

Badler (1975) presents a temporal scene analysis for the conceptual description of changes in a scene, in terms of objects and events. Object movements are described at successively higher levels by procedures which manipulate a database of objects and events. Events are defined contextually using lower level data computed from the picture sequence. A close correspondence between event representation and the case structure for motion verbs in English is established. Object properties relevant to motion are identified and event descriptions are based on motion.

Tsotsos, Mylopoulos, Covvey, & Zucker (1980) describe a motion understanding system which takes off from Badler's method for the conceptual description of object movements. They define motion understanding from a sequence of images as the provision of *sequence-spanning* descriptions, or one motion concept to explain many changes. Motion concepts are represented as frames in a semantic network. The verbal and qualitative knowledge of motion is interfaced to quantitative image data using a scheme based on Badler's analysis of movements. Five primitive motion descriptors are used to build higher level motion concepts, to define a hierarchy of motions.

Thibadeau (1986) presents a method for action definition which relies on deriving conceptualizations from physical events. The effective input into the perceptual system is assumed to be a sequence of states, where a state is an interpreted image at time t. The domain of possible descriptions of an event is obtained by evaluating all change descriptors for all moments in time. Action perception is then viewed as problem solving and action schemes are formulated in terms of a search method through a space of descriptions. The space of descriptions is formalized as action schemas, inspired by the action definitions of Miller and Johnson-Laird (1976) described earlier. Unlike their definitions, however, the schemas are computational and trigger the action conceptualizations from the bottom-up cues. A taxonomic organization of schemas for recognition is built up by instantiations and compositions of the instantiations of a parent schema.

AMR DEVELOPMENT METHODOLOGY

A formalism to describe an autonomous mobile robot has been described earlier (Sowmya, Ramesh, & Isaac, 1990a). I recapitulate only the relevant aspects in this chapter. In that paper, a formal specification and verification methodology for an AMR, which employs a top-down specification of motion components, has been proposed. This part of the research was inspired by the analysis of motion described in the previous section, and specifically by the motion hierarchies due to Thibadeau and Tsotsos.

Briefly, an AMR is modeled as a real-time reactive system, which continually interacts with its environment and is driven by both external stimuli and internal events. The AMR is specified by describing its two strands: the *behavior*, which is the external manifestation of its actions, and the *function*, which is the causal and temporal relationships between the component behaviors. The behavioral specification is based on a visual language called *statecharts* while the functional specification is written in a new logic-based functional specification language called FNLOG, presented in Sowmya, Ramesh, and Isaac (1990a).

The building blocks of FNLOG are instantaneous events and durative activities. For every AMR, one could define the *primitive* events and activities, which may be left unrefined. Logical and temporal operations on the events and activities are defined using the standard logical operators and past-time temporal operators. These operators permit the composition of events and activities into higher level events and activities. Though not enjoined by the language, FNLOG facilitates hierarchical decomposition of a motion into simpler motions, as discussed in the previous section.

As an example, consider an AMR functioning within a complex environment. *Translate* and *Rotate* are the primitive motions possessed by the AMR. These are primitive activities, and the corresponding initiation and termination of translation and rotation are primitive events in the domain.

A *move* activity of the robot might be either a translate or rotate or a combination of both. Hence, if $\odot_t$ stands for the current operator, which says that the event or activity it operates on is true at time t, we have

$$\odot_t \text{ (move)} = \odot_t \text{ (translate)} \vee \odot_t \text{ (rotate)}$$

Higher level motions may now be defined by combinations of these activities and other events. For example, a *run* activity consists of a move above a certain speed. Of course, the temporal operators would enable more complex definitions, but that is not the focus of this paper. By successive refinement, a hierarchy of motions may be defined for the AMR.

I have shown that the specification of an AMR based on this formalism is verifiable (Sowmya, Ramesh, & Isaac, 1990a). Thus, tools and programs which would enable systematic development may be based on this formalism.

CONCLUSION

This chapter has discussed the lack of formalisms to capture the cognitive processes that must operate within an AMR. Autonomy and mobility must be accounted for by any model of the AMR. Since autonomy is studied in great detail in artificial intelligence, I have not considered it in this discussion. The modeling of motion itself requires an understanding of the robot-environment interactions and the conceptualization of motion components. The recognition and interpretation schemes for motion patterns already developed in linguistics, vision and pattern recognition are utilized to propose a conceptualization of robot motion, on which development may be based.

REFERENCES

Badler, N. I. (1975). *Temporal scene analysis: conceptual descriptions of object movements* (Tech. Rep. #80), Toronto, Canada: University of Toronto, Department of Computer Science.

Brady, M. (1984). Artificial intelligence and robotics. In M. Brady, L.A. Gerhardt, & H.F. Davidson (Eds.), *Robotics and artificial intelligence* (NATO ASI series, F11; pp. 47-64). New York: Springer-Verlag.

Brooks, R.A. (1986). A robust layered control system for a mobile robot. *IEEE Journal of Robotics Automation, 2* (1), 14-23.

Collins, A., & Smith, E.E. (1988). A perspective on cognitive science. In *Readings in cognitive science: A perspective from psychology and artificial intelligence* (pp. 1-4). A. Collins & E.E. Smith (Eds.) San Mateo, CA: Morgan Kaufmann.

Georgeff, M.P., & Lansky, A.L. (1987). Reactive reasoning and planning. In *AAAI-87, Proceedings of the Sixth National Conference on Artificial Intelligence* (pp. 677-682), Seattle, Washington.

Miller, G.A., & Johnson-Laird, P.N. (1976). *Language and perception*. Cambridge, MA: Belknap Press.

Rasmussen, J. (1986). *A cognitive engineering approach to the modeling of decision-making and its organization* (Tech. Rep.). Denmark: Riso National Laboratory, Riso.

Schank, R. (1975). *Conceptual information processing.* Amsterdam: Reston.

Smithers, T., & Malcolm, C. (1987). *A behavioural approach to robot task planning and off-line programming* (DAI Research Paper #306). Edinburgh, Scotland: University of Edinburgh.

Sowmya, A. (1990, September). Motion specification in robotics: A review. In *Proceedings of the International Conference on Automation, Robotics, and Computer Vision* (ICARCV '90; pp. 544-548), Singapore: McGraw-Hill.

Sowmya, A., Ramesh, S., & Isaac, J.R. (1990a). A statechart approach to specification and verification of autonomous mobile robot control. In *Proceedings of the International Conference on Automation, Robotics, and Computer Vision* (ICARCV '90; pp. 499-503), Singapore: McGraw-Hill.

Thibadeau, R. (1986). Artificial perception of actions. *Cognitive Science, 10,* 117-149.

Thring, M.W. (1983). *Robots and telechirs.* New York: Wiley.

Tsotsos, J.K., Mylopoulos, J., Covvey, H.D., & Zucker, S.W. (1980). A framework for visual motion understanding. *IEEE Transactions on Pattern Analysis of Machine Intelligence, 2,* 563-573.

CHAPTER 14

Categorization and Prototypes in Design

M.A. Rosenman and F. Sudweeks

Key Centre of Design Computing
University of Sydney

INTRODUCTION

Research in the Key Centre of Design Computing at the University of Sydney over the past few years has been concerned with the development of a framework for design using generalized knowledge elements referred to as *prototypes* (Gero & Maher, 1988; Gero & Rosenman, 1990; Gero, 1990). However, this work has progressed without a deeper theoretical basis of the meaning of prototype.

In the field of cognitive psychology, Rosch (1978) associates a prototype with typicality effects; that is, it refers to a typical or ideal representation of a category which may or may not be a member of that category. When this typical representation is an actual member of the category it is referred to as an exemplar (Medin & Wattenmaker, 1987; Smith & Medin, 1981). In contrast, the interpretation of prototype in our work is that of a type or schema (Kant, 1787; Sowa, 1984); that is, a generalized class of elements more in accord with that used by Addanki and Davis (1985). Research into generalization and related areas, such as induction and machine learning, has been carried out in many areas including artificial intelligence, cognitive science, cluster analysis, conceptual programming, and parallel distributed processing, as well as design. To prevent confusion, we now use the term *design prototype* to describe a generalized class of design elements, and the typical or representative example of the class is referred to as an *archetype*. The thrust of our work is to draw on the commonalities in these areas and to clarify the use of the term 'prototype' in the context of design and, more specifically, computer-aided design.

Design is defined as a purposeful human activity concerned with changing the state of things by producing a specific description of an entity so as to satisfy some need in the form of a set of given functional requirements. Computer-aided design is concerned with formalizing design descriptions and processes in a manner that can be manipulated by computers in order to aid a human designer. To this end, we wish to encode generalized information about classes of design elements so that it can be used to design specific entities for a range of specific situations. As we are attempting to form categories of design elements, we must first turn our attention to what categories are, why they are useful, and how they can best be represented. We will then describe the special needs of design prototypes as a basis for modeling design processes.

CATEGORIZATION

What are Categories?

Categorization is an integral aspect of human thought in that representations of unique experiences or stimuli are encoded into an organized system that economizes and simplifies cognitive processing. Categories are distinct, discrete classifications of information which help to give order to a confusing, continuous mass of information. In some way, this continuum of information has been divided into discrete regions where points within each such region (category) bear qualitative similarities to each other, whereas points in different regions bear qualitative differences to each other. One view on the nature of categories is, therefore, that they carve the world according to defined boundaries. A completely different view is that the boundaries are not well-defined, if at all existing. What does exist are points of reference to which comparisons are made and which are combined in different ways depending on the particular context.

Most models of categorization assume that category members can be analyzed into attributes, which may themselves be concepts, and that similarity of category members depends on common and distinctive attributes. However, there is little agreement about any similarity function of attributes apart from agreement that the similarity of any two entities increases with the number of shared features and decreases with the number of distinctive ones. There is also little agreement on what constitutes an attribute. One view is that attributes are identified by detectors in the nervous system, while an alternative view is that attributes are a convenient fiction that allows relationships among concepts to be identified (Medin & Wattenmaker, 1987). Smith and Medin (1981) point out that there need to be constraints on which attributes form part of a category. An attribute is useful to the degree that it reveals relationships between categories; that is, attributes posited for a category should serve as inputs for categorization.

There is a general insufficiency, so far at least, of attribute-matching approaches, in that categories are assumed to be little more than the 'sum' of their components. All the attributes that are characteristic of a bird, for example, do not make it a bird unless held together in a 'bird structure.'

A category is not just a simple set of lists of attributes because relations exist between these attributes (Smith & Medin, 1981). Rather than matching a list of attributes, categorization may be an inference process based on relationships between attributes. What is required, therefore, is a set of relational properties.

A theory-based approach argues that what is needed is a method of measuring similarity without prior knowledge about category membership (Medin & Wattenmaker, 1987). This implies that to categorize knowledge about a concept, we must include a complex web of relations involving that concept and any other concepts that depend on it. Theories may constrain correlated attributes in at least two ways. First, theories may influence the saliency of individual properties. Second, and more importantly, the role of theories is to link attributes in an explanatory system. The correlation between certain attributes is not a chance occurrence — for example, the correlation between certain types of feathers and webbed feet in certain water birds is a logical and biological necessity.

Categories are only coherent to the extent that they fit people's existing knowledge or theories about the world and are very much context-dependent. If we take the set of {children, jewelery, paintings, TV set, ...} out of context we cannot see much similarity and we may not recognize them as forming a category. In the context of things to take during a fire, however, they make more sense. While such ad hoc categories may not be natural, they nevertheless hang together in their own context.

Why are Categories Useful?

Categories are essentially pattern-recognition devices (Smith & Medin, 1981), allowing for the classification of new experiences, for the inferencing of information given that an entity is a member of some category, and for the generation of instances.

Classification. Classification entails going from the specific to the general; that is, from an example to a category. Classification may be carried out using functional information with or without perceptual information. For example, given that an entity is to be used for eating on rather than for writing on will serve to classify it as a table rather than a desk.

Inferencing. The purpose of classification is to enable inferencing of information based on certain properties of the category. Once an entity is classified as a member of some category, a vast amount of information, not explicitly presented, becomes accessible. For example, given a particular fruit which we recognize (classify) as an apple, we infer that it has a core, has pits and, depending on the type of apple, that it is sweet or sour, even if we cannot see these attributes. Even if we cannot see the apple in question, we will have some expectations about its shape, size and color (although we may be wrong).

Generation. Generation, in contrast to classification, entails going from the general to the specific; that is, generation takes the form of instantiation of categories. This is the special concern of design. The role of categorization is central in the formation of new instances and hence in creative thinking and creative design. People who see relations between things which look as though they are seemingly unrelated are more likely to make unusual combinations (Cropley, 1970). The kind of person who codes in this way is referred to as a 'wide categorizer' whereas the opposite is referred to as a 'narrow categorizer.' Treating entities whose connections are not readily apparent as roughly equivalent would tend to allow creativity to take place. Creative thinking thus appears to be related to the width of categorizing.

Models of Categories

Smith and Medin (1981) present three models of categorization — the classical view, the probabilistic view and the exemplar view (Figure 14.1). Medin and Barsalou (1987) describe these models as defined categories and fuzzy categories. The defined categories include well-defined categories (the classical view) and ill-defined categories (the probabilistic view). Fuzzy categories (or graded structures) map onto the exemplar model. Barsalou (1987), on the other hand, presents a completely different model based on distributed knowledge.

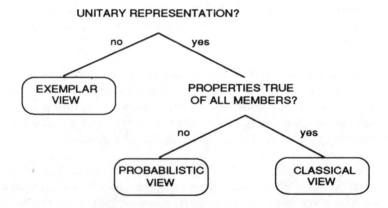

Figure 14.1. Three models of categorization

The classical model. The classical model is based on a summary representation of an entire class, often as the result of an abstraction process. There is a concept of essentialism — that a category has some intrinsic nature — in that there is a set of defining features which are necessary and sufficient. All members of the class possess those features and any entity possessing those features is a member of that class. The classical view is fine for formal concepts, basically constructed to fit the model. In geometric concepts, for example, all triangles have three edges and having three edges is sufficient to classify a geometric entity as a triangle. Problems appear, however, with other types of categories, such as natural or general knowledge categories. It is difficult to posit the defining feature of a cup, such that they define a cup and not other categories such as a glass, bowl, vase, or mug. Many categories seem to be accessed by nonnecessary features. Features such as flying (for birds) or having a handle (for cups) are important or salient but they are not true of all members of the class. The classical view also does not account for disjunctive members of a category and for typicality effects.

The probabilistic model. The probabilistic model, like the classical model, assumes a category is a summary representation of an entire class, but the representation is not restricted to a set of necessary and defining features. The features that represent a category are salient and have a substantial probability of occurring. Thus the probability model overcomes the problem of nonnecessary features. However, the aggregation of a weighted sum has the usual problems associated with multiattribute descriptions. In some cases, the same sum can be arrived at with totally different sets of features so it is possible, on this basis, to adjudge a very atypical member of a category as belonging to some other category.

The exemplar model. Rosch's experimental findings regarding typicality effects (1978; Mervis & Rosch, 1981) seem to challenge the notions of traditional set theory models. These studies have shown that people often use exemplars (or prototypes) when dealing with a category. When asked to indicate members of a category, people specify typical members more often and more quickly and they classify these members as belonging to that category faster than less typical exemplars. An exemplar may be a concept itself or an instance (Figure 14.2).

While the exemplar or prototype model removes the problem of boundaries to categories, it begs the question of how 'typical' representations are formed; that is, why are some things judged more typical and what does that mean. Also, it offers no solution to the problem of how instances are judged to be similar to exemplars. Additionally, typical design deals with the modification of existing category descriptions and is often concerned with atypical members. Therefore it would seem that what is also required is some process for moving away from this 'central tendency' while still being within its 'sphere of influence.' In addition, it has been found that people recognize atypical instances more readily than either typical instances or remembered instances

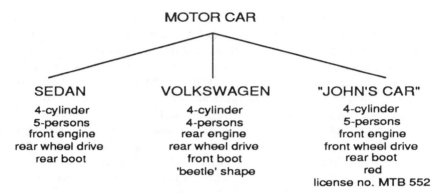

Figure 14.2. An exemplar representation using both concepts and instances

(Purcell, 1984, 1990), and retain instances which are interesting in some way but are certainly not typical. A designer may, for example, retain an interesting solution for some design and, when asked to design some object of that type, recall that design rather than a more mundane typical example.

The distributed model. Barsalou (1987) argues that the graded structure (prototype) of a category is unstable and notions of typicality vary widely across contexts. In the context of a farm, for example, a cow is a more typical animal; in the context of jungle, a tiger is more typical. Ad hoc categories are constructed as required depending on context. Graded structures do not reflect invariant properties of categories but, instead, are highly dependent on constraints inherent in different situations. Barsalou proposes a model of distributed knowledge in long-term memory from which concepts are formed as temporary constructs in working memory tailored to current situations. This model of distributed knowledge is then compared to the architecture of parallel distributed processing (PDP) systems where various aspects of the current context combine to drive the system into a unique state each time a concept is activated.

McCauley (1987) asks how do we organize, store, or retrieve this material in long-term memory without using concepts? What is this material in long-term memory anyway? Is it formed of concepts or something 'more basic' and if so what is this more basic unit? McCauley points out that there must be some criterion for recognizing the concepts as belonging to the same category. Such judgments are impossible without presupposition of either innate processes or some stable basis for representing the category's local integrity within the cognitive system. It is only because we have theories disposed to perceive and react to the world in certain ways that we can have any empirical knowledge at all.

Discussion and Issues Raised in Cognitive Science

So where does all this leave us? Notwithstanding the dissatisfaction with the classical model and its requirement of necessary and sufficient features, and with the current emphasis on the prototype and graded structure models, there is universal agreement that there must exist some similarities between members of a category, although there is no agreement as to what constitutes a similarity. It is often pointed out that two concepts which are totally disjunctive in that they share nothing in common cannot be similar in any respect and therefore cannot be members of the same category. The examples that are given, however, do not reflect concepts that have nothing in common. The examples are human fabricated concepts and these concepts are thus fabricated to serve a human purpose. What the different forms of getting out in baseball or cricket have in common is exactly that, that they perform the function of getting a striker or batsman out.

Attributes. One of the main issues is the preoccupation of cognitive psychologists with perceptive attributes. The role of functional attributes has only recently begun to receive sufficient attention and it has been pointed out already that many of the problems associated with defining features and disjunctive concepts disappear when functional attributes are taken into account. Many structurally different objects can perform the same function. It is difficult, if not impossible and certainly not desirable, to comprehensibly define the range of structure that an object may take, but it is not so difficult to define its functional attributes. For example, a cup may take many forms — it may or may not have a handle, it may be made of many materials, and soon — but its intended function of enabling a person to drink hot liquids in a comfortable manner remains the same. While this is not sufficient to distinguish a cup from a mug, other features, such as size and the way it is intended to be held, do.

Articulation of attributes. Much experimental work involves subjects listing attributes for given categories or making decisions about category membership based on given lists of attributes. However it is contended that, in most cases, people do not know or cannot articulate verbally the precise attributes on which they base their judgment of similarity. As Harnad (1987) points out, a picture is worth more than an infinite number of words.

Saliency of attributes. The issue of the relative importance of attributes (either existing or perceived) is generally neglected, although it does feature somewhat in the probabilistic model. If we simply list attributes for two entities then they may share many attributes in common and, if we simply use the number of attributes in common as a basis for categorization, we may decide that the two entities belong to the same category. Similarly, if we decide that two entities only possess one or two attributes in common out of a total of many attributes we may decide that these entities do not belong to the same category. For example, if we compare a Swiss chalet to an igloo there will be few perceptual attributes in common, yet both can be categorized as houses on one functional attribute in common — providing an environment suitable for living. So it seems that members of a particular category may possess many features, but only some of the features are essential to the definition of the category and are considered when classifying entities. Moreover, even though it is difficult to articulate essential or important features, we do seem able to act as if they exist.

The key issue in categorization, therefore, is the selection of relevant attributes on which to judge similarity. This has to do with the judgment of saliency of attributes with respect to the category. It seems that what constitutes the constituents of a category is any information which is deemed either essential or relevant at the time. As of yet, no machine learning system can perform this task, which is the central task in generalization or induction.

Approximation. Another important issue is that of approximation (Harnad, 1987). Humans operate entirely with approximate systems. No human system is perfect. The legal system is based on the premise 'beyond a reasonable doubt,' democracy and other social systems are presumed to be 'best' for the majority or selected group but not necessarily for every single individual. All decisions which concern the future are based on informed plausible consequences to some degree. We use generalizations everywhere even though they do not hold in every case. We just note the exceptions, but do not invalidate the generalization. Our grammar abounds with general rules of the type 'to form plural nouns add -*s* to the end of the singular noun except in the case of ... where we do the following ... .' Why do we not accept that categories may have the same standing of being applicable in the majority of cases but may fail in some exceptional cases which should be noted? Even using approximate systems, it appears that humans are very accurate when it comes to classifying entities (Medin & Barsalou, 1987).

The recent preoccupation with the exemplar model ignores arguments, such as those of Lakoff (1987), that prototype effects are just that, effects, and do not represent a model of categorization. What is totally missing from such a model is a description of what constitutes similarity between candidates for the same category. If this can be articulated then we have what we are looking for — the similarity description, defining or invariant features, or whatever we wish to call them.

Probability. The probabilistic model seems to provide many of the properties we are looking for in a model of categorization and even provides a mechanism for assessing similarity through the use of some aggregation or probability theory (Shastri, 1989). It is also possible to use subjective probability values (Fox, 1987) using terms such as possible, plausible, and probable. However the use of probabilities, even subjectively, has been discounted as a way in which humans reason. Kahneman and Tversky (1982) argue that representativeness is an important factor in our perception as to the likelihood of events. Examples are cited whereby the results based on probability theory are misjudged and prior odds are ignored. Instead, the probability of an event or item is evaluated by the degree to which it is similar to the most representative member of the category to which it belongs.

Category structure. Most of the examples on categorization given in the literature are very simple examples of category structure. The examples are usually of natural categories, only three levels deep and have a simple tree structure where each category has only one parent (Figure 14.3). This taxonomy may hold for natural categories or formal systems such as geometry, but not necessarily for other conceived entities. A screwdriver may be both a tool and a weapon; a cup may be both a drinking implement and a measuring instrument; a wall may be a structural element, a space divider, an acoustic barrier, and an environmental filter (Figure 14.4).

It is possible to categorize a certain house as an example of a single-story, Spanish-style, courtyard type, low-cost house. While each of these could be classified as subcategories of the category 'house,' this would mean that each of these subcategories would have to include information relating to the other subcategories. In fact, what this means is that a large number of very specific subcategories (e.g., 'single-story, Spanish-style, courtyard type, low-cost house'; 'single-story, Spanish-style, courtyard type, medium-cost house') would need to be formed (Figure 14.5).

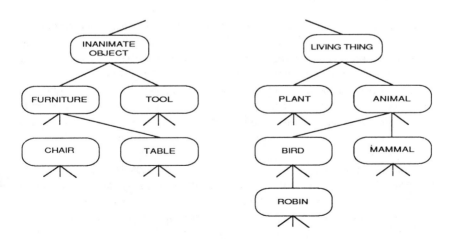

Figure 14.3. A simple tree category taxonomy

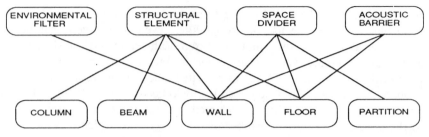

Figure 14.4. A lattice taxonomy with multiple parents

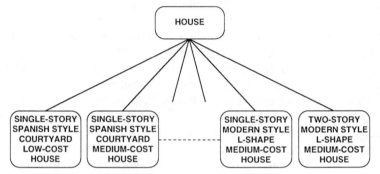

Figure 14.5. Subcategory combinatorial explosion

This type of taxonomy would lead to a combinatorial explosion of categories with much redundant information being repeated in each one. It would seem that, for the sake of efficiency, each subcategory should be a description of some aspect of an entity rather than a complete description of the entity. The complete description should be an aggregation of a member from each of the subcategories (Figure 14.6).

Categorization and learning. Categorization and learning are related to each other through the concept of generalization. It is mostly accepted, though there are dissenting views (e.g., Dreyfus & Dreyfus, 1986), that we do not store all individual experiences or episodes as such but that we form generalizations of these episodes and store these generalizations with indices to the episodes. That is, learning is the process of forming generalizations or categories — learning to recognize patterns in the world. This process prevents an overload of redundant information while allowing special episodes to be stored.

There are approaches to learning which either deny the preexistence of generalizations or deny our ability to correctly express them in a formal system. Thus, we have machine learning approaches based on induction of examples (Michalski, 1983) and PDP approaches (Coyne, Newton, & Sudweeks, 1989; Rumelhart & McClelland, 1986). However, humans use both inductive and generalization processes when learning. We continually take

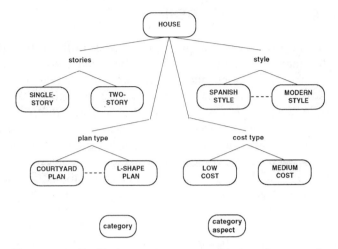

Figure 14.6. Partitioning a category according to various aspects

in information from our environment and form our own particular generalizations but we are also taught generalizations. We may learn the rules of chess by watching several games being played and some gifted individuals may even learn to play good chess through their own playing and perception. Most of us, however, would never be able to induce such general strategies as 'control the center,' 'develop your pieces quickly,' 'open up files,' and so on. Even if we could, it would take so many games that it would be impractical, especially as there is so much literature and personnel willing to impart this compiled knowledge and help shortcut the induction process. Some events are obviously impossible to experience personally and we accept experiences told to us (in various ways) depending on the reliability we place in the source. We do not need to experience death to know that firing a gun at one's head is not conducive to a long life. When the generalizations do not exist, or if we wish to investigate the possibility of other relationships existing, then we must have recourse to induction. It is totally unnecessary to throw away knowledge if we do possess it.

It has been pointed out previously that reasoning using generalizations is imperfect and we make mistakes but that, on the whole, humans do quite well within this framework of uncertainty. Systems that demand certainty would be rendered totally inactive. Most of the time we demand of our systems that they perform above the performance of humans and this concentration on the absolute may be an impossible demand. On the one hand we are dealing with human intelligence and in some way trying to emulate it; on the other hand we are not willing to accept its nature. It may well be that the very nature of human intelligence and reasoning is implicitly bound with the ability to work in an uncertain and imprecise environment in an approximate manner.

DESIGN

Research in categorization has been mostly concerned with representational issues rather than procedural issues. It has been concerned with how we perceive and form categories, and with the structure of categories — that is, going from the specific to the general or from an instance to a category. In contrast, the main concern in design is using generalized constructs to create specific instances — that is, going from the general to the specific.

We now turn our attention to showing how categorization is an integral part of the design process. Apart from a couple of examples in the animal world, which are still the subject of controversy, humans are the only entity that can design in a general manner. Design is a conscious cognitive process employed to satisfy some particular needs. It is a process which alters or, more precisely, has the potential to alter, the state of the environment from some state with which we are dissatisfied to a new state with which we hope to be satisfied. Whereas the role of logic is to deduce facts and the role of science is to induce knowledge, the role of design is to arrive at solutions in the form of entities. Given a set of requirements, usually in general or functional terms, we wish to produce a description of an entity, in structural terms, where the properties of that entity are such that they satisfy the given requirements. Entities may be physical objects (cars), symbolic entities (posters), or more abstract concepts (plans). That is, design is about specialization, going from the general to the specific, going from a category to an instance. In routine design (Coyne, Rosenman, Radford, Balachandran, & Gero, 1990) the instances of the category are well-known and well-defined. In innovative design none of the known instances of the category or categories is suitable for the problem at hand, while in creative design, the category itself may need to be formulated and some instance generated.

Design is a human activity because it employs the human capabilities of formulating goals and reasoning abductively from the general to the specific in order to fulfil those goals. We will argue that no design at all can be carried out unless we have some experience, no matter how little, on which to ground the process of abduction and that this experience is in the form of generalized concepts.

Function, Behavior, and Structure

In the discussion on categorization above, we mentioned perceptual and functional attributes. Since we stated that design is the translation of function into structure we need to have a look at these aspects of function and structure. However, we also need to introduce the notion of behavior (Gero & Rosenman, 1990; Rosenman & Gero, 1989; Umeda, Takeda, Tomiyama, & Yoshikawa, 1990). Function is the purpose which we require to be provided to meet some needs; behavior is what an entity does or exhibits and structure is the form of the entity itself. For example, if the function is to perform surgery, the behavior of the entity may be that it cuts and the structure may be that it is a piece of sharpened steel. Structure is the entity itself and behavior is intrinsically related to this structure and its relation with its environment. There is, however, no intrinsic relationship between structure and function or behavior and function. There is no concept of purpose associated with the mere existence of an entity; it exists and it behaves in a certain way by virtue of its existence in a certain state. There is nothing implicit in, say, a very sharp instrument which can cut very precisely being used as a surgical instrument. Function is purely a human construct imposed on the entity. However, having said that, this human construct is just what design is about: formulating needs as required functions to be performed and arriving at an entity to perform these functions. Once we have this construct of function, we can make relationships between structure, behavior and function.

Given this distinction between function, behavior, and structure let us look at their relationships. Two entities which are identical in all aspects of their structure (apart from being the one and the same) will both behave in the same way (within tolerances of inexactitude) and hence perform the same function, for example, two exact cups (Figure 14.7). Two entities which differ either partly or wholly in their structure but which exhibit the same behavior will also perform the same function; for example, hydraulic and mechanical systems which allow force to be applied can be used in elevator systems (Figure 14.8). The problem of whether two entities exhibiting different behaviors can perform the same function is more difficult to answer. It depends on the granularity of how we look at both the behavior and the function.

The role of function, behavior and structure in classification. Structure, behavior and function can be used in assessing the similarity of entities. One of the problems that was mentioned with the exemplar or prototype model of categorization is how new entities would be judged to be sufficiently similar to the exemplar or prototype to be adjudged a member, albeit an atypical member, of that category; for example, if the prototype of a house is a description of something resembling a suburban cottage, how it would be possible to recognize an igloo as a house. The answer lies in the emphasis on the structural attributes of the two entities. As mentioned previously, entities with the same structure in every respect are very similar; there will be little problem to classify them as belonging to the same category. As their structure differs, so will the judgment of similarity. Based purely on structural attributes it may not be possible to judge the two entities as belonging to the same category. However, their behavior may be very similar. Both the cottage and the igloo have an envelope which encloses the same sort of scale of space and they both modify the external environment to an

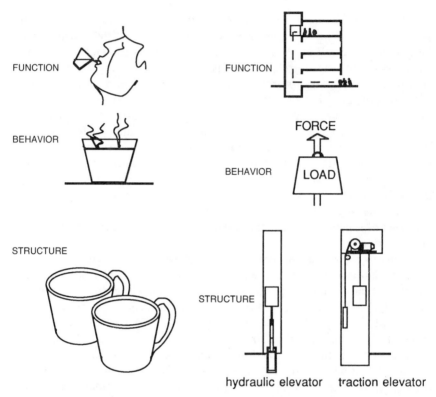

FUNCTION

BEHAVIOR

STRUCTURE

FUNCTION

FORCE

BEHAVIOR   LOAD

STRUCTURE

hydraulic elevator   traction elevator

Figure 14.7. Same structure, same behavior, and same function

Figure 14.8. Different structure producing similar behavior and same function

acceptable degree. Their function is similar in that they both provide an internal environment suitable for certain similar activities to take place. They can thus be classified as belonging to the same category but given their structural difference, the igloo will be noted as an unusual or atypical member. If we accept that different behaviors can perform the same function then we may need to look at the function of the entities to find similarities. The scalpel and the laser beam can both be used to perform surgery. The constant element in all of these is the function. *Entities with similar functions are similar.*

This discussion of finding similarities still does not solve the problem of how to measure similarity. Similarity depends upon some totality of similarity of attributes along certain dimensions. If the dimensions change so does the view of similarity. This ability to change the dimensions on which we measure similarity is the factor which allows us to dynamically create categories for different contexts. Many entities which are categorized as belonging to different categories still may have some properties in common and when those properties are chosen as relevant to the context, a new category being chosen, then those entities will be reclassified as belonging to the new category. For example, a diary and a stapler are usually classified as belonging to different categories. However, in the context of holding down papers on a desk, both have a weight which is adequate and both may be found on a desk. Therefore, along the dimensions of adequate weight (to hold paper down) and availability (in context of desk) they may be classified as belonging to the category of paperweights.

It would seem, therefore, that not only is a category itself not precisely definable but that the whole category structure is itself dynamic in that it can change according to context. Notwithstanding this, stability is achieved in that the structure we keep is the one which itself is general to most contexts or to the context which holds most of the time.

Function is subjective in that it is culturally based. Different cultures have different needs and values and hence the functions they need performed will differ. A posited function is an intended function. That is, an entity is required with the intention that its behavior will be such that it performs the required function. Of course, entities behave in a multiplicity of ways and, hence, can subsequently perform many functions, not all of which may have been intended or are necessarily immediately recognized. Windows can be used to provide light to a space, ventilation, and even access. Cups may have been intended for drinking hot liquids but they are just as useful for drinking cold liquids, and because of their volumetric capabilities can be used for measuring. Once a required function is posited we can only arrive at the entity which carries out that function if we have prior knowledge of that entity and its relation to that function; otherwise we need to generate a new entity. It is, generally, difficult to go directly from a function to a physical entity since there are few, if any, apparent intrinsic clues in a functional description as to its physical realization, unless we have fairly specific prior experience of entities in relation to this function. However, we can more easily make relationships between structure and behavior, and between behavior and function.

Since behavior is a manifestation of structure, it is relatively easy to go from structure to behavior. The behavior of a known entity can be tested (observed) either directly, analogically, or modeled symbolically. Deriving behavior from a structural description of an element depends on the application of interpretative knowledge. This may take the form of mathematical formulae or more qualitative or heuristic knowledge, as may be expressed in rule form. The derivation of qualitative behavior from structure is the subject of work in qualitative physics (Bobrow, 1984; DeKleer & Brown, 1984; Kuipers, 1984).

To derive function from behavior, however, requires relating the behavior of an entity to an existing need. It is only because we have a need to move around or to transport heavy objects that we may recognize that a moving animal exhibits the necessary behavior to perform the functions of carrying us or a load. This recognition process is that which we use in finding new functions for existing entities. There are obviously clues in the behavior of entities which allow us to associate this behavior with required needs. Looking at the design problem, going from function to behavior is impossible unless we have some prior experiences of behavior – function relationships. If we want to render a quarry unconscious we cannot just surmise that what is required is an object which is hard and weighty and needs to be applied to the head with force unless we already know that the attributes hard and weighty somehow produce the desired effect — that is, we have had some experience with hard and weighty objects being applied to a head. For example, we may have struck our own head on a rock or tree or have seen someone else do it. Through that experience we still have had to recognize the causes of the effect otherwise the only thing that could be applied at a future stage would be the same rock or tree that caused the experience. That is, having experienced something, we have recognized and generalized the attributes relevant to that experience. This allows us at some stage to relate required function to a set of required behavior attributes.

Similarly, to go from required behavior attributes to some structure requires prior experience of the behavior of various structural entities. When we require an entity with the behavioral attribute of transparency, we cannot say that what is required is glass unless we know that glass is transparent. At times, however, we may realize that we need something to allow light to pass through, but we do not have such an entity. In that case, we need to carry out research to discover what it is that could allow light to pass through an entity.

What the above discussion aims to point out is that design cannot be performed without recourse to prior experiences in a generalized form. Design is about experience and about generalizations. Except for very mundane tasks, where a problem is solved by recourse to some exact previous experience we need to apply generalized knowledge, sometimes seemingly from another context, to our specific problem. Therefore, design involves specifying required attributes, matching these as closely as possible to existing attributes inferring other properties as necessary and arriving at the required instance.

What is thus required for a system to aid in the design process is a framework in which generalized experiences can be represented, stored, accessed, and made use of so as to be applied to specific design tasks. To be useful in a design context, these generalized experiences will need to address the function, behavior and structure relationships. Thus any such description needs to represent information regarding functional, behavioral and structural attributes as well as all the relevant relationships among these. These relationships may take the form of causal or inferential knowledge, procedural knowledge, and/or constraints. Moreover, information needs also be available as to the context in which this information is applicable.

Routine design is characterized by the existence of categories which have well-defined functional, behavioral, and structural attributes and relationships between these. Nonroutine design is characterized by the incompleteness of some of these attributes, especially the structural attributes. The more a design problem is stated in behavioural and/or functional terms, the less constraining it is in terms of the possible design solutions. Any generalized design description is in fact a category in which all relevant attributes as well as their relationships are represented. The representation needs be general enough to allow a wide variety of entities to be designed for a given functional problem. Where the structural attributes are narrowly defined, both as to their existence and as to their possible range of values, then the representation allows for a very rigidly defined class of entities in that category. Where the behavior and/or functional attributes are posited but the structural attributes are left very general then the actual instances of entities which may be included in that class of entities are not rigidly defined.

Abduction and Attribute Matching

We have stated above that the process of design is an abductive process going from function to behavior to structure and that this abductive process necessarily involves finding appropriate general experiences. Finding these experiences is a pattern matching process, in which a set of required attributes needs to be matched by the attributes of an entity. The design problem, however, is given in terms of required functional and behavioral attributes and the solution to be found is in terms of structural attributes. Therefore, matching to a generalization or category is done through these functional and/or behavioral attributes. The specificity of these attributes will determine the specificity of the category matched. For example, if the functional requirements only state that passage is required through a wall, then an opening or a door will do. However, if these requirements specify that security is also required, then a door will do but an opening will not. If in addition to the security requirement there is also a minimum space occupation requirement then a match may be made, say, to a sliding door.

There remain problems regarding what set of attributes to match and how exact a match needs to be to be acceptable. If we require an entity with attributes A and B and C do we only want those entities that have all three attributes? What if no single entity that we know about has all three attributes but there are entities that have two or even just one such attribute? Are they of any use in helping us configure a new entity from those entities? Can we, say, extract those features from those entities which contribute to the required attributes and configure the various separate parts into a new entity? There is, first a problem of consistency. The parts in themselves may contribute to some abstracted requirement, but their structural manifestation, as selected, may not be compatible. Yoshikawa (1981) points out this problem with his 'frodird' configuration. Matching also depends on the attributes themselves and the question of generality and relevancy. For example if one of the required attributes is 'costs less than \$2,000,' this, by itself, may match to a large number of entities with no relevancy to the problem at hand. In order to match only to relevant entities we must always include some essential defining attribute which must be matched. This would seem to be some sort of functional attribute which the entity must perform.

The question of matching also entails the question of closeness of match. What if an entity matches approximately, either by matching all of the required attributes approximately or by matching some exactly and some approximately? What is meant by approximately and when is close enough good enough? What if many 'unimportant' attributes are matched closely but some 'important' ones matched only approximately? Humans seem to be able to operate quite efficiently within this environment, making decisions about whether to accept such matches or not. We need some sort of aggregate of fit.

DESIGN PROTOTYPES

The main concern of cognitive science with categorization is the representation of categories and how these are formed, that is with perception and learning. While learning is an essential activity of any human cognitive process, we are more concerned with the representation and use of already-acquired experience for a computer-aided design system. The main concern of design is the generation of specific entities, not the generation of general knowledge or the classification of entities, though these processes may be used in design. To this end we have stressed the roles of function, behavior, and structure. We have previously discussed the various views regarding categories and discussed various models. In capturing generalized design experiences we are, in fact, forming categories or classes of design entities. In the design context we will use the term design prototype to mean a class of generalized design experiences. The term archetype will be used to describe a typical member of a design prototype. In order to describe a class of entities the design prototype will contain all information deemed to be essential or important to the description of the class or to the identification of members of the class. The model used is one comprising all salient features deemed important. In some sense, it is akin to the probabilistic model, although it makes no use of probabilistic distribution.

Requirements for Design Prototypes

The design prototype is thus a category of entities related to design and includes all the necessary information related to that category. The information must allow for the recognition of the design prototype as suitable for a given design problem, for the specialization of that prototype, and for the process of satisfying requirements by finding instantiating values for the structural attributes or variables. Not only does the design prototype include information describing an entity but also the necessary relationships and processes to arrive at this description. The information must, therefore, include the following elements: functional properties; behavioral properties; structural properties; context; and relations between these elements. Note how the knowledge regarding the relations between the various attributes relates to the theory-based approaches to categorization discussed previously. There will, inevitably, be relationships among the design prototypes and an efficient structural framework is required to represent these relationships.

Implementation of a Design Prototype System

The model. Since we are principally interested in generating entities, that is, specific instances from a class, the exemplar model is insufficient for this purpose. To this end we would need not only the exemplar description but also a modification process (e.g., design grammar) which would allow us to generate other members of the class no matter how atypical. The exemplar model has the advantage, however, that a description of a typical member of the class is always available. That is, when we think of a class of entities we have some image or representation present depending on the context. The classical model would allow us to describe only the necessary and sufficient features of the class and, as previously discussed, would be insufficient in many cases where nonnecessary features are deemed important. For example, in the case of windows, there are windows which allow light, provide ventilation, and provide a view; others allow light but do not provide ventilation or a view; yet others may allow light and ventilation but do not provide a view (for this argument we will not call panels which do not allow some measure of light to be called windows). The only feature (functional) that all the three types of windows have in common (intersection of features) is that they allow light in and this would be the only such feature that could be included in a classical model. This would mean that if we were searching for an entity to provide a view we would not match 'window' but rather some other design prototype such as 'picture window.' This seems unnatural and we feel that these important features of members of the class should somehow be mentioned in the class itself while being fully aware that not all members will necessarily possess all those attributes. The model which seems most appropriate for the design prototype is one which contains all salient features as deemed by the person generating the design prototype; that is, the design prototype will not contain only necessary and sufficient attributes, nor will it contain all the specific attributes of all members of the class, the union of all the attributes of the members, but it will contain the union of the salient attributes of the members (Figure 14.9).

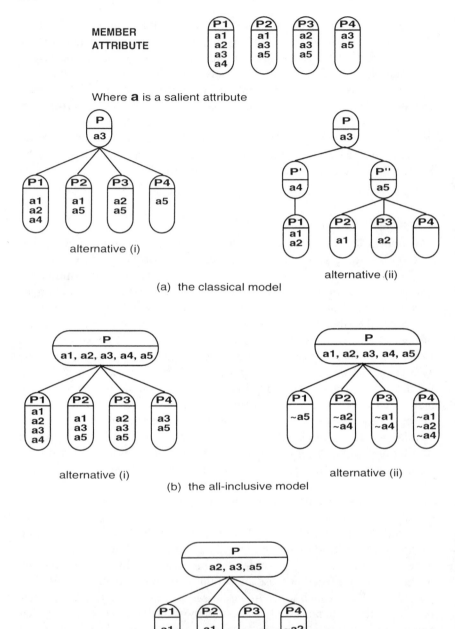

Figure 14.9. Models of design prototype structure

We can formalize our model as follows:

      if   *S1* is set of attributes of prototype *P1*
             S2 is set of attributes of prototype *P2*
             S3 is set of attributes of prototype *P3*

             s1 (*s1 S1*) is set of SALIENT attributes of *P1*
             s2 (*s2 S2*) is set of SALIENT attributes of *P2*
             s3 (*s3 S3*) is set of SALIENT attributes of *P3*

   then   prototype *P*
  where   *P1, P2, P3* $<$ *P* (i.e., *P* is a superclass of *P1, P2,P3*)
is given by *s1* » *s2* » *s3*

In the classical model, since the design prototype contains only those attributes common to all members then the members do not need to repeat that information (Figure 14.9a). In an all-inclusive model where every attribute of every member is contained in the design prototype, it is possible to either repeat fully the attributes of each member or else negate those attributes which each member does not possess (Figure 14.9b). In either case this amounts to a large amount of redundant information. In the salient attribute model proposed, only salient attributes are contained in the design prototype and it seems more efficient to then negate those attributes not contained in the description of the members themselves (Figure 14.9c).

    The typical member of the class will be a representation called the archetype of a design prototype. In accordance with an exemplar representation having more than one exemplar, a design prototype may have more than one archetype. Each archetype contains a fairly specific description of a member of the class. Many, if not all, the attributes of the entity will have a specific value. In addition, atypical members may also be represented. The use of typical and atypical members is to serve as representations of the class when no information is given. They may then serve as a starting point for the design of other instances.

CONCLUSION

This chapter accepts the existence of categories and their usefulness. It accepts that there is no universal agreement as to what constitutes a category yet notes that all researchers agree that a category defines some measure of similarity between entities in a given context. Various views were explored and their merits and demerits noted. It has been shown that processes in design involving generalizations are based on the more general cognitive process of categorization. At the same time, it has been shown that certain problems, owing to the particular domain and the emphasis on the use of categories rather than on their representation, raise additional issues in the realm of categorization theory.

REFERENCES

Addanki, S., & Davis, E. (1985). A representation for complex physical domains, *IJCAI85, 1*, 443-446.

Barsalou, L. W. (1987). The instability of graded structure. In U. Neisser (Ed.), *Concepts and conceptual development, ecological and intellectual factors in categorization* (pp. 101-140). Cambridge, UK: Cambridge University Press.

Bobrow, D. G. (1984). Qualitative reasoning about physical systems: An introduction. *Artificial Intelligence, 24*, 1-5.

Borgida, A., Myplopoulos, J., & Wong, H. K. T. (1984). Generalization/specialization as a basis for software specification. In M. L. Brodie, J. Myplopoulos, & J. W. Schmidt (Eds.), *On conceptual modeling* (pp. 87-114), New York: Springer-Verlag.

Coyne, R., Newton, S., & Sudweeks, F. (1989). Modeling the emergence of schemas in design reasoning. *Preprints Modeling Creativity and Knowledge-based Creative Design* (pp. 173-205). Sydney: University of Sydney, Department of Architectural and Design Science, also, A connectionist view of creative design reasoning. In J.S. Gero and M.L. Maher (Eds.) (1993), *Modeling Creativity and Knowledge-Based Creative Design* (pp. 177-209). Hillsdale, NJ: Erlbaum.

Coyne, R.D., Rosenman, M. A., Radford, A. D., Balachandran, M., & Gero, J. S. (1990). *Knowledge-based design systems.* Reading, MA: Addison-Wesley.

Cropley, A. J. (1970). S-R psychology and cognitive psychology. In P. E. Vernon (Ed.), *Creativity* (pp. 116-125). New York: Penguin.

DeKleer, J., & Brown, J. S. (1984). A qualitative physics based on confluences. *Artificial Intelligence, 24*, 7-83.

Dreyfus, H., & Dreyfus, S. (1986, January). Why computers may never think like people. *Technology Review*, 42-61.

Fox, J. (1987). Making decisions under the influence of knowledge. In P. Morris (Ed.), *Modeling cognition* (pp. 199-212). Chichester, UK: Wiley.

Gero, J.S. (1990). Design prototypes: a knowledge representation scheme for design. *AI Magazine, 11 (4)*, 26-36.

Gero, J. S., & Maher, M. L. (1988). Designing with prototypes. In V. Hubka, J. Baratossy, & U. Pighini (Eds), *ICED88* (Vol.1, pp. 74-81). Zurich: Heurista.

Gero, J. S., & Rosenman, M. A. (1990). A conceptual framework for knowledge-based design research at Sydney University's Design Computing Unit. *Artificial Intelligence in Engineering, 5*(2), 65-77.

Harnad, S. (1987). Category induction and representation. In S. Harnad (Ed.), *Categorical perception* (pp. 535-565). Cambridge, UK: Cambridge University Press.

Kahneman, D., & Tversky, P. (1982). On the study of statistical intuitions. *Cognition, 11*, 123-141.

Kant, I. (1787). *The critique of pure reason.* London: Dent.

Kuipers, B. (1984). Commonsense reasoning about causality: Deriving behaviour from structure. *Artificial Intelligence, 24*, 169-203.

Lakoff, G. (1987). Cognitive models and prototype theory. In U. Neisser (Ed.), *Concepts and conceptual development, ecological and intellectual factors in categorization* (pp. 63-100). Cambridge, UK: Cambridge University Press.

McCauley, R. N. (1987). The role of theories in a theory of concepts. In U. Neisser (Ed.), *Concepts and conceptual development, ecological and intellectual factors in categorization* (pp. 288-309). Cambridge, UK: Cambridge University Press.

Medin, D. L., & Barsalou, L. W. (1987). Categorization processes and categorical perception. In S. Harnad (Ed.), *Categorical perception* (pp. 455-490). Cambridge, UK: Cambridge University Press.

Medin, D. L., & Wattenmaker, W. D. (1987). Category cohesiveness, theories and cognitive archeology. In U. Neisser (Ed.), *Concepts and conceptual development, ecological and intellectual factors in categorization* (pp. 25-62). Cambridge, UK: Cambridge University Press, Cambridge.

Mervis, C., & Rosch, E. (1981). Categorization of natural objects. *Annual Review of Psychology, 32,* 89-115.

Michalski, R. S. (1983). A theory and methodology of inductive learning. *Artificial Intelligence, 20,* 111-161.

Purcell, A. T. (1984). The organisation of the experience of the built environment. *Environment and Planning B: Planning and Design, 22,* 173-192.

Purcell, A. T. (1990, November). *Consistency with expectations effects with complex representations of everyday scenes.* Submitted to Australasian Society for Cognitive Science First Annual Conference, University of New South Wales, Sydney.

Rosch, E. H. (1978). Principles of categorization. In E. Rosch & B. B. Lloyd (Eds.), *Cognition and categorization.* Hillsdale, NJ: Erlbaum.

Rosenman, M. A., & Gero, J. S. (1989). Creativity in design using a prototype approach. *Preprints modeling creativity and knowledge-based creative design* (pp. 207-232). Department of Architectural and Design Science, University of Sydney; also, in J.S. Gero and M.L. Maher (Eds.) (1993). *Modeling Creativity and Knowledge-Based Creative Design* (pp. 111-138). Hillsdale, NJ: Erlbaum.

Rumelhart, D. E., & McClelland, J. L. (Ed.). (1986). *Parallel distributed processing: Explorations in the microstructure of cognition — Volume 2, psychological and biological models.* Cambridge, MA: MIT Press.

Shastri, L. (1989). Default reasoning in semantic networks: A formalization of recognition and inheritance. *Artificial Intelligence, 39* (3), 283-355.

Smith, E. E., & Medin, D. L. (1981). *Categories and concepts.* Cambridge, MA: Harvard University Press.

Sowa, J.F. (1984). *Conceptual structures: information processing in mind and machine.* Reading, MA: Addison-Wesley.

Umeda, Y., Takeda, H., Tomiyama, T., & Yoshikawa, H. (1990). Function, behaviour and structure. In J. S. Gero (Ed.), *Applications of artificial engineering V: Design* (pp. 177-193). Southampton, UK: CMP.

Yoshikawa, H. (1981). General design theory and a CAD system. In T. Sata & E. Warman (Eds.), *Man-machine communication in CAD/CAM* (pp. 1-19). Amsterdam: North-Holland.

CHAPTER 15

Multiple Reasoning Contexts in Health Care Planning

Carol Ingrid Bradburn and John Zeleznikow

Database Research Laboratory
Applied Computing Research Institute

INTRODUCTION

An expert system may be used to assist a nonexpert person to achieve apparent decision-making skills comparable to those of the expert whose knowledge is encapsulated into the system. However, the nonexpert often would benefit more from insight into the reasoning processes of the expert than from the simple provision of a correct problem solution. This is especially important if the nonexpert is a novice practitioner in the area of expertise; understanding of reasoning methodologies in problem solving may accelerate growth toward competency.

A good case may therefore be made for designing expert systems which simulate expert reasoning in process as well as in content. The knowledge of an expert may be from many differing sources and organizations; the knowledge types appropriate to the present circumstances must be applied. In addition, an expert continues to refine and enrich his knowledge on the basis of experience.

This paper proposes a model of reasoning appropriate to planning by health care professionals. It is argued that, while case-based reasoning is used, decision making is not normally based on the remembering and adapting of individual cases. Rather, the health care practitioner bases decisions on a framework of "standard" cases. These standard cases initially comprise formally learned knowledge but, in the course of clinical practice, become enriched and extended by the addition of detail derived from actual cases. Individual cases are only remembered when they cannot be linked with a standard case. In addition, reasoning is supported by an underlying base model of "how things work." This is also based on learned knowledge and may be used to explain difficult cases or solve unique problems. The reasoning model is used in the design of the FLORENCE nursing care planning system.

Firstly, we discuss the rationale of using multiple knowledge sources. Details are then given of the individual knowledge sources and a reasoning model using these sources is proposed. Finally an example is given of the application of the model to the field of nursing care planning.

EXTENDING CASE-BASED REASONING

As much of health care practice is concerned with the management of individual patients, clients or "cases," a case-based reasoning paradigm would seem a logical starting point.

Considerable recent attention has been paid to case-based reasoning as a mechanism of human and machine problem solving. The underlying concept is that "a case-based reasoner solves new problems by adapting solutions that were used to solve old problems" (Riesbeck & Schank, 1989). It is suggested that humans, when faced with a new situation, make decisions or form plans by "remembering" similar situations in the past. They adapt successful past solutions to current circumstances whilst avoiding old solutions that did not work. Computer simulation of case based reasoning has been applied to such diverse domains as menu planning and medical diagnosis. (Kolodner, 1988; Koton, 1988).

However, while professional health care workers may draw upon knowledge of previous cases in the planning of care, simple case-based reasoning is an overly simplistic representation of the process. Health care workers, like other professionals, do not reason entirely from their own experiences. Such practitioners normally commence clinical practice after an undergraduate course of study in which they learn the basic principles of their professions. This initial knowledge is used as a basis for decision making and is itself modified during the process; they hold a concept of an idealized case before encountering real cases and these idealized or "standard" cases form a basic framework for memory and reasoning.

It is suggested that complete details of individual cases are only stored in memory when they cannot be classified within the framework of standard cases. More commonly, details of individual cases are abstracted into standard cases, initially formed during professional education, and enriched throughout ongoing clinical practice. The enrichment process may be viewed as one of recording extensions and exceptions to the features of the standard cases. Experience then allows the expert to recognize that while a new client may not display the classic features of standard case S, an S situation does exist and plans relating to the management of S may be applicable.

Finally, an underlay of basic knowledge is used to provide explanation for features of standard cases and to hypothesize about the nature of novel or unique cases. This knowledge may, depending on the discipline, include principles of physical sciences, biological sciences, sociology, or psychology.

It provides a rationale for decisions and actions. The process of generalizing cases in the medical domain has been previously recognized (Kolodner & Simpson, 1986). However, little attention has been paid to the integration of basic theoretical knowledge, and theoretical knowledge about cases, with that of knowledge gained by experience. We suggest a tentative paradigm of knowledge representation which might achieve such integration.

KNOWLEDGE SOURCES

When planning care for a new client, we may consider the professional as drawing upon three intersecting knowledge sources, explained in the following sections.

Base Knowledge

This includes an understanding of the principles of biological sciences, psychology, and sociology and their relevance to health care. The majority of this knowledge is obtained from professional education prior to practice, although it may be updated on a need-to-know basis throughout the individual's career.

In the prepractice educational process, this material is commonly presented in the form of a detailed systems model. For example, a functional model of the human body is presented in a physiology course or of human society in a sociology course. However, the detailed models do not necessarily represent material used in clinical reasoning. Much of the complexity is forgotten; indeed, few of us would claim to remember the detailed content of introductory undergraduate courses. What is remembered is a simplified model of how things work in general. For example, the details of muscular physiology may be forgotten but it will be remembered that muscles require a good supply of oxygen and an intact nerve supply for normal functioning.

These simplified models, and their interactions, form a background to the specific cases encountered in practice.

Standard Case Knowledge

This may be viewed as a collection of descriptions of the typical features of a case type. These descriptions are in the form of a listing of the salient features of a case:

- name and description of condition
- causes
- presenting features
- recommended treatments
- probable outcomes

This broad outline could be applied to the types of cases encountered in any health care discipline. Individual disciplines might include extra features.

Much of this standard case knowledge is also obtained prior to clinical practice in a formal learning situation. However, it may be regarded as the professional foreground knowledge and is remembered in more complete detail than the background base knowledge. These standard cases would seem to be intermediate between the ossified and the paradigmatic cases of Riesbeck and Schank (1989). While the standard cases represent abstractions from real life, as do ossified cases, they are not static but subject to modification in the face of new experiences. The major source of modification of standard case knowledge is the learning that comes from experience with the unique cases of clinical practice.

Unique Case Knowledge

This is the practical knowledge, based on experience. The practitioner sees and cares for specific clients. Many present as examples of the recognized conditions described by the standard cases; others may show atypical features of the standard cases; a few will prove to have conditions for which standard cases do not exist.

Unique case knowledge may be used in three ways:

1. modifying the standard cases by incorporating into them new significant features derived from specific client cases. As the practitioner acquires experience, the standard cases become enriched by the addition of new knowledge.
2. developing a library of "exceptions" to standard cases. This would be required when features of a standard case were found to be applicable to a situation that failed to fully meet the specified criteria. With repeated experience, these exceptions may be reclassified as usual parts of standard features.
3. storing details of specific cases in memory. This would occur in those situations where the new case was of a rare type for which no standard case was recognized. The specific case might remain as an example of an isolated instance, redefined as an exception to a standard case, or it might form the basis for a new standard case if more specific instances were seen.

The three identified knowledge sources of base knowledge, standard cases, and unique cases may be regarded as having individual and combined contributions to the planning process.

- At the interface of base knowledge and standard cases are the explanations or rationales for the material contained within the standard cases.

- At the interface of standard cases and unique cases are those cases that, while not standard, may be categorized as exceptions or extensions to standard cases.
- At the interface of base knowledge and unique cases are found the tentative analyses of a hypothesis about unique cases.

These relationships are shown diagrammatically in Figure 15.1.

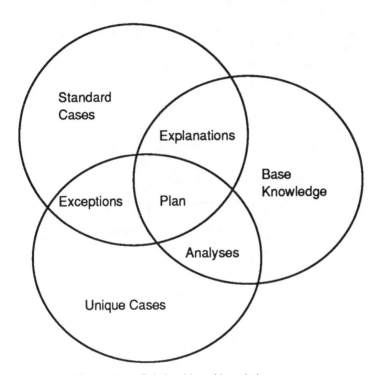

Figure 15.1. Relationships of knowledge sources

THE REASONING PROCESS

When planning care for a new client, the professional will attempt to retrieve a standard plan that may be adapted to meet the needs of the present circumstances. The search process requires the answering of certain questions:

1. Is this a typical standardized case? A case may be defined as standard if the presenting features are essentially those of a stored standard case. This will involve a review of the standardized case and its associated exception library.

2. If this is not a typical standardized case, can its unusual features be explained by extension to a standardized case? Basic knowledge will be applied to the unusual features to see if they may be explained within the standard case context. The standard case may then be adjusted to take account of the new knowledge.
3. If this is not an extension of a standardized case, is it similar to a remembered specific case? In this eventuality, the prescriptions of the remembered case may be implemented and (possibly) a tentative standard case formulated.
4. If this is a unique case, what can be hypothesized about it from basic general knowledge? An attempt is made to reason about the case using basic knowledge. A hypothesis is either formed or a need for further information is identified.

This reasoning process is illustrated in Figure 15.2.

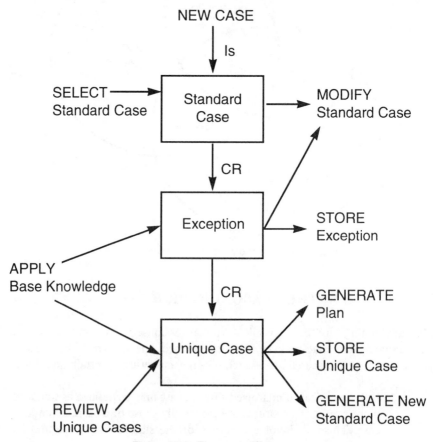

Figure 15.2. The reasoning process

AN EXAMPLE: NURSING CARE PLANNING

This section relates to work on the development of FLORENCE, an expert system to advise student and novice nurses on the formulation of nursing care plans. Present research relates to mechanisms of retrieving a standard or unique plan that can be adapted to the needs of a new client. A prototype system has been implemented using PEARL, a Franz Lisp extension which creates hierarchical slot-filler representations.[1] This allows representation, manipulation, and storage of cases in a standard format.

When a client comes under the care of a nurse, his condition is assessed and nursing needs are identified. Nursing assessment differs from medical assessment in that the emphasis is on identifying functional problems that interfere with the person's daily living activities, rather than on the formulation of a clinical diagnosis. Nursing assessment may be divided into assessment of specific "functional health patterns." The FLORENCE prototype handles problems within the activity-exercise functional group. Problems are identified concerning the ability of a nursing client to be independently mobile, to exercise and to pursue normal daily activities.

Assessment will identify deviations from normal which may indicate the presence of actual or potential nursing problems, commonly known as "nursing diagnoses." Attempts have been made to formalize these nursing diagnoses and the North American Nursing Diagnosis Association (NANDA) has produced listings of nursing diagnoses which are recommended for use by the practicing nurse (Carpenito, 1989a). Suggested problems that may be identified within the Activity-Exercise Pattern assessment are listed in Figure 15.3.

Activity intolerance
Cardiac output, decreased
Disuse syndrome, potential for
Diversional activity deficit
Home maintenance management, impaired
mobility, impaired physical
respiratory function, potential altered
   ineffective airway clearance
   ineffective breathing patterns
   impaired gas exchange
(Specify) Self-care deficit: (Total, Feeding, Bathing/hygiene,
Dressing/grooming, Toileting)
Tissue perfusion, altered: (Specify) (Cerebral, Cardiopulmonary,
Renal, Gastrointestinal, Peripheral)

Figure 15.3. Nursing diagnostic categories by functional health pattern
— Activity-Exercise adapted from Carpenito (1989a)

---

[1] PEARL (Package for Efficient Access to Representations in Lisp), developed by M. Deering, J. Faletti, and R. Wilsensky at Computer Science Division, University of California, Berkeley.

Retrieval of cases in FLORENCE is based on the presence of major defining characteristics, which must be present for the diagnosis to be made, and minor characteristics, which may be present. The representation of the diagnosis "ineffective airways clearance" is shown in Figure 15.4.

```
(dbcreate individual diagnosis ineffective__airways__clearance

    (name ineffective__airways__clearance)

    (majf
         (ineffective__cough
inability__to__remove__airway__secretions))

    (minf
         (abnormal__breath__sounds abnormal__respiratory__rate
         abnormal__respiratory__rhythm
     abnormal__respiratory__depth)))
```

Figure 15.4. Nursing diagnosis — ineffective airways clearance

Each diagnosis will have an associated standard plan of care. It is usual in nursing for a particular client to have multiple nursing diagnoses. In addition, expected diagnoses may be clustered around medical diagnosis, age, social environment, or other background features. Thus a standard "super-plan" is available. Volumes of such standard care plans have been produced (Carpenito, 1989b). The selected plan may then be modified for the particular client. In the FLORENCE prototype a standard case is defined as a cluster of nursing diagnoses based on the client's medical diagnosis.

An initial search is made for confirming evidence of the expected cluster of nursing diagnoses, based on the presence of the diagnostic defining characteristics. If we consider the major defining characteristics (MDC) of which all are required to be present for a diagnosis to be accepted, five situations may occur for a particular diagnosis:

If M is a set of MDC, $\{x_1, x_2, \ldots x_n\}$, of diagnosis **D**

and

F is a set of abnormalities in a particular functional group, $\{y_1, y_2, \ldots y_n\}$, detected in client **C**

then

1. If $M - F = \Delta$ then client **C** exhibits all of the features of diagnosis **D** and of no other diagnosis
2. If $M \ll F = \Delta$ then client **C** exhibits none of the features of diagnosis **D**
3. If $M \ll F \pi \Delta$ and $M - F \pi \Delta$ then client **C** displays some of the features of diagnosis **D**

4. If $F \ldots M$ then client **C** exhibits all of the features of diagnosis **D** plus additional features

5. If $M \ll F \pi \Delta$ and $M - F \pi \Delta$ and $F - (M \ll F) \pi \Delta$ then client **C** displays some of the features of diagnosis **D** plus additional features.

If all major features are present (1 or 4) then it is probable that **D** can be accepted. In practice this is somewhat simplistic. Although the published NANDA diagnoses list major features as "must be present," experienced nurses recognize that this is not always so. Assessment data may be incomplete or a single major feature may be sufficiently convincing even in the absence of others. It is planned to introduce a weighting system for the major features of each diagnosis.

If no major features are present, **D** may be rejected. If **D** was an expected diagnosis, based on the client's medical condition or age, the absence of **D** must be evaluated.

If some major features are present, (3 or 5) confirming evidence must be sought before **D** is accepted or rejected.

Three selection problems may arise:

1. an individual diagnosis may have some, but not all, major features present.
2. some of the expected cluster of nursing diagnoses may not be supported by abnormal assessment data.
3. abnormal assessment data may exist which appears unrelated to any of the cluster of expected diagnoses.

Resolution is attempted by consideration of the presence of minor defining characteristics. Again, a weighting of the significance of specific factors is required.

Following this phase of the assessment there may be two outstanding data items:

1. the presence of expected diagnoses for which no evidence has been found
2. the presence of assessment abnormalities which do not fit any expected diagnosis.

It is necessary to investigate whether these items can be explained as exceptions to the standard case or whether the present client must be classified as displaying unique features.

For this purpose the items are referred to the base model. The base model may be viewed as consisting of "nodes of influence." Each node represents a functional structure which is influenced by preceding structures and in turn influences following structures. An example of a model representing the

activity-exercise functional group is shown in Figure 15.5. Recall that this
is a broad, nondetailed model which represents the base knowledge stored
in the memory of the practitioner. In this way it is possible to represent normal
rather than abnormal behavior. Detailed models of a medical domain have
been found excessively complex (Torasso & Console, 1989) and it has been
more usual to represent a model of faulty behavior.

FLORENCE defines each node as having inputs and outputs, each of which
is weighted in terms of importance of effect. Attached to each node are listings
of abnormalities that may indicate malfunction in the node and, if they exist,
nursing diagnoses that may be associated with malfunction. An example of
such a node is given in Figure 15.6.

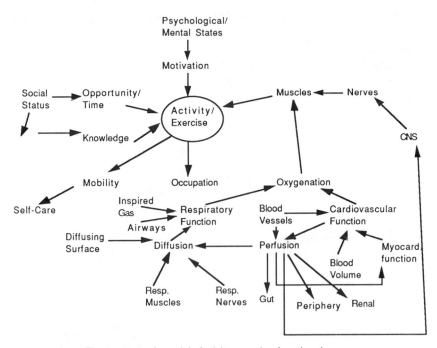

Figure 15.5. A model: Activity-exercise functional group

It is possible to enter the model at any node and to follow forward or reverse
pathways. Search may be made more efficient by following high-value input
and output paths first. If there is a data abnormality that has not been
associated with a diagnosis, following a forward path may indicate a potential
diagnosis and following a backward path may indicate a possible diagnostic
cause.

If outstanding data items may be fitted into the model in such a way that
they could be caused by, or could cause, the expected diagnoses of the
standard case, the present case is classified as an exception to the standard

case. If nonexpected diagnoses are suggested or if residual, unexplained data items remain, the present case is classified as a unique case. In the case of exceptions, only the unusual data items are stored, with reference to the standard case. Cases classified as unique are stored in their entirety.

```
(dbcreate individual model__node activity__exercise
    (node activity__exercise )
    (type (type
        (main__type physical)
        (sub__type muscular))
    (inputs ((input__output
        (node motivation)
        (value 5))
        (input__output
      (node opportunity)
        (value 4))
        (input__output
        (node knowledge)
        (value 4))
        (input__output
        (node muscles)
        (value 6))))
    (outputs ((input__output
        (node mobility)
        (value 7))
        (input__output
        (node occupation)
        (value 6))))
    (abnormalities (altered__response__to__activity ) )
    (diagnoses (activity__intolerance)))
```

Figure 15.6. Model node — activity-exercise

CONCLUSION

This chapter has described preliminary work in the analysis and modeling of the planning behavior of health care professionals. The novice practitioner begins practice with a broad knowledge of basic principles and a bank of standard cases which act as a guide to the care of particular client groups. With more experience in the care of real clients, features of actual cases are abstracted into the standard cases. The standardized cases become richer and more predictive of reality. Individual real cases in their entirety tend only to be remembered if they are unique or if they display exceptions that do not fit readily into the standardized cases. FLORENCE, a prototype nursing care planning expert system, attempts to compare new client cases with standard cases on the basis of assessment abnormalities. If this is not successful, an underlying model is searched for possible explanation of unusual client features. A new client case may be classified as an example of a standard cases, as an exception to a standard case or as a unique case.

Future development of FLORENCE will be concerned with the refinement of the current, rather simplistic, classification mechanisms. Heuristic material obtained from experienced clinical nurses is to be incorporated particularly in the area of exception identification. In addition, mechanisms are to be incorporated for the ongoing review and reclassification of exception and unique cases.

REFERENCES

Carpenito, L.J. (1989a). *Handbook of nursing diagnosis 1989-90.* Philadelphia, PA: J.B. Lippincott.

Carpenito, L.J. (1989b). *Nursing diagnosis: Application to clinical practice* (3rd ed.). Philadelphia, PA: J.B. Lippincott.

Kolodner, J., & Simpson, R. (1986). Problem solving and dynamic memory. In J. Kolodner, & C. Riesbeck (Eds.), *Experience, memory and reasoning.* Hillsdale, NJ: Erlbaum.

Kolodner, J. (1988). Extending problem solver capabilities through case-based inference. In J. Kolodner (Ed.), *Proceedings of Case-Based Reasoning Workshop,* pp. 21-30. San Mateo, California: Morgan Kaufman.

Koton, P. (1988). Reasoning about evidence in causal explanations. In J. Kolodner (Ed.), *Proceedings of Case-Based Reasoning Workshop,* pp. 260-270. San Mateo, California: Morgan Kaufman.

Riesbeck, K. & Schank, R. (1989). *Inside case based reasoning.* Hillsdale, NJ: Lawrence Erlbaum.

Torasso, P., & Console, L. (1989). *Diagnostic problem solving.* Oxford, UK: North Oxford Academic.

CHAPTER 16

Some Reflections on Procedural and Declarative Representations for Cognitive Processes

Terry Caelli and Roger Wales

Departments of Computer Science and Psychology
The University of Melbourne

INTRODUCTION

Describing how you get to work would usually involve some script about getting up, eating, walking or driving, and so on — a representation of a series of acts which are linked together in a symbolic, linguistic, way that is understood by most. We call this a *declarative* representation for how you get to work. However, each of these acts involves the initiation of complex procedures of muscle innovation, complex neurophysiological information processing, and planning which are not explicitly included in the symbolic description of the acts. We call this level of representation *procedural*, each of whose components, of course, can, in turn, be described symbolically and which, again, can invoke lower-level procedural representations. This chapter is about how these two apparently different types of representations can be integrated.

Studies of intelligent information processing in either man or machine have employed these two types of representations typically as a function of the domain of analysis. Again, the terms *declarative* or *symbolic*, refer to representations which employ an explicit and discrete formulation in terms of languages involving explicit grammars varying from predicate calculus through to complex grammars endemic to models for natural languages. The *procedural* representations, more typically associated with numerical domains apply where the representation is defined by a set of procedures or processes which evolve from the physical description of the input through to complex decision-making processes which index some networks which can be generally analyzed in terms of control systems, or, in general, discrete time dynamical systems.

Though, in a deeper sense, both types of representations, for communication purposes, are defined by some formal symbolic system, the inherent representations of such processes seem quite different at least on the surface. Indeed, one of the fundamental problems in artificial intelligence has been the problem of relating numerical representations to categorical symbolic types. Further to this, in the area of cognitive psychology, an example of the distinction between declarative and procedural representations is embodied in the "direct versus indirect perception issue" and the problem of stimulus transduction raised over the last 20 years. Put simply, such problems are focused on the issue as to where, in the biological information processing system, specific transformations of information occur which result in a different level of symbolic processing. An example of this is in the idea that the conscious brain works purely at the symbolic level whereas the *preattentive* or *automatic* stage of information processing occurs at a procedural level which is devoid of any explicit or conscious symbolic state.

Another area where the issue of procedural and declarative representations is most important is expert systems. Expert systems typically have symbolic knowledge representations and, more often than not, are concerned with producing diagnoses, predictions, or analysis at this level. For example, in PROSPECTOR (Duda, Gaschnig, & Hart, 1979), the input information is contained within well-log data and the problem is to generate some symbolic rules based on specific patterns of this numerical information. In this area the numerical and symbolic descriptions are typically bound by weighting the *truth* or *strength* of given rules (Pearl, 1988). This type of direct binding also occurs in computer object recognition systems, expert systems where the symbolic description of object features are given evidence weights for indexing each object in the model database (see Jain, & Hoffman, 1988).

In the following section we will show that in the areas of artificial intelligence, cognitive psychology, and expert systems, further analyses of the relationship between procedural and declarative representations, per se, is still needed. To do this adequately we must have some formal way of analyzing the differences between these representations, to create bridges between the structures used within each type of representation, and develop objective criteria for assessment of whether such connections are valid or not.

CURRENT STATUS OF DECLARATIVE AND PROCEDURAL MODELS IN COGNITIVE SCIENCE

Cognitive Psychology

Although cognitive psychology covers a wide variety of information-processing problems, here we focus upon the issue of representing perceptual events: how such events emerge from the characteristics of sensory-processing structures and the degree to which the evolution of symbolic "descriptions" of the world from within the brain are real or whether they are epiphenomena generated by "observers" to explicitly represent a set of procedures that lie beyond the scope of such symbolic systems.

The area of perception has many examples of incomplete integration of these two components of a model, varying from the analysis of sensory encoding through to higher-order domains of object recognition and issues about spatial organization. In the former case, many physiologists and psychologists have proposed an organization of the visual system to fit in with what we have assumed to be important "dimensions" based upon the ways physicists and engineers have symbolically defined features of objects. Consequently, motion, color, orientation, and size-specific *channels* have been discovered which, again, from a symbolic perspective, are intended to encode such image qualities as are current in our normal language. All these dimensions have states and, for many years, the search was for detectors, encoders, and so on, which would delimit the actual number of states in each channel. However, as Teller (1984) has recently pointed out, the underlying neural networks which process signals are highly interactive, nonlinear, and sufficiently adaptive to task demands so that it is incorrect to explain or bind such symbolic descriptions with elementary isolated, parameter-state indexed processing units. This is not to imply that our inherited descriptions of spatial information have no foundations in neurophysiology — such a claim would be ludicrous from a functionalist's perspective. Rather, Teller's point is that the *linking hypotheses* used by many psychologists to "explain" human behavior are not logically consistent, mainly due to the fallacy of the Neuron Doctrine (see, for example, Barlow, 1972), that an individual neuron constitutes the fundamental encoding element independent of its connections and control by others.

Another area of perceptual analysis where there is inadequate connection between symbolic and procedural levels of representation is that of mental imagery or spatial cognition: the study of our abilities to store, manipulate, and retrieve information about the three-dimensional (3D) world. For the past two decades, a number of authors have argued that there are processes (undefined) within the brain which allow us to have a 3D model of the world analogous to what is "out there." Examples include explanations for the time taken to mentally rotate 3D objects in terms of the physical analog: Time varies with degree of rotation (Shepard, & Metzler, 1988). Other examples include "models" for 3D object recognition in terms of an internal system which compares stored model parts with image parts, all being encoded by generalized cylinders (*geons*; Biederman, 1987).

The limitations of such theories are that they do not provide any symbolic calculus which delimits how "parts" are defined, how many there are, what their unary and binary predicates are, and how they are learned. Secondly, such descriptions of spatial cognition do not relate symbolic representations to processing characteristics. For example, there are many ways in which model parts can be matched to data parts, including depth-first search, parallel search, and efficient decision-tree procedures which produce very different predictions about search time.

In summary, then, there still exist fundamental problems as to how declarative and procedural representations for cognitive function are related. Most "models" fall down on the procedural side and solutions to this imbalance are recently being approached through the application of neural networks or connectionist ideas and paradigms. However, we will argue in a following section that additional constraints must be added to basic neural networks in order to produce adequate syntheses of both levels of representation.

Artificial Intelligence/Expert Systems

Artificial intelligence, like cognitive psychology, focuses on a variety of different intelligent information-processing domains from computer vision, language understanding, memory, and the creation of systems that behave in complex tasks as humans do. As in cognitive psychology, the choice of representations has largely been determined by the substantive characteristics of the specific problem domain to the extent that, for example, much of computer vision has been concerned with numerical or procedural representations whereas in the area of logic, spatial reasoning, and so on, the emphasis has been on symbolic or declarative language. This latter level of analysis has dominated artificial intelligence over the last 30 years. A good example of this is in the area of machine learning. Symbolic learning is much more difficult than numerical learning: Not only are there challenges to classical first-order (monotonic) logic approaches since learning, per se, involves the accumulation and assimilation of new knowledge within a logical framework, but also the very process of symbolic generalization (induction) as a symbolic process is impossible to restrict, by definition, to a fixed set of elements.

Broadly speaking, symbolic tools in artificial intelligence involve the implementation of the predicate calculus (logic) into data structures and program flow which will allow verification (true/false); the storage of data in clause form or simple logical data structures; and the ability to deduce conclusions from axioms based on a variety of logical devices like resolution proof, modus ponens, modus tolens, and instantiation. Each verification procedure determines the type of search algorithm involved. For example, when verification requires simple instantiation then the data structure is usually a tree where children of a given node constitute instances of that node with respect to other features.

In contrast, numerical or procedural representations usually involve a selection of discrete or continuous variables which permit rules with graded evaluation functions which also must satisfy given algebraic structures (for example, satisfy group axioms, etc).

Perhaps the most distinguishing factor in declarative representation is that the verification predicates themselves are typically categorical: a clause, rule, or fact is either true or false in accord with traditional logic. In contrast, numerical or procedural processes are not necessarily "true" or "false" in the same way. Verification of procedural representations usually lies within the domains of internal consistency, completeness, and production of interpretations of physical events that can predict or "fit" states of the world by criteria which are analytic or continuous in nature.

Whether it be with declarative or procedural representations, true insight into intelligent processing comes about by *delimiting (constraining) the processes* which operate in a given problem-solving situation. Indeed, an example of such insight is one of the fundamental axioms of artificial intelligence — namely that solutions to problems which reflect human behavior do not employ or check all possible states of a system but operate on a limited set of "default" states which are more likely (bounded rationally). We hope to show, in the next section, that such constraints are expressively incorporated in known constraint satisfaction networks and the integration between declarative and procedural representations must occur in terms of how symbolic descriptions of such networks are made parsimonious with what they do by such constraints.

Two important differences are visible in the comparison of the tools generated for analysis from these two perspectives. First, the level of domain "resolution" and domain "structures" in the symbolic area is not as rich as that of the numerical areas. Generic symbols, in contrast to number (symbols), do not necessarily have the properties that numerical forms have. Secondly, declarative levels or representation usually define the system constraints and problem goals explicitly. This is particularly evident in the evolution of "shells" which allow system developers to choose the database structures, rule and inference preferences, and search procedures to fit in with the problem being analyzed.

An example of such "control" properties of declarative procedures is the area of *picture languages* and, in particular, the works of Waltz (1975) and Tenenbaum and Barrow (1976). Waltz's task was the now classical problem of identifying polyhedral objects from line and line intersection types. Tenenbaum and Barrow's task was interpreting regions corresponding to parts of the interior of a room through constraint satisfaction procedures: Region labels are updated as a function of their compatibilities with others. Both analyses were based upon symbolic constraint satisfaction on line and region relations, respectively. However, what differentiated them was the *way* in which constraints were used to update labels. In Waltz's case the models were stored in a tree structure and so the matching was accomplished by (serial) tree search methods (pruning, etc). Tenenbaum and Barrow's method was based upon relaxation where the model data was stored in terms of relational matrices, or tables. The reason for such differences in underlying search procedures lies in the different symbolic structures employed. Objects defined by part unary and binary predicates are easily mapped into relaxation labeling procedures while objects defined by critical line features are more recognized through, essentially, decision trees.

A UNIFIED PERSPECTIVE

We conclude from the above discussion that symbolic descriptions or representations are supported, validated, and implemented through data structures and search algorithms which are based on specific procedures which underpin each symbolic state. Each such processing unit itself can be represented symbolically only to be subserved by another procedural level which is used to verify that particular element of the system. In other words, we see the difference between declarative and procedural representations to be relative: procedural representations subserving declarative structures, and this dependency may be duplicated across many levels. In other words, declarative and procedural differences are not absolute but relative to the "scale of analysis." Our unified perspective is that all cognitive processes are represented by predicates (symbolic representations) and processing networks (procedural components), and the relationship between these predicates, and associated network processing constraints, define a model.

In the case of picture languages, image symbols are associated with object world symbols. However, for such a symbolic system to produce "intepretations" of real-world data, a host of processes must be activated, from fundamental feature extraction through to symbolic search procedures. The symbolic representation indicates the types of constraints which must apply to define consistency, transitivities, and completeness. Representations can be viewed as extensions of current neural networks in the sense that they are *model based* where specific weights or specific connections are defined to capture different parts of the system for the information flow between input and output. In this sense, the declarative model not only serves as a description at the higher level but also defines *intentionality* in the system. Intentionality, in this sense, is a defining characteristic of the declarative representation insofar as it constrains the type of network connections and also determines the expected types of inputs and outputs in the system. In the following three subsections, we consider three specific ways in which declarative and procedural information can be integrated.

Solution 1: Model-Based Neural Networks

In an unconstrained (neural) network, be it associative (correlation-type) or additive memory, connections between elements are defined by a connectivity matrix w_{ij} and, across all hidden layers, each connection is assumed to be independent of the other and is normally estimated as an independent element. Techniques like stochastic relaxation and back-propagation are used to estimate the appropriate feature weights in extremely high-dimensional network state spaces, and such solutions do not usually generalize very well (see Hinton, 1989). Model-based methods essentially constrain the search by placing algebraic functional constraints on the relationships between connections (w_{ij}) and actual node (x_i, x_j) states at the *declarative* level. For example, it may well be the case that at one level, say e, w_{ij}^e is Gaussian distributed over all j for each i with the same sigma (variance). This would render w_{ij}^e, a low-pass filter which produces a Gaussian weighted input to each node i (level e) from all elements x_j at level e-1.

Further, the choice of sigma may be determined by the known size or aperture required to obtain such measures — again, an explicit (symbolic) constraint on the network. Alternatively such sigmas may be estimated to minimize some objective criterion, like maximizing signal-to-noise ratio, guaranteeing that specific sized regions can be detected, and so on. The estimation of w_{ij}'s in this case is defined by the theory of *adaptive filters* (Haykin, 1986). It is the authors' belief that more appropriate and successful use of neural networks comes from the involvement of such symbolic constraints on the information flow through the system, an integration of procedural and declarative levels of representation.

To illustrate these points consider the recent study by Plaut and Hinton (1987) on the recognition of "risers" and "non-risers" in speech recognition. The task of their neural network was to determine weights between input, one hidden layer, and one output (2 nodes) layer of elements which discriminate between the two types of audiograms. Since such input data is defined by a two-dimensional (causal) array of time/frequency amplitude information (in discrete form), the task essentially reduces to that of finding a specific edge or curved line in the data $I(t,f)$. Rather than estimate the appropriate weights in a high-dimensional feature space, the problem could have been reformulated in terms of determining the edges or curves in these images and then using the edge strength, orientation, or estimated curve parameters to decide the existence of a riser or not. Such prior (symbolic) constraints on the recognition problem reduce the parameter estimation task to very few parameters, in contrast to the basic neural network method used, with no constraints, on the system identification procedure. In these cases, model-based neural networks reduce to adaptive filters which involve procedures which are *constrained* by a symbolic or declarative level of representing the network *and* the goals of the system (for example, maximizing between class and minimizing within class variance).

Solution 2: Hybrid Numerical/Symbolic Constraint Satisfaction

Another area where it seems possible, already, to see how declarative and procedural representations can fit into a single network is that of parallel relaxation labeling as used in the areas of picture languages or image interpretation. In general, (parallel) relaxation labeling assumes the form:

$$P_j^{t+1}(\text{i}) = N \{p_j^t(\text{i}) + \sum_{hk} c(i,j;h,k) \cdot p_k^t(h)\} \qquad (1)$$

where i and h correspond to data parts, j and k to their respective labels, $p_j^t(i)$ to the probability that part i is labeled j at time t, and N is a normalization function to guarantee all probabilities (weights) fall within the unit interval and sum of one. Finally, $c(i,j;h,k)$ corresponds to the label "compatibility function," which is usually defined as positive for situations where the pair of labels are "compatible," negative if "incompatible," and zero if "irrelevant."

Such compatibility functions (network weighting functions) can be replaced by higher level symbolic rules which can be used to update label probabilities. As with Tenenbaum and Barrow's region identification process, we can set up rules in terms of tables of possible combinations of labels, as a function of given relationships between positions. Within each table is a weight value which defines the "compatibility" between such labels. That is, conditional rules can be defined by such functions as:

$$C_R(i,j;h,k) \equiv R(h(i,j),k(i,j)) \qquad (2)$$

where R defines the specific relation, and $h(i,j)$ and $k(i,j)$ define the contingencies between labels h,k as a function of the part positions. Such weights can vary from (± 1), equivalent to (TRUE/FALSE) and so differ from the analytic form of the compatibility function insofar as they assume discrete values and is explicitly contingent on label and position states. For example, such C_R tables Equation 2 would involve the types of labels (h,k) which can occur between adjacent parts (defined by (i,j)). The symbolic characteristics of the set of C_R tables defines the image interpretation system and so controls the relaxation network in Equation 1: the control of a procedural process by, again, symbolic constraints.

A CASE STUDY:
EVIDENCE-BASED OBJECT RECOGNITION SYSTEMS

The study of object recognition systems is interesting (and difficult) since the systems usually involve reasoning with incomplete data insofar as image data only contains parts of objects. Secondly, except for defining objects by some explicit view-independent continuous numerical representation, most models are defined by parts (usually surface parts) and their unary, binary features. Though such features usually have parametric states, they are defined, as operators, symbolically. For example, unary predicates like area,

$(A(x))$, perimeter $(P(x))$, curvature $(C(x))$ and binary predicates such as adjacency $(Ad(x,y))$, distance $(D(x,y))$, surface normal angular differences $(N(x,y))$, are predicates defined over numerical images which delimit different object models.

Jain and Hoffman's (1988) recognition system shows how both procedural and declarative representations can be integrated in this domain. First a database is formed by determining all unary and binary predicates of parts[1] over sufficient views of all objects to cover all surface information or parts. Such features are then converted into a rule-based database where the rules are automatically generated to optimize the recognition procedure. Object recognition is difficult insofar as each object is not defined by a set of common features which occur in every instance, the feature ranges cannot be partitioned into bins as is typical of inductive learning procedures (Michalski & Stepp, 1983), and not every feature is defined for every instance (view). Consequently their rulebase generation strategy proceeds as follows. For n 3D objects (n "classes"), each class, c, is assumed to have n_c sample views ("instances"), giving a total of $N = \sum\limits_{c=1}^{n} n_c$ views. For each view m, $1 \leqslant m \leqslant N$ a number feature properties are observed, making a representation R_m of the view:

$$R_m = \{V_m^1, V_m^2, \ldots, V_m^h\}$$

where each V_m is a *list* of features (vectors) of a specific type of property, predefined (for example, unary, binary, etc). Given all representations $\{R_1, \ldots, R_N\}$ the collection of all features V_t can be determined as:

$$V_t = \bigcup\limits_{m=1}^{N} V_m^t.$$

Jain and Hoffman define a rule Σ as consisting of the 4-tuple:

$$\Sigma \equiv \{F, B, \theta, W\}$$

where F is the feature list (corresponding to V^t), B the feature list bounds, θ a morphological feature (to be ignored in this discussion), and most importantly, W, a list of evidence weights (vector) corresponding to the degree to which satisfying the feature list bounds supports the hypothesis that the observed object is of class (type) n.

---

[1] For simplicity, we will omit the issue related to model and data-part generation and simply assume that both are compatible such that all unary and binary predicates can be evaluated in both domains.

The rule-base generation method attempts to ensure that every instance (i) of every class (c) should satisfy:

$A(i,c)$ = true, if, and only if, instance i of class c is satisfied by at least one rule whose W has:

$$w_c \neq 1 \text{ (major evidence constraint) and}$$
$$w_j \neq 1 \; \forall_j \neq c \text{ (uniqueness constraint).}$$

Given a set of individual features, the rule generation process determines feature bounds (ranges) which, over all objects and instances (views), retain only those feature groupings which satisfy the above uniqueness condition, including negative weights ($w_c < 0$) for cases where evidence refutes the presence of a given object.

The rule structure Σ is the basis of the *parallel certainty inference technique* (PCIT) as used in a number of expert systems including MYCIN (Shortliffe & Buchanan, 1975) and PROSPECTOR (Duda, Gaschnig, & Hart, 1979). In such systems, recognition occurs by determining which rules are satisfied in the data and by comparing the evidence weights across objects over all rules. Examples of rules are (Jain & Hoffman, 1988):

1. The perimeter is greater than 20 < general rule >

   {-0.5, -0.5, -0.5, -0.5, 0.5, -1.0, -0.5, -0.5, 0.5, 0.5}

2. There is a jump edge between a convex surface of area 6 to 16 and a concave surface of area 2 to 8, and the jump gap is between 2.5 and 3.5 < cup rule >:

   {-1.0, 1.0, 0.0, -1.0, 0.5, -1.0, -1.0, -1.0, -1.0, 0.0}

Here the rules are either individual features (Equation 1) or combination of features (Equation 2) and the weights correspond to the degree to which support for this rule indicates the existence of a given object (in this case there were 10 objects).

The PCIT is similar to Baysian inference techniques and the Dempster-Shafer theory (Shafer, 1976) insofar as weights are generated conditional on hypotheses about the presence of objects: how the declarative (rule) and numerical (evidence weights) components are related.

Further, procedural issues like the ordering or rule evaluation (etc.), can be determined from a comparison between the weights. For example, the rules can even be arranged into a decision-tree structure or simple linear list as a function of their relative strengths, or ability to differentiate classes of objects.

CONCLUSIONS

We have argued here that procedural and declarative representations complement each other and that both are necessary for the evolution of a model for cognitive function. Declarative representations are devoid of processing characteristics except for those which implicitly delimit the types of data structures, rules, and inference mechanisms required in the explication of the symbolic analysis. On the other hand, procedural representations can neither be analyzed, per se, or constrained to produce what we would accept as "tractable" models for function, without the use of explicit symbolic representations for the system, its goals and processing characteristics.

Three major ways of integrating both levels of analysis have been discussed: model-based networks, rule-based relaxation techniques, and evidence-based inference techniques. In all cases the transformations between symbolic and numerical domains are defined, essentially, by conditional and/or compatibility tables. However, they differ in the types of search techniques and ways the rules are defined. In the first two methods compatibility or consistency is checked at the procedural level insofar as information flow is dynamically controlled by compatibility (for example, dynamical update of labels). In the latter case, however, compatibility is defined and derived in the establishment of rules, which include all unary and binary predicates.

REFERENCES

Barlow, H. (1972). Single units and sensation: A neuron doctrine for perceptical psychology? *Perception, 1,* 371-394.

Biederman, I. (1987). Recognition-by-components: A theory of human image understanding. *Psychological Review, 94,* 115-147.

Duda, R., Gaschnig, J., & Hart, P. (1979). Model design in the prospector consultant system for mineral exploration. In D. Michie (Ed.), *Expert systems in the microelectronic age* (pp. 153-167). Edinburgh, Scotland: Edinburgh University Press.

Haykin, S. (1986). *Adaptive filter theory.* Englewood Cliffs, NJ: Prentice-Hall.

Hinton, G. (1989). Connectionist learning procedures. *Artificial Intelligence, 40,* 185-234.

Jain, A., & Hoffman, R. (1988). Evidence-based recognition of 3-D objects. *IEEE Transactions on Pattern Analysis and Machine Intelligence, 10* (6), 783-802.

Michaelski, R., & Stepp, R. (1983) Automated construction of classification: conceptual clustering versus numerical taxonomy. *IEEE Transactions on Pattern Analysis and Machine Intelligence, 5,* 396-409.

Pearl, J. (1988). *Probabilistic reasoning in intelligent systems.* San Mateo, CA: Morgan Kaufman.

Plaut, D., & Hinton, G. (1987). Learning set of filters using back-propagation. *Computer Speech Language, 2,* 36-61.

Shafer, G. (1976). *A mathematical theory of evidence.* New Brunswick, NJ: Princeton University Press.

Shepard, S., & Metzler, D. (1988). Mental rotation: Effects of dimensionality of objects and type of task. *Journal of Experimental Psychology: Human Perception and Performance, 14* (1), 3-11.

Shortliffe, E., & Buchanan, B. (1975). A model of inexact reasoning in medicine. *Mathematical Biosciences, 23,* 351-379.

Teller, D. (1984). Linking propositions. *Vision Research, 24,* 1233-1246.

Tenenbaum, J., & Barrow, H. (1976). Experiments in interpretation — Guided segmentation. *Stanford Research Institute Technology, Note 123.* Palo Alto, CA: Stanford University.

Waltz, D. (1975). Understanding line drawings of scenes with shadows. In P. Winston (Ed.), *The psychology of computer vision* (pp. 19-91). New York: McGraw-Hill.

CHAPTER 17

The "Philosophical" Case Against Visual Imagery *

Peter Slezak

*Program in Cognitive Science,
University of New South Wales*

IMPASSE IN THE IMAGERY DEBATE:
PICTURES OR 'TACIT KNOWLEDGE'

The "Imagery Debate" concerning the iconic or pictorial explanation of visual imagery was characterized as "one of the hottest topics" in cognitive science a few years ago (Block, 1981, p.1). This followed upon the now familiar claims which Block describes as "amazing" by Shepard and Metzler (1971) and Kosslyn, Pinker, Smith & Schwartz (1979) concerning the rotation and scanning of images. Based on these investigations, the representational medium underlying imagery has been taken to represent in the manner of pictures by virtue of some relation of resemblance to its referents. On the other side, opposed to this conception have been what are usually characterized as "philosophical" arguments in favor of a descriptive or propositional mode of representation which takes the representational medium to have a 'format' which is more abstract and, in particular, more

* The title is intended to be doubly ironic. The term "philosophical" to characterize the 'tacit knowledge' theory is used as a pejorative epithet by its psychologist critics in order to distinguish it from "empirical," "theoretical" or perhaps even "scientific" theories. Likewise, the title's implication that the theory in question rejects visual imagery is a common misconception which the paper is concerned to reject. Preliminary reports of this work have been presented to Brisbane Cognitive Science Society at Griffiths University, Queensland on August 7, 1989, Australasian Association of Philosophy, University of Sydney on July 1 1990, Australasian Society for Cognitive Science, November 5, 1990, Department of Psychology at the University of Sydney on March 18, 1991, 13th Annual Meeting of the U.S. Cognitive Science Society at the University of Chicago on August 8th, 1991, AAAI Spring Symposium at Stanford University, March 25, 1992, 14th Annual Meeting of the U.S. Cognitive Science Society at the University of Indiana August, 1992. I am grateful to Max Coltheart, Ronald Finke, Jim Franklin, Gillian Rhodes, Daniel Reisberg, Irvin Rock and Mark Rollins for valuable comments and criticism of earlier versions of the paper. I am especially indebted to Nigel Thomas for his most extensive, detailed comments and discussion which have led to many improvements. Thanks also to Graham Mann for assistance with the experiments. The research reported here was partly supported by a grant from the Centre for Cognitive Science at the University of New South Wales.

highly cognitive. Principal advocate of this alternative 'tacit knowledge' view
has been Zenon Pylyshyn (1973, 1981).

Central to the debate has been the notorious difficulty of explaining the
precise sense in which mental representations might be pictorial without being
literally pictures in the head. Nigel Thomas (1989, 1990) has made the
important point that pictorialist assumptions are built into the word *image*
itself, prejudicing the very formulation of the problem and making it difficult
to express and conceive criticisms which do not seem to deny the empirical
phenomena themselves. Thus, although fully aware of the problem *in
principle,* the leading theorists have nonetheless failed to convince critics that
they have avoided the difficulties *in practice* in the formulation of their
theories. Finke (1989) accurately captures the issue, saying:

> Most people doing imagery research today acknowledge that the picture
> metaphor should not be taken too literally. The question of current
> interest is not whether images function in exactly the same way as pictures,
> but *whether images share any properties in common with pictures.* (1989,
> p.18; emphasis added)

Although Finke is clearly sensitive to the problem, his question may be
seen as still embodying pictorialist assumptions in the very idea that there
might be some kind of objects such as "images" of which one can meaningfully
inquire whether they have properties shared by pictures. However, alternative
theoretical conceptions of the phenomena need not share these assumptions
and this entire conception of the problem is subtly biased in favor of pictorial
theories. The fundamental question, then, is whether it is possible to have
some of the apparent advantages of pictures without incurring their notorious
problems. It is noteworthy that these problems are precisely the same ones
against which Bartlett (1932) warned in his classical work when criticizing
theories of memory as "reduplicative" and images as "fixed, lifeless and
fragmentary traces" (p.213), "made complete at one moment, stored up
somewhere, and then re-excited at some much later moment" (p. 211).

Nontheless, Kosslyn, Van Kleeck and Kirby (1990) have recently discussed
the results of certain chemical treatments of the monkey or rat brain which
they suggest will clinch the argument in favor of the pictorial theory. Kosslyn
et al. (1990) use the metaphor of "developing" the cortex like a photographic
plate to reveal a retinotopic "picture" of the original stimulus. In the light
of this optimism, there is a certain irony in much earlier remarks by B.F.
Skinner which challenged the pictorialist account:

> At some point the organism must do more than create duplicates. . . . .
> The need for something beyond and quite different from copying is not
> widely understood. Suppose someone were to coat the occipital lobes
> of the brain with a special photographic emulsion which, when developed,

yielded a reasonable copy of a current visual stimulus. In many quarters this would be regarded as a triumph in the physiology of vision. Yet nothing could be more disastrous . . . (1963).

Although we are unable to accept Skinner's particular solution, it is perhaps not surprising that he should see the *problem* very clearly in the dangers of homunculus pseudo-explanations.[1] As we will note below, the same insights were clearly articulated by Descartes 300 years earlier.

NEW FOCUS ON REINTERPRETING IMAGES

The extraordinary persistence of the debate suggests that the fundamental problems are not straightforward empirical issues as some psychologists have suggested (Finke, 1989). The "new" solution of Kosslyn et al. (1990) suggests that, notwithstanding the extensive research, there appears to have been little progress on the fundamental theoretical questions. After 20 years of the recent controversy, the debate is widely regarded as having become stalled, with no new ideas on how to break the impasse by bringing some decisive evidence to bear. If there has been some waning of interest in the "imagery debate" since its heyday as the "hottest topic" in cognitive science, this is not because of any evident resolution of the issues. On the contrary, the contending positions are as entrenched as ever, declaring the demise of their opposition. For example, in the light of the accumulated evidence, Finke (1990, p. 19) asserts that propositional accounts "no longer present a serious challenge to imagery research," whereas, on the other side, Thomas (1990, p. 5) says "When all the empirical objections are taken together, the [pictorial] theory can hardly stand against them, being, if not refuted, at best so compromised and qualified as to become effectively empty."

Clearly, the intellectual challenge remains, although the deadlock has even led some (Anderson 1978) to conclude that the issue between pictorialism and the propositional alternative is undecidable in principle on the basis of behavioral evidence. On the contrary, however, the experiments reported here show that divergent predictions from the contending theories may be readily formulated and tested with an appropriate experimental paradigm.

More recently, experimental research appears simply to have ignored the original imagery debate concerning the "format" question, focussing instead on the more direct empirical issue of whether, and under what conditions, images can be re-interpreted (Chambers and Reisberg 1992, Peterson, Kihlstrom, Rose and Glisky 1992, Riesberg and Chambers 1991). Although these investigations neglect the theoretical question at the heart of "the" imagery debate, they may be seen to have the most direct bearing as tests of the competing theories.

---

[1] See D. Dennett's 'Skinner Skinned' in Dennett (1978).

UNDERDETERMINATION OF THEORY
BY CHRONOMETRIC EVIDENCE

The celebrated experiments of Shepard on mental rotation and those of Kosslyn on mental scanning have provided undeniably striking linearities which require explanation. The postulate of an analog medium having spatial properties purports to be one such explanation since the reaction-time data are taken to be a predictable consequence of the intrinsic properties of the medium. However, this particular postulate does not exhaust the explanations which might be given for these data and Pylyshyn's tacit knowledge account purports to be an alternative explanation of the *same data*. The imagery debate has come to appear intractable because of the fact that the two theories make *identical predictions* for chronometric evidence and, accordingly, adducing new experimental evidence of time-dependent measures — as Kosslyn has repeatedly done — cannot strengthen the case for a pictorial, spatial medium against the tacit knowledge theory. Resort must be made to some alternative kind of experimental data. Our own investigations, like those of Chambers and Reisberg (1985), derive their interest for the imagery debate by resorting to independent kinds of evidence on which the contending theories give divergent predictions.

The issue of reinterpreting visual patterns in mental imagery may be seen in this way as a new focus for the controversy, since the question of whether, and under what conditions, novel information may be discovered from images provides a new means for testing the properties of the conjectured pictorial medium and the claimed parallel between imagery and perception. Our own evidence concerns perceptual organization tasks which provide unequivocal, non-chronometric evidence of the successful rotation, inspection and re-interpretation of images using "recognition processes" and "shape classification" procedures. Despite the demonstrated ease of our tasks under perceptual conditions, naive subjects have generally been unable to succeed in the tasks under imagery conditions as would be predicted on the pictorial theory. Just as in the case of the "crucial experiment" of Michelson and Morley concerning the speed of light, one might conclude from our null results that the pictorial medium, like the luminiferous ether, does not exist. However, as familiar from the history of science, and indeed as our own experiments have shown, the situation is somewhat more complicated. Historians and philosophers of science well know there can be no such thing as a "crucial experiment" as such, since there are always means of avoiding the implications of what is *prima facie* negative evidence for any theory. Thus, the situation in the imagery debate has now become less a matter of deciding between predictively equivalent theories than a matter of comparing their respective virtues according to the usual criteria of explanatory adequacy, comprehensiveness and simplicity etc., in relation to the full set of available evidence. Above all, rather than *supporting* evidence being proferred in a partisan manner as "refuting" the competing theory (Finke, Pinker, and Farah 1989), there is a need to show how the theories can accommodate the seemingly *inconsistent* data. That is, there is an acute need for both accounts to develop theoretically motivated explanations for their respective *anomalies* rather than merely adducing supporting evidence. The recent studies generating seemingly inconsistent evidence on image reconstrual provide an opportunity for considering the precise significance of the varying experimental conditions.

DIVERGENT PREDICTIONS

The possibility of reinterpreting an image follows as a direct implication of pictorial theories of the imaginal medium, since on such accounts the image is taken to be a display in a visual buffer having spatial properties to which the perceptual apparatus itself is applied. Thus, Kosslyn explains that his model entails that "images depict visual information, and that this information is interpreted by some of the same sorts of classificatory procedures used in classifying sensory input during vision" (1980, p. 32). Kosslyn explains further that "the purposes of imagery, in large part, parallel those of vision" and "one may 'recognize' parts and properties of imaged objects that had not been previously considered" through the "use of recognition processes" (1987, p. 149). Thus, the significance of reinterpreting images as a crucial test of the pictorial theory is evident in Kosslyn's explicit predictions:

> The image is formed by forcing a change of state in the visual buffer in the attended region, *which can then be reprocessed as if it were perceptual input (e.g., the shape could be recategorized),* thereby accomplishing the purposes of imagery that parallel those of perception. (1987, p. 155; emphasis added)

By contrast with the direct implications of the quasiperceptual, pictorial-medium theory, the 'tacit knowledge' account would predict that the reinterpretation of images is difficult because it takes the mental representations to be highly abstract entities which are the output of 'higher' cognitive processes; these are encodings of conceptualizations or beliefs and, in this sense, already meaningful and not requiring interpretation, nor susceptible to *easy* reinterpretation (Pylyshyn 1973, 1978).

CONFLICTING EVIDENCE

The experiments reported here tested the radically divergent predictions of the two contending theories on this question of reinterpretation of images.

In particular, we tested the ability of subjects to perform tasks in imagery which have been widely taken as firmly established, namely, those of rotating and inspecting figures in order to apply "recognition processes," "shape classification" procedures and "creative mental synthesis" in order to discover a new intepretation of the figures. These are, after all, the abilities which Kosslyn has taken to be the very function and central purpose of imagery.

This question of reinterpreting visual images had been brought into sharp relief with the work of Chambers and Reisberg (1985) who found that subjects were uniformly unable to reverse their mental images of the familiar ambiguous figures such as the duck/rabbit and Necker Cube. Chambers and Reisberg concluded that their results show that images cannot be re-construed because they are not independent entities to be construed at all in the first place, but are intrinsically meaningful symbols. Since the close parallel, indeed "equivalence" of imagery with the mechanisms of perception has been one of the central tenets of the pictorialist theory (Farah, 1988; Finke, 1980; Podgorny & Shepard, 1978), the results of Chambers and Reisberg are surprising and may be seen as posing a fundamental challenge for the pictorial orthodoxy.

Of course, the negative results of Chambers and Reisberg provided experimental support for the specific claims made over a decade ago by Pylyshyn (1973, 1978) in his critiques of pictorial theories:

> Although there are similarities between cognitive operations in perception and in imagining, there are also some outstanding differences that may be more revealing of the underlying processes. For example, the order of scanning and the sorts of things that can be "noticed" in imaging are much more constrained than in perception. The reason for this is partly that a scene has a stable independent existence and can be reexamined at will to produce new interpretations. In contrast, the construction of an internal description from stored knowledge can hardly be divorced from its interpretation. While some reinterpretation is certainly possible, it surely is more like the derivation of new entailments from stored knowledge than like the discovery of new aspects of an environment by the usual visual means. Discovering even moderately novel readings from a mental image ... have been shown to be exceedingly difficult. (1978, p. 37)

Despite these earlier skeptical claims, in the intervening period there has been experimental evidence of just such abilities of people to detect novel properties in imagined or remembered scenes. Thus, for example, Pinker and Finke (1980) report subjects' ability to "see" novel properties which should emerge in images only after mental rotation. Subjects were asked to perform tasks which demanded the ability to "see" new two-dimensional patterns that should emerge after rotating an image only if the image depicts the new perspective accurately. Central to the present study is just this possibility of pattern recognition within imagery which is a clear entailment of the pictorial theory. As Pinker and Finke claim, the properties of images "can be 'read off' the display" (1980, p. 262). Finke and Slayton (1988) have extended this work, providing further evidence "that people are capable of making unexpected discoveries in imagery" and that novel patterns can "emerge" from within imaged patterns.

Most recently in this vein, Finke, Pinker, and Farah (1989) have sought to reinforce these claims with new experiments which also purport to show that subjects can inspect and reinterpret their images by "applying shape classification procedures to the information in imagery" (1989, p. 51). This latter work is of particular interest because it has been specifically designed to counter the skeptical conclusions warranted by the negative results of Chambers and Reisberg (1985). Thus, it is in the light of this clash of experimental results and theoretical claims that our own experiments are to be understood: Though *prima facie* falsifying central entailments of the pictorial medium theory, our own negative results can be seen more neutrally as illuminating the precise conditions under which such seemingly contradictory results can be obtained.[2]

Of course, only theories, and not the world, can embody contradictions. Thus it is ultimately fruitless for the protagonists in the imagery debate to continue counterposing empirical results with only a minimum of theoretical analysis as if these speak for themselves. The cloudiness of the present situation and the intractability of the debate is symptomatic of fundamental conceptual problems rather than straightforward empirical issues. Consequently, even more than new experiments, there is a need for careful theoretical analysis which will clarify the causes of discrepant results and their implications.

THE "PHILOSOPHICAL" AND THE "STRICTLY EMPIRICAL"

A certain impatience with such theoretical analyses is evident in Finke's (1989) recent comments on the issue: After acknowledging the seriousness of the challenge posed by the investigation of Chambers and Reisberg (1985), Finke (1989) only mentions the principal alternative theory (Fodor, 1975) in passing, and implies its relative unimportance saying that, by contrast with such

---

[2] Independently, Reisberg and Chambers (1991) have conducted experiments in a similar vein which illuminate precisely these more specific questions of "when we *can* and when we *cannot* make new discoveries in our own mental images." Notwithstanding methodological similarities, differences in important details between the two inquiries makes them complement one another with regard to this central question. Furthermore, although both investigations bear on this issue of the exact conditions under which learning from images is possible, our own work here is concerned specifically with the notoriously unresolved 'format' question. By contrast, Reisberg and Chambers are not concerned with this issue and, indeed, where Kosslyn's pictorial theory is mentioned in passing, they say "we find these arguments [of Kosslyn's] fully persuasive."

considerations, "this is strictly an empirical question" which will be settled by the "evidence that mental images can be reinterpreted" (1989, p. 129). The seemingly contrary evidence of Finke, Pinker, and Farah (1989) undoubtedly shows, as Finke says, that "images *can* be reinterpreted." But, of course, this only begs the central question: What is the reason for the discrepancy? That is, since the *prima facie* conflict among the data is the source of the problem, they cannot be appealed to on either side as "strictly an empirical question" which can settle the matter.

The common designation of "philosophical" for the tacit knowledge position by its critics is a peculiar, though telling, terminological symptom of the difficulties we have been intimating: the conception of the tacit knowledge account as "philosophical" reflects some invidious, if obscure, comparison between rival theories which are, in fact, identical in status as competing explanations of the evidence. We see the same notion that the central issues are somehow really "empirical" where Finke et al. (1989) write: "Arguments in the philosophical literature on imagery, such as those cited by Chambers and Reisberg, have no relevance to this strictly empirical question" (p. 54). On the contrary, however, I will indicate certain long-familiar philosophical arguments have the most direct bearing on the "strictly empirical question", and a greater sensitivity to these arguments might have helped avoid the persistent misunderstandings. The views just noted betray a certain vestige of positivist or behaviorist faith in the unambiguous and supposedly definitive deliverances of observational evidence. However, among the insights familiar to philosophers is the fact that there is no such thing as a "strictly empirical question." As Duhem, Quine, Hanson, Kuhn and others have made well-known, all possible empirical evidence must under-determine any theory. Correspondingly, on the other hand, a theory is just a theory and the tacit knowledge account is no more and no less than a competing explanation on a par with its pictorial rival. Misunderstanding on this point has not been irrelevant to the persistence of the dispute, since the characterization of the tacit knowledge theory as "philosophical" has led to its peremptory dismissal and to a systematic neglect of its explanatory force. Accordingly, it is instructive to survey some of the confusions which have bedevilled the dispute.

TACIT KNOWLEDGE OF WHAT?

"No imagery account"?

I have noted that the alleged import of additional *chronometric* evidence has been misunderstood. Just as adducing further reaction-time evidence of the very kind in dispute cannot support pictorialism, so it has been a related mistake to construe the tacit knowledge theory as denying the reality of imagery phenomena. Kosslyn (1980, p. 30) has tellingly described the tacit knowledge opposition as a "no imagery" account as if it purported to deny the existence or reality of visual imagery which his data confirms. This is a serious misunderstanding, since the tacit knowledge account denies only a *pictorial medium* as explanation of the imagery data and proposes another explanation of the *very same data.* Kosslyn's two related tactics — namely, adducing further chronometric data and misconstruing the tacit knowledge theory as denying imagery — amount to resolving the issue by fiat. This approach is simply legislating pictorialism true by taking the chronometric evidence to somehow uniquely favor or even establish the pictorial theory.

Knowledge of laboratory experiments?

This misunderstanding of the tacit knowledge account is manifest in the methodological design of experiments which have been taken to bear on the dispute. Thus, it is significant that Kosslyn (1983) has tried to deflect tacit knowledge explanations of imagery phenomena by noting that subjects could not have produced the data in question from tacit knowledge because they could not have known about such surprising experimental phenomena as the McCullough effect and, therefore, could not plausibly be thought to have employed such knowledge in their performance. Kosslyn explains that "virtually nobody outside the field knows about the McCullough effect" and therefore "subjects could not have intentionally or unconsciously produced these results *without using imagery*" (1983, p. 81; emphasis added).

First, however, the issue cannot be whether the subjects used imagery as Kosslyn suggests here, since this is not in dispute. As already noted, the tacit knowledge theory does not deny that imagery is being used by subjects, but only offers a different explanation of it. The question is only how best to explain the phenomena in which subjects are, on all accounts, taken to be using imagery. In particular, it is no argument against the tacit knowledge theory to demonstrate how control subjects *not* using imagery give different results from those who do (Kosslyn, 1981, p. 61, Kosslyn, 1983, p. 59). Although this experimental design is conceived as having empirical bearing on the debate between the pictorial medium and the "philosophical" tacit knowledge accounts, it is *in principle* incapable of doing so. The control group in all of these cases is presumed not to be using imagery and therefore becomes utterly *irrelevant* to the disputed question of how the results are to be explained in the case when subjects *are* using imagery. Patently, controlling for the use of imagery can only establish the empirical importance of imagery as a variable and does not favor the pictorial medium account, unless the two are implicitly and illegitimately taken to be the same question.

Furthermore, the undoubted ignorance of the subjects concerning such experimental results is entirely irrelevant to the possibility of explaining them through tacit knowledge since there is nothing in the claim which requires that the relevant beliefs be *this* kind of belief. On the contrary, the idea of tacit knowledge is precisely the idea of beliefs which are unavailable to conscious awareness. Pylyshyn has been quite explicit on this question, noting that "much of it is not introspectable or verbally articulable" (1981, p. 161). Pylyshyn's notion of tacit knowledge is derived from what he describes as "one of the most powerful ideas to emerge from contemporary cognitive science" (1981, p. 161), citing Fodor's (1968) important articulation of the concept, which is paradigmatically exemplified in Chomsky's conception of our knowledge of grammatical rules. Accordingly, the appeal to tacit knowledge in the explanation of imagery is an appeal to rules and representations which are largely inaccessible to the subject and used automatically in the relevant behavior. In the present context, the appeal to tacit knowledge is to invoke what the subject knows implicitly about the *phenomena* being imagined, and emphatically not about the psychological experiment or its results as Kosslyn seems to think. Kosslyn makes the same serious mistake when he suggests that certain properties of imagery "are only manifest in highly novel laboratory settings, which precludes the subject from developing tacit knowledge about them from prior experience" (1981, p. 62). However, the relevant prior experience for acquiring tacit knowledge is not with the laboratory experiments, but with the normal use of the visual apparatus itself. The error of Kosslyn's argument can readily be seen if applied to the linguistic case: There are vastly many subtle properties of grammars which are "surprising and only manifest in highly novel laboratory settings," but it is transparently mistaken to suggest that this fact "precludes the subject from developing tacit knowledge about them from prior experience," as Kosslyn has suggested in the case of vision. The attribution of tacit knowledge is an attribution of principles which are acquired and employed in the normal use of the faculty in question. Like the rules of a grammar, these might be innate or learned, but are certainly not themselves dependent on having access to the psychologist's results and theories. Obviously humans develop their tacit knowledge of grammatical rules independently of the linguists' theory of them.

To serve the explanatory purpose for which it is intended, the idea of tacit knowledge must explain why imagined scanning or rotation should preserve certain response regularities. This explanatory goal is achieved (rightly or wrongly) through crediting the observed results to what subjects know and, therefore, expect to see. To appreciate the force of this kind of explanation, it is important to notice what *kind* of knowledge can serve this explanatory purpose. As already noted, in the present case, the imagery results are claimed to depend on what the subject believes about the "actual behavior *of the things represented*" (Pylyshyn, 1981, p. 157), that is, about what regularities hold *"in the world."* The observed regularities are attributed to the subject's beliefs and expectations rather than the biological properties of the representational medium. This is because the images *represent* rather than *instantiate* all the properties such as distance, shape, and so on, which are being tested for. In order for this point be as clear as possible, it must be emphasized that the content of the tacit knowledge is supposed to be the semantically interpreted entities which represent the objects being imagined. That is, the representations constitute "the subject's tacit knowledge *about the physical world*" (Pylyshyn, 1981, p. 162). Thus, the tacit beliefs are about the way objects move, or about the properties of space, or other such facts about the way the physical world behaves. Without rehearsing Pylyshyn's arguments here, it is important nevertheless to emphasize this point because it appears to be crucial to the misunderstandings in the imagery debate. The claim of the tacit knowledge account, then, is that the imagery phenomena are "a function of what principles one believes govern *the events in question*" (Pylyshyn, 1981, p. 169; emphasis added) or "what subjects believe about the world" (ibid, p. 164).

Non-visual knowledge?

Among pictorialists, Farah (1988) has described Pylyshyn's view as the argument "according to which subjects use *nonvisual* representations to simulate the use of visual representations during imagery tasks, guided by their tacit knowledge of their visual systems" (1988, p. 307, emphasis added). However, there is nothing in the tacit knowledge claims which entail that the representations employed are "nonvisual." The idea that a tacit knowledge theory denies the visual character of imagery is to conflate the "format" and "equivalence" claims, since imagery may be visual on the tacit knowledge theory, as well.

Knowledge of Visual System?

Nor, second, can the knowledge in question be construed as knowledge "of their visual systems" in the manner that Farah has taken it. Farah has considered "a tacit knowledge account of the electrophysiological and blood flow data" (1988, p. 314), and the tacit knowledge subjects might have of their normal and impaired brain. Assuming (on behalf of the alleged tacit knowledge view) that even patients with cerebral rather than peripheral disorders would be most likely to "simulate" a normal visual system leads to the prediction that they would give normal imagery performance in experiments. However, this prediction is not borne out by the available evidence and Farah takes this to count against a tacit knowledge theory. However, once again, it is only a *reductio ad absurdum* of the particular version of the theory which she has put forward. Just as the tacit knowledge position does not need to postulate a simulation of the visual system as such, it does not predict normal imagery in cases of cerebral disorders. Indeed, Farah's striking evidence of abnormal imagery in cases of cortical damage is entirely consistent with the tacit knowledge account, since it is not an intact visual system which is the actual *subject matter* of the beliefs posited, but only the real-world objects which would normally be perceived by an intact visual system. That such real-world knowledge should be impaired with cerebral disorders is exactly what the tacit knowledge account would predict, in line with the evidence. Farah notes the obvious implausibility of the supposition that subjects could know which parts of their brains are normally active during vision and, although she takes this as an objection to such tacit knowledge claims, it is clear that this conception could not be, and has not been, seriously proposed. Pylyshyn's conception of the relevant knowledge is an implicit physical theory about properties and regularities in the world. It is a tacit knowledge of "geometry and dynamics" (1981, p. 194), not physiology.

EQUIVALENCE OF IMAGERY AND PERCEPTION

The significance of nonchronometric tasks as "crucial experiments" derives from their testing direct implications of the pictorial theory. On the pictorial view, a mental image is conceived to be a "surrogate percept, allowing people to detect some pattern or property in a remembered scene that they did not encode explicitly when they saw the scene initially" (Pinker & Finke, 1980, p. 246). As already noted, Kosslyn, too, has argued that "the purposes of imagery, in large part, parallel those of vision" specifically in "the use of recognition processes" (1987, p. 149). Thus, Kosslyn claims that "one may 'recognize' parts and properties of imaged objects that had not been previously considered" (ibid). In particular, the *general* possibility of *re*interpreting an image follows as a direct implication of the pictorial account of the medium, since on this view the image is like the perceptual representations of early vision in the sense of being a raw display in a visual buffer having spatial properties.

   The general nature of this commitment to the possibility of reconstruing images is perfectly explicit in Finke et al. (1989), and Kosslyn also explains that his model entails that "images depict visual information, and that this information is interpreted by some of the same sorts of classificatory procedures used in classifying sensory input during vision" (1980, p. 32). Clearly a conception of images as quasipictorial "surface representations" which requires that they must be interpreted will also be committed to the claim that they may be *re*interpreted in general. It is in this spirit that Kosslyn has elaborated his model of the imaginal medium in terms of a CRT (cathode ray tube) spatial display in a visual buffer to which interpretive and other classificatory processes must be applied (1980, p. 34). It is in this sense that the uninterpreted images in a spatial medium are themselves "functionally equivalent to physical objects or events" (Finke, 1980, p. 113), and cause the same mechanisms to be activated as in actual visual perception itself (ibid, p. 130). On the orthodox pictorialist view, images are construed as 'surrogate percepts' (Pinker & Finke 1980, p. 246). Kosslyn (1987, p. 149) explains that one purpose of imagery involves "recognition processes" to discover information which is not stored explicitly in memory, and thus we "look" at our images in a way which is analogous to the way we look at external objects in order to inspect them.

The close modeling of visual imagery processes on those of visual perception is the source of its profound difficulties. It is important to notice the full extent and generality of this quasiperceptual conception of imagery. Pinker's recent survey explains:

> The study of [perceptual] shape recognition has led people to posit many types of operations that take as input array-like data structures created by sensory receptors, such as the $2_1/2$-D sketch, and it would be a short step to claim that *the same processes could access such data structures generated from memory rather than from the eyes.* (Pinker, 1984, p. 38; emphasis added).

Kosslyn, too, explains the way in which imagery is essentially identical in its mechanisms to perception:

> One purpose of imagery apparently relies on the use of recognition processes to make explicit information stored implicitly in memory. That is, people encode patterns without classifying them in all possible ways. ... In order to make explicit a particular aspect of a remembered pattern, one may form an image and 'internally recognize' that aspect of it. That is, *one may 'recognize' parts and properties of imaged objects that had not been previously considered.* (1987, p. 149; emphasis added.)

We see here the extent to which the possibility of reconstrual in imagery must be a quite general one which is, moreover, founded on the fundamental mechanisms postulated for imagery. Indeed, the very same higher mechanisms are invoked in imagery as in perception itself, as Finke has explained:

> I now wish to propose that the mental images themselves, once formed, cause these visual mechanisms to become activated. That is, I propose that images are the source of this activation, not the product of it.
>
> According to this view, mental images can stimulate visual processing mechanisms directly. Thus, when mental images are formed, these mechanisms would respond in much the same way as they do when objects and events are observed, resulting in the sensation that an image can be "seen" as if it were an actual object or event. (1980, p. 130)

By assimilating imagery so closely with vision, indeed by claiming their "equivalence," the pictorialists are inevitably committed to predicting closely similar "perceptual" phenomena in imagery to those found in perception itself. It is this deep commitment to the perceptual character of imagery which is the source of its vulnerability to such asymmetries as those of Chambers and Reisberg's and our own results reported here.

PERCEPTS AS OBJECTS

A true idea is something different from its correlate; thus a circle is different from the idea of a circle. The idea of a circle is not something having a circumference and a centre as a circle has; nor is the idea of a body that body itself.

Spinoza, *On the Improvement of the Understanding*

We see a symptom of the problems inherent in the pictorial approach in Finke's (1980) discussion where he speaks of "physical objects" instead of *percepts* of physical objects. He writes: One can think of mental images as being functionally equivalent to physical objects or events, with respect to certain types of effects" (p. 113). Despite Finke's comparison in these terms, it should be evident that one cannot make any meaningful comparison between images and physical objects per se, if the latter are taken seriously and literally as the relevant items of comparison. That is, if taken *literally*, it is somewhat anomalous to speak of "functional equivalences between mental images and physical objects." That is, we should not be concerned to compare the properties of mental representations *qua* psychological entities with those of tables and chairs. Rather, we must construe such talk as intending to compare images or imagery processes with *perceptions* of tables and chairs. This correction is not merely an inconsequential matter of usage or nitpicking philosophical pedantry. We had earlier noted Thomas's (1989) important caution regarding the assumptions built into the very word *image*. Even if only a *façon de parler,* the systematic category mistake in speaking of images as objects reflects a significant theoretical commitment to some kind of direct, literal object of apprehension. Specifically, this is the controversial conception of images as some kind of raw, unconceptualized pictorial substrate for viewing with the "mind's eye." Just as in perception we apprehend objects, so in imagery we apprehend our images.

We see Pylyshyn warn against the dangers inherent in the notions of analogical representations and the mistake of a too literal object-apprehension view of imagery:

> I shall argue that much of the attraction of this notion stems from a failure to recognize some fundamental differences between the objects of perception (i.e., the physical environment) and the objects of cognition (i.e., mental representations). (1978, p. 20).

On a descriptive or tacit knowledge account of imagery, the internal representations involved are taken to have a much more abstract nature and are consequently not objects in need of perceptual interpretation. Instead, the interpretation is intrinsic to the image. It is in this vein that, like Chambers and Reisberg, Hinton (1979) earlier suggested that structural descriptions of objects "form an integral part of a mental image" (1979, p. 248).

THE HOMUNCULUS AGAIN

Notoriously, the danger of falling into homunculus pseudoexplanations arises from modeling visual imagery too closely on visual perception itself. Repeated confident assertions that the homunculus problem has been avoided in recent accounts of imagery cannot be taken at face value: Mere disavowals and an awareness of the problem in principle are not enough to avoid the dangers *in practice*. Thus, Pinker (1984) in his recent survey of theories of visual cognition asks how the mind could contain images without some little man in the head to look at the images and he asserts

> This is simply not a problem under the computational theory of mind: images may be construed as data structures, and there is no more of a conceptual problem with positing mechanistic operations that can access those data structures than there is in positing mechanistic operations that access other mental representations such as linguistic or logical structures, or positing operations that access data in a computer. (1984, p. 38)

However, in the first place, adverting to these other domains in which data structures need to be accessed does not help here because they are equally prone to the explanatory dangers of the homunculus problem. Secondly, their mere use of mechanistic computational notions is not *ipso facto* sufficient to avoid the homunculus problem in practice; these approaches have only showed us how they *might* do so, and whether or not the explanatory vacuity is actually avoided depends on the specific character of the models postulated and how they are conceived. It is not enough to merely cite their computational character as if this on its own precludes falling prey to the notorious difficulty. Computational models are just as prone to the vacuity of homunculus pseudoexplanations as any other, though Kosslyn, too, seems to miss this point when he declares in frustration: "Once and for all, the 'homunculus problem' is simply not a problem. We thought this would be obvious given that the theory is realized in a computer program, but it seems necessary to address this complaint again" (Kosslyn et al., 1979, p. 574).

Being realized in a computer program would only make a theory *ipso facto* immune to the homunculus problem in the case when the model was a more or less complete working simulation of the cognitive phenomenon in question.

However this familiar virtue of the computational approach is unavailable as a guarantee of coherence and consistency in a theory unless the model actually works. At this stage it is far from clear what it would mean to have a fully working computational model which had visual images, but it is evident that the computational idiom in which Kosslyn's theory has been articulated leaves his model far from this ideal (see Pylyshyn, 1979, p. 562).

Dennett (1978) has clearly articulated the problem and its solution, and so it is particularly revealing that Kosslyn appeals to Dennett's analysis here. I am suggesting that the specific postulate of a pictorial medium has inescapably introduced a full-blown homunculus, and its proponents have hardly avoided the explanatory problem as they believe. At best, these approaches rely on much more intelligent homunculi in the hierarchy than they have evidently realized, and to this extent have not "discharged" the little man in the head in one stroke. The issue is to what extent the pictorial medium postulate advances the understanding of imagery phenomena and to what extent it has merely deferred it instead. My suggestion has been that the pictorial analog medium does no work in the explanations, and the burden has been simply transferred to the apparatus which is supposed to access the imaginal medium, thereby begging the question in the traditional manner. Moreover, the computational idiom does not itself advance our understanding with respect to this particular problem and does not alter the fundamental flaw in a postulate of this kind. It is, of course, correct but irrelevant for Kosslyn to plead that "computer programmers have known for years" that "it makes perfect sense to talk about a routine constructing, 'looking at,' or 'altering' a data structure," but he is not warranted in concluding from this fact alone that "notions of question begging, circularity, or infinite regress simply do not arise" (1979, p. 574). The problem arises not with these notions as such, only with certain ways they might be deployed in a particular case.

FUNCTIONS OF IMAGERY

The writings of pictorialists are noteworthy for the conspicuous neglect of the fundamental question of the *functional role* of images in the larger cognitive mechanisms of which they must be a part. In this regard, little has changed since Bartlett (1932) wrote that "... most statements that have been made about images in traditional psychology concern their nature rather than their functions, what they are rather than what they make it possible to do" (1932, p. 215). It is in this respect that the pictorial theory seems curiously lacking in explanatory depth and this is perhaps a clue to its inadequacies. That is, knowing that images may have pictorial properties tells us very little about their functional or causal role. Indeed, the conception of images as objects to be apprehended by the visual system is one in which they have no cognitive function at all, since this function is entirely ascribed to the apprehending apparatus. Admittedly, the question concerning the purpose or function of imagery has been asked by Kosslyn et al. (1990; p. 74; Kosslyn, 1988, p. 264), but his answer is to assimilate it with vision whereas the problem is precisely to differentiate it from vision. To assert, as Kosslyn et al. do, that "one purpose of imagery is to 'recognize' properties of imaged objects" (1990, p. 74) is to do little more than articulate our introspections and, thereby, to beg the crucial question of how imagery *differs* from visual perception.

Indeed, if we are concerned about understanding the functional role of imagery in cognition, it is far from clear that the entire approach which considers what an image *is* — in the sense of determining the *properties of images* — is theoretically well-conceived, since this conception implicitly incorporates a commitment to some kind of *object* or *entity* whose intrinsic properties we are concerned to elucidate. This bias may have prevented serious consideration of quite different properties which would naturally be posited given an alternative way of formulating the problem. Thus, a significantly different conception of the phenomena might avoid the implicit hypostatizing of the term 'image' as the basis for our systematic theorizing. There are grounds for seeing our idiom here as encouraging a Rylean category mistake which can lead us astray. For example, it is natural to speak not only of images and their properties as if they were mental entities, but also to talk of our ability to "generate images" (Kosslyn et al., 1990, p. 75) as if they were objects of some kind. But having the *experience* of imagery is not necessarily a warrant for the theoretical commitment to literally 'having' objects called 'images' which we generate in any sense. More specifically, as already noted, the reification of images entails a questionable doctrine according to which mental representations may *have* parts, as distinct from *representing* parts (see Kosslyn & Shwartz, 1981, p. 243). However, notwithstanding our folk psychology and its idioms, an alternative conception might relinquish altogether the idea of *images* as *entities* in favor of the notion of *imagery* as a *process*. The point is perhaps made clearer by means of an analogy. We are far less inclined to hypostatize other complex processes in the same way despite an analogous idiom: Thus, for example, we speak of indigestion or headaches, their properties, and even of 'having' headaches, but we are unlikely to conceive of these as objects of some kind. Instead, we would naturally take a headache to be a process we undergo. In the same way, it might be preferable to say that there are no images in the sense of internal objects of any kind which we apprehend, but only that we undergo the process of imaging. The issue is not merely terminological, but rather one of radically different theoretical conceptions for which the terminology is only a superficial symptom. Though entirely overlooked by pictorialists, a radically alternative conception has long been articulated in the philosophical literature under the title of 'the adverbial theory' of sensory experience (see Sellars, 1975; Jackson, 1975; Tye 1984).

Focusing attention on the functional role of images can bring into relief the difficulties of the pictorial medium along the lines just suggested: Apprehending or "inspecting" images is taken to exploit pattern recognition processes and other "visual routines" and in particular the comparison with information in long-term visual memory. However, the "image proper" in the visual buffer which is being inspected in this way is originally supposed to be generated from these very same long-term memory representations with which they are now being compared. That is, long-term visual memories are used to generate an image, which are then used again to inspect it. The explanatory circularity and the redundancy of the pictorial medium is obvious. Whatever its details, an alternative account would dispense with the visual buffer and explain the phenomena entirely in terms of the memory mechanisms where the relevant information is encoded even on the pictorial account.

Notoriously, if the purpose or function of imagery is taken to be fundamentally the same as that of perception, it requires the inner eyes of the inner man to "see" the image. The problem is seriously aggravated by the fact that imagery and like-modality perception are likely to be closely connected, as persuasive evidence suggests (Farah, 1988; Finke, 1980). This question of equivalence or commonality between imagery and perceptual processes must be sharply distinguished from the medium format question as Block (1981) has noted. Clearly, the extent to which visual imagery mechanisms might share those of visual perception is a distinct empirical matter from the issue of the nature of the representational medium and the character of imagery processes. How much the two phenomena may overlap or share mechanisms is a quite distinct empirical issue from what these mechanisms might be like in the sense of how they function. Thus, the danger arises from taking perceptual processes to be too close a *model* for those of imagery. Notwithstanding their intimate connections, the two phenomena are likely to be very different in their character and mechanisms, as would be expected given their different roles in cognition. Nevertheless, the "equivalence" question concerning the extent of *shared* processes appears not to have been clearly separated from the distinct theoretical issue of the nature of the imagery mechanisms themselves. This latter issue is the question of how far imagery may be similar in its fundamental operation to that of perception. Recall that it is this latter question which raises the spectre of the homunculus and its vacuous pseudoexplanation.

"REFUTATION" BY FINKE, PINKER, AND FARAH (1989)

The import of our own investigations is best appreciated by seeing them in the context of the preceding developments. Specifically, we have already noted the way in which the issue of reinterpreting visual images has become a new focus for the long-standing debate, even though it has not explicitly been taken as a testing ground for the rival 'format' theories. Our own data can illuminate this question by providing not merely a confirmation of the negative Chambers and Reisberg results, but by giving a further elaboration of the precise conditions under which images can or cannot be transformed. By testing new and quite different "perceptual" phenomena, our work shows yet further respects in which the alleged "equivalence" breaks down. Moreover, our investigation can be seen to serve as a direct response to the attempt of Finke, Pinker, and Farah (1989) to defuse the damaging implications of the Chambers and Reisberg (1985) evidence. Finke et al. (1989) have sought to reinforce pictorialist claims with new experiments which purport to show that subjects can inspect and reinterpret their images by "applying shape classification procedures to the information in imagery" (1989, p. 51). This work is of particular interest because it has been specifically designed to counter the skeptical conclusions warranted by the negative results of Chambers and Reisberg and sets the scene for our own investigation.

METHODOLOGY OF FALSIFICATION

As their bald appeal to the "data" suggests, Finke et al. (1989), appear to be arguing that Chambers and Reisberg have been shown to be mistaken on a "strictly empirical" claim that mental images are not subject to reconstrual, since the results of Finke et al. have demonstrated otherwise. Construing the question at stake in this way as the strictly empirical one of whether images can be reinterpreted, Finke et al. assert "our experiments show that the answer to it is that such reinterpretation is possible" (1989, p. 74). However, it is essential to notice the logic of their case before concurring in their judgment.
  Assuming that their experiments do, in fact, demonstrate what they claim — namely that "reinterpretation is possible" — Finke et al. have not yet vindicated their cause by refuting Chambers and Reisberg. This notion of refutation is to trivialize the issue by uncharitably construing the Chambers and Reisberg case in its most implausible and most uninteresting form. The logic of their claim cannot be seriously interpreted as being merely that images cannot be interpreted in some unqualified and completely general sense, and consequently refuted by finding any contrary case. The Chambers and Reisberg investigation derives its significance not merely from making such a bald claim but rather from having shown the inability for image reconstrual precisely under conditions in which we would have expected it according to the quasiperceptual account. To be sure, whether images can be reinterpreted is a strictly empirical question in an unproblematic sense, but it is not the question raised by the investigation of Chambers and Reisberg. Undeniably, *"given suitable conditions,"* as Finke et al. say, people *are* able to reconstrue their images. But clearly, it only begs the deeper questions raised by Chambers

and Reisberg — questions which are, moreover, inescapably the "philosophical" (that is, theoretical) ones Finke et al. have wished to dismiss.

INTERPRETATION AND NOTHING BUT INTERPRETATION

For example, in their attempt to deflect the consequences of the negative findings of Chambers and Reisberg, Finke et al. claim that they "refute one kind of explanation for this difficulty: [namely] that visual images *do not contain information about the geometry of a shape* necessary for reinterpreting it." (1989, p. 51; emphasis added). That is, Finke et al. devote much of their effort to refuting what they refer to as "the strong position that images are nothing but interpretations" and consistently attribute to Chambers and Reisberg the conclusion that "images *do not contain* uninterpreted information; the implication is that images are nothing but interpretations or construals" (1989, p. 54). They take Chambers and Reisberg to claim "that images lack 'uninterpreted' information pertaining to the geometry of an object" (ibid, p. 54), and "the image itself contains no information that is not part of a conceptual information" (p. 60) or images are "lacking in nonconceptual geometric information" (p. 76). However, Chambers and Reisberg do not need to go so far as to deny the presence of any purely geometric information in images, but only to assert the intrinsic association of such information with a semantic interpretation. It is evident that people are capable of answering questions about the geometric properties of their images even when they do have some interpretation. For example, we can imagine a doughnut or a dog's ear and also describe their geometric properties. That is, the lesson to be learned from the failure of subjects to reverse their images is not that they do not contain geometric information, but only that this information is not readily dissociated from the old interpretation and reassociated with a new one. This is the specific issue which will be further illuminated by the results of our own experiments. The logic of the claim and its force are misrepresented by Finke et al., since the claim is only that images are "created as symbols of something and hence *need no interpretive process*" (1985, p. 317). The emphasis on the *intrinsically interpreted* character of images is not the same as *denying the presence* of purely geometric information.

STIMULI OF FINKE ET AL. (1989) AS MEANINGLESS

Chambers and Reisberg explicitly identify their conception of interpretation with Brentano's idea that every mental phenomenon has "reference to a content" or "direction toward an object" (1985, p. 318). On this view, the interpretation of a symbol or image consists of the fact that they are *about* some object or scene in the world. The neglect of such "philosophical" matters is reflected in a feature of the experiments of Finke et al. (1989), which may weaken their relevance to the results of Chambers and Reisberg. Finke et al. want to show that "people *can* assign novel interpretations to ambiguous images" (1989, p. 51), but the stimulus figures or patterns employed were all of a highly geometric character including letters and numbers. That is, there is at best only a very attenuated sense in which one can speak of 'reinterpretation' in regard to these patterns at all, and certainly there is nothing which corresponds to the full-bodied interpretations of the ambiguous duck/rabbit, for example, or to the real world object represented by the Necker cube. It is significant, therefore, that our own stimuli revert to figures which have a semantic interpretation in the fullest sense and once again subjects are unable to accomplish the reconstruals in imagery which are instantaneous in perception.

Finke et al. (1989), consider related criticisms of their stimuli in an effort to preempt them, but their discussion does not appear to address the central problems of their experiment. They anticipate a possible objection that their subjects' performances might not be regarded as legitimate examples of reversing an ambiguous figure in imagery since there was no initial construal that had to be switched away from. They answer this possible criticism by claiming that all of their "stimuli" had at least two interpretations, notwithstanding their need for a complex description:

> The fact that one of the two interpretations was invariably characterised by a complex articulated description rather than by a single word, unlike the case of a duck/rabbit, is of little theoretical importance. There is no basis for considering the patterns used in this experiment to be any less ambiguous than the duck/rabbit ... For that matter, some of the ambiguous figures used by Chambers and Reisberg, such as the Necker cube and Schroeder staircase, also do not have one-word labels attached to each interpretation. (1989, p. 69)

The focus of Finke et al. upon the issue of interpretations being couched in a "complex articulated description" rather than a "single word" misses the point here: The issue is not the complexity or otherwise of descriptions but rather the nature of a *perceptual gestalt*. In particular, it is not the one-word *labels* which might attach to the ambiguous figures such as 'duck' or 'rabbit' which are the relevant factor for Chambers and Reisberg, but the fact that the figure permits a perceptual identification and interpretation *as* something in the first place — that is, other than the geometrical figure itself. The possibility of such a meaning or interpretation is clearly independent of any linguistic label (simple or complex) which might become associated with the figure. It is precisely this kind of interpretation which is absent from the geometrical figures in Finke et al.'s experiment. The force of the Chambers and Reisberg result derives from the parallel of their experiment with the phenomena of perception itself. If imagery is quasiperceptual in the sense of using interpretive visual mechanisms to operate on a pictorial medium, then the existence of verbal labels is irrelevant. Rather, the point is that we would expect to find parallels to perceptual phenomena in imagery like those tested by Chambers and Reisberg and our own experiments.

More importantly, however, these arguments offered by Finke et al. are specific to the mechanisms for reversal of ambiguous figures and these will be of no avail where completely different kinds of reinterpretation may be involved — as in our own experiments. Thus, whatever its merits for the Chambers and Reisberg results, the appeal to specific mechanisms for reversal of ambiguous figures will begin to look very ad hoc when appeals will need to be made to quite different mechanisms in every other case of failure of image reinterpretation. For example, it is clear that the mechanisms of figure-ground separation and imposition of Kanizsa illusory contours, for example, will be quite different from those of ambiguity switching.

"SUITABLE CONDITIONS"

In a significant departure from the experimental paradigm of Chambers and Reisberg (1985), the "stimuli" used by Finke et al. (1989) were not visually presented perceptual objects at all. Instead, Finke et al. used *verbal descriptions* of certain patterns and, although Finke et al. speak of the "patterns" used in their experiment, this disguises the fact that these were constructed entirely in imagination from verbal descriptions and were not constrained by perceptual input for the subjects. As a matter of experimental procedure, Finke et al. rightly require that any *new* interpretation of a pattern should not have been the result of "having encoded that interpretation while the stimulus was *actually visible*" (1989, p. 55; emphasis added), but they manage to avoid this problem of perceptual confounding by avoiding perception altogether. The absence of such explicit theoretical justification for this strategem obscures the relevance of their results. Accordingly, a particular virtue of our own experiments is to revert to visual stimuli, while avoiding perceptual reconstrual in other ways.

EXPERIMENTS

In the most general terms, our experiments were designed to test the direct predictions of the spatial medium or 'pictorial' account. Specifically, the experiments were concerned with testing the 'quasiperceptual' and 'equivalence' claims of the theory articulated by Kosslyn and others according to which "the purposes of imagery, in large part, parallel those of vision" specifically in "the use of recognition processes" (1987, p. 149) through which Kosslyn claims "one may 'recognize' parts and properties of imaged objects that had not been previously considered" (ibid). The abilities being tested are exactly those which are claimed to have been demonstrated by Pinker and Finke (1980) who reported subjects' ability to "see" novel properties which could emerge from images only after they had been mentally rotated where new properties of images "can be 'read off' the display" (1980, p. 262). Their task, just as our own, demands "the ability to 'see' the two dimensional patterns that should emerge in their images if the images depicted the new perspective accurately" (1980, p. 244). The ability to "re-parse" an image by using perceptual shape classification procedures has been claimed by Finke et al. (1989), just as Finke and Slayton (1988) claim to have shown "that people are capable of making unexpected discoveries in imagery."

Mental Rotation

Stimulus materials were designed to have two distinct interpretations which are highly orientation specific. Thus, the figures are recognizable as a certain object in one orientation, but are interpretable as an entirely different object when rotated by 90 degrees. These stimuli are variants of the stimuli used by Rock (1973), and are considerably improved in their recognizability. In this respect, the shapes have the important feature that the alternative interpretations are readily obtained by rotation under *perceptual* conditions.

Figure 17.1

It is important that the task of reinterpretation can be readily accomplished in this way during perception because this makes the conditions for reconstrual under imagery conditions as favorable as possible. Thus, for example, when subjects are shown Figure 17.1 in one orientation, it is immediately recognized (as, say, the duckling or penguin); then upon rotating the figure by 90 degrees, subjects immediately notice (with frequent expressions of surprise and delight) the alternative interpretation (in this case the rabbit).

Figure 17.2

The direct expectation of the pictorial medium theory is that the same effect should be obtainable under imagery conditions. That is, if subjects are shown the figures in only one orientation, it would be expected that they could *rotate their image* and *discover* the alternative construal by inspection *from their rotated image.* Of course, the tacit knowledge alternative account takes images to be highly abstract, intrinsically interpreted conceptualizations and would predict that such reinterpretation would be difficult or impossible for subjects to perform in this way on their rotated images.

Indeed, under suitable controls to prevent either perceptual confounding or degraded images, there were only eight percent successful reconstruals. Moreover, these successes were largely confined to the two stimuli (snail/seahorse and boat/toucan) which have telling clues (e.g. curly tail of the snail) which subjects reported as enabling a reasoning strategy quite different from "visual" apprehension or "inspection" of their image. Thus, typical of the predicted difficulty of reconstrual was the reaction of subjects when pressed to reinterpret their rotated image of the duckling: Just as we would expect on a tacit knowledge account according to which the image is intrinsically encoded with its interpretation, many subjects would volunteer the response that it is a "duckling on its back!"

It is important to note that our figures are geometrically simpler than Shepard and Metzler's (1971) representations of blocks stacked in three

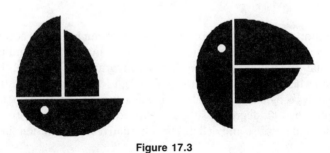

Figure 17.3

Figure 17.4

dimensions for which mental rotation has been claimed. Moreover, our shapes are no more complex than those of Cooper (1975) for which complexity was specifically found not to be a factor in the ease of rotation. Among the further conditions favoring ease of mental rotation is the fact that our experiment utilizes *recognizable* shapes, unlike those of Rock, Wheeler and Tudor (1989).

The significance of our negative results in these experiments derives from the fact that the mental rotation and reinterpretation are not only explicitly predicted by pictorial theorists, but involve precisely the mental transformations which have been classically taken as well established. Of additional importance is the fact that our task is readily performed under perceptual conditions, thereby entitling us to expect it in imagery as well according to the pictorial theory.

As already noted, even if the response by Finke et al. (1989) to Chambers and Reisberg (1985) is not problematic in various ways noted earlier (see also Slezak, 1991), their "refutation" is specific to the case of ambiguous stimuli and, therefore, irrelevant to our entirely different imagery tasks. A pattern of such failures on other perceptual phenomena would leave only ad hoc ways of avoiding their significance for the pictorial theory. Accordingly, as a follow-up, we have devised additional experiments having the same logic — namely, they test yet other perceptual phenomena in imagery for the claimed "equivalence."

Figure-Ground Separation

The figures illustrated in the left half of Figures 17.5 and 17.6 are such to encourage a perceptual organization into several black objects which may, however, be reversed to become the ground and thereby reveal the letters "EI" and "HI." Since the reversal in this form is somewhat difficult in perception itself, the effect can be readily elicited by asking subjects to imagine bringing the horizontal black lines together to touch the shapes as illustrated in the right-hand figures, clearly revealing the letters.

Figure 17.5

Despite the ease of the imagery task, not a single subject in 20 trials was able to reconstrue their image to reveal the alternative construal as letters. This was despite the fact subjects' subsequent drawings of their memorized images were highly accurate.

Figure 17.6

Kanizsa Illusory or 'Subjective' Contours

The stimuli of the kind illustrated in Figures 17.7 and 17.8 were designed to produce the familiar illusory or subjective contours, but they were not presented to subjects in this form since the effect would then be created in perception. In order to test the parallel with imagery, circumstances must be contrived which generate the figure only in imagination and, accordingly, the entire figure was not presented visually all at once. Instead the black shapes were designed to have good gestalt properties and to discourage any inferences about other shapes of which they might be a part. The black shapes were presented one at a time for 30 seconds at their respective positions and then removed from view. Having seen them only one at a time, subjects were asked to imagine them together and were then asked whether they were able to detect any other shape, figure, or object in their reconstructed image.

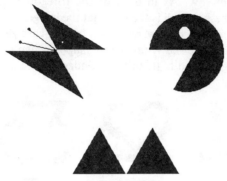

Figure 17.7

Despite research on "creative mental synthesis" which suggests that people can use imagery to mentally assemble the separately presented parts of a pattern (Finke, 1990, p. 21), only one subject out of 30 trials reported seeing a geometrical shape, correctly identifying the emergent white figure. Again, this overwhelming difficulty with the task was despite the fact that in most cases, subjects' drawings from memory were highly accurate and they were frequently able to notice the alternative construal from their own drawing.

Figure 17.8

Creative Mental Synthesis

In this experiment again, subjects were tested for their alleged ability to discover something from their images which they had not noticed during perceptual exposure. The shapes illustrated on the top row in Figure 17.9

("M," "heart" and "pot") are such as to be generally unfamiliar in the sense that subjects see them as a whole without noticing that they are composed of a familiar numeral on the right joined to its mirror image on the left, as shown in the bottom row. As in each of the foregoing experiments, an essential feature of these stimuli is the fact that the imagery task is one which can be readily accomplished *in perception*. In this case, although people invariably fail to recognize the symmetrical shapes, when partially covered to reveal only the right-hand half, this remainder is instantly recognized as the familiar numeral.

Figure 17.9

The symmetrical shapes were shown to subjects with the instruction to memorize them as accurately as possible and were then asked, in the fashion of an illustration provided, to imagine their right halves standing alone. When subjects confirmed that they were visualizing the right half of the figure by itself, they were asked whether it looked like any familiar shape or object.

With these stimuli, the results were strikingly different from those of the previous experiments. A significant proportion (65%) of subjects were easily able to report the numerals 1, 2, and 3 as a discovery made from their image. In each case they had not noticed the familiar shape when shown the figures and had only discovered its meaning from "inspecting" their image. The ease of reconstrual in these cases is in marked contrast with the earlier experiments, despite the essentially similar logic of the imagery task. The overall success rate should be qualified by noting an order effect in which there was a consistent improvement from only a 50% success rate on the first stimulus to 66% on the second and 77% on the third. From subjects' reports it appeared that if they once discovered a numeral from their image, this helped to make the subsequent discovery by directing their search in a specific way. Though no less genuine discoveries from imagery, this improvement gives further insight into the scope and limitations of operations with images. The facilitation effect evident here is not a matter of perceptual confounding, but nonetheless suggests that later stimuli should be considered separately from the first naive attempt at discovery in imagery. In the case of this first, naive test, the 50% success rate in imagery is still evidence of some significant difficulty in reinterpretation, despite the instantaneous result in perception. The subsequent discoveries could plausibly be explained as a kind of reasoning rather than a quasiperceptual "inspection." Though qualified in the ways just noted, it remains that our results in this experiment provide more positive results of imagery reconstrual like those of Finke et al. (1989).

It is perhaps significant that the stimulus figures in this experiment bear a similarity to those of Finke et al. (1989), namely, line drawings of geometrical shapes with more or less attenuated meanings, and certainly not having the robust interpretation of the orientation-dependent silhouettes. This is consistent with the supposition of the tacit knowledge theory that it is the intrinsic conceptual meaningfulness of images which makes reconstrual difficult or impossible.

CONCLUSIONS

Overall, our results can be seen as casting further light on the precise conditions under which visual imagery transformations are possible. Notwithstanding the claim by Finke et al. (1989) to have given a straightforward "refutation" of Chambers and Reisberg (1985), we have shown that image reconstrual is generally difficult or impossible to perform under certain conditions in which one would have expected it according to the pictorial theory. These negative results are precisely as one would expect on the tacit knowledge account according to which imagery is highly abstract and cognitive, and does not involve any internal surrogate objects to be apprehended by the visual system. On the other hand, our positive evidence of image reconstrual, like that of Finke et al. (1989), must be accommodated into any theory of imagery and there is a need to consider how any account can explain what are *prima facie* counterexamples to its generalizations.

FURTHER PREDICTIONS

Zenon Kulpa's (1983, 1987) investigations have led him to suggest[4] a further elegant test of the competing pictorial and tacit knowledge theories in the same spirit as our foregoing experiments. If images are depictive displays which can be manipulated by the processes postulated by Kosslyn, then subjects could be presented with two figures independently and asked to juxtapose them in their imagination — as if sliding together two drawings — essentially in the manner already claimed by Finke et al. (1989) in which different shapes are imagined being joined together to make a new one. In particular, the separately presented figures could be representations of the two halves of various objects such as simple wooden frames. However, on the pictorial theory, we would not expect greater difficulty in such imagined

---

[4] Personal correspondence

juxtapositions when the two halves belong to the representation of impossible objects such as the Penrose Triangle than with representations of possible objects of similar complexity. In both cases, on the pictorial theory, the task presumably involves some transformation of the *uninterpreted* "image proper" in the visual buffer. However, on the tacit knowledge theory, the internal representations are inherently interpreted in the sense of being structural descriptions of real world objects (Hinton 1979). Accordingly, this theory would predict that the operation of juxtaposing two parts of a figure in imagery is an attempt to imagine the fitting together of two real objects. On this account one would predict that joining two possible halves of an *impossible* object in imagery would be harder than in the case of a possible object. Kulpa's elegant idea provides further non-chronometric means for testing the contrasting predictions of pictorial and tacit knowledge theories and can add to the store of growing evidence concerning the scope and limits of image reinterpretation.

WHAT IS RESEMBLANCE?

As Chambers and Reisberg (1985) explicitly recognize, it is through the postulate of picture-like representations which refer by *resemblance* that the traditional difficulties arise.[5] The problem is familiar from Chomsky's related complaint against traditional grammars which tacitly relied on the linguistic knowledge of the *user or theorist* rather than explicit theory. Here too, in a similar fashion, the conception of a pictorial medium which refers through resemblance inherently requires the implicit contribution of the theorist to provide the illusion that the theory works: This is because the notion of resemblance can do no work in the theory on its own as a purported mechanism of reference; mental representations (unlike pictures) cannot resemble their objects, since the resemblance of one thing for another requires that a perceptual judgement be made by a third party external to them both. That is, the claim that an image or picture resembles something is necessarily a perceptual *judgement* made by *comparing* one with the other. However it is just this comparison which is impossible in the case of mental images, since we have no independent vantage point from which to judge our own images in order to make the comparison. Introspection aside, it seems clear that the salient property of mental representations in this domain cannot be that they *look like* their referents which is what the claim of pictorial resemblance entails.

---

[5] In their more recent work, Reisberg and Chambers (1991) appear to accept the explanatory value of this notion.

On this very point, "philosophical" theories at least since Descartes have been sensitive to the difficulties which beset recent psychological accounts[6]:

> It is necessary to beware of assuming that in order to sense, the mind needs to perceive certain images transmitted by the objects to the brain, as our philosophers commonly suppose; or, at least, the nature of these images must be conceived quite otherwise than as they do. For, inasmuch as [these philosophers] do not consider anything about these images except that they must resemble the objects they represent, it is impossible for them to show us how they can be formed by these objects, received by the external sense organs, and transmitted by the nerves to the brain. And they have had no other reason for positing them except that, observing that a picture can easily stimulate our minds to conceive the object painted there, it seemed to them that in the same way, the mind should be stimulated by little pictures which form in our head to conceive of those objects that touch our senses; instead we should consider that there are many other things besides pictures which can stimulate our thought, such as, for example, signs and words, which do not in any way resemble the things which they signify. . . . So that often, in order to be more perfect as images and to represent an object better, they must not resemble it. Now we must think in the same way about the images that are formed in our brain, and we must note that it is only a question of knowing how they can enable the mind to perceive all the diverse qualities of the objects to which they refer; not of [knowing] how the images themselves resemble their objects." (Descartes, pp. 89-90)

It would seem that the theoretical postulate of resemblance is an illegitimate extrapolation from a misguided introspection. We can see the problem emerge as a tension in Finke's account. Thus, he begins his recent book acknowledging "that imagery is a subjective phenomenon" (1989, p. 1) and appropriately defines mental imagery as "recreation of an experience that in at least some respects resembles the experience of actually perceiving an object or an event" (ibid., p. 2). So far so good: Notice that Finke has only asserted the resemblance of one kind of *experience* with another. However, Finke proceeds to endorse a piece of dubious, if compelling, folk psychology according to which most people claim that their images often resemble *actual objects*. Thus, he concludes that "a mental image must be more like a 'picture' of something than a verbal description" (ibid., p. 4).[7] However, this is simply a

---

[6] It is important to note, however, that despite seeing the problems of resemblance, by virtue of his dualism, Descartes was inevitably committed to an homunculus model and to a pictorialism not unlike Kosslyn's. I am grateful to Nigel Thomas for forcing me to clarify this point.

[7] In passing it should be noted that the tacit knowledge and descriptive accounts of imagery have not been committed to the exceedingly implausible view that the descriptions in question are "verbal" in any sense deriving from natural language. This is a straw man which is consistently presented as the opposing account by pictorialists despite explicit disclaimers (see Pylyshyn, 1973).

nonsequitur and Finke is only entitled to assert that a mental image is more like the *experience of seeing a picture,* and not like the picture itself.

The problem is also familiar to philosophers, at least, from Berkeley's answer to Locke:

> But say you, though the ideas themselves do not exist without [i.e. outside] the mind, yet there may be things like them, whereof they are copies or resemblances . . . I answer, an idea can be like nothing but an idea; a colour or figure can be like nothing but another colour or figure. If we look ever so little into our own thoughts, we shall find it impossible for us to conceive a likeness except only between our ideas. (1710, p. 64)

It is thus only through pretending to be external to our own images and imposing the judgment of resemblance from outside that the pictorial account appears to work. In ascribing pictorial properties to images, in fact it is *we* as theorists who have thereby implicitly taken on the explanatory burden and not the image as a construct in the pictorial account. It is in this sense that the representational medium cannot function as claimed by virtue of its pictorial qualities. Our own spurious attribution of resemblance is tacitly assumed to be a capacity of the mechanisms which access the pictorial data structure, thereby endowing them with precisely the intelligence we are trying to explain. The visual characteristics of imagery are not objective properties which can be assumed, but rather they are precisely what needs to be explained. It is thus the claim of resemblance for our mental representations (essential to the pictorial medium account) which is the key to its elaborate question begging. The idea that images can "resemble" something requires that we can *look* at them, hence a medium conceived as pictorial imposes the full perceiving homunculus on the theory. As the literature on machine vision makes acutely clear, a visual buffer containing only the spatial array of light intensity information leaves the entire task of object recognition unsolved. In particular, the pictorial resemblance of one such spatial array to another will be the *end product* of complex computational processes and not their input. Despite a computational idiom, scare quotes and metaphorical talk of "seeing" with the "mind's eye," there has been no indication by Kosslyn of how the pictorial images and their accessing mechanisms have managed to reduce the cognitive task to more stupid homunculi, as required on Dennett's model and to which he explicitly adverts. As Descartes recognized, the solution is to explain how sensory patterns in memory might serve the functions of imagery without needing to resemble their referents. In particular, it is important to recognize that just because the *experience* of imaging may resemble the *experience* of seeing, it does not follow that there are any *images* which resemble the *objects* of seeing.

IMAGES TO "SEE THEMSELVES"

Discussing the work of Fodor (1975), Dennett (1978) drew attention some time ago to the general difficulty which also confronts pictorialism. Dennett refers to it as Hume's Problem which arises because "nothing is intrinsically a representation of anything; something is a representation only for or to someone." Dennett explains:

> The problem is an old one. Hume wisely shunned the notion of an inner self that would intelligently manipulate the ideas and impressions, but this left him with the necessity of getting the ideas to "think for themselves". . . . Fodor's analogous problem is to get the internal representations to "understand themselves." (1978, 101)

The analogous challenge for theories of imagery is to get the images to "see themselves." If, as Kosslyn says, the "pattern in the visual buffer (i.e., the image proper) is formed on the basis of information stored in long-term memory" (in Pinker, 1984, p. 201), then the question is: What additional function does the visual buffer — the image proper — serve? It seems to be an entirely superfluous entity with no discernable function or explanatory role, since, *ex hypothesi*, all the information it contains was already encoded and available in long-term memory. Of course, in one sense, the "function" of the visual buffer is evident: Because it is accorded pictorial properties, it is something which we, *as theorists,* can see and interpret as depicting something. Kosslyn has failed to notice that without this illegitimate factor, the spatial display cannot serve its supposed role as representing visual appearances. Notice that Kosslyn and Finke et al. (1989) are demanding what Searle had illegitimately demanded in another context: they want the internal symbols to be intelligible to a full-blown interpreting mind. But however we explain mental symbols generally, it cannot be by demanding their interpretability to a conscious intelligence following Searle; nor, by parity, can the representations subserving imagery require their visual perceptibility.

REFERENCES

Anderson, J.R. (1978). Arguments concerning representations for mental imagery. *Psychological Review, 85,* 249-277.

Bartlett, F.C. (1932). *Remembering: A Study in Experimental and Social Psychology.* Cambridge: Cambridge University Press, reprinted 1961.

Berkeley, G. (1710/1965). The principles of human knowledge. In D.M. Armstrong (Ed.), *Berkeley's philosophical writings.* New York: Collier MacMillan.

Block, N. (Ed.). (1981). *Imagery.* Cambridge, MA: Bradford/MIT Press.

Chambers, D., & Reisberg, D. (1985). Can mental images be ambiguous? *Journal of Experimental Psychology: Human Perception and Performance, 11,* 317-28.

Chambers, D., & Reisberg, D. (1992). What an image depicts depends on what an image means. *Cognitive Psychology, 24,* 145-174.

Cooper, L.A. (1975). Mental rotation of random two-dimensional shapes. *Cognitive Psychology, 7,* 20-43.

Dennett, D. (1978). *Brainstorms.* Montgomery, Vermont. Bradford.

Descartes, R. (1965). *Discourse on method, optics, geometry and meteorology.* (Trans. by P.J. Olscamp). New York: Bobbs-Merrill.

Farah, M.J. (1988). Is visual imagery really visual? Overlooked evidence from neuropsychology. Psychological Review, 95, 307-317.

Finke, R.A. (1980). Levels of equivalence in imagery and perception. *Psychological Review, 87,* 113-132.

Finke, R.A. (1989). *Principles of mental imagery.* Cambridge, MA: Bradford/MIT Press.

Finke, R.A. (1990). *Creative imagery: Discoveries and inventions in visualization.* Hillsdale, NJ: Erlbaum.

Finke, R.A., Pinker, S., & Farah, M.J. (1989). Reinterpreting visual patterns in mental imagery. *Cognitive Science, 13,* 51-78.

Finke, R.A., & Slayton, K. (1988). Explorations of creative visual synthesis in mental imagery. *Memory and Cognition, 16,* 252-257.

Fodor, J. (1968). The appeal to tacit knowledge in psychological explanation. *Journal of Philosophy, 65,* 627-640.

Fodor, J. (1975). *The language of thought.* New York: Crowell.

Hinton, G. (1979). Some demonstrations of the effects of structural descriptions in mental imagery. *Cognitive Science, 3,* 231-250.

Jackson, F. (1975). On the adverbial analysis of visual experience. *Metaphilosophy, 6,* 127-135.

Kosslyn, S.M. (1980). *Image and mind.* Cambridge, MA: Harvard University Press.

Kosslyn, S.M. (1981). The medium and the message in mental imagery: A theory. *Psychological Review, 88,* 46-66.

Kosslyn, S.M. (1983). *Ghosts in the mind's machine.* New York: Norton.

Kosslyn, S.M. (1987). Seeing and imagining in the cerebral hemispheres: A computational approach. *Psychological Review, 94,* 148-175.

Kosslyn, S.M. (1988). Imagery in learning. In Michael S. Gazzaniga (Ed.), *Perspectives in memory research,* Cambridge, MA: Bradford/MIT Press.

Kosslyn, S.M., Pinker, S., Smith, G.E., & Schwartz, S.P. (1979). On the demystification of mental imagery. *The Behavioral and Brain Sciences, 2,* 535-581.

Kossly, S.M., & Shwartz, S.P. (1981). Empirical constraints on theories of visual mental imagery. In J. Long & A. Baddeley (Eds.), *Attention and performance IX.* Hillsdale, NJ: Erlbaum, 242-257.

Kosslyn, S.M., Van Kleeck, M.H., & Kirby, K.N. (1990). A neurologically plausible model of individual differences in visual mental imagery. In P.J. Hampson, D.F. Marks, & J.T.E. Richardson (Eds.), *Imagery: Current developments.* London: Routledge.

Kulpa, Z. (1983). Are impossible figures possible? *Signal processing, 5,* 201-220.

Kulpa, Z. (1987). Putting order in the impossible. *Perception, 16,* 201-214.

Peterson, M.A., Kihlstrom, J.F., Rose, P.M., & Glisky, M.L. (1992). Mental images can be ambiguous: Reconstruals and reference-frame reversals. *Memory and Cognition, 20* (2), 107-123.

Pinker, S. (1984). Visual cognition: An introduction. In S. Pinker (Ed.), *Visual Cognition,* Cambridge, MA: Bradford/MIT Press.

Pinker, S. & Finke, R. (1980). Emergent two-dimensional patterns in images rotated in depth. *Journal of Experimental Psychology: Human Perception and Performance, 6,* (2), 244-264.

Podgorny, P., & Shepard, R.N. (1978). Functional representations common to visual perception and imagination. *Journal of Experimental Psychology: Human Perception and Performance, 4,* 21-35.

Pylyshyn, Z. (1973). What the mind's eye tells the mind's brain: A critique of mental imagery. *Psychological Bulletin, 80* (1), 1-24.

Pylyshyn, Z. (1979). Imagery theory: Not mysterious — just wrong. *The Behavioral and Brain Sciences, 2* (4), 561-563.

Pylyshyn, Z. (1978). Imagery and artificial intelligence. In C.W. Savage (Ed.), *Minnesota Studies in the Philosophy of Science,* Vol. IX. Minneapolis: University of Minnesota Press.

Pylyshyn, Z. (1981). The imagery debate: Analog media versus tacit knowledge. *Psychological Review, 88,* 16-45.

Reisberg, D., & Chambers, D. (1991). Neither pictures nor propositions: What can we learn from a mental image? *Canadian Journal of Psychology, 45* (3), 336-352.

Rock, I. (1973). *Orientation and Form.* New York: Academic Press.

Rock, I., Wheeler, D., & Tudor, L. (1989). Can we imagine how objects look from other viewpoints? *Cognitive Psychology, 21* (2), 185-210.

Sellars, W. (1975). On the objects of the adverbial theory of sensation. *Metaphilosophy, 6,* 144-160.

Shepard, R.N., & Metzler, J. (1971). Mental rotation of three-dimensional objects. *Science, 171,* 701-703.

Skinner, B.F. (1963). Behaviorism at fifty. *Science, 140,* 951-958.

Slezak, P. (1990). Re-interpreting images. *Analysis, 50* (4), 231-243.

Slezak, P. (1991). Can images be rotated and inspected? *Proceedings of the Thirteenth Annual Conference of the Cognitive Science Society.* Hillsdale, NJ: Erlbaum.

Slezak, P. (1992). When can visual images be re-interpreted? *Proceedings of the Fourteenth Annual Conference of the Cognitive Science Society.* Hillsdale, NJ: Erlbaum.

Thomas, N.J.T. (1989). Experience and theory as determinants of attitudes toward mental representation: The case of Knight Dunlap and the vanishing images of J.B. Watson. *American Journal of Psychology, 103* (3), 395-412.

Thomas, N.J.T. (1990). *Are theories of imagery theories of imagination?* Paper read at 16th Annual Meeting of the Society for Philosophy and Psychology, University of Maryland, College Park, June 10.

Tye, M. (1984). The adverbial approach to visual experience. *The Philosophical Review, 93* (2), 195-225.

CHAPTER 18

Communication and Uncertainty

Roderic A. Girle

School of Computing and Information Technology
Griffith University

INTRODUCTION

How many times have you been involved in the business of producing some computer software? You know how it goes. First, the real computing problem has to be solved. This usually means that we have to be clear about the type of data to be dealt with, and we have to discover the algorithms for processing the data. Once this has all been done, and the back of the problem broken, then there comes the time-consuming secondary task of putting on a pretty front end. The annoying thing is that the front end will take far more time than the real job, but it has to be done.

That's how many people think of the task of the production of software. I want to argue here that this way of thinking has bred, and is breeding dangerous attitudes, and a dangerous set of priorities. These attitudes and priorities disregard the human context in which computing is carried out. This disregard for the human context expresses itself both directly and indirectly. I want to consider three cases which exemplify this disregard. The first of the cases comes from Scheme programming (Scheme is a dialect of Lisp). The second comes from a discussion of the teaching of computer science. The third is from the computational approach to discourse and dialogue.

But before looking at these cases, it must be insisted that this disregard for the human context has profound consequences for a range of things in computing and cognitive science. I will return to those consequences later, and in particular to their impact on the growing research into the management of uncertainty in computing. In the final section of the chapter I will make some remarks on the consequences for cognitive science and some areas of research which need to be explored.

THREE CASES

Processing and Programming

The first of the cases concerns a particular way of seeing programming languages. It is exemplified in a highly regarded text in programming. The text is Abelson and Sussman's *Structure and Interpretation of Computer Programs* (1985). In the preface of this text the authors say:

> First, we want to establish the idea that a computer language is not just a way of getting a computer to perform operations but rather that it is a novel formal medium for expressing ideas about methodology. Second, we believe that the essential material to be addressed by a subject at this level is . . . the techniques used to control the intellectual complexity of large software systems. (p. xv)

These remarks can be taken very broadly or much more narrowly. Taken broadly they can be applied to the working of a machine in a human context. We could use the language Scheme, to express ideas about the way in which a machine interacts with the people who surround it. A methodology would then indicate what sorts of interactions there should be and how they should be handled. We might expect considerable facility in the area of human input, and machine output. (Those of you who know something about Lisp (or have ever tried to write a windows system in Prolog) are requested to cease rolling in the aisles with tears running down your cheeks.)

So we could go looking in the textbook for some examples of human-machine interaction. In fact there are a couple, but I can only describe them as user-hostile. My own attempts to do any programming in Scheme, programming which tries to deal with the input of sentences of either English or of propositional logic have left me with the clear impression that, though it may be theoretically possible, it is not a practical possiblity to use Scheme to express ideas about the machine's interaction with the people who surround it. Even at square one, people do not speak or write "in quotation."

It may be stating the obvious, but most dialects of Lisp are focused on internal processing, and are turned away from input and output. Now, if a machine is to interact, it must do it by input and output. That is its method of interacting with the world, and with the people who are in the world around it. It just might be that, despite the supposedly marvelous syntactic, modular, decompositional problem-solving features of Lisp and its dialects, it has never gained the popularity of the wicked, syntactically rich, nonmodular languages which have lots of input and output facilities. Dare I say that these languages seem to be more basic.

Formality and Context

The second case is the recent debate in Communications of the ACM entitled "On the Cruelty of Really Teaching Computer Science" (1989). The debate was prompted by a talk given by Dijkstra at a computer science conference. Dijkstra says three main things: First, the computer is a radical novelty. Second, we must deanthropomorphize programming. Third, we must emphasize the formal nature of programming.

Dijkstra contends that too much of computing is influenced by an anthropomorphic metaphor. This metaphor was introduced, he says, by von Neumann. Dijkstra wants this metaphor to be thoroughly rejected. He says of the anthropormorphic metaphor that:

> It is paralyzing in the sense that because persons exist and act in time, its adoption effectively prevents a departure from operational semantics, and, thus forces people to think about programs in terms of computational behaviors, based on an underlying computational model This is bad because operational reasoning is a tremendous waste of mental effort. (1989, p. 1403)

and goes on to insist:

> We should reason about programs without even mentioning their possible behaviors. (1989, p. 1403)

It is important to see that Dijkstra does not only want formal methods to be given an equal or strong running. He wants computing to be seen in essentially formal and nonbehavioral terms, and with no consideration for computational models. Cognitive scientists might ponder on what this means for their work.

In my view, the reply given by Terry Winograd (1989) was the best. His reply emphasizes the fact that computers have their most fundamental role in a community of people. He insists that Dijkstra is wrong about what computers do, about what their programmers do, and about what knowledge engineers do. I want to draw attention to Winograd's remarks about knowledge engineering. These remarks are most relevant to what I have to say later about the management of uncertainty and ignorance.

Winograd says:

> In this last question — the relation between mechanism and use — the current vision of "software engineering" is too narrow and needs to be expanded into a vision of design. A building is created by a combination of people including both engineers and architects. The architect's skill includes knowledge of materials and building techniques, but has a primary focus on function. The key questions go beyond construction

to "What will make the building be appropriate to its use? What will function as a good design when people move in?" We need the develop effective (and rigorous) training that builds the skills to answer these questions in designing computer systems. (1989, p. 1413)

Dialogue and Metacommunication

The third case has to do with the handling of discourse and dialogue. This was reported in a keynote address at the FLAIRS 89 Conference. Since the full text of the address is not available, you will have to rely on my report. The keynote address was given by John Roach on "Parsing Pragmatics in Natural Language Dialogue."

Roach was involved in a project to build a voice-driven navigational computer for an aircraft. The idea was that the pilot would tell the computer the destination coordinates, and then tell it to take the plane to that destination.

The team soon found out that this was no simple task. They needed to program the machine with some sort of dialogue handling abilities. To do this they turned to the computational linguists, and began with the orthodox approach. The orthodox approach is essentially a language-centered approach. The focus is on the syntax and semantics of sentences. The pilot's sentences are to be taken in, parsed, analyzed, matched, and acted upon. This process is quite computationally expensive.

Almost straight away the team ran into the standard problems that vex this approach. The discourse and dialogue literature is filled with examples. Many come from situations such as railway station information desk conversations. For example, if someone comes to the desk and says, "When does the next train go to Edinburgh?" then there is no problem. The utterance parses into a query for which there is an appropriate answer. But, if someone comes to the desk and says, "Do you know when the next train goes to Edinburgh?" then, according to the language-centered approach, the answer would quite correctly be "Yes." And if someone comes to the desk and says, "My poor old Mum wants to know when the next train goes to Edinburgh," then, since there is no question, a nil response would be linguistically correct. Or perhaps the attendant might say, "How interesting, we'll start a file on your poor old Mum with a special field on her desires, for future reference." Unfortunately for Roach's team, these were not funny.

Now, just note that if an attendant on an information desk did give these linguistically correct answers, then we would consider the attendant to be rude and uncooperative. Many computation linguists and computer programmers would think that our classification of the attendant as rude and uncooperative is irrelevant to the writing of programs, and so it was at first with Roach's team. The idea that a computer could be rude and uncooperative was mere anthropomorphism.

Many of the interactions between the prototype navigational computer and the pilot were hilarious. In many cases the pilot lost his temper and shut the thing down. Basically, the computer was rude, thoughtless, and demanding.

Just when the team was about to give up, someone suggested to them, probably a clown from humanities, that they might consult the experts. This person dared to suggest that the real experts for this sort of interaction were not the computational linguists with their language-centered approach, but the rhetoricians. The team were prepared to try almost anything, so they took a look. They discovered a developed discipline which had many things to say about dialogue and discourse. The emphasis was on the social setting of discourse, and the social conventions within which dialogue takes place. Furthermore, there was the notion that the bulk, up to 90%, of what goes on is noninformational. Questions are asked, and responded to with very heavy emphasis on politeness, social hierarchy considerations, and emphasis on how to elicit responses without offense.

The informational content of an utterance will very often be conveyed in an envelope of meta-information. For example, say you wish to walk down a hallway during a conference. There are lots of people in the way. What you really need to do is issue a command: "Move out of my way." Try it one day. What you usually do is say "Excuse me," or "Can I get past?" The latter is a question. If someone responded, "Not unless I move," then you would consider them to be something else. The question is a polite way of issuing a command. The request, "Excuse me," is an even politer way of issuing the command. This way of looking at utterances looks at the social context in which things are said.

Roach's team took a look at some common examples. They discovered at least 1200 ways of issuing the command, "Tell me the time." There were various levels of politeness ranging from grovelling obsequiousness to rude commands. There were exercises of social pecking order such as, "My boss wants to know what the time is."

Roach's team developed a system which took much of this into account, and he says, in the abstract of his paper:

> Our system is based on the human communication theory known as "metacommunication" in which every utterance is said to consist of both a semantic content portion and a communication management portion. (1989, p. 4)

The processing concentrated *first* on the social dimension of what was said. When that had been sorted out, the second thing was to determine what the content was. It turned out that this approach was far more computationally efficient than the language-centered approach.

The details of the successes of the Roach team are not the important point for this chapter. The important point about Roach's paper, and the work it describes, is that it emphasizes not only that computers must interact with people in the way in which people interact with each other, but that whilesoever this community of people was ignored, the computing solutions were up the spout. As Winograd insists, the design of computing systems must take full account of:

> the design considerations that come from their embedding in situations of use. . . . The key questions go beyond construction to . . . "What will function as a good design when people move in ?" (1989, p. 1413)

APPROACHES TO UNCERTAINTY MANAGEMENT

Skepticism and Probabilities

The literature on uncertainty management is dominated by a strong emphasis on processing and formal systems. In a recent summary article, Peter Rothman (1989) sets out various approaches to the handling of uncertainty. In every case there is little attention to the problem in terms of the way in which people approach the question, and how they communicate their uncertainty to each other. The focus is on probability processing, or on evidential weight processing, or on fuzzy processing, or on the processing of degrees of certainty.

There is evidence in the article of an impatience with the sorts of conceptual distinctions which underlie the ways in which people deal with their own certainty and uncertainty, knowledge, and ignorance. In the same article Rothman says that "Virtually all knowledge outside of pure mathematics involves some level of uncertainty" (1989, p. 56)

He goes on to say that, "The term uncertainty is often equated with the concept of randomness. Randomness refers to uncertainty arising from the observation of random processes." (1989, p. 56).

In the face of such blasé assertions of philosophical views which are at least highly controversial, if not completely wrong, it is hard to know where to start. Maybe we should ask Rothman whether or not he knows the difference between an armchair and a steam train. Most people do!

Epistemology

But perhaps the better place to start is with a bit of straightforward epistemology. Let me draw attention to John Austin's classic paper "Other Minds" (1961). Although the paper is essentially an analysis of the concept of knowledge, it accomplishes this by drawing attention to ways in which people distinguish knowledge from belief.

Austin argues that the difference between knowledge and belief is to be found in three areas. One of these is quite uncontroversial. It is that a claim to know something will be a false claim if that something is not true, whereas, the claim to believe something can be a correct claim even if the something is false as a matter of fact. This leads to the notion that it is possible to have false beliefs, but it is not possible to know something which is false. It might also be added that it is not possible to know something which is uncertain.

The second distinction concerns the difference between the questions which can be put to those who claim to know and those which can be put to those who claim to believe. If someone claims to know that P, we can ask "How do you know that P?" But if someone claims to believe that P, we ask "Why do you believe that P?" The former question implies that if a knowledge claim is correct then the claimant should be able to give anyone an account which guarantees the claim is correct. Acceptable responses to "How do you know that P?" are determined by a range of issues having to do with the knowledge domain, the community of experts, and the status of the claimant. If the correct type of response is not given, then the claim to knowledge is called into question. The response that someone "just knows" might not be logically unsatisfactory, but it does call the claim to knowledge into question.

In answer to the latter question, "Why do you believe that P?" it is usual for the believer to cite the reasons and arguments which support the belief. Although it is not logically unsatisfactory for someone to respond that they "just believe," this response might not persuade many to adopt the same beliefs. But it is a legitimate response, and does not call the claim to believe into question.

It should be noted that the conceptual distinction outlined here is a distinction about human interaction. It relies upon the notion that some interactions are correct and some are not. It does not focus on the content of the assertions but on their context.

The third distinction concerns what Austin (1961) claims to be the promissory nature of knowledge. A claim to know, he says, is when "I give others my word: I give others my authority for saying that 'S is P.'" (p. 67) But when one claims to believe, or even to be certain but not to know, then one is not prepared to enter that unqualified promissory note. The claim to know puts the onus on the knowledge claimant to come up with the goods. The claim to believe is the claim of caution. The caution can arise from uncertainty, or from something else.

Again, this third distinction is very much oriented to social interaction. It is a promissory distinction. It has to do with being cautious, and protecting oneself from criticism. "I did not say I knew, I only said that I believed it."

Communication Management

It is important to note that in these kinds of terms, the communication of uncertainty is not handled by some declaration about the probability of the content of an assertion being true. Uncertainty is handled by guarding oneself from social responsibility of a particular kind. People say things like, "I believe he is at the dentist, *but I am not certain.*"

People do not react like Mr. Spock in *Star Trek*. When Spock responds to Kirk's question about life on a planet with the utterence, "The probability of life on that planet is only one in 156,728.507," we know that Spock is an alien. For all the sense it makes, he might as well have said, "The probability of life on that planet is only one in buzz buzz buzz." A human respondent might have said, "I can't tell." or "I don't believe so, but I can't rule it out entirely." or "I don't believe so, but I can't prove it."

The real problem with much of the uncertainty management in computing is that it is Spock processing, alien processing. The danger is that people will take seriously the figures used. And even if that is not a great danger, if the figures are not ignored, they will be converted to something else.

When people are asked to put data into a machine in the demanded format, they will make all sorts of leaps. They might always declare firm belief to be 90% certainty. They might always declare disbelief to be 10% certainty. Not knowing which way to go might be declared as 50% certainty. And so on. This might seem fair enough until we consider the problem cases.

Lack of belief is one problem case. This is the case where a person might want to say, "I don't know whether or not P, and I have no opinion as to whether or not P." To classify P as 50% probable as a consequence is at best quite misleading, and at worst farcical. Then there are the insuperable difficulties of ordering the probabilities of propositions. Even when these are not ordered in terms of probabilities but in terms of some partial or linear order, people more often than not cannot sensibly order propositions in terms of degrees of certainty, uncertainty, or ignorance. General hypotheses are another problem case. Given the usual facts about the general hypotheses of science, are we to give them a probability of 0 ? Of course not.

These problems turn the entry of data into a nightmare of arbitrary decisions. So I introduce the new slogan NINO — Nightmare In Nightmare Out. At this point I must insist that we reject appeals from programmers in terms of "What else can we do? At least we understand probability calculus (or evidential calculus, or certainty-ordering calculus)." These appeals are just like the appeal which might come from a doctor who, when confronted with with a difficult medical case says, "Well at least we know how to amputate legs, so let's take the left one."

The problem is not insoluble. Indeed, the scene is not as bleak as I have so far painted. We need not only to look at alternative ways of handling uncertainty, but we need the cognitive scientists to do some research on the way in which people handle uncertainty and ignorance. The philosophical framework set out by Austin is one viable starting point. It is also a starting point for some work in parallel by programmers and knowledge engineers.

Consider Austin's distinctions for a moment. At some sort of *prima face* level we should be able to indicate what the distinctions mean for the handling of information in machines. If the machine is to have some functional structure for distinguishing between knowledge and belief, then what part, if any, will the Austinian distinctions play? The first distinction is the least problematic and can be handled by some sort of autoepistemic logic.

The second distinction, if accepted, has some strong practical consequences for machines. The consequences are best thought of in terms of machine responses to queries about what the machine knows. In the first place, for example, if the machine answers the question "Do you know whether the temperature was over 100?" with "Yes, it was," then it should typically also be able to answer the question, "How do you know that the temperature was over 100?" In the second place, given that each knowledge domain has its own type of acceptable explanatory response, a machine asked the question above would have to be able to answer the "How" question with an appropriate answer such as, "Two independent thermometers gave a reading of 103 at that time." In the third place, it may well be decided that there are to be some areas in which the machine "just knows." These might have to do with direct input from peripherals, or with certain logical or mathematical claims. So, there would be a subset of the machine's knowledge which has some kind of privileged status.

Similar consequences follow for belief. If the machine answers the question posed above with, "No, but I believe that it is," then it should typically be able answer the question, "*Why* do you believe that the temperature was over 100?" In answer to this the machine might report on the source of the answer, or on some nonconclusive reasoning process which supports, but does not guarantee the claim that the temperature was over 100. It might report that it was "told" by someone that the temperature was over 100, but that the reporter was not always reliable, and so on. In all such cases the report given would give both the reasons and the cause for caution.

These consequences mean that any machine system for knowledge and belief which took Austin's second distinction seriously would have to have explanatory and reason-giving modules to go with knowledge and belief representation.

The third distinction consequences are important when we are considering the status of information. Some might be beyond question; it is basic knowledge. But some portions of the information which a machine has in store, or to which it has access, might be information about which some sort of caution needs to be entered. This information can be properly categorized as believed information. There has to be some provision for keeping track of information qualified by caution and the inferences that are drawn from such information.

I also have the suspicion that the status of information, from a human point of view, relates to the theories and sets of beliefs which people have about the world. This raises the point that ignorance and uncertainty, like belief and knowledge, are strongly related to theory formation and theory change.

COMPUTERS AND PEOPLE

All of this has an impact on cognitive science. The Dijkstra philosophy of computing is clearly hostile to cognitive science, but the philosophy which I am advocating has the consequence that cognitive science must look carefully at human interaction and its impact. If machines are to be used as models for cognitive activity, then we must be able to model in them the ability to make some of the conceptual distinctions which are at the center of cognitive activity. It is no good to keep offering machines as the basis for cognitive modeling, but not be able to program any machine to make the distinctions which a child can make. And if the child's distinctions are driven by social imperatives, then the models must allow for that dimension.

Michie and Johnston, in *The Creative Computer* (1985), point out that "It is the task of knowledge engineering to design and construct . . . conceptual interfaces to allow people . . . and machines . . . to understand each other" (p. 65), and "in order for any beings, human or machine, to talk to each other, they must share the same mental structures" (p. 72).

They must also make those distinctions in the same way that people make the distinctions, or in highly analogous and understandable ways. If machines do not have the same or highly analogous mental structures as people, but use the same terminology for radically differing structures, then the firm foundations are being laid for serious misunderstandings and consequent communication breakdown.

It is important that when descriptions are given of some area of machine implementation that there is a sensible understanding of what is being done. Even if the label is misleading to a layperson, the people working in the area should understand what is at the heart of what they are doing.

There is a real need for research here. Of course, research will not start in epistemology, then go on to cognitive science and then to computing. All will happen in parallel. So what's the problem with that ?

REFERENCES

Abelson, H. & Sussman, G.J. (1985). *Structure and interpretation of computer programs.* Cambridge, MA: MIT Press.

Austin, J.L. (1961). "Other minds". In *Philosophical papers* (pp. 44-84). Oxford, UK: Clarendon Press.

Dijkstra, E.W. (1989). On the cruelty of really teaching computer science. *Communications of the ACM,* December, 1398-1404.

Michie, D., & Johnston, R. (1985). *The creative computer.* Harmondsworth, UK: Penguin Books.

Roach, J.W. (1989). Parsing pragmatics in natural language dialogue. *Proceedings of the Second Florida Artifical Intelligence Research Symposium,* April 3-6, Orlando, FL.

Rothman, P. (1989). Selecting an uncertainty management system. *AI Expert,* July, 56-62.

Winograd, T. (1989). Reply to Dijkstra. *Communications of the ACM,* December, 1989, 1412-1413.

CHAPTER 19

Levels of Description

Paul Griffiths

Department of Philosophy,
University of Otago

INTRODUCTION

Levels of nature are becoming a fashionable philosophical "technology," somewhat after the manner of possible worlds. But like talk of possible worlds, talk of levels stands in need of explication. Accounts of theoretical reduction abound with references to higher and lower level theories and entities, but it is rare to find any sustained account of what it is to occupy a higher or a lower level. To address questions like "Do all levels reduce to the subatomic" or "Is the social level independent of the psychological?", we need to know something about the structure of levels of nature. Is the relation "at a higher level than" transitive? Is it symmetric or asymetric? Does it form a complete ordering of the contents of the universe, or only a partial ordering? If levels of nature are to be a basic notion of our metaphysics, then we need a systematic metaphysic of levels.

It is outside the scope of this chapter, and probably of my philosophical abilities, to provide such a systematic metaphysic of levels of nature. I have, therefore, two more limited aims. First, I advance some tentative arguments concerning the structure of the system of levels. Secondly, I draw attention to various unresolved issues, in the hope that others will be stimulated to give them their attention.

ORDERING THE LEVELS

Two separate strands of thought run through previous discussions of levels of nature. The first is often found in literature on theoretical reduction and the unity of science. Here we find the idea of broad levels of natural phenomena, the subatomic, atomic, molecular, biochemical, cellular, organismic, and social levels. I shall refer to this as the theoretical reduction tradition. In this tradition levels are ordered by the part/whole relationship between lower and higher level entities. The second strand of thought is found in the postfunctionalist theories of W.G. Lycan (1987) and others. These generalize the role/occupant distinction of functionalism to create a multiplicity of levels of description which successively realize one another. I shall refer to this as the functional level tradition. In this tradition, levels are differentiated by the multiple realizability of higher-level descriptions by lower-level ones. It is frequently assumed that both traditions are concerned with the same phenomena when they talk of levels, but this is far from obvious. In particular, it is not clear that the various ordering relations that have been suggested generate the same hierachical structure.

H.A. Simon in his *The Sciences of the Artificial* (1969) suggests that a series of levels[1] can be recovered from a distinctive pattern in the causal structure of certain complex systems. Certain complex systems, he suggests, exhibit a property of "near-decomposability." A system is "near-decomposable" if there are discrete subsets of the phenomena that occur in the system such that the short-term behavior of each subset is largely independent of the others. This, he argues, allows "entification," or the division of the system into a number of subsystems. Suppose the system we are describing is the biosphere. Taking cells as the elementary level, we discover that there are subsets of cells whose short-term behavior is very strongly inter-dependent. The short-term evolution of these subsystems can be predicted fairly well while ignoring the influence of other cells. These are the plants and animals.

Now suppose that each of these plants or animals is considered as a complex system, links to other plants and animals being ignored. If a similar pattern emerges within each system, then another level of entities has been discerned, nested within the first. In this case, these will be the organs. Alternatively, take the plants and animals as elementary, and consider the domain of these entities as a complex system in virtue of the interactions between them. If there are differences in the relative density of these interactions amongst the entities, then another level of entities can be discerned, which nests the first. These may be family groups, colonies, or herds.

I call this the "causal-clustering" model of levels. It is an ingenious idea, but it faces a number of problems. Simon describes how to determine whether a system is near-decomposable from a matrix representing strengths of interaction between elements of the complex system. But the interactions he has in mind in real cases are causal ones of every kind, and it is far from clear how this notion of strength of interaction is to be cashed out. Individuating causal relationships of every kind in a way that would make sense of counting them would require considerable ingenuity. It is not unreasonable to be skeptical about the applicability, even in principle, of Simon's criterion of entification.

---

[1] Which he refers to as a "hierachical structure."

There are more principled problems for Simon's model as well. The model is primarily designed for cases where the lower level entities stand in part/whole relationships to higher level entities. But some of the levels of nature that are referred to in current philosophical discussion are not of this kind. Consider, for example, the idea that a functional description of an animal's system of organs is at a higher level than an anatomical one. It does seem correct to say that a description of an animal as possessing a blood pump, a waste filter, an oxygen interface, and so on, is at a higher level than a description of it as having a heart, lung, and kidneys. But Simon's model would not place these at different levels. Anatomical entities do not stand in a part/whole relationship to functional entities. Instead, the functional categories seem to be at a higher level because they are more abstract. The anatomical *category* stands in a part/whole relationship to the functional *category*. It is this feature that allows the functional level theorist to place them at different levels.

W.C. Wimsatt presents a similar account to Simon's in his seminal paper *Reductionism, Levels of Organization and the Mind/Body "Problem"* (1976). This is very much a view from the theoretical reduction tradition. Once again, the stress is on entities, and it is taken for granted that movement up the structure of levels will mean movement from smaller to larger entities. However, Wimsatt introduces two important new ideas. First, he notices that what he calls "the same system" will occur at a number of levels, although it will be individuated *as a system* at only one level. Secondly, he suggests that entities collect at levels because there are regularities at levels. Wimsatt's advance here is to realize that it may not be the existence of higher level entities that leads to the existence of higher level regularities, and thus to the need for higher level theories. The direction of explanation may be quite the reverse. The presence of discernible entities may be explained by the presence of new regularities at higher levels of generality.

Because of these two features Wimsatt's model of levels has something in common with more recent accounts of levels, such as Lycan's. The same system can exist at many levels, although, as Wimsatt notes, it exists as a system at only one level. This suggests that levels are essentially levels of *description*, since systems at many levels can be composed of exactly the same basic, ontological material. The sense in which there are different entities at different levels is that the same material answers to different descriptions at each level, and new regularities can be expressed when the material is redescribed in higher level terms. Wimsatt shares an insight which is central to Lycan's account of levels. The levels of nature are the nexus of laws or generalizations that can be discerned when our classifications of things are arranged along an axis of increasing generality.

However, Wimsatt's ordering relation is still basically compositional. One level is higher than another if the entities at one level are composed of the entities at the other. I have already mentioned a major problem for the compositional view. There are theoretical perspectives on organisms — functional and anatomical perspectives, for example — whose descriptions do not seem to relate to one another compositionally, but which are arguably at different levels. In the next section, I discuss attempts to define the ordering relation in terms of multiple realizability.

MULTIPLE REALIZABILITY

Recent accounts in the functional level tradition, such as Lycan's, have assumed a tight connection between the ordering relation between levels and the relation of multiple realizability. This is because these "functional" levels are concieved as successive abstractions from the level below. At each level a class of features discernible at the lower level is declared irrelevant to descriptions at the higher level. Thus, in the functional/structural anatomy case, the functional description abstracts away from the nature of the physical mechanisms that perform certain functions. Blood pumps may be either hearts or prostheses. The physical differences between the two are irrelevant to the application of the description "blood pump." So blood pumps are multiply realizable at the anatomical level. It is usually assumed that if one level is higher than another, then descriptions at the higher level are multiply realizable at the lower level.

Functional level accounts also standardly assume that it is multiple realizability that makes the levels of nature independent. The idea is that multiple realizability blocks the reduction of one level to another. But consider the following criteria of ordering:

(C1) A level L1 is higher than a level L2 iff descriptions at L1 can be realized by more than one description at L2.

On this criterion, higher levels can be produced trivially by introducing predicates that abbreviate disjunctions of lower-level descriptions and calling these higher-level descriptions. So it is not just multiple realizability that separates out levels of nature. The additional element in most accounts is a demand that the higher-level descriptions yield regularities (laws, causal connections) which cannot be stated at any lower level. In this way the functional level account will preserve the insight that levels of nature are the nexus of new regularities at successive levels of generality.

As I have already noted, this insight is also found in the theoretical reduction tradition. According to Wimsatt, new patterns of causation become visible as successively larger entities are considered. But functional-level theorists will differ from Wimsatt in not thinking that all new patterns of causation are equally significant. Suppose the larger, higher level entities are just agglomerations of smaller entities. Type identities between the larger entities are mapped by type identities between their constituents. In this case, any causal links they enter into will exist at lower levels as what we may call "macrolaws." Macrolaws are of the form "such-and-such a cluster of events is nomically related to such-and-such a cluster of events." The functional level theorist standardly argues that the existence of macrolaws at the lower level renders the higher level explanatorily redundant. The higher level explanatorily redundant. The higher level predicates can be treated as names of structures at the lower level.

However, the higher level entities need not be simple agglomerations of this kind. Higher level entities may be type identical with other higher level entities without the sets of lower level entities of which they are composed being type identical with one another. In other words, the higher level entity type may be multiply realizable at the lower level. These are the cases which the functional-level theorists think significant. In such cases, any attempt to restate the causal conections between the higher level entities as macrolaws at the lower level will either involve a loss of generality or require disjunctive laws. The functional-level theorists standardly maintain that it is because of this that the higher level is not reducible to the lower. Adding the new level adds something substantial to our ability to explain phenomena, because it gives us nondisjunctive laws at a higher degree of generality.

The revised criterion of order that emerges from this discussion is:

(C2) A level L1 is higher than a level L2 iff descriptions at L1 can be realized by more than one description at L2, and there are generalizations at L1 that cannot be nondisjunctively stated at L2.

But there are still problems with C2. Suppose that the disjunctions required to state the higher level generalizations at the lower-level are relatively short. Do we really lose explanatory power by moving from the L_1 generalization that all As are Bs to the L_2 generalization that all things that are either a_1 or a_2, or a_3 are either b_1, b_2, or b_3?

Whatever the intuitive response to this, C2 will have to be rejected. Higher levels can be generated quite trivially using this criterion. Suppose that at L2 A events cause B events, and C events cause D events. Now take the L1 predicate X which applies to whatever is A or C at L2, and L1 predicate Y, which applies to whatever is either B or D at L2. X and Y are multiply realizable at L2, and the generalization that X-type events cause Y-type events cannot be nondisjunctively stated at the lower level.

It might be possible to rest content with C2, despite the fact that it generates more levels of description than we have any use for. Pragmatic factors, such as the simplicity of the resulting theories, might be allowed to determine which levels we take seriously. I am inclined, however, to look for a stronger notion of level, one which will preserve the idea that the theories of special sciences that discuss those levels are genuinely irreducible.

This can be achieved by requiring that the generalizations which emerge at a level cannot be *finitely* stated at lower levels. In other words, the significant form of multiple realizability occurs when a potentially infinite number of lower level descriptions could realize the higher level description, and the higher level generalizations could only be stated by a correspondingly infinite disjunction. This will block the trivial generation of additional levels[2]. The new criterion of ordering will be:

(C3) A level L1 is higher than a level L2 iff descriptions at L1 can be realized by more than one description at L2, and there are generalizations at L1 that cannot be finitely stated at L2.

This may seem a very strong requirement, but this is not the case. A higher level description need not actually have an infinite number of realizations. It is enough that no limit can be put on how it might be realized. This is guaranteed whenever the higher level description has criteria of application that are independent of the lower level. This explains why the mere *conceivability* of alternative realizations for the mind was fatal to the Identity Theory of Mind. Even if minds were uniquely physically realized in the actual world, the fact that the conditions for applying mental predicates are independent of any facts about how they are realized implies that the predicate "has a mind" and does not correspond to any finite disjunction of physical predicates. So if there are any true generalizations in psychology, they cannot be stated as a finite disjunction of connections between physical predicates.

It can be argued that potentially infinite realisability of this sort does not block certain important kinds of reduction. Although minds on Mars may be hydraulic, and minds in the future may be electronic, human minds are all neural. So domain-specific reductions remain possible. Normal human psychology can be reduced to neuroscience if human minds turn out to be uniform enough. But I can admit the importance of this sort of reduction while still holding that potentially infinite multiple realizability marks off new levels of nature. There may be considerable scientific utility in establishing universal but contingent facts about realization (which is what these domain-specific reductions really are). Nevertheless, information (generality) is lost in the move to the lower level. The higher level vocabulary allows the

---

[2] Pavel Tichy has pointed out that C3 allows the creation of higher levels by the use of vague predicates denoting a continuum of precise values for a determinable. Thus, the description "weighs between one and two grams" is at a higher level than descriptions like "weighs exactly one and a half grams." The former can be realized by a potentially infinite number of the later, and generalizations featuring the former, such as "anything that weighs between one and two grams will activate this device" cannot be finitely stated in terms of the lower level. One response might be to say that there is a genuine explanatory gain from the introduction of such vague predicates. Such an "outsmarter" can argue that if we eschewed the use of any but precise measurements we would not be able to capture generalizations about the properties of stretches of continua.

formulation of more general laws, although this additional generality is not actually needed to explain currently observed phenomena.

A similar situation arises when it is logically possible for a higher level predicate to be realized in an infinite number of ways, but nomologically impossible. There is an important sense in which the generality that is lost in moving to the lower level is unnecessary generality. It does not increase our ability to explain the way things are in the actual world, although it does increase our ability to give a partitioning of overall logical space. Some of the classic "contingent identities" of the physical sciences may fit into this category. Lightning may be nomologically uniquely realizable, and thus, in this important sense, reducible to the phenomena of electrical discharge.[3] We could then explain why the assimilation of mind/brain reduction to such cases was mistaken. Although minds are realized in brains, it is not nomologically impossible for them to be realized in other ways.

In summary, we have three senses of reducibility: domain-specific, or extensional reductions, nomological reductions, and full or logical reductions. These will all have significance for different purposes. C3 is intended to capture full or logical irreducibility. Descriptions that are seperated by C3 may still be nomologically or domain specifically reducible to one another.

THE LOGIC OF REALIZABILITY

If multiple realizability is to play the central role in differentiating levels, then we need to examine the logic of the multiple realizability relation.

It is easy to see that the relation is transitive. If a description at L1 has a potentially infinite number of realizers at L2 and if at least one of the realizers at L2 has a potentially infinite number of realizers at L3, then the L1 description has a potentially infinite number of realizers at L3.

It is more important, and more difficult, to show that the multiple-realizability relation is asymmetric. It is desirable for the criteria of higher leveledness to be asymmetric if it is to explicate the informal notion of a level of nature. Simon and Wimsatt's compositional approach guarantees the direction of the hierachy of levels because the part/whole relationship is asymmetrical. The entities at each successive level are made up of entities at the lower levels. This seems to exclude the hierachy looping back, so that lower level entities are composed of the higher level entities which they

---

[3] I don't mean to suggest that the original decision to identify lightning with electrical discharge rested on a claim about nomologically unique realization. The domain-specific identity of the two phenomena was probably all that was required. However, there is an important distinction to be drawn between identities which are nomologically guaranteed and identities which we can only really assert for the domain we have investigated. I suggest that some of the classic "contingent identities" may lie on the nomological side of this dichotomy, whilst mind/brain identity lies on the domain specific side.

themselves compose.[4] Some assurance is needed that loops of this kind cannot occur with the multiple-realizability relation.

It may seem self-evident that multiple realizability is asymetric, because talk of realization still has overtones of composition, and thus of the part/whole relationship. But this is not reflected in any explicit conditions on multiple realizability that I have given so far. So far I have assumed that a description at L1 is multiply realizable at L2 iff two systems can share the L1 description without sharing an L2 description (or, to exclude illicit disjunctive descriptions, any nondisjunctive L2 description). But the following story seems to show that this is not enough to guarantee asymmetry.

Suppose that at LF organs are described in terms of their functions, while at LA they are described anatomically. At LF we have the descriptions blood pump and blood filter. At LA we have anatomical descriptions of the heart, the kidney, and an imaginary organ. Now suppose that in different animals the imaginary anatomically described organ could serve as a blood pump, or as blood filter.[5] The LF descriptions blood pump and blood filter are multiply realizable at LA because they can be realized by two different anatomically described organs. But the imaginary anatomically described organ is multiply realizable at LF because it can be realized either by a blood pump or a blood filter.

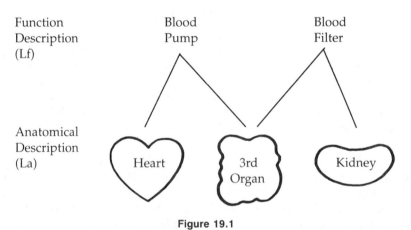

Figure 19.1

---

[4] Although more work is probably needed before it is safe to conclude that the causal clustering criteria for "entification" of a level always yields entities which stand in appropriate part/whole relationships.

[5] It is quite common for the same anatomical item to serve different roles at different stages in the evolution of a lineage.

In order to see why multiple realizability is asymmetric it is necessary to draw attention to the role of supervenience. It is usually assumed in discussions of multiple realizability that the realized level supervenes on the realizing level. Historically, this is because multiple realizability is introduced as an *explanation* of the irreducibility of certain supervenient descriptions. I shall now explicitly state that a level L2 cannot realize a level L1 unless L1 supervenes on L2.

This has implications for the story about the imaginary organ. In the story, each functional description can be realized by more than one anatomical description. I have required that realized levels supervene on realizing levels, so the functional must supervene on the anatomical. Thus, if there is to be any change at the functional level, there must be change at the anatomical level. Now consider the two situations, in one of which the imaginary organ is a blood pump, and in the other of which it is a blood filter. These two situations differ at the functional level, so they must differ at the anatomical level. I have stipulated that the imaginary organ is the same at the anatomical level in both these situations, so there must be changes elsewhere at that level.

At this stage the story still seems to work. But it ceases to work if we try to apply it to *total* descriptions of a system at the two levels. The system description S-at-LF, which includes the claim that the system has a blood pump, could be realized by the system description S-at-LA or by S'-at-LA. These correspond to the two ways the blood pump could be realized, as a heart, or as the imaginary organ. According to the story, the system description S'-at-LA can also stand in the realisation relation to a system description S'-at-LF. This corresponds to the claim that the imaginary organ could also be a kidney. But if S'-at-LF differs from S-at-LF, then there must be a difference in the supervenience base level at LA, which contradicts the assumption that the supervenience base in both cases is the same, namely S'-at-LA.

Function   S at Lf   S' at Lf
Description

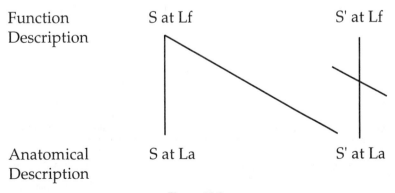

Anatomical   S at La   S' at La
Description

Figure 19.2

The key to this argument is that a lower level description which describes the whole supervenience base[6] for a higher level description cannot correspond to more than one description at that higher level. To suppose that it does is to violate the assumption that it captures the whole supervenience base. The lesson to be drawn from this is that a higher level description applies in virtue of the whole of its supervenience base at a lower level. Thus, whilst it is true that the heart, in virtue of its salience in the blood-pumping system, is the blood pump, the description "system with a blood pump" is not made true by the system containing a heart, but by the state of the whole system which constitutes it being organized so as to pump blood.[7]

So we have the following pair of conclusions. First, a level L1 cannot be realized at a level L2 unless L1 supervenes on L2. Second, a higher level description is made true by its complete supervenience base at the lower level.

In the light of these conclusions we need to revise C3:

(C4) A level L1 is higher than a level L2 iff there are L1 descriptions for each of which there is more than one complete supervenience base at L2, and there are generalizations at L1 that cannot be finitely stated at L2.

THE SYSTEM OF LEVELS

So the multiple-realization ordering relation is transitive and asymmetric. The question I now want to consider is the overall structure of the system of levels. Do the several levels at which different systems are described link up to form broad "levels of nature" as in the traditional theory-reduction picture? This would require the ordering relation to be complete, that is, to determine for any two descriptions that are not at the same level which is higher than the other. Alternatively, are there many incomparable types of higher level description, each applicable to some limited domain of systems? This would require the ordering relation to form a partial ordering, leaving some descriptions incommensurable in terms of level.

---

[6] That is, a minimal set of lower level properties which is sufficient to fix the truth of the higher level description.

[7] I do not intend to deny that a functional term like "blood pump" can properly be applied to some salient component of a blood-pumping system. I merely maintain that the term applies to the component in virtue of the overall blood-pumping organization of the system at that level. The situation is also complicated by the fact that the *biological* function of the heart, namely to pump blood, can properly be assigned to the heart alone. According to the etiological theory of biological function, such functions supervene on past states of the organism. In those past states the organism was so organized that the functional part played an appropriate functional role, although it may no longer do so.

The criterion C4 is only applicable to descriptions which potentially stand in the realization relation to one another. It cannot determine, for example, whether a description of a tiger at the cellular level is at a higher or lower level than a description of the activity of some computer given in a low-level programming language. In order to determine this, I would have to find descriptions that were at the same level as, say, the description of the computer, but which were either potential realizers of, or potentially realized by, the description of the tiger. In other words, to determine whether C4 yields a partial or a complete ordering of descriptions, I require some account of the horizontal identity of levels.

Turning our attention to horizontal identity of levels brings out two major gaps in the account of levels given so far. I will attempt to fill these gaps before directly confronting the problem of horizontal identity of levels. The two gaps are as follows. First, I have assumed that the relation of multiple realizability relative to some level L2 will be distributed over all descriptions at L1. I have not considered the possibility that some L1 descriptions may be multiply realizable at L2 whilst others are not. Secondly, I have referred to the existence of various alternative realizations of a higher level state at some lower level. But I have given no criteria for determining that the various potential realizers are at one and the same level. I have talked as if the mere fact that states are the realizers of the same higher level state places them at a single level.

I have the following argument for supposing that multiple realizability relative to some lower level will be distributed over all the descriptions at a higher level. Suppose that we have two clusters of descriptions, one of which we suppose to be at a higher level than another. Now suppose that some of the putatively higher level descriptions do not turn out to be multiply realizable at the lower level. Quite simply, these will be descriptions that are reducible to the lower level, and thus should not be regarded as being at the higher level at all.

The same argument can be put in terms of the functional-level theorists' idea that levels are generated by successive abstractions. Suppose there is an initial level L2, and we abstract away from L2 by ignoring some list of features fi-fn to obtain a new level L1. Now suppose that we describe a domain of systems at L1. This yields a set of new descriptions. Some of these may turn out to be reducible to the existing L2 descriptions, as fi-fn are not relevant to the application of those L2 descriptions. In this case, it would seem that we have failed to create any higher level descriptions in that subdomain.

To make this more concrete, imagine generating a cellular level by ignoring certain classes of differences in the constitution of molecular systems. Things count as cells of a certain type if they satisfy certain structural conditions, irrespective of the details of how those structures are implemented. Now imagine trying to describe non-organic systems at the new, higher level. The non-organic systems fail to satisfy any of the new, structural descriptions that apply in the organic subdomain, and if we make up new terms that refer to the way the nonorganic things are structured, it turns out that one and only one thing at the lower level could occupy that structure. Once again, the higher level contains only terms that are multiply realizable at the lower level, because if they were not, they would drop back to the lower level.

This leaves me with the second gap in my account, the unargued assumption that the various realizers of an L1 description will be at the same level. This reflects the wider assumption that if there are two distinct levels L1 and L2, where L1 is higher than L2, every realization of an L1 description must have an L2 description. However, this assumption is simply incorrect. Consider a psychological description, with potential realizations in both biological and nonbiological systems. Some of its realizations will have descriptions at the cellular level, but others will not, so C4 should be revised to avoid this assumption.

C4 can be revised to avoid this problem by dropping the requirement that all of the supervenience bases that give rise to the multiple realizability of the higher-level description are at the same lower level. There is a slight complication to doing this. Every description is realized by many different descriptions at various lower levels. It is realized by the whole vertical array of descriptions that realize one another down to the lowest level (if there is one). Since the realization relation is transitive, each of these realizes the high-level description. But this is not what is meant by multiple realizability. To avoid counting the vertical series of realizations as multiple realizations, I introduce the idea of horizontally separated supervenience bases. Two supervenience bases are horizontally separated if neither realizes the other. We can now revise C4, making use of this notion.

> (C5) A level L1 is higher than a level L2 iff there are L1 descriptions for each of which there is more than one complete, horizontally separated supervenience base, and some of these bases are at L2, and there are generalizations at L1 that cannot be finitely stated at the level(s) containing realizations of L1 descriptions.[8]

C5 sidesteps the problem of determining whether various realizations are at one and the same level, but it still gives no positive account of what it is for two descriptions to be at the same level. It does not provide a criterion of the horizontal identity of levels. It is to this major problem that I now turn.

---

[8] It would be sufficient to require that the generalizations not be finitely statable at L2 if it were not for one problematic case. Suppose there are two levels, L2 and L3, such that they are themselves incommensurable as regards level (a possibility discussed below). If the descriptions that enter into an L1 generalization have a finite number of potential realizations at each of L2 and L3, the generalization will not be finitely statable at either L2 or L3, but will be finitely statable using the combined vocabularies of L2 and L3.

Intuitively, levels derive their unity from being occupied by the same sorts of things. The molecular level is occupied solely by molecules, the cellular by cells, and the organismic by organisms. In other words, the contents of a level are type-identical in respect of certain of their general features.

The problem of the horizontal identity of levels is overlooked in the compositional accounts of Simon (1969) and Wimsatt (1976). These authors seem to assume that each level is occupied by a particular type of entity, but this is not guaranteed by the compositional ordering relation. The notion that each level consists of the same kind of basic entities is an additional element in the account, not something which follows from their basic mechanism for generating levels. To see this, suppose we admit that there is some unproblematic unity to the molecular level. Then apply the compositional criteria to locate higher level entities. There will be some collections of molecules that compose the cells that will later compose organisms, but there will be other collections of molecules that will compose complex but nonbiological systems. Are these two classes of newly isolated entities on the same level? The compositional criteria provides no answer. The idea that the cells are on the same level seems relatively unproblematic because they are all cells, not because they are products of the same stage of Simon's entification process.

This problem for Simon and Wimsatt has its analog on the multiple-realizability view. We cannot generate an account of being at the same level from our account of being at a higher level. Suppose there is some unproblematic lower level, and that two descriptions have realizations at that level, but not at any intermediate level. There is no reason to conclude from this that they are themselves at the same level.

Although the idea that levels consist of particular kinds of entities is important to our intuitive grasp of the idea of a level, it is not easy to see how this idea can be made precise. Even where the idea seems unproblematically applicable, as in the case of the molecular or cellular levels, it may be difficult to determine the extension of the entity type without referring to the level it occurs at. It seems clear that plant and animal cells, despite their considerable differences, are the same type of entity, and constitute a single level of description for the biosphere. But should descriptions of viruses as single-celled organisms be placed at the same level? According to the 'same entities' approach, we should ask whether these purported cells really are type-identical with the other cells. But in determining this, one of the critical questions is whether they are at a higher or lower level than molecular descriptions of the same viruses.

So the "same entities" approach to horizontal identity is at best problematic. One other approach to horizontal identity suggests itself. In the functional-level tradition, levels are generated by successive abstractions. At each stage some class of features is declared irrelevant to the type identity of systems, thus generating a new, more abstract set of categories. Each level will have some classes of features that are relevant to type identity at that level, and others that are not. Perhaps this proprietory vocabulary can be used to unify a level.

This line of thought might be developed in the following way. If a level is primarily a level of multiply realizable descriptions, then each description is a specification of a role that may have many occupants. This role will be specified in terms of input and output properties, so each level has a proprietory vocabulary of inputs and outputs. A description of a system that uses this vocabulary is a description at that level. This is a promising idea, but it faces a major difficulty. When a particular role is specified, only a fragment of the available vocabulary need be used, so different fragments must be judged to be part of the same vocabulary. Therefore, if this account of levels is not to be circular, there must be a way of determining the unity of a vocabulary of inputs and outputs which is independent of the fact that they determine descriptions at the same level. This seems likely to be as difficult of a task as that of determining the unity of a class of entities.

So the problem of horizontal identity of level remains unsolved. This makes it difficult to give any definitive picture of the structure of the system of levels, and to answer my initial query about the completeness of the ordering relation. In the remainder of this section I shall give a picture of the structure that I think has some immediate plausibility. I hope that a suggestive picture may provide useful feedback into an account of horizontal identity.

Wimsatt (Figure 19.3) suggests that certain levels of nature cover the whole domain of existent systems. In particular, his physicalist metaphysical assumptions make it plausible that every system has a subatomic decomposition. However, nothing in Wimsatt's account suggests that higher levels are similarly complete. The compositional ordering relation allows judgments about level to be made only where one kind of system is composed of another kind. There is, presumably, no account at the cellular or organismic level of higher level nonorganic systems, since these are not composed of cells or organisms. So in Wimsatt's model, where higher level entities must be composed of lower level ones, the hierachy of levels of nature looks likely to divide into branches. Each branch will consist of a set of levels applicable to subdomains of natural phenomena. Levels on different branches will be incommensurable as regards level. Furthermore, because higher level systems may be assembled out of various different materials, previously separated branches may converge at still higher levels, so the "higher than" relation defines a reticulate structure.

This seems an intuitively plausible model of levels of nature. Interestingly, we get the same picture by two different routes. First, there is the intuitive idea that a level consists of a class of entities. The "same entities" conception of the horizontal identity of levels seemed to give the right answers in the cases where it has application. This idea suggests a structure of levels very similar to Wimsatt's model. There will be very broad subatomic, atomic, and

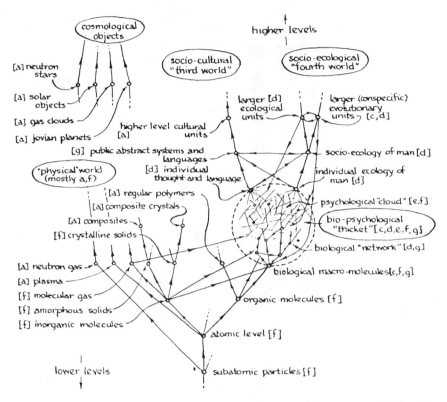

Figure 19.3. An 'illustrative' (i.e., tentative) "ontology of our world." From Wimsatt (1976) p. 253.

molecular levels; a branch of partial levels for biological organisms; and various still-higher partial levels for psychological and sociological entities.

Secondly, this picture of levels is at least compatible with the C5 ordering relation. The kinds of judgments that can be made with C5 will often track those produced by the compositional ordering relation, because the realization of many systems is related to their composition. It will leave incommensurabilities between various levels which have no capacity to realize one another, and these include the incommensurabilities left on the compositional account. However, C5 will also provide an ordering for various levels of abstraction, such as the functional/anatomical and perhaps the psychological/neural, which are not explicable in terms of composition. There may be further incommensurabilites here that will complicate the picture.

A revised speculation about the structure of the system of levels, incorporating the treatment of informational systems allowed by using a multiple realizability ordering relation is shown in Figure 19.4.

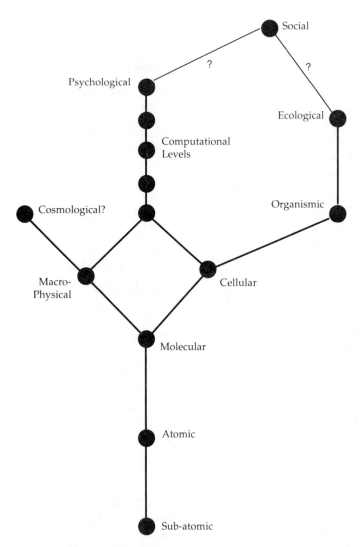

Figure 19.4. Speculations about the system of levels produced by C5

If this picture were accepted it would have implications for the idea of
levels as levels of abstraction. Rather than thinking of levels as produced
in an orderly series by successive abstractions, we would have to think of
different abstractions occurring from the same starting level, giving rise to
bifurcations in the system of levels. Thus, starting from the same basis, say
at the molecular level, ignoring a certain subset of differences between
molecular descriptions might allow the generation of the hierachy of biological
levels. Ignoring a different, although perhaps overlapping sub-set might allow
the generation of the astronomical level (if this is distinct from the physical).

CAUSATION AND THE SYSTEM OF LEVELS

I have described a picture in which the same ontological material must be described at many levels in order to capture all available generalizations. The facts expressed at each level of description supervene on those expressed at lower levels, but are not finitely expressible at those levels. This picture has implications for an account of causation.

Because of the supervenience assumption, the evolution of systems at higher levels of description is sufficiently determined by the evolution of the lowest level systems on which they ultimately supervene. Any higher level causation which is not, in some sense, supervenient on the lowest level, will overdetermine higher level occurrences. There are various responses to this. One is to consider the causal relationships at the lowest level as locus of real, ontologically significant causal influence. Another is to regard causation as something inadequately described when any of the levels are omitted. This would parallel the attitude I have suggested to the reality which we describe at various levels.

There is no space to discuss these issues here, but causation is clearly another area where a systematic theory of levels would be illuminating.

REFERENCES

Lycan, W.G. (1987). *Consciousness*. Cambridge, MA: Bradford Books.
Simon, A.H. (1969). *The sciences of the artificial*. Cambridge, MA: MIT Press.
Wimsatt, W.C. (1976). Reductionism, levels of nature & the mind-body problem. In *Consciousness & the Brain*. G.G. Globus, G. Maxwell, & I. Savodnik (Eds). New York: Plenum Press.

CHAPTER 20

Empty-Headed Animals?
– Eliminativist Prose and Cons *

Drew Khlentzos

*Department of Philosophy,
University of New England*

INTRODUCTION

Eliminativism presents us with a conundrum. If it is true no one, least of all the eliminativist, can believe that it is, and if any further proof of its incoherence be demanded, one need only point to the fact that to the eliminativist, Moore's Paradox[1] not only is *not* paradoxical but tells us the sober truth about belief.

Is it any wonder that armchair critics who have advanced smug and facile arguments such as the preceding one have not exactly endeared themselves to cognitive scientists? Indeed, the eliminativist has a plausible reply to it: What better proof could there be of the incoherence of the folk notion of *belief* than that one *can believe* in eliminativism if and only if one *cannot believe* in eliminativism? This tells *not* against the coherence of eliminativism, the eliminativist will contend, but against the coherence of the concept of *belief*.

To be sure, recent eliminativist critics of folk psychology, such as the Churchlands (1981, 1983, 1986) and Stephen Stich (1983), have not advanced the bold thesis that our attributions of beliefs and desires to other people and to ourselves are *incoherent*. They have insisted, rather, that they may very well be revealed by cognitive science or neuroscience as systematically false, drawing upon analogies with discredited scientific theories in other domains of inquiry, such as geocentric theories of planetary motion and the

* My thanks to my colleagues at U.N.E. — Dr. Fred D'Agostino, Dr. William Grey, Dr. Robert Elliot, Emeritus Professor Richard Franklin — and to participants in a philosophy seminar at A.N.U., especially Dr. Peter Roeper, Professor Frank Jackson, and Dr. Timothy Williamson. Special thanks to Don Arthur for convincing me that eliminativism *ought* to be taken seriously.

[1] Moore's Paradox concerns how to explain the puzzling status of the possibly true "p but I do not believe p."

caloric theory of heat to show how this might come to pass. Still, it is clear that any demonstration that no psychological state *could* have the properties ascribed to beliefs, desires, intentions, and their ilk by folk psychology would be welcome news to any eliminativist ear and as we shall see (though without going in to details) the most cogent extant arguments against folk psychology precisely *do* contend that our attributions of beliefs and desires *are* incoherent.

As poor as the toy antieliminativist argument with which we started was, I think we would be deluding ourselves if we pretended that there is *nothing* to the sentiments which give rise to it. The plain fact is that eliminativism has won comparatively few converts and many of those who resist it do so not for antiscientific reasons, but because they suspect that the eliminativist's own theory really is, at bottom, incoherent. How so? Well it is very difficult to see how it can be legitimate for the eliminativist to *simultaneously* condemn folk psychology as false and make use of the very notions implicated in this condemnation (viz. folk semantic ones) to formulate the charge. More perspicuously, eliminativism, as articulated by Paul and Patricia Churchland, alleges that all attributions of states with representational content are false, yet in order to *interpret* the eliminativist's own thesis we must prescind from ascribing any semantic content to it, which leaves us wondering "How are we supposed to interpret it *at all*?" The worry is *not* the crude one that eliminativists really do *believe* their thesis despite their disavowals. That criticism can be silenced in any number of ways, the crudest way being to respond that it is question begging for the antieliminativist to accuse his/her opponent of *believing* the thesis that there *are no* beliefs. The problem is rather that we do not know what thesis we are supposed to be evaluating or whether it is even right to talk of theses or evaluation of theses at all. We do not know which, if any, principles of inference are sanctioned by the eliminativist; we do not know what, if any, response to the eliminativist's claims would be appropriate; we do not know whether *any* of our previous ways of talking or acting — that is of comporting ourselves — as we supposed, *rationally,* can have any chance of surviving the radical demise of folk psychology recommended by eliminativism.

In short, we do not know what rationality could possibly consist of for the eliminativist. We do not know and, we suspect, the eliminativist cannot possibly tell us.

It is this suspicion, I feel, that restrains many from giving any serious credence to eliminativism. What I wish to do in this chapter is to allay this suspicion as best I can. Eliminativism may be mistaken but it is *not*, I shall argue, incoherent. There is only one way I can succeed in this project — I must outline a coherent version of eliminativism. I intend to do this by way of criticizing a recent attempt to prove the incoherence of eliminativism.

I need to address a more pressing question before doing that: What interest attaches to the Eliminativist's theory? Are there any grounds *at all* for believing it? Plainly, if eliminativism were just an idle possibility dreamt up by bored philosophers or if the best empirical evidence from cognitive science and neuroscience held strongly against it there would be little of interest to people engaged in research on the mind in a project such as mine. After all, the thesis that our present economic woes are due to the spells of malevolent goblins is a perfectly coherent one, it is just that no one, not even Paul Keating, seriously entertains it. This is not how the situation stands with eliminativism. There are compelling theoretical reasons for discarding folk psychology and eschewing all talk of mental representation modeled on the notion of belief. What are those reasons? Let me sketch the most important ones. There are three different sorts of consideration that speak in favor of eliminativism, at least two of which I can reasonably expect cognitive scientists to be familiar with:

1.   The first has to do with what used to be called materialism but is now often referred to as physicalism. Physicalism requires that all properties either reduce to or supervene upon *physical* properties. But, the argument goes, to attribute a belief or a desire or an intention to a person is to attribute a state which has a certain representational content. However, this content neither reduces to nor supervenes upon physical properties. Hence there can be no such states.

2.   The second focuses on recent work on neural networks. The point is perhaps most easily expressed by means of a Language of Thought (LOT) model of belief, though it in no way *requires* that model. According to LOT proponents, for an agent to believe that the Australian economy is in a mess is for that agent to stand in a certain relation to a sequence of mental symbols s_1 which *means*: the Australian economy is in a mess and for that agent to later acquire the belief that if the Australian economy is in a mess then the present Labor government is solely responsible for that deplorable state of affairs is for the agent to token another sequence of mental symbols s_2 in which the previous sequence s_1 (meaning that the Australian economy is in a mess) will occur as a physical (syntactic) part. But in a PDP model there need be *no* discrete representation of either proposition. No element or cluster of elements need represent the proposition that the Australian economy is in a mess, similarly no element or cluster need represent the proposition that if the Australian economy is in a mess then the present Labor government is solely responsible for that deplorable state of affairs. Moreover even if there *were* to be stable configurations of elements within the network that represented these propositions, it still would not thereby *have* to be the case that the configuration representing the compound (conditional) proposition contain some cluster of elements representing the atomic proposition. Instead there may simply be a certain distribution of weights throughout the network

that causes the network to respond "Yes" to the question "Is it the case that the Australian economy is in a mess?" and a quite different distribution of weights inducing the network to later respond "Yes" to the very different stimulus "Is it the case that if the Australian economy is in a mess then the present Labor government is solely responsible for that deplorable state of affairs?" The transition from the old state to the new one is not even partially caused by the tokening of a mental representation of the Australian economy being in a mess (within the syntactic context of a representation of the more complex state of affairs). The transition from one state to another is brought about instead by a widespread readjustment of weights throughout the network. A connectionist network in other words need not, and typically will not, contain representations of propositions; neither need it mirror the logicosemantic relations between propositions. So if the mind-brain just *is* a PDP machine as opposed to a 'classical' von Neumann machine, beliefs and desires as attitudes to certain propositions need not feature in *its* behavior either.

3.   The third set of considerations in favor of eliminativism may be less familiar to cognitive scientists. These considerations all seek to cast doubt on the notion of content that folk psychology appears committed to in characterizing beliefs, desires, and so forth as states with content. Some arguments attack the causal efficacy of contentful states, delegating to them an epiphenomenal status and thus withdrawing them from service in science. Others make the more serious accusation that contentful states lack any objectivity. The most radical objections claim that the very notion of content is incoherent. Thus we have:

1. W.V. Quine's (1960) famous arguments against the determinacy of content first advanced in the form of an argument to show that translation between languages was indeterminate. There can be no fact of the matter as to what some foreign expression or sentence really and truly *means*. Indeed, there can be no fact of the matter concerning what the expressions of one's *own* language really mean.

2. Arguments (again originally due to Quine) to the effect that attributions of content are irredeemably holistic and context-sensitive. These arguments have received an interesting recent formulation in Stephen Stich's work (1983).

3. Arguments from what may be termed the *queerness* of content. How can anything *physical* have a representational content? Isn't it at least a *puzzling* fact about the world, if indeed it is a fact, that certain distributions of particles (or perhaps certain higher order physical properties of such) represent of and by themselves certain *other* distributions of particles? How could this come about? How would

a world in which *no* physical state intrinsically represented any other physical state *differ* from our world? Scientific realism seems to urge us to say that such a world without content just *is* our world. An elegant formulation of this style of argument, freed from any commitment to physicalism, is due to Saul Kripke (1982). Kripke's arguments cause problems for the intuitive conception of following a rule but they generalize to any sort of contentful state. According to the folk theory, when one follows a rule one is in a certain type of mental state which has some very interesting properties. In particular, by being in that mental state one knows how one *ought* to act so as to accord with the rule and one also knows how to act in accord with the rule in the indefinitely many possible situations that comprise the diverse applications of the rule. Kripke argues that no mental state *could* have these 'queer' properties of normativity and indefinite extensibility.

It is not my purpose to evaluate the strength of any of these types of considerations in favor of eliminativism, although the position which I recommend the eliminativist adopt owes a lot to Kripke's arguments, as we shall see. What I want to do instead is develop a version of eliminativism which differs from the usual one propounded by its more vocal advocates (such as the Churchlands). The chief point in favor of my version is that it appears to be coherent, whereas the Churchland version is at best only dubiously so. That at any rate is what I hope to show. I am not endorsing this view myself. In fact I believe that it is most probably mistaken but it is not incoherent. As I can think of no better way to introduce it than by recounting its historical origins I turn to that task now.

Paul Boghossian (1990) has recently attempted to show that eliminativism is incoherent. Eliminativism is one species of a generic view he calls *content irrealism*. An *irrealist* view of a given type of discourse according to Boghossian is the view that "no real properties answer to the central predicates" of the discourse in question. One may be led to adopt content irrealism *either* because one thinks that folk psychological sentences have truth-conditions but are systematically false *or* because one believes that such sentences do not express facts in the first place. The first alternative represents an *error thesis* about folk psychological claims and, it would appear, the Churchlands' variety of eliminativism is such an error thesis. In the second case, one is adopting a *nonfactualist thesis*.

How does Boghossian propose to show content irrealism in general and eliminativism in particular to be incoherent? By showing that content irrealism is an *unstable* position in that "we cannot make sense of the claim that our thoughts and utterances do *not* possess robust truth-conditions" (Boghossian, 1990, p. 157) owing to the fact that "the claim that they do possess robust truth-conditions is a presupposition of the most refined attempt to deny that they do" (ibid.).

Suppose Boghossian were to succeed in this endeavor. What would he have shown? Certainly not that content attributions *do* possess robust truth-conditions (though Boghossian clearly does not think that he *has* shown that). At best he would have established that we cannot make sense of a certain claim, viz. "Content attributions might not possess robust truth-conditions." Boghossian might be giving expression to the worry voiced earlier, as an eliminativist of the Churchland/Stich hue provides no hint as to what rationality might *really* consist of once purged of the mistaken folk dross of belief and desire we are at a loss as to how to rationally construe the eliminativist's own thesis. It is not misleading to describe that situation as one wherein we "cannot make sense of" content irrealism. But in fact I doubt that Boghossian *does* mean this. I think that he believes himself to have shown that there is an incoherence located within the content irrealist's acceptance of his/her own thesis rather than that the intended interpretation of the thesis is ineradicably anomalous. The incoherence is of this form: If the thesis is true then it must be false; the thesis is, in popular parlance, self-defeating, or, in philosophical jargon, epistemically unstable.

My response on behalf of the content irrealist is this:

1. Even if Boghossian *were* right in thinking that we can recognize that the content irrealist's thesis is self-defeating this fact would not *of itself* undermine content irrealism.
2. In fact he is not right at all.

Let me take the latter contention first. Why do I maintain that Boghossian is mistaken in thinking that no one can make sense of the claim that content attributions might not possess robust truth conditions? Because *I* can make at least partial sense of it. I can conceive of how something like it might be true.[2]

I can conceive how content attributions might not possess truth-conditions very simply. Just as noncognitivists in ethics have held ethical evaluations to be expressive of emotions or attitudes of approval or disapproval rather than descriptive of some objective feature of the world — the objective goodness or badness of some action, for example — so it might also be that content attributions are similarly expressive of attitudes held by the content *ascriber* rather than objectively descriptive of any inner mental state of the agent to whom the 'state' is *ascribed*. Now these 'attitudes' had better *not* be states with content. Something less theoretically loaded or at least with a different theoretical loading would *have* to suffice: complex dispositions to behave may be. Granted. But I see no reason to rule out this possibility a priori. Boghossian thinks he can block this type of nonfactualist response and I think he *does* establish that there is a genuine problem for it as stated in this crude form, but a refinement of it can survive his objections.

More importantly, however, even if Boghossian *were* right about our inability to coherently conceive of the possibility that our content attributions lack truth-conditions this would not of itself provide a reprieve from eliminativist attacks for the folk attitudes. We have already seen why. Recall that Boghossian's view is that eliminativism is an epistemically unstable position: One can believe the eliminativist's thesis if and only if that thesis is not true. Alternatively one can believe that no content attribution possesses truth conditions if and only if some content attributions *do* possess truth conditions. It doesn't matter which version we take, the problem is the same: While it might be plausible to claim that no truly rational agent can believe these epistemically unstable theses so long as we continue to found our theories of rationality upon a central theoretical notion of belief,[3] such theories simply enshrine the very notions the eliminativist seeks to attack. Our projected epistemic instability, pursuant on acceptance of eliminativism is, once more, further evidence that the notion of belief and the theories of rationality and epistemology which are parasitic upon it are all scientifically disreputable. At least, that is what the eliminativist will say.

Let me just say, before proceeding further, what I think Boghossian *does* establish:

1. I think he does succeed in showing that any grounds for adopting differential attitudes to mental and semantic contents would have

---

[2] Why the hedging about being able to partially grasp it or grasp something like it? Because there is something objectionable about the notion of robust *truth conditions.* I think I understand what is meant by the assertion that *truth* is robust − it is the denial of the claim that the truth predicate is a trivial disquotational device or the affirmation of the claim that truth is a substantive property which has interesting and deep connections with the notions of meaning, belief, rationality, and with the metaphysical question of realism. I therefore think I also understand the assertion that truth is *not* robust, the 'Deflationist' thesis that "when we've pointed to certain formal features of the truth predicate (notably its disquotational features) and explained why it's useful to have a predicate like this (e.g. as a device for asserting infinite conjunctions) we've said just about all that can be said about truth." What I do not understand is how truth *conditions* can be either robust or deflationary. For irrespective of one's views about the status of the property of truth (whether it's robust or not), one can agree upon the truth conditions that any given statement has. For truth conditions are just certain sorts of states of affairs and while one can indeed ask interesting questions about the epistemological or metaphysical status of those states of affairs, these questions are all quite orthogonal to the question of whether any substantial property would be marked out were the state of affairs that makes a given statement true to actually obtain in the world. That is, the truth theorist who takes truth to be a substantial property, who believes that truth is *robust*, and the truth theorist who takes truth to be insubstantial or *deflationary* can agree about what states of affairs would make a given statement true. Their disagreement is over the *interest* attaching to the *actual obtaining of* these states of affairs. Both robust and deflationary theories will agree that the truth condition of "snow is white" is *snow's being white*, it is just that the 'robust' theorist will add "and when the truth condition obtains this is AN INTERESTING FACT" while his 'deflationary' counterpart will add "but when the truth condition obtains this is A WHOLLY UNINTERESTING FACT." The states of affairs are the same; they just come with different labels attached: 'philosophically interesting' in the one case, 'utterly trivial' in the other.

[3] Roy Sorensen (1988) makes out a compelling case for this claim.

to be rather tenuous. For, as he notes, the most compelling arguments against the existence of contentful psychological states or contentful semantic states turn on skepticism about *content* (and not on content's being embedded in a mental rather than linguistic context). I have already sketched those arguments.

2. It would seem a rather uncontentious, even obvious, point that linguistic and semantic contents ought not to be treated differentially by the content skeptic. Yet if it is, it is one that eliminativists such as Paul Churchland find difficult to acknowledge. The reason isn't hard to discern, and this brings me to the second point on which I agree with Boghossian:

Insofar as s/he is an error theorist about content, an eliminativist holds that:

All sentences of the form "∅" have the content that ∅ are false.

But then it would appear that we could never truly articulate the content of the eliminativist's *own* thesis. Thus consigned to ineffability, eliminativism would no longer be able to sustain its claim to theoretical superiority over folk psychology. Perhaps this is why eliminativism provokes the resistance it does? Perhaps the silent majority who suspect that eliminativism is incoherent do so because they think that *there can be no telling* what it is that an eliminativist believes, what it is that s/he is trying to persuade us of.

I can now state my main disagreement with Boghossian: Boghossian takes the issue of realism or irrealism about content to be, at bottom, an issue about the nature of truth; namely, whether truth is robust or deflationary.[4]

To that end, he ultimately *identifies* content irrealism with deflationism about truth. Recall that deflationism about truth is the thesis that truth is not a substantial property.

Now Boghossian does not explicitly say why he believes that the denial that truth is a substantial property is, in his terms, "an impeccably content irrealist position" (Boghossian, 1990, p. 177) but he says enough to enable us to work it out. The reasoning goes like this:

(DeflT) Truth is not a substantial property
But (TC) Whatever content is, it must *at least* be truth conditional.
Hence (Cont Irr) Content is not a substantial property

So far as I can see, there is no way Boghossian could have been led to the view that deflationism about truth *just is* a version of content irrealism except through the intermediary of (TC). Moreover, he tells us that (TC) is uncontroversial and even more forcefully that "a skepticism about content,

---

[4] Note that 'robust' theories of truth need not be correspondence theories; a coherence theory of truth is also a robust theory.

if it is to be interesting, must be directed primarily at the idea of a truth-condition" (1990, p. 173).

The argument for identifying content irrealism with deflationism about truth is unconvincing. There are two separate weaknesses. The first is that deflationists about truth need not, and typically do not, accept a truth-conditional model of meaning. The second, and far more serious one, is that the argument requires a highly dubious suppressed premise in order to make it valid.

Why is a deflationist about truth *not* obliged to accept (TC)? Well consider the Tarskian Schema:

> (*T*) *s* is true iff *p*

where '*s*' is a structural-descriptive term referring to the object language sentence whose translation in the metalanguage is *p*. One version of deflationism contends that truth has *no* important attributes apart from those specified in this schema. Tarski himself referred to natural-language instances of the (T) scheme such as:

> (TI) "The mind is a neural network" is true iff the mind is a neural
> network

as partial definitions of truth. Given that we understand the metalanguage and know that the sentence on the right-hand side of the biconditional is the metalinguistic translation of the object language sentence referred to by 'The mind is a neural network,' we can recognize (TI) as a correct applica-tion of the predicate 'is true.' Now it *may* be that we understand the metalanguage by grasping the truth conditions of its sentences. But it need not be; perhaps we need only grasp the assertibility conditions or deniability conditions of the sentences of the metalanguage in order to understand them or again perhaps it suffices if we grasp their conceptual or inferential or functional roles. The deflationist need not proffer *any* view — in particular, s/he need not be committed to a *truth-conditional* model of meaning or content.

I claimed that Boghossian's argument was not valid as it stood. In order to repair it we need a suppressed premise, viz:

> (P) If truth is not a substantial property of a sentence then neither is
> the sentence's having the truth condition it has a substantial property
> of that sentence.

An incautious interpretation of deflationism about truth might suggest that commitment to the insubstantiality of truth entails a commitment to the insubstantiality of truth conditions. Not so. One might think that truth per se is a property of a belief or sentence that explains very little whilst insisting that the *truth conditions* of these beliefs or sentences *do* have an important explanatory role to discharge, in accounting for the validity of inference or for the rationality of an agent's decisions, for example. We can imagine a cognitive scientist designing a computer which believed *it* was a cognitive scientist designing a computer which believed it was a cognitive scientist. All of the unfortunate machine's beliefs about itself might turn out false — indeed, a malevolent cognitive scientist might ensure that all of its beliefs in toto turn out false. Yet the actual truth value of its beliefs would not enter into any explanation of why the machine behaved in the rational manner in which it did. A decision theory for the machine qua rational agent might, however, take the truth conditions of its beliefs to be of central theoretical importance. Why couldn't the same be true of us? There are good grounds — methodological solipsistic grounds — to regard the actual *truth value* of our beliefs to be of no relevance to the explanation of our behavior. *Those* grounds do not support the claim that the *truth conditions* of our beliefs are psychologically inert. I conclude that (P) is at best highly dubious. So Boghossian's identification of content irrealism with deflationism about truth cannot be motivated in the way he seeks to motivate it.

Content irrealism is conceptually independent of deflationism about truth. Nonetheless, a plausible version of eliminativism, qua content irrealism, *requires* deflationism simply because the eliminativist wishes to convey certain truths about content, namely that content is irreal (i.e., that content attributions do not express facts in some proprietary sense of "express facts"). This is on pain of not being able to truly articulate the content of his/her own eliminativist thesis. Boghossian *does* succeed, in my view, in establishing that a plausible version of eliminativism must assume a nonfactualist form.

My eliminativist argument allows that ascriptions of propositional attitudes and other contentful states have truth conditions; they have to, since they feature in inferences of various sorts. So no invidious comparison between the sentences of physical theory and the sentences of folk psychology (such as Quine wishes to draw) can be made out in terms of the notion of a *truth condition*. Hence my nonfactualist eliminativist must look elsewhere to ground the fact/nonfact-stating distinction.

Boghossian claims that a nonfactualist content irrealist *cannot* maintain that "the difference (between folk psychological discourse and scientific discourse) consists in their differential capacity for stating facts" (Boghossian, 1990, p. 178).[5] I think that this is precisely what the nonfactualist

---

[5] One curious thing about Boghossian's article is that he notices (p. 178) that "irrealists about content tend to be realists about physics, and, indeed, the former because the latter" and goes on to pose the correct question, vis "... how is a realist/irrealist contrast between physics and semantics to be formulated, if content irrealism is expressed as a deflationism about truth?" and yet *still* does not question his identification of content irrealism with deflationism about truth. This *is* curious if only because *none* of the philosophers who subscribe to Scientific Realism cotenably with Content Irrealism — Quine, Churchlands, Schiffer, Stich — arrive at their irrealism by musing about the nature of truth.

eliminativist *must* say, but is s/he entitled to? I say yes.

How then *is* the fact/nonfact distinction to be drawn if not in terms of a contrast between sentences (or beliefs) that do and sentences (or beliefs) that do not possess truthconditions?

W.V. Quine has long championed the eliminativist cause. What motivates Quine to espouse the views he does is a philosophical naturalism − a principled and obstinate refusal to countenance any vantage point from which the deliverances of physical science could be assessed to see if they are in good conceptual order. In his book on Quine, Christopher Hookway (1989) has noted this and as I cannot hope to improve on his exemplary presentation of the following points, let me quote him in full:

> It is tempting to account for the virtues of physics, or of whatever sciences are included in the canonical list, by claiming that they alone yield truths. It is only in these sciences that propositions are accepted because they are *true*: expressive discourse lacks this kind of link with truth. ... This is not Quine's strategy. In order to carry it out, we should need some sort of substantive characterisation of what it is for a claim to be true and then demonstrate that scientific results fit this characterisation. We should risk circularity if we took our account of truth from the sciences so the strategy will only work if there is a philosophical discipline, independent of and more fundamental than science, whose task is to provide such a substantive characterisation of what it is for a claim to be true. It is a consequence of Quine's naturalism that there can be no such discipline .... Indeed, Quine's remarks about truth indicate that he thinks this strategy deeply misconceived. ... The property of truth cannot be used to mark fundamental philosophical distinctions: it simply follows our practice concerning what is assertible or 'rightly affirmed.' It cannot be exploited to justify it. Indeed, someone who denies the objectivity of (say) values could happily admit that 'cruelty is wrong' is *true*: since to say *that* is just to say the cruelty is wrong, it is just as expressive or subjective as the latter claim. ... If not via an account of truth or through some idealised model of scientific method, how are we to decide which disciplines are truly scientific or truly descriptive? Granted Quine's constant insistence that we start inquiry in the middle of things, equipped with a body of beliefs and prejudices, concerned to rebuild our boat at sea, perhaps we rely upon a list of those disciplines which, we would all agree, are sciences .... This seems a sensible Quinean starting point. ... We can begin from our untutored sense of what is scientific, refining our list as we compare the controversial cases with the straightforward ones. (p. 68-69)

Let me sketch the theoretical position of my nonfactualist eliminativist:

1. Some sentences of a language are derivable from (some ideal extension of) physical theory, most are not.

2. The sentences that are so derivable express facts, the rest do not.
3. All declarative sentences of the appropriate form have truth conditions but truth is simply deflationary truth and has nothing at all to do with whether the sentence is factual or not.
4. Amongst the nonfactual sentences are content attributions which have what we might call weak assertibility conditions: There are recognizable conditions in which we assert them and these assertions subserve a useful social function, promoting social cohesiveness.
5. The sentences of scientific theory have what we might call strong assertibility conditions: Unlike content attributions, they are useful in predicting and controlling phenomena in the world.
6. The entities and properties and relations that the sentences of scientific theory quantify over exist. Nothing else does. There are no witches or goblins. Neither are there any beliefs, desires, intentions, values, or actions. So:
7. Qua protoscience folk psychology is simply *false*. Yet:
8. Certain content attributions are true (i.e., we're prepared to assert them).
9. Correctly understood, our folk psychological practice is perfectly in order as it is. There is no foreseeable prospect of our radically revising, it let alone *discarding* it, though there is no telling what impact dramatic discoveries in neuroscience or cognitive science may have upon it.

The model that I have for the weak assertibility conditions of content-attributions is that provided by Saul Kripke (1982) in his marvelous book on Wittgenstein's private language argument. That no facts correspond to statements such as "Jones means addition by +" is the result, according to Kripke's *Wittgenstein* (henceforth KW) of an ingenious skeptical argument. What KW says of rule-following, my eliminativist says of content attribution in general: Our intuitive model of content attribution, fed by a philosophical distortion of our actual linguistic practice of ascribing beliefs, desires, and other contentful states to people has it that in attributing a contentful state to some agent like myself I am attributing a state in which "I have achieved something that depends only on my own inner state, and that is immune to Cartesian doubt about the entire external world" (Kripke, 1982, p. 80). To straighten out this confused model of content ascription "the picture of correspondence-to-facts must be cleared away" (p. 79). It will then emerge that "all that is necessary to legitimate assertions that someone means (or believes or desires or intends) something is that there be roughly specifiable circumstances under which they are legitimately assertable, and that the game of asserting them under such circumstances has a role in our lives" (pp. 77-78). Prior to KW we took conditionals such as "If Alfonse believes that it is raining then if he is asked 'Is it raining?' He will reply 'yes'." to be true because some mental state of Alfonse's within his head causally results in his issuing the vocable "yes" in response to questions such as this. But KW's skeptical paradox precisely denies this. So now we must understand such a conditional contrapositively: If Alfonse does *not* come out with "yes" when asked "Is it raining?" then *ceteris paribus* we cannot assert "Alfonse believes that it is raining." Content attribution according to my eliminativist (following KW) is not a scientific activity at all. We are not uncovering the aetiology of behavior or of anything else in ascribing contentful states to others. We are merely bestowing an honorific label upon those who behave and respond as we do.

I should emphasize, in conclusion, that my nonfactualist eliminativist takes issue with a Churchland-Stich eliminativist over several points. The most marked disagreements concern the theoretical status of folk psychology and the semantic status of content attributions. The Churchland-Stich view is that folk psychology is a protean scientific theory and that content attributions are systematically false. My nonfactualist claims that, on the contrary, folk psychology is not a theory at all, let alone a nascent scientific one, and that many content attributions are true. Is it legitimate to call this view *eliminativist* at all then?

I think it is. My eliminativist and the Churchland-Stich variety are agreed on one central point: *There are no* contentful states such as folk psychology imagines there to be. But while the Churchland-Stich eliminativist thinks that folk psychological sentences really do possess truth conditions and that truth is a deep and interesting property that such truth-evaluable sentences can miss out on, my eliminativist holds that truth is not a real property at all and folk psychological claims are true only insofar as we are inclined to assert them in recognizable and repeatable contexts. But s/he will insist that we must not therefore leap to the unwarranted Churchland-Stich conclusion that we *thereby* intend to state scientifically interesting facts by our folk psychological claims.

It might be suggestive to call my nonfactualist eliminativism *soft* eliminativism and the Churchland-Stich variety *hard* eliminativism, suggestive of the dispute between soft and hard determinists, that is.[6] To be sure, my eliminativist does claim, along with the soft determinist, that our present practice in applying the central concepts of folk psychology (of which free action is one) is perfectly acceptable once we disentangle it from the mistaken philosophical construal of that practice which has insinuated itself so effectively into the minds of the folk.

But we should be careful of overworking either this analogy or the analogy with noncognitivism in ethics — content attributions are *not* expressions of conative attitudes after all. Furthermore, my Kripkean eliminativist is in many ways a more radical skeptic about the scientific pretensions of folk psychology

---

[6] I owe this suggestion to Dr. Fred D'Agostino.

than is his/her Churchland-Stich counterpart. For the latter holds it to be a straightforwardly empirical question whether future cognitive science or neurophysiology will uncover sentential or other sorts of internal symbolic structures which can physically implement the propositional attitudes whereas the Kripkean eliminativist contends that no internal physical state (or nonphysical state for that matter) *could* realize a belief or a desire or an intention.[7]

A better analogy in some ways is provided by finitism in the philosophy of mathematics. Hilbert (1983) took combinatorial mathematical statements to be epistemologically and semantically secure: We could tell directly whether one finite string of symbols was longer than another, for example, and we could thereby understand the claim that it was. Statements quantifying over infinite totalities were regarded as strictly meaningless: They could not be finitely verified/falsified by any number of combinatorial facts. However they were extremely useful. We can state mathematical laws more simply for example. Such statements functioned in theorizing *about* mathematics as ideal elements such as 'points at infinity' functioned *within* mathematics. Moreover, if it could be shown by finitistically acceptable methods of proof that no inconsistency can result if these quantified statements are added to the corpus of finitistic mathematics, then their use could be justified on finitistic grounds.

Much the same holds for this case. Content attributions are scientifically meaningless: They have no strong assertibility conditions since they cannot be verified or falsified by any number of scientific facts, but they are extremely useful. They build up expectations and allow predictions of the behavior of others. Without them our efforts to coordinate our scientific investigative activities would be thwarted. So if we can show that no actual inconsistency results in our scientific theories if we allow these assertions as ways of coordinating our activities then those assertions are legitimate. This is precisely what I have attempted to do — I've tried to show that there is a coherent way of understanding folk psychology from the eliminativist point of view. Needless to say, I don't believe a word of it.

REFERENCES

Boghossian, P. (1990). The status of content. *Philosophical Review, 99* (2), 157-184.
Churchland, P.M. (1981). Eliminative Materialism and Propositional Attitudes, *Journal of Philosophy, 78*, 67-90.

---

[7] This point may ease the worry that a Kripkean eliminativism could be adopted towards the four humours or the theory of nested crystal spheres. We do not presume that it is logically impossible that the central theoretical entities of discredited scientific theories such as these exist. Hence, on these grounds alone no such eliminativism could be sustained. Furthermore, these theories are discredited scientific theories. The burden of the Kripkean eliminativist position which I have just sketched is that folk psychology is not such a theory; indeed, it is no theory at all.

Churchland, P.M., & Churchland, P.S. (1983). Stalking the Wild Epistemic Engine *Nous 17,* 5-18.

Churchland, P.S. (1986). *Neurophilosophy,* Bradford Books/MIT Press.

Hilbert, D. (1983), On the Infinite in P. Benacerraf, & H. Putnam (Eds.), *Philosophy of Mathematics — Selected Readings,* Second Edition, 183-201. Cambridge University Press.

Hookway, C. (1989). *Quine.* Oxford, UK: Polity Press.

Kripke, S. (1982). *Wittgenstein on rules and private language: An elementary exposition.* Oxford, UK: Blackwell.

Quine, W.V. (1960). *Word and Object.* Cambridge, Mass.: MIT Press.

Sorensen, R. (1988). *Blindspots.* Oxford, UK: Clarendon Press.

Stich, S. (1983). *From folk psychology to cognitive science: The case against belief.* Cambridge, MA: MIT Press.

CHAPTER 21

Which Symbols Have "Meaning for the Machine"?

Hugh Clapin

Faculty of Arts,
Australian National University

The computational view of the mind holds that important properties are shared by human thought, and computational processes on Von Neumann architectures. Critics of this view like Searle (1980) have claimed that it is inconceivable that intentionality can arise from such computational processes, since they simply amount to a series of purely formal operations over symbols which are meaningless to the manipulator. One response to this criticism, found in Aaron Sloman's papers *What Sorts of Machines Can Understand the Symbols They Use?* (1986) and *Reference Without Causal Links* (1987), suggests that some symbols — the program instructions — do have intrinsic meaning for a computer, and from this basic level of intrinsic meaning the semantics of other representations in the computer can be constructed.

It is important to address this issue because Sloman makes explicit a claim that I think underlies the intuitive plausibility of many computationalist models of cognition. The idea, roughly, is that there is a sense of "understanding" in which computers can be said to understand programming languages. This sort of understanding looks to be a basis on which to build more sophisticated semantic properties into the symbols manipulated by computers.

My aim in this chapter is to show that the data symbols a computer manipulates cannot get any of their semantic properties in virtue of the semantic properties of programming instructions. The reason is that a running program has no direct access to the machine language instructions which comprise it, thus the running program's relation to symbols which represent program rules is significantly different from its relation to symbols which represent data. Since the running program has no access to the programming language rules which underlie it, these rules can have no meaning at all to the running program.

SLOMAN'S ARGUMENT

In his paper *What Sorts of Machines Can Understand the Symbols They Use?* (1986), Sloman claims that computers can be said to refer to their internal states and processes by the use of the symbols of programming languages, and by extension through various causal mechanisms, to objects in the outside world. In order to make this claim, Sloman presents a set of prototypical conditions for an agent to use a language to refer to a world.

The fifteen or so conditions he sets out are intended to be treated as a cluster of attributes of which a number of different subsets would characterize different degrees of understanding in a computer toward the symbols it manipulates. Sloman argues that computers can, in one way or another, satisfy each of the fifteen conditions. Thus, says Sloman, computers can be said to understand symbols which refer to internal states, to numbers and to symbolic patterns because the "semantic links between symbols and things in the world are directly derived from simple causal links and the way the symbols are used" (1986, p. 71).

Sloman suggests that a harder problem than that of the internal semantic linkage of computer symbols is that of external semantic linkage. He then proposes that external semantic linkage might be achieved through a combination of the internal semantics he claims to demonstrate, and a Tarskian semantics.

Here is a taste of the sort of conditions for understanding that Sloman presents:

> (2) [Agent] U associates some symbols of [language] L with objects in [world] W, and other symbols with properties, relations, or actions in W. (1986, p. 66)

> (3) If U is a computer and L its machine code, the semantic relation is causal:
> $'S$ refers to O for $U' =$
> $'S$ makes U's activities relate to or involve O, and facts involving O affect U's use of S'
> where O may be an object, property, relation, or type of action. Some objects referred to in world W may be abstract, e.g. numbers. (1986, p. 67)

> (12) U can make *inferences* by deriving new symbols in L from old ones, in order to determine some semantic relation (e.g., proofs preserve truth, refutations demonstrate falsity). (1986, p. 69)

In a later paper, *Reference Without Causal Links* (1987), Sloman makes further claims about the semantics of computer languages and the data the computer operates on. He continues with the claim that it is internal causal links which provide machine code instructions with semantics. From this basis, he builds up a story about how the data manipulated by the computer can also come to have semantic properties, even in cases where such data do not have direct causal links to whatever it is in the world that they represent.

Perhaps the most striking aspect of Sloman's 15 prototypical conditions for understanding is his free use of intentional idioms such as "associate" and "derive." Despite Sloman's claim that he is using these in an entirely innocent way, I'm sure many readers would feel that these apparent attributions of intentionality are doing a lot of work in Sloman's arguments for the ability of computers to understand symbols. These criticisms will not be pursued here, however, because even if we grant Sloman all his claims, we find that he trades on the ambiguity involved in his use of the term "the computer."

An important point to note with regard to any discussion of cognitive representation is that representations are only representations for agents who can understand them. According to Daniel Dennett:

> Nothing is intrinsically a representation of anything; something is a representation only *for* or *to* someone; any representation or system of representations requires at least one user of the system who is external to the system. Call such a user an *exempt agent*. (Dennett, 1977, p. 101).

On this understanding of representation, there are at least two levels of analysis that Sloman fails to recognize in his all-embracing term "the computer." The first level is that of the CPU and the machine language instructions which affect the way the CPU processes data symbols. The second level is the running process which is comprised of a list of machine language instructions as followed by a CPU and abstract data symbols. The CPU manipulates binary numerals a few at a time, but cannot be said to recognize or manipulate complex or abstract data structures. A running process is the correct level of explanation for the manipulation of data structures, but it has virtually no access to the machine code instructions which make it up.

What this view of computers entails is that machine code symbols and complex or abstract data symbols are significantly different types of things, and more importantly, they exist as symbols for two quite different machines. Machine code tokens are symbols for the CPU, data tokens are symbols for a process. Any semantic properties machine code tokens have for "the computer" are semantic properties for the CPU, while any semantic properties data symbols have are for the process, or so I hope to show.

Sloman shows himself to be partly aware of the distinction being urged here when he clearly distinguishes between cases where the language under discussion is machine code, and when it is a system of data representations. What he fails to recognize is that if these two sorts of symbols carry any meaning, they carry that meaning for different exempt agents. If the language referred to is machine code, then the "computer" which understands this language is merely the hardware. If the language referred to is the system of symbols in which the data is stored, then the "computer" would be a running process, an instantiation of a program. The "understander" in question will vary with the system of symbols under discussion.

A third possibility, and perhaps the one Sloman has partly in mind, is that the language is a high-level programming language. We should remember here that in almost all von Neumann computers, when a program is written in a language higher than machine language, it is first compiled into machine language. A program written in Pascal or C is stored in the computer's memory and used as data by another process called a compiler. The compiler is a program which takes the symbols of high-level languages and translates them into machine language instructions. Thus any program whatsoever, when running, is in fact a machine language program. Thus if what Sloman has in mind is that the language that a computer can understand is a high-level language, then this is either a special case of the computer being a process, where the program being instantiated is a compiler or interpreter, and the higher level language is in fact the data on which the process operates; or else he is referring to the compiled program, and thus to machine code. I will assume that he is referring to machine code.

To clarify these points, we should take a quick look at a real CPU. This will allow us to have a more definite image of what Sloman is proposing. In talking about the CPU we will attempt to determine the exempt agent for the systems of representation Sloman discusses.

INSIDE A CPU

At the heart of the von Neumann computer is the CPU. Within the CPU is the lowest level of explicit representation used by a computer. For the purposes of this account, I will take as my characterization of the CPU of a von Neumann computer that given in Goldschlager and Lister (1982, pp. 147ff), and in particular the figure reproduced here as Figure 21.1.

From the diagram (Figure 21.1), we can see that this CPU operates with two memories: the main memory, which stores data, and the micro memory, which stores the microinstructions. The CPU as a whole follows the instructions represented by the microcode, instructions about adding numbers together, storing results in registers, reading data from the memory and so on.

- Registers A-D are each short-term storage registers for one 16-bit data symbol.
- The MPC is the microprogram counter, which holds the micromemory address of the current microinstruction.

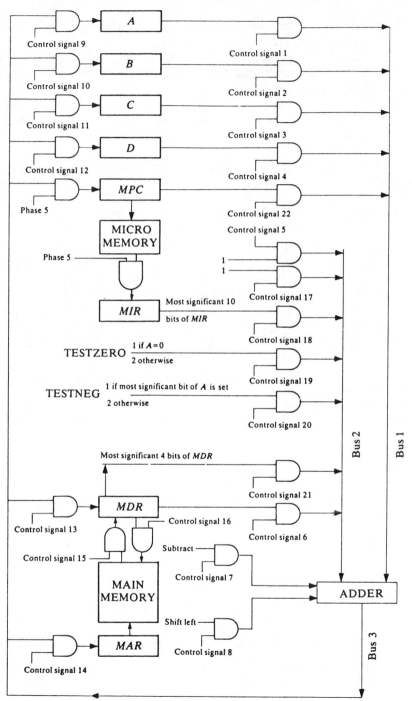

Figure 21.1

- The MIR is the microinstruction register, which holds the current microinstruction.
- The MDR is the memory data register, which holds data symbols as they are read from the main memory, or symbols to be written to the main memory.
- The MAR is the memory address register, which holds the main memory address of the data symbol currently being read to or written from the MDR.

Each microinstruction is a 22-bit binary numeral, and each bit of the microinstruction corresponds to a control signal in the CPU. Thus if the first bit of the current microinstruction is set, then control signal 1 is set, and so on.

To take an example, if the first bit of the current microinstruction is set, the CPU will carry out the operation "Place contents of register A onto Bus 1," because control signal ONE is set, which allows the contents of register A to pass through the AND gate onto Bus 1. If the fifteenth bit of the microinstruction is set, the CPU will read from the memory location currently in the MAR, and place this value into the MDR. If the seventh bit of the microinstruction is set, then the Adder unit will perform subtraction, rather than addition, on the values currently represented on Bus 1 and Bus 2.[1]

The CPU operates according to an ordered set of microinstructions (a microprogram) in the micromemory. Microinstructions are 22-bit binary numerals (each bit corresponds to a control signal), while data and addresses are 16-bit numerals. On some occasions the first 10 bits of the current microinstruction are treated as data. This would typically be a case where these 10 bits hold a micromemory address to which the program should jump.[2]

A few points need to be cleared up at this stage. First, Sloman refers to a computer's "machine language." Machine languages are typically higher level languages than microcode. The example CPU illustrated here is useful because the interaction between the physical nature of the microcode symbols and their functional purpose is made clear. The point here is that any program

---

[1] The effect of each microinstruction is constrained by five clock phases. Each microinstruction lasts in the MIR for the whole five clock phases, but on each clock phase, only certain of the bits of the microinstruction are active. On clock phase 1, only bits $1-8$ are permitted to have any effect, on phase 2, bits $9-14$, on phase 3, bits $15-16$, and on phase 4, bits $17-22$. On clock phase 5, none of the bits are allowed to be active. This basically means that on clock phase 1, addition (or subtraction, etc., depending on bits 7 and 8) of the contents of the registers $A-D$, the value '1', and the value in the MDR can take place. On phase 2, the output of the adder can be placed into a register. On clock phase 3, the CPU can either read from memory, or write to memory, and on clock phase 4, other special values can be added together (these are values like microinstruction addresses, or the result of a test for negation). During clock phase 5, the next microinstruction is read into the MIR, the address of which is taken to be the current output of the adder. Example programs, and a far more detailed explanation of the workings of this CPU can be found in Goldschlager and Lister (1982, pp. 147ff).

[2] This distinction is regulated where necessary by control signal 18.

running on this CPU must be first compiled or translated into microcode, and thus any running process is implemented by a microcode program. Thus any claim Sloman makes for causal links (and thus semantics) between the machine language and other parts or states of the computer will be treated as claims for causal links (and thus semantics) between microcode and other parts of the computer.

The second point is that this CPU shows the micromemory to be distinct from the main memory. For almost any running process this is effectively the case. Compilers, however, must be able to write to the micromemory, and this cannot be done by the CPU here. Thus this CPU is functionally equivalent to any running process except a compiler.

TWO DIFFERENT COMPUTERS

Sloman distinguishes symbolic reference to the computer's internal world and reference to its external world. Under our present description there is no clear indication that the CPU is a device with inputs and outputs, nor do we have a description of the environment in which it operates.

Since the diagram shows the memories to be encapsulated within the CPU, the CPU seems to be totally disconnected from the world. If instead we view the memories as external to the core device we are dealing with (which I will call the 'Core CPU'), the memory registers become more like input and output devices and the main memory becomes the system's environment. Remember that the Core CPU, and a process constituted by the CPU running a program, are considered as quite distinct systems.

Specifically, the inputs to the Core CPU are: the MDR, the four most significant bits of the MDR, the MPC, and the ten most significant bits of the MIR.[3] The outputs are the MDR, the MAR, and the MPC (see Figure 21.2). In the normal case, where the contents of the MIR are to be interpreted as instructions, we will not treat them as an input, but rather as a special section of the Core CPU which is involved in changing the way the Core CPU processes its inputs.

For the Core CPU then, the micromemory is *outside* the system, and the MPC is just a way of manipulating the environment (as are the MDR and the MAR). The current microinstruction, however, is internal to the Core CPU, and determines (amongst other things) the state of the MPC at the end of each clock cycle, and thus (through the outside world which includes the micromemory), produces a new instruction.

The contents of the data and address registers are associated in fixed ways

---

[3] Note that where different portions of a given register are introduced to the CPU for calculation according to different rules (as is the case with the MDR and the four most significant bits of the MDR), I have treated these as two separate inputs.

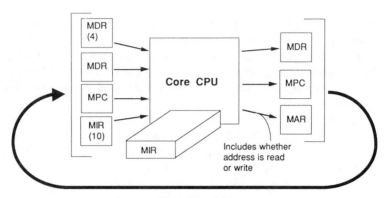

The World

Figure 21.2

(given the current contents of the MIR). Only a limited number of very simple operations and associations are possible within the Core CPU. Certainly the sort of semantic content *we* would ascribe the data symbols cannot be available to the Core CPU. Given the current microinstruction, the Core CPU will behave in exactly the same way toward the current contents of the various registers, regardless of what *we* think those contents refer to. If the MDR held the numeral 000000000000001000001 on one occasion it might refer to the number 65, on another it might refer to the letter *A*. The Core CPU will not, and cannot, treat that numeral differently according to its interpretation or functional role within a running process.

Thus the data and address symbols cannot have any meaning for the Core CPU.

The important aspects of the Core CPU are as follows:

- Its inputs and outputs are the address and data registers.
- Its environment consists of fixed length (16-bit) binary numerals.
- Its input/output relationship is determined by the combination of the current microinstruction and the current clock phase.
- Micromemory addresses have no special significance for the Core CPU. They are just another binary numeral to be shuffled around.
- Data numerals and main memory address numerals are treated identically and have no special significance.

As with the Core CPU, the running process is also defined in terms of its environment. When we talk of "the computer" manipulating abstract data structures like characters and so on, we are referring to a program which is being run on the Core CPU. The abstract data types can be as simple as characters or as complex as multidimensional matrices. Since the CPU only manipulates binary numerals, these come to be treated as abstract data types by virtue of the way in which they are manipulated and moved around; that is, by virtue of their functional role in a running process.

For Sloman to be at all justified in making claims such as that in Condition 12 — that the computer can make inferences — the representational system with which the agent in question operates must be one that can be said to support a logical syntax and logical relations between symbols. Thus the system of representation in question must be an organized system of symbols whose functional relationships are such that logical operations over those symbols can be said to take place. The symbols would have to be abstract entities (with respect to the 16-bit binary numerals which are actually shuffled around the machine). For the functional relationships in question to obtain, the symbols must be a part of an active computational environment.

The Core CPU is only capable of some very simple operations over two or three binary numerals — addition, subtraction, and moving numerals to different registers. Any other sort of representational operation demands a more sophisticated (or at least different) functional environment of which it can be a part. Different functional environments are brought about on a computer by running a process which can set up the required functional relationships between abstract data items.

The contents of the micromemory, in conjunction with the physical structure of the CPU and the clock pulses, wholly defines the running process. Thus the micromemory is internal to the process, but it is also inaccessible to the process. A running process cannot manipulate the symbols of microcode which constitute it. It manipulates micromemory addresses, thus affecting the flow of control, but it cannot directly read or write microcode symbols.

To contrast the running process with the Core CPU we should note that:

- Microcode is inaccessible to the process.
- Micromemory addresses refer to states of the process.
- In virtue of their functional role, data numerals can act like a huge variety of symbolic tokens or subparts of such tokens.
- Main memory addresses refer to locations in the environment of various data structures.
- The process' immediate environment consists of abstract data structures which are referenced via memory addresses.

Another way of making this point would be to say that we are dealing with two functional architectures, as in Pylyshyn (1980; 1984). The Core CPU is the basic architecture of the von Neumann computer which is capable of a small range of symbolic operations over 16-bit binary numerals. On this basic functional architecture we then implement another virtual architecture — the running process — which may be capable of a huge range of symbolic operations over a huge range of symbol types. However, since the process architecture is implemented in the Core CPU architecture, the Core CPU architecture has no direct relationship to the symbolic operations of the process architecture, and *vice versa*. The Core CPU architecture constrains the process architecture, but does not interact with it. The symbolic operations of these two different architectures are quite distinct.

SLOMAN'S AMBIGUITY

A major aspect to both of Sloman's arguments in the papers discussed here is the move from internal semantics to external semantics. Sloman claims that the computer has a primitive sort of original intentionality with respect to its internal states and components because:

> Associations between program elements and things in the computer's world define a primitive type of meaning that *the computer itself* attaches to the use of symbols. Its use of the symbols has features analogous to simpler cases of human understanding. (Sloman, 1986, pp. 70-71)

By "things in the computer's world" I take it that Sloman means things like memory locations and contents. His discussion of the fifteen conditions for understanding indicates that "computers" are capable of a range of impressive feats with respect to representational systems. Unfortunately, the reference of the word "computer" varies significantly throughout the discussion.

Thus in Conditions 2 and 3 (see above), where Sloman quite explicitly refers to the language in question as the computer's machine language, the agent in question (the "computer") can only be the Core CPU, since a running process has no access to microcode. However in Condition 12 Sloman refers to the representation system as one which could support logical inference. In this case (as we observed above) the representations involved must be abstract structures, and their functional relationships determined by a running process.

Essentially then, I take Sloman to be claiming that: (a) Machine language commands 'have imperative meanings because they systematically cause actions to occur';[4] and (b) Systems of data representation manipulated by a computer can support inference. These are only two of Sloman's many conditions, but between them they would seem to be pretty powerful. A machine which can obey instructions about how to manipulate symbols and make inferences involving those instructions could display some fairly impressive feats. This computer might, for example, look ahead a few instructions and infer that the current course of the program leads to an infinite loop, and so change the state of control to a different part of the program.

---

[4] Sloman, 1986, p. 66.

But this is incoherent. "The computer" here is none other than the process instantiated by the sequence of microinstructions. To carry out an operation like "infer that the current course of the program leads to an infinite loop" requires processing, which of course involves a sequence of microinstructions. The inference, were it possible, would necessarily lead the process into a different state of control, and hence the referent of "the current course of the program" would change.

For the process to make inferences about the current course of the program is not impossible, but it would require the process to model its own instructions as data, since it does not have direct access to the instructions which make it up. But having carried out the inference using the model in memory, the architecture of the von Neumann CPU prevents the process from changing the set of microinstructions which are currently running.

The combination of the imperative meaning of instructions and the inferential ability of a logical language implied by Sloman is thus illusory. If microcode commands have imperative meaning at all, it is to the Core CPU, not the process, since the process has no access to microcode symbols.[5] If inference can be supported, then it is supported by a running process, not by the Core CPU. On our two-level view, two questions remain: Could data have imperative meaning for the process, and could microcode symbols support inference?

The answer to the first is "maybe," and to the second "no." The Core CPU does not manipulate microcode. As we have described it here, the Core CPU is a static device and can only be said to be related to one microcode instruction at a time. The most complicated relation the Core CPU might be said to recognize between microcode instructions would be that of succession (i.e., that one instruction is the predecessor of another), since at the end of one clock cycle, the output of the adder has the address of the next instruction. But this is not enough, I think, to support inference.

The answer to the first question (Can data have imperative meaning to the process?) is unresolved. Certainly the rules held as data in a production system might be said to have imperative meaning for the process. Sloman would then be claiming only that the computer's data symbols have meaning for the computer, which is an interesting claim which might have some merit. But if he must retreat to this position, he has lost the intuitive force of the meaning which programming language instructions seem to have for "computers."

Bringing these points together suggests that one and the same language

---

[5] Perhaps this would be a good point at which to mention that the process might be said to have access to the *addresses* of microcode instructions which of course refer to the instructions. On Sloman's sort of view, however, addresses, for the process, refer to something like states of the system rather than being commands. That is, they are descriptive (not prescriptive) for the process.

cannot obviously have all the properties ascribed to it by Sloman. Throughout his arguments, Sloman moves between treating the computer as an understander of machine language instructions and treating it as an understander of abstract symbolic representations. My main point here is that a "computer" has a vastly different relationship with microcode instructions than it does with abstract data structures.

In the first case, any sort of meaning which a microcode symbol has must be meaning to the Core CPU, since this is the computational system which is functionally arranged in order that microcode symbols have a relevant effect. The Core CPU, however, cannot be said to operate with abstract data symbols. In the second case, any sort of meaning which abstract data symbols have must be meaning to a process, since abstract data types only arise as a result of the interaction between a running process and the main memory. But a running process has no meaningful access to symbols of microcode.

CONCLUSION

Sloman's implicit reliance on there being a relation between the meaning program instructions have for a computer, and the meaning data symbols have for a computer, has proved to be unfounded. As is the case in many discussions of computational abilities, Sloman has shown scant regard for the underlying mechanisms of von Neumann computation.

It should be noted, however, that I have perhaps been a little unfair to target Sloman in this manner. In neither paper does he make an explicit appeal to the combination of machine language semantics and data semantics in the way I have suggested. His claim is simply that a computer can exhibit a number of competences with respect to symbol systems, and that combinations of these competences may bring to the computer true understanding of some symbols.

My reasons for choosing Sloman as a target have been twofold. First, I think he gains credence for his arguments through the intuitive idea that programming languages do have a special kind of meaning for computers which is closely related to the meaning people find in natural language instructions. My argument here is that these instructions have this meaning for the CPU, not for a running process.

Secondly, I think Sloman (like many who discuss cognitive representation) forgets that one symbol can mean vastly different things to different exempt agents. The hardware of a computer defines a functional architecture which supports program instructions. The program instantiated on this functional architecture defines another functional architecture (a virtual architecture) which supports data representations. There is often ambiguity in the literature about whether the term "computer" refers to one of these architectures or the other. I hope to have shown that distinguishing between the two is important in any discussion of the relationship between computers and symbols.

REFERENCES

Dennett, D. C. (1977). A cure for the common code? In *Brainstorms,* Brighton: Harvester Press 1978.

Goldschlager, L. & Lister, A. (1982). *Computer science: A modern introduction.* London: Prentice Hall.

Pylyshyn, Z. (1980). Computation and cognition: Issues in the foundations of cognitive science. *Behavioural and Brain Sciences, 3,* 111-169.

Pylyshyn, Z. (1984). *Computation and cognition.* Cambridge, MA: MIT Press.

Searle, J. R. (1980). Minds, brains, and programs. *Behavioral and Brain Sciences, 3,* 417-424.

Sloman, A. (1986). What sorts of machines can understand the symbols they use? *Proceedings of the Aristotelian Society, Supplement 60,* 61-80.

Sloman, A. (1987). Reference without causal links. In B. du Boulay, D. Hogg, & L.J. Steels (Eds.), *Seventh European Conference on Artificial Intelligence* (pp. 369-381). Amsterdam: North Holland.

CHAPTER 22

Why Knowledge Engineers Should Study the Humanities *

Damien Laker

Australian Mutual Provident Society

Knowledge engineering is the acquisition and clarification of knowledge. This is usually done with a view to representing knowledge in an expert system. This chapter argues that, broadly construed, knowledge engineering is not a new human activity. We have records of distinguished achievements in knowledge engineering which date back over 2,000 years. This is no flippant claim: Socrates (as we shall see) made significant contributions to the art of knowledge acquisition.

The central argument of this chapter is that knowledge engineers can learn much from knowledge processing work which has been done in the humanities and social sciences. To neglect this earlier work is wasteful of time and money, as it leads to intellectual impoverishment.

SOCRATES AND KNOWLEDGE ENGINEERING

As an example of early knowledge acquisition, we might consider Socrates (469-399 B.C.). Socrates used an interviewing technique (sometimes called "the Socratic method") which we now recognize as using two tools of informal logic: adduction and general definition. In so doing, he intended to elicit knowledge from his subjects, just as his mother — a midwife — had assisted the birth of children. Without doubt, his intention was to foster knowledge acquisition:

> There is one way, then, in which a man can be free from all anxiety about the fate of his soul; if in life he has abandoned bodily pleasures and adornments, as foreign to his purpose and likely to do more harm than good, and has devoted himself to the pleasures of acquiring knowledge. (Plato, 1969, p. 178)

---

* Tim Menzies and Terry White made many helpful comments and corrections while I was preparing this article.

Typically, Socrates would use the following tactics when interviewing an "expert" about some particular concept:

1. Asking the "expert" for a provisional definition of the concept
2. Intuitively proposing several examples of the concept, to see whether its meaning has been correctly apprehended
3. Seeking a general principle in the examples
4. Testing whether the general principle contradicts the provisional definition

This technique thus demands conversational skills (eliciting a provisional definition, proposing several examples that you think may conform with it), and the adroit use of informal logic (seeking a general principle in the examples, and testing this principle for contradiction with the provisional definition given by the "expert").

We see these principles at work in Socrates' dialogue with Euthyphro (Plato, 1969). The question at stake is the nature of piety. However, the logic of the conversation is equally appropriate to a more secular subject, such as what the concept of a "reverse takeover" means. This dialogue can be considered, then, as a paradigm of knowledge elicitation:

SOCRATES: If piety is a kind of moral rectitude, then presumably we ought to discover what kind of moral rectitude piety is.

EUTHYPHRO: Well, Socrates, it seems to me that reverence or piety is that kind of rectitude which is concerned with tendance of the gods, and the remaining kind of rectitude is that which is concerned with the tendance of human beings.

[The provisional definition has now been elicited: piety is that kind of rectitude which concerns tendance of the gods.]

SOCRATES: And an excellent answer too, in my opinion, Euthyphro; but I still haven't got all that I want, because I'm not sure yet what you mean by tendance. I presume you don't mean by tendance in the case of the gods just the same sort of tendance as in all other uses of the word, because surely we use the term — Well, for instance, we say that not everyone knows how to tend horses, but only the horse trainer. Isn't that so?

EUTHYPHRO: Certainly.

SOCRATES: Because horse training is the tendance of horses?

EUTHYPHRO: Yes.

SOCRATES: And in the same way not everyone knows how to tend dogs, but only the dog trainer.

EUTHYPHRO: Quite so.

SOCRATES: Because dog training is the tendance of dogs.

EUTHYPHRO: Yes.

SOCRATES: And cattle farming is the tendance of cattle.

EUTHYPHRO: Certainly.

[Several examples of "tendance" have now been accepted.]

SOCRATES: Then is piety or reverence the tendance of the gods, Euthyphro? Is that what you mean?

EUTHYPHRO: Yes.

[The provisional definition has been sharpened by the examples: piety is tendance of the gods where tendance accords with the examples of horse training, etc.]

SOCRATES: Isn't the effect of all tendance the same? What I mean is that it is for the good or benefit of the thing tended: as you can see that horses tended by horse training are benefited and improved. Don't you agree?

EUTHYPHRO: Yes I do.

SOCRATES: And so, I presume, are dogs by dog training and cattle by cattle farming, and so on with all the rest. Or do you think that the tendance aims at the hurt of the thing intended?

EUTHYPHRO: Certainly not.

SOCRATES: It aims at the benefit of it?

EUTHYPHRO: Of course.

[A general principle of tendance has been agreed on: it benefits the thing tended]

SOCRATES: Then if piety is tendance of the gods, is it a benefit to the gods, and does it make them better? Would you agree that when you do a pious act you make some of the gods better? Would you agree that when you do a pious act you make some of the gods better?

EUTHYPHRO: No, certainly not.

[It is now seen that the reasoning so far leads to a contradiction. Piety cannot mean tendance in the sense which had been agreed on. Socrates and Euthyphro then go on to see whether any other sense of 'tendance' is more acceptable.]

Using this method, Socrates was able to understand and clarify other people's ideas. This extract, had it been on another topic (for example, reverse takeovers), could pass quite easily as a transcript of a contemporary knowledge engineer's interview. Especially for beginners, it might serve as an admirable paradigm. It shows the strength of a logical approach: that ideas are clarified, concepts are defined, and contradictions are exposed. However, it also shows a danger of logical analysis: Euthyphro eventually became infuriated when his ideas were shown to be riddled with contradiction. Antipathy of this sort contributed substantially to Socrates' demise. Those with experience in knowledge engineering will surely agree that one of the main dangers for a novice is to undiplomatically expose the equivocations and contradictions which the domain expert seems to make.

Contemporary textbook writers are constructing knowledge elicitation techniques from scratch, as if they believed that knowledge elicitation is a new technology. However, the novelty of contemporary techniques consists more in the enforcement of implementation restrictions during knowledge acquisition than in any substantive contribution to interviewing technique. For example, a recent textbook (Debenham, 1989) urges the knowledge engineer to accept from the domain expert only statements which are expressible in the form of Horn clauses (possibly augmented by modal operators). Debenham bases his knowledge acquisition methodology on the distinction between the "GEF" and the "PAF" (these terms abbreviate "general fact" and "particular fact"). His advice on the treatment of GEFs and PAFs during the interview runs like this:

> If the analyst regards a fact as a GEF, then the fact is recorded. In particular, if the GEF is the definition of a new thing-population, then the analyst should immediately inquire what the identifying name-population is. No matter what the GEF states, the analyst should then attempt to identify sufficient PAFs to fully define that GEF. We might describe this process as particularization. When the analyst is advised that sufficient PAFs have been presented to specify the given GEF fully, then the GEF is called a complete GEF.
>
> If the analyst regards a fact as a PAF, then the fact is recorded and the analyst will then attempt to "generalize" the PAF as we now describe. The generalization of a PAF is a particular GEF to which the given PAF belongs. (Debenham, 1989, pp. 134-5)

This process of particularization and generalization has much in common with Socrates' method of adduction and general definition. We might compare particularization (i.e., "attempt[ing] to identify sufficient PAFs to fully define that GEF") with Socrates' tactic of understanding "tendance" in terms of horse training, dog training, and cattle farming. Also, generalization is comparable with Socrates' postulation that horse training, dog training, and cattle farming conform with the principle that they are intended to cause benefit rather than harm. To this extent, the proposed knowledge acquisition technique is not substantially novel.

Furthermore, it seems reasonable to suggest that from a pedagogical point of view, Socratic dialogues are superior to abstract methodological recommendations. The student's ability to retain principles exemplified by the Socratic method is no doubt far superior to their grasp of using PAFs and GEFs in an interview. (If any reader doubts this, they may care to attempt one interview in the Socratic style, and another in the textbook style. The advantages of a tangible paradigm soon become apparent.)

What lesson can we draw from this? Apparently there is some theoretical justification for the anecdotal reports that humanities graduates are unexpectedly talented for expert systems work. Socratic philosophy may be a useful component in the education and training of knowledge engineers. Certainly, if the field of expert systems is to attain strong intellectual foundations, it should acknowledge its debt to the earlier work on which it (consciously or otherwise) depends.

CULTURAL PERSPECTIVE ON KNOWLEDGE

The nexus between expert systems and social science has been discussed by Harry Collins (1987, 1990). Lest it be thought that Collins — a sociologist of science — is indulging in hubris by publishing on expert systems, it is interesting to note that Collins was the main author of a paper which shared the prize for "best technical paper" at the British Computer Society's Expert Systems 85 conference (Collins, Green, & Draper, 1986). Collins explains one aspect of the relationship between expert systems and social science thus:

> As much as history of technology and sociology of knowledge can learn by looking to AI, they in turn can shed light on the possibilities, limitations, and fruitful routes for development of knowledgeable machines. ... This means that the findings of the whole research program of modern science studies, as well as specific examinations of AI, have implications for what AI researchers are trying to do. Whereas for most science and technology the visitor from science studies can be an onlooker, in this case he or she is also an expert, a knowledge specialist. (Collins, Green, & Draper, 1986, p. 329)

The point Collins is making is that social scientists were doing knowledge engineering (by a different name, of course) years before computer scientists "invented" it. The abundant work which researchers in "modern science studies" (i.e. history of science, sociology of scientific knowledge) have been doing is recorded in the social sciences literature. However, the AI community remains almost completely oblivious to this literature. We can verify this obliviousness through an examination of expert systems textbooks, where hardly any reference to social science is found.

A particular technique which social scientists use is known as participant observation. This involves working together with the subjects of one's study with a view to absorbing something of their culture. This facilitates greater insight into the thoughts and customs of one's subjects, and this in turn is an indispensable basis for a subsequent written report, which makes the activities of the subjects accessible to an audience which has no prior knowledge about the subject. The goal of participant observation is quite similar to the goal of knowledge engineering: to make the beliefs and practices of a certain group sufficiently explicit that they can be documented.

Many fine examples of the participant observation technique have been written up in the social science literature (for example Collins, 1984, 1985). It is a terrible waste that knowledge engineering techniques are being developed with no reference to this published work. This is surely an opportunity for expert systems workers to learn from social scientists.

Collins has outlined some aspects of knowledge which give theoretical support to the emphasis on social factors which we find in the participant observation technique. He compares two models of knowledge: algorithmic and enculturational. The algorithmic view of knowledge is that knowledge is something "hard" which can be communicated adequately through verbal media (whether spoken or written). This corresponds to communication through journals, conferences, and (less formally) via letters and telephone.

On the other hand, the enculturational model regards knowledge as something which ramifies indefinitely, and which is ultimately transmitted through shared enculturation. In other words, concepts are explicable only in terms of other concepts; and this explanation of concepts in terms of other concepts would regress infinitely were it not for the existence of shared culture, which requires no explanation. Hence the emphasis on practical work and the repetition of "classic" experiments which characterize most university science courses: These endow students with a cultural competence (habits of thought, speech, and action) which they hold in common with colleagues internationally.

FOURFOLD KNOWLEDGE TYPOLOGY

This fundamental dichotomy between the algorithmic and enculturational models motivates a fourfold knowledge typology which surpasses traditional AI views of knowledge. According to this typology, the kinds of knowledge which are involved in the transmission of expertise are "1) Facts and formal rules; 2) Heuristics; 3) Manual and perceptual skills; 4) Cultural skills" (Collins, 1987, p. 335).

Traditionally in AI, the all-important distinction has been between heuristics on one hand, and facts and formal rules on the other. The expert systems literature has popularized a dualistic epistemology in which expert knowledge consists of facts and heuristics. The possibility that facts and heuristics might together only account for a relatively small proportion of expert knowledge is hardly countenanced. For example, Oxman and Gero (1987) write:

> The knowledge incorporated within an expert system consists of facts and heuristics. The facts constitute the body of information and the heuristics are methodological statements and the rules of good guessing which together characterise expert level decision making within the field. (p. 4)

The fourfold typology proposed by Collins is quite different from the traditional expert systems view. Collins regards facts and heuristics as fundamentally alike, since they can both be explicitly verbalized (i.e., they both accord with the algorithmic model of knowledge). Furthermore, the amount of knowledge and skill that belongs in the enculturational categories of knowledge is considerably greater than the amount in the algorithmic categories. This is represented schematically in Figure 22.1 by the size of the boxes.

The categories of manual and perceptual skills and cultural skills fall onto the other side of the algorithmic/enculturational dichotomy. They also correspond broadly to the notion of "tacit knowledge," which was propagated by philosopher Michael Polanyi (1967). There is no strong division between these "enculturational" categories of knowledge, since manual and perceptual skills are generally theory-laden (i.e., suffused with the theoretical perspective furnished by the technical culture within which a scientist acts).

Examples of manual and perceptual skills abound in medical diagnosis: for instance, cardiac auscultation, esophagoscopy, interpretation of electrocardiograms. There is good reason to regard observations like these as theory-laden, since the layman undoubtedly could not make them; they depend on complex theories (e.g., the principles of cardiology). Financial skills such as the interpretation of share price charts also fall into the category of manual and perceptual skills.

The fourfold typology is a useful perspective for analyzing knowledge. Interestingly, particular pieces of knowledge are not necessarily "fixed" in some category: Sometimes knowledge can be moved from one category to the other (and surely this process is a kind of "knowledge engineering"). For instance, Collins observed Dr. Robert Harrison (who was attempting to construct a TEA laser) discard a theoretical rule in favor of an empirically derived heuristic. Initially, Harrision used "theoretically derived" figures to measure the permissible tolerances for clearance between the trigger wires and bottom electrode in the TEA laser. Careful measurements were required to ensure the satisfaction of these tolerances. Later, however, he found that it was sufficient to ensure that the tubes holding the trigger wires appeared roughly flat. This corresponds to the knowledge transformation labeled "b" in Figure 22.1.

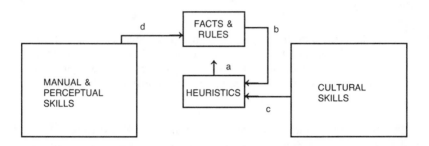

Figure 22.1

The transformation labeled "a" is also well known to laboratory scientists. In this case, a rule of thumb is replaced by principles which are more theoretically adequate. For instance, as an undergraduate computer scientist, I constructed several digital circuits known as "counters." The laboratory demonstrators introduced us to the heuristic that if a counter circuit behaved unexpectedly, it could often be fixed by placing a capacitor across the power supply wires (this smoothed out power supply fluctuations). As an undergraduate laboratory practice, this rule of thumb proved perfectly adequate. However, had we progressed to an industrial situation where counter circuits were designed and manufactured, we would have explored the effect of power supply fluctuations on our circuits from a theoretically rigorous perspective. This would have involved timing diagrams (published by the digital component manufacturers), logic analyzers (expensive diagnostic machines), and general principles of electronics. In this case, we would have made transformation "a."

ENCULTURATIONAL SKILLS ARE THE MOST PROBLEMATIC

AI workers have often tried to solve problems using the formalisms of facts and rules (e.g., predicate calculus, algebra, production rules). More recently, expert systems work in particular has become more pragmatic, using heuristics which may lack theoretical rigor, but which encapsulate the experience of skilled practitioners. Collins' typology of knowledge helps us to see both why the introduction of heuristics is useful (since it eliminates the need to express knowledge precisely at the level of facts and rules), and yet why it is limited (since it still fails to address the vast bulk of knowledge which exists at the enculturational level).

Attempts to derive formal methods which are generally applicable to problem solving have been largely unsuccessful. In fact, it is well known that AI workers have found "basic" skills such as facial recognition or understanding natural language much harder to replicate than fact-processing skills which we take to be diagnostic for intelligence when we find them in a human being: playing chess at grandmaster level, proving theorems in logic, or solving equations. This seems paradoxical if we accept the computationalist metaphor (expounded by Pylyshyn, 1984) that human cognition is most usefully viewed as a computational process.

Yet, according to Collins' model, this is exactly what we should expect. Fact-processing skills are readily implemented on a computer using a rule-based formalism, since the knowledge transformation required here is rather minimal. On the other hand, implementation of a skill such as facial recognition involves transforming "enculturational" skills (in the human) into "algorithmic" skills (in the computer). This transformation is extraordinarily difficult, since these two classes of skill are rather incommensurable. Humans are in a privileged position, since we are participants in a culture where we interactively relate to other people's facial expressions. In the limit, computers may somehow approach this level of interactive participation, but they will never fully achieve it, since they will never be fully human.

For many purposes, however, approximation to human skills is perfectly adequate for a commercially useful system. Hence I am not arguing, for instance, that computer systems for facial recognition will never outperform humans in particular applications. What I do argue is that the principal design limitation on these systems is that they are not participants in human culture. This will make them hard to build, and will also constrain the shape of their "performance envelope." To construct systems with greater functionality, expert systems practitioners will need to work on the transformations labeled "c" and "d" in Figure 22.1.

GENERALITY IN ARTIFICIAL INTELLIGENCE

Using Collins' insights, we can also consider afresh the problem of generality in artificial intelligence. This perplexing issue was addressed by John McCarthy in his 1971 Turing Award Lecture. McCarthy waited 16 years before attempting an exposition of this issue in written form. As he observed, "The topic turned out to have been overambitious in that I discovered I was unable to put my thoughts on the subject in a satisfactory written form at that time." (McCarthy, 1987, p. 1030).

In the same article, McCarthy claims that "getting a language for expressing general commonsense knowledge for inclusion in a general database is the key problem of generality in AI." He reports on various lines of research which have grappled with achieving more general techniques for knowledge processing. In logic, a central problem has been how to manage nonmonotonic reasoning. Techniques such as circumscription have certainly furthered our knowledge of this field. However, despite this progress, the goal of realizing some general technique for machine intelligence seems as distant as ever. As McCarthy concludes, "All this is unpleasantly vague, but it is a lot more than could be said in 1971" (p. 1035).

From the history of science it seems reasonable to conclude that when a problem has been this resistant to solution, satisfactory progress comes only through some sort of paradigm shift. In other words, there is a general recognition that an alternative conceptualization of the problem will facilitate a more fruitful research program. One doesn't need to adhere to Kuhn's theory of the history of science in order to accept this basic perspective on how scientific research proceeds (although this perspective is substantially Kuhnian). The key point is merely the common-sense observation that often a problem becomes more tractable when we view it a different way.

Collins' approach seems to be a suitable candidate for a new way of viewing the problem of generality in artificial intelligence.

We have already seen that facts, formal rules, and heuristics (the kinds of knowledge which are generally amenable to explicit transmission through verbal media) are ready-made for automatic processing since it is relatively easy to state them explicitly. However, cultural, manual, and perceptual skills have a substantially tacit component. This tacit component might be innate, or transmitted through culture, or some combination of both. Collins does not mention the possibility of innateness, yet it seems clear that there is often a component of innate ability underlying the manual and perceptual skills practiced by such diverse groups as surgeons and stock market analysts.

Regardless of whether these tacit skills are innate or encultured, humans have a distinct advantage over computers in acquiring them (since humans receive innate skills as part of their genetic endowment, and receive enculturational skills through the normal processes of living in a society). This explains why this sort of skill is so difficult to embed in a computer. We know, however that this is not impossible in the general case, because of the transformations illustrated in Figure 22.1.

This prompts the proposal that we could replace one large problem (of achieving generality in artificial intelligence) with several more tractable subproblems (of classifying knowledge and skills according to the fourfold typology, and of working on stronger techniques for making the transformations illustrated in Figure 22.1).

This might have at least two beneficial effects. The first would be at least a modest improvement in the capabilities of AI systems. The second (and probably more important) effect would be a clearer perception of why certain tasks are feasible for AI and others are not. For instance, tasks such as the control of a bipedal robot moving over rough terrain may be difficult, but at least they are not usually constrained by anything more volatile than the vagaries of geography, weather, and so on. On the other hand, determining the motivations of a human being (which is sometimes necessary in a court of law) would be more difficult, since all sorts of ephemeral contingencies of culture are likely to impinge.

KNOWLEDGE ENGINEERING METHODOLOGIES

Knowledge engineers seem to be in quest of methods or methodologies. Several authors have made efforts toward developing a knowledge engineering methodology (Cooke & McDonald, 1986; Debenham, 1989; Freiling, Alexander, Messick, Rehfuss, & Shulman, 1985; Kitakami, Kunifuji, Miyachi, & Furukawa, 1984; Mettrey, 1987). What do these authors mean when they refer to method or methodology?

It seems they mean something more comprehensive than a technique or procedure; perhaps a guideline which is intended to provide for almost every contingency a knowledge engineer may face in their work. Webster's Dictionary describes methodology as "a body of methods, procedures, working concepts, rules and postulates employed by a science, art or discipline." Another description offered by Webster is "the theoretical foundations of a philosophical doctrine. The basic premises, postulates and concepts of a philosophy."

These definitions seem to indicate that methodology aims to be all-embracing. This impression is confirmed by Debenham (1989), who offers "a detailed description of a method for designing expert knowledge-based systems and deductive database systems. This method is complete and extends from initial knowledge acquisition to knowledge base implementation and knowledge base maintenance" (p. 1).

In the light of this, it seems reasonable to conclude that the quest for methodology is the quest for an all-embracing approach, and is much more ambitious than the study of various tools and techniques.

Now it so happens that one of the main areas of study in the history and philosophy of science is the question of scientific method. The work which has been done on this question is relevant to the notion of knowledge engineering methodologies.

Despite the vigorous search for knowledge engineering methodologies, there does not seem to have been any serious debate about why methodologies are desirable. Surely we must justify the desirability of having methodologies for knowledge engineering before we start building and using these methodologies. In other words, the question "Would it be useful to have a methodology for knowledge engineering?" logically precedes the question "What should our knowledge engineering methodology be?"

It may seem self-evident that a methodology must be a good thing. After all, since the notion of a methodology entails organized and systematic activity, it seems plausible that the absence of methodology will tend toward unproductive chaos. However, this may not be true. In *Against Method,* Paul Feyerabend (1975) argues that the quest for methodologies in science has been somewhat like chasing after the wind. He announces:

> My intention is not to replace one set of general rules by another such set; my intention is, rather, to convince the reader that all methodologies, even the most obvious ones, have their limits. The best way to show this is to demonstrate the limits and even the irrationality of some rules which she, or he, is likely to regard as basic. (p. 32)

Consequently, Feyerabend presents a re-examination of substantial portions of the history of science. He challenges the rational reconstructions favored by many philosophers and historians of science, where scientific achievements throughout history are interpreted to show their accord with certain beliefs about rationality and the proper methods for intelligent discovery. Since believers in methodology construe the history of science according to their methodological assumptions, it is not surprising that the history they write seems to reveal method at work in scientific discovery.

Most textbook science presents the history of science according to this methodological bias: The work of early scientists is interpreted as significant only so far as it is a precursor to modern science. This style of writing history was identified as the "Whig interpretation" by Butterfield (1932). Whig history is generally regarded by professional historians as an inferior style.

So the history written in science texts appears to show early scientists succeeding in direct proportion to the extent that they stumble on modern scientific method. Galileo is almost universally portrayed in the science texts as a pioneer of experimental method. High school students are urged to replicate some of his crucial experiments. However, Feyerabend emphasizes something which others before him recognized: many of Galileo's experiments cannot be replicated, and appear to be physically impossible. Cohen (1984) presents evidence of the physical impossibility of various experiments Galileo claimed to have done.

So much for the view of Galileo as a pioneer of experimental methodology! Feyerabend's re-examination of Galileo reveals work based more on intuition and rhetoric than on objective experiments. Yet this is not to discount the value of what Galileo did. It is just to point out that if Galileo worked to method, it was a method substantially different from the method attributed to him in most textbooks. Shouldn't this be taken into account before we slip into a habit of thinking that knowledge engineering must be conducted according to some particular method?

In actual fact the prescription of methodologies has been a theme in the philosophy of science for many decades. It perhaps reached its heyday in the work of Karl Popper, who in turn had been influenced by the Vienna Circle (otherwise known as the logical positivists). Popper was engaged in studying the growth of knowledge, a topic now embraced by knowledge engineers. As Popper (1959) wrote, "The central problem of epistemology has always been and still is the growth of knowledge. And the growth of knowledge can be studied best by studying the growth of scientific knowledge" (p. 15).

Since many AI workers are leaning heavily toward logic-based methodologies, it is interesting to observe that Popper proposed a logicist scientific method to avoid defective scientific maneuvers which he called "conventionalist stratagems." He enumerated these stratagems along with his prescribed antidote in the *Logic of Scientific Discovery*. Unfortunately for advocates of knowledge engineering methodologies, Popper's scientific method never really caught on.

Feyerabend is blunt in his assessment of Popper's insistence on methodology:

> [The methodological principles of Popper and the Vienna Circle] ... give an inadequate account of science because science is much more "sloppy" and "irrational" than its methodological image. ... The difference between science and methodology which is such an obvious fact of history, therefore, indicates a weakness of the latter, and perhaps of the 'laws of reason' as well. For what appears as 'sloppiness,' 'chaos,' or 'opportunism' when compared with such laws has a most important function in the development of those very theories which we today regard as essential parts of our knowledge of nature. ... Without chaos, no knowledge. (p. 179)

Therefore, according to Feyerabend, the absence of methodology is not, as we suggested before, an unproductive chaos. On the contrary, it is a productive chaos whose productivity and chaotic nature are demonstrable from a careful study of the history of science. It is reasonable, therefore, to demand of prescriptive methodologists some historical evidence that prescribed methodologies have brought more progress than we might otherwise have expected.

Hall and Kibler (1985) have identified the harm involved in prescribing methodologies for AI work:

> We argue that prescriptive methodological analysis of AI simply adds to the prevailing sense of confusion. We propose instead a descriptive analysis of what participants in the field actually do. (p. 166)

This sentiment can only be endorsed. Modern science studies (such as Feyerabend's work) are practically unanimous in rejecting a prescriptive approach to methodology. Much creative work achieves its excellent results precisely because it ignores standard methodologies of the day. Particularly in expert systems and knowledge engineering, adherence to methodologies prescribed so early in the development of the field will more likely stifle rather than promote any worthwhile advances.

As Hall and Kibler rightly point out, reflection on AI methodologies is valuable; but the value lies in describing (or understanding) the perspective of other workers in the field, not in prescribing some canonical approach which will supposedly obtain the best results. It is worth reiterating here that descriptive analysis of scientific methodologies is a well-established area of study in the humanities (for example, Barnes, 1982; Collins, 1985; Latour, 1987; Latour & Woolgar, 1979). There is no need for AI workers to develop this field independently.

It is also worth noting Feyerabend's claim that adherence to methodology can be a terrible self-deception, since science when practiced as a methodology is actually very much like religion and mythology, while supposing itself virtually antithetical to them. For instance, religions are commonly supposed to have the characteristics of taboo beliefs, an elite priesthood, and a fiduciary commitment which undermines the possibility of any rational self-criticism. In actual fact, says Feyerabend, these characteristics are more descriptive of methodological science than of religion.

Each methodology has its "gurus" who create and preserve the teachings in the methodology. Also, by their nature, methodologies propagate some basic world view that cannot be abandoned without abandoning the methodology itself.

For instance, many AI paradigms have a logicist emphasis. A fundamental characteristic of inferencing with a two-valued logic is that contradictions (whether explicit or derivable) in the knowledge base cannot be tolerated, since they effectively make all propositions provable. Therefore if we enshrine two-valued logic in a methodology (rather than merely using it as a convenient tool), we practically prohibit ourselves from coming to grips with the possibility that experts might function at a high level while maintaining a belief system with contradictions in it. At this point, the reader, engaging in candid introspection, may admit that their capacity for intelligent behavior has not been eliminated by the occasional self-contradiction.

However, in a thoroughly logicist methodology, the possibility of intelligent agents with contradictory knowledge bases becomes tantamount to a taboo belief: It cannot meaningfully be challenged within the system.

To sum this up, the study of techniques (such as logic) is unquestionably useful, but the creation of all-embracing methodologies can be a trap. Those who wish to promote methodologies should publish proof that methodologies have advanced computer science in the past. Otherwise, we should perhaps join Feyerabend in regarding method[ology] as the "most recent, most aggressive, and most dogmatic religious institution" (p. 295).

CONCLUSION

This chapter has advocated the view that links between knowledge engineering and the humanities and social sciences should be recognized and actively explored. In actual fact, this process has already begun; mostly from the humanities side (for example, Boden, 1977; Ringle, 1979; Collins, 1985; Collins et al., 1986; Bloomfield, 1985; Darden, 1987), but also to a certain extent from the AI side (Hall & Kibler 1985). Furthermore, this process is a natural extension and deepening of the links which AI already enjoys with philosophy and cognitive psychology.

One of the hallmarks of a professional engineer is basic competence in the scientific fields which support the engineering discipline. Accordingly, mechanical engineers are expected to have some familiarity with the basic principles of mathematics, thermodynamics, materials science, and other such sciences. In which scientific disciplines should a knowledge engineer have competence?

The AI literature already reveals an awareness that principles of philosophy and cognitive psychology are relevant to knowledge engineering, and intellectually profitable to the development of the field. This article supports the argument of Collins (1987) that modern science studies — history, philosophy, and sociology of science — constitute a body of "knowledge science." Several examples have demonstrated the potential foder profitable interaction between knowledge engineering and the humanities. It is therefore argued that knowledge engineering will needlessly be stunted in its development if it fails to draw on the humanities, including the "soft" areas such as the history and sociology of science.

In our time, many people are resigned to a chasm between the "two cultures" described by C.P. Snow (1964). These two cultures are, broadly speaking, the sciences and the humanities. It may seem fanciful to suggest that knowledge engineers should immerse themselves, for instance, in the sociology of science. Yet the fact is that some sociologists of science have plenty of experience in knowledge elicitation from which knowledge engineers may benefit.

Perhaps not too distantly in the future, the knowledge engineering literature will interact fruitfully with the sociology of scientific knowledge, and trainee knowledge engineers will cut their teeth on Socrates and Wittgenstein.

REFERENCES

Bloomfield, B.P. (1985). *The question of artificial intelligence: Philosophical and sociological studies*. London: Croom Helm.

Boden, M.A. (1977). *Artificial intelligence and natural man*. New York: Basic Books.

Barnes, B. (1982). *T.S. Kuhn and social science*. New York: Columbia University Press.

Butterfield, H. (1932). *The Whig interpretation of history.* London: Bell.

Cohen, H.F. (1984). *Quantifying music: The science of music at the first stage of the scientific revolution, 1580-1650.* Dordecht, Germany: D. Reidel.

Collins, H.M. (1984). Concepts and practice of participatory fieldwork. In C. Bell & H. Roberts (Ed.), *Social researching* (pp. 54-64). London: Routledge and Kegan Paul.

Collins, H.M. (1985). *Changing order: Replication and induction in scientific practice,* Beverly Hills, CA: Sage.

Collins, H.M. (1987). Expert systems and the science of knowledge. In W.E. Bijker, T.P. Hughes, & T.T. Pinch (Eds.), *Social construction of technological systems: New directions in the sociology and history of technology* (pp. 329-348). Cambridge, MA: MIT Press.

Collins, H.M. (1990). *Artifical Experts: Social Knowledge and Intelligent Machines,* Cambridge, MA: MIT Press.

Collins, H.M., Green, R.H., & Draper, R.C. (1986). Where's the expertise: Expert systems as a medium of knowledge transfer. In M.J. Merry (Ed.), *Expert systems 85,* (pp. 323-334). Cambridge, UK: Cambridge University Press.

Cooke, N.M., & McDonald, J.E. (1986). A formal methodology for acquiring and representing expert knowledge. *Proceedings of IEEE, 74,* 1422-1430.

Darden, L. (1987). Viewing the history of science as compiled hindsight. *AI Magazine, 8* (2), 33-41.

Debenham, J. K. (1989). *Knowledge systems design.* Sydney: Prentice-Hall.

Feyerabend, P.K. (1975). *Against method: Outline of an anarchistic theory of knowledge.* London: New Left Books.

Freiling, M., Alexander, J., Messick, S., Rehfuss, S. & Shulman, S. (1985). Starting a knowledge engineering project: A step-by-step approach. *AI Magazine, 6* (3), 150-164.

Hall, R.P., & Kibler, D.F. (1985). Differing methodological perspectives in artificial intelligence research. *AI Magazine, 6* (3), 166-178.

Kitakami, H., Kunifuji, S., Miyachi, T., & Furukawa, K. (1984). A methodology for implementation of a knowledge acquisition system. *1984 International Symposium on Logic Programming,* IEEE Computer Society.

Kuhn, T.S. (1962). *The structure of scientific revolutions.* Chicago, IL: Chicago University Press.

Latour, B. (1987). *Science in action: How to follow scientists and engineers through society.* Cambridge, MA: Harvard University Press.

Latour, B., & Woolgar, S. (1979). *Laboratory life: The social construction of scientific facts.* Beverly Hills, CA: Sage Publications.

McCarthy, J. (1958). Programs with common sense. In M. Minsky (Ed.), *Semantic information processing* (pp. 403-410). Cambridge, MA: MIT Press.

McCarthy, J. (1987). Generality in artificial intelligence. *Communications of the ACM, 30,* 1030-1035.

Mettrey, W. (1987). An assessment of tools for building large knowledge-based systems. *AI Magazine, 8* (4), 81-89.

Oxman, R., & Gero, J.S. (1987). Using an expert system for design diagnosis and design synthesis. *Expert Systems, 4,* 4-15.

Plato (1969). *The last days of Socrates* (Trans. by H. Tredennick), Harmondsworth, UK: Penguin.

Polanyi, M. (1967). *The tacit dimension.* London: Routledge and Kegan Paul.

Popper, K.R. (1959). *The logic of scientific discovery.* London: Hutchison.

Pylyshyn, Z. W. (1984). *Computation and cognition: Toward a foundation for cognitive science.* Cambridge, MA: MIT Press.

Ringle, M. (1979). Philosophy and artificial intelligence. In M. Ringle (Ed.), *Philosophical perspectives in artificial intelligence.* Atlantic Highlands, NJ: Humanities Press.

Snow, C.P. (1964). *The two cultures and a second look: An expanded version of the two cultures and the scientific revolution.* Cambridge, UK: Cambridge University Press.

Wittgenstein, L. (1974). *Tractatus logico-philosophicus* (Trans. D.F. Pears & B.F. McGuinness.) London: Routledge and Kegan Paul.

CHAPTER 23

Reduction and Levels of Explanation in Connectionism*

John Sutton

Department of Philosophy
Macquarie University

INTRODUCTION

Recent work in the methodology of connectionist explanation has focused on the notion of levels of explanation. Specific issues in connectionism here intersect with wider areas of debate in the philosophy of psychology and the philosophy of science generally. The issues I raise in this chapter, then, are not unique to cognitive science; but they arise in new and important contexts when connectionism is taken seriously as a model of cognition. The general questions are the relation between levels and the status of levels which have no obvious relation to others. In speaking of levels, what is the connection, if there is one, between explanation and ontology? Which, if any, concept of reduction is applicable to connectionist systems? What kind of legitimacy can the constructs of common sense psychology, or of that version of intentional realism represented by classical symbol-systems AI, have in a full-scale connectionist theory of mind?

In this chapter I address the promising and sophisticated picture of connectionist explanation developed by Andy Clark in his book *Microcognition* (Clark, 1989a) and in a number of recent papers (Clark, 1988a, 1989b, 1990a). The drift is to suggest that, while Clark makes clear the radical nature of the connectionist explanatory framework, his view fails to account successfully for the value of high-level explanations and for why such explanations work. In particular, Clark doesn't provide a sufficiently robust account of the kind of mental causation which seems to be necessary if realism about propositional attitudes is to be maintained. A weak

* Many thanks and my acknowledgements to Daniel Stoljar, with whom I wrote and delivered an ancestor of this paper at the University of Adelaide in March 1990. The outline of A Theory of Reduction and Levels of Explanation presented here was worked out in collaboration with him. Thanks too to George Couvalis and Graham Nerlich for comments on that paper, and to Gerard O'Brien, Huw Price, and Doris McIlwain for many helpful discussions.

requirement of reducibility on a level of explanation, which I will spell out and defend at some length, will explicate the relations between levels in a way Clark's position cannot. It will then serve as a defense of the "condition of causal efficacy" on explanations which Clark, following Jackson and Pettit, rejects. Finally I apply this weak reducibility constraint back specifically to explanation in connectionism, and discuss the status of high-level explanations of connectionist systems.

I will deliberately be blurring some allegedly vital distinctions here. I won't be drawing sharp distinctions between levels of description and levels of explanation, between intertheoretic and interlevel reductions, nor between type and token reductions. The metaphysics of reduction I advance has a number of gaps of detail, but its general drift is so appropriate to connectionist explanation, and such a useful counterweight to Clark's thoroughgoing antireductionism, that its introduction to these specific debates might excuse the compressed form it takes here.

To situate the issue I am addressing, consider the long-running dispute about the legitimacy of causal explanations in terms of propositional attitudes, between robust "big-R" realists and eliminativists (P.M. Churchland, 1981, 1988b, Fodor, 1987). From the perspective of this chapter, the differences between these two positions are relatively minor: The requirement of reducibility on explanation to be expounded is, I claim, weak enough to be accepted by Fodor and by philosophical functionalists as well as by eliminativists. But Clark sees both extremes as misguided (along with others whose specific views I won't be discussing here but who include Dennett, 1978, 1987, 1988; Wilkes, 1984, 1986; Rorty, 1980, 1983; and Price, 1988). Concerning requirements for the legitimacy of common sense psychological explanation, Clark laments,

> We can find two sets of otherwise opposed philosophers united in mutual error. Both Fodor's (1987) defence of ordinary mental talk and various eliminativist attacks on it are committed to a principle of scientific legitimation which can be stated thus:
> The goodness of Folk Psychological talk depends on its being legitimised by the discovery of an engineering story which shares its form. (Clark, 1988a, p.275)

It is Clark's rejection of this principle which is open to dispute. The range of reductive possibilities in the development of cognitive science includes, as extremes, Fodorian realism and San Diego eliminativism. But Clark's wish to accept and justify ordinary mental talk and its theoretical derivatives without "scientific legitimation" is, I maintain, neither a genuine option nor a good enough defense.

CLARK'S LIBERALISM ABOUT CAUSATION AND LEVELS

Levels of Connectionist Explanation

Clark offers a neat, innovative model of explanation in connectionist systems (1989a, especially pp. 83-105, 184), and discusses its departures from traditional theories of explanation in cognitive science (1990a). He acknowledges that connectionism simply fails to fit Marr's classical view of levels of explanation (Marr, 1977, 1982). As I am almost wholly in agreement with Clark on these points, I will only sketch, from his presentation, those levels of explanation the status of which make them relevant to my argument.

Starting only with a general task specification, connectionist models with distributed representation are simply set running with random weights, and trained up to better performance, by a variety of supervised or unsupervised learning procedures. The first steps in connectionist explanation, then, are not detailed specifications of the function to be computed and the information on which algorithms are to draw, as in classical models (Peacocke, 1986). Rather they deal with a fully working system. At this stage, the network can be described only by precise mathematical specification of the connections and weights of its individual units. Differential equations can specify both the state of the system at a given time (by stating a vector of numerical values), and its dynamic learning pattern. Explanation of this sort is at what Clark calls "the numerical level" (1989a, pp. 188-189). At this level, as Smolensky notes, "the explanations of behavior are like those traditional in the physical sciences" (1988, p. 1).

Only at this stage can the observer of the connectionist system work backwards, up the levels, toward an understanding of larger-scale patterns of hidden-unit activity, through, for instance, network pathology caused by artificial lesions and hierarchical cluster analysis. I will be concentrating on cluster analysis as an example of an interesting intermediate level of analysis, because it is well-known and already much discussed in the present context.

Cluster analysis reveals the "sorts of internal representations the network has developed to carry out a particular task" (Elman, 1989, p. 5). For each class of input, a mean vector of hidden unit activation patterns is computed. These mean vectors are all then subjected to hierarchical cluster analysis. "The hierarchical interpretation is achieved through the way in which the spatial relations of the representations are organized. Representations which are near one another in representational space form classes, and higher level categories correspond to larger and more general regions of this space" (Elman, 1989, p. 7; 1990, pp. 205-207). Through such analysis the observer can display a hierarchy of partitions, portraying the shape of the representational space of the possible hidden-unit activations that power the network's performance (for more examples and detail see Rosenberg & Sejnowski, 1987; P.S. Churchland & Sejnowski, 1989; P.M. Churchland,

1989a, 1989b; Clark, 1989a, 1990a; Elman, 1989, 1990).

Understanding of connectionist systems, then, comes not through detailed prior analysis of the structure of the task domain, but through statistical glimpses into the running of an already operational network. This "explanatory inversion," which Clark describes as "Marr-through-the-looking-glass" (1990a, p. 215), does not imply a lack of explanatory power. In letting the task organize the network, rather than "imposing the form of our conscious, sentential thought on our models of unconscious processing" (p. 218), the connectionist is able to avoid "ad-hoc organizing principles and sentential, linguistic bias" (p. 219) projected downwards from our conscious understanding[1].

So far so good: Connectionism, in Clark's rendering, is a means to escape what Patricia Churchland called philosophers' "fetishism with respect to logic as the model for inner processes" (1986, p. 381). But what of the status of the levels, discovered in such post hoc strategies as artificial lesioning and cluster analysis, which are higher than that of mere numerical specification of connection weights? There is an intuitive sense in which it is the latter, the base level of connection weights which, as Paul Churchland has put it, drives the dynamic cognitive evolution of the system over time (P.M. Churchland, 1989a, Section 5). What implications does this have for explanation? This question is the focus of some debate, and is central to my concerns in this chapter.

For now I want to bring into play other high levels of description of connectionist systems. Firstly, what Clark calls "the symbolic-AI level": Connectionist systems are described at this level as if they were classical, as if they follow rules, access schemas, fire productions, and so on. These are descriptions according to which the system seems to be satisfying "hard, symbolic constraints in serial order" (1989a, p. 194). The descriptions will tend to break down, to fail to explain, under suboptimal conditions, for "solutions" to ill-posed problems, or with curtailed processing time. In these conditions, connectionist systems will still give "sensible performance" by satisfying as many soft constraints as well as possible. So the formal descriptions of the symbolic AI level cannot provide a unified account of genuinely connectionist cognition, even if they appear to be accurate descriptions of a system's behavior under ideal conditions (see Clark, 1989a, pp. 194-195, and Smolensky, 1988 for detail on this level).

The final relevant level is that of common sense psychology. Here too there is a prima facie tension with the base numerical level. The words and concepts of ordinary language have, it initially seems, no obvious discrete analogs in distributed connectionist systems, since in any particular case they will be

---

[1] Compare Clark's description of Fodor's search for in-the-head structures which mirror the structures of conscious thought-ascription as "polishing the tip of the iceberg" (Clark 1988b, p. 616).

represented as a complex activation vector across a large set of units in state space. It is this point which drives the recent suggestion that eliminative materialism would be confirmed by the success of connectionism (Stich, 1988a, 1988b; Ramsay, Stich, & Garon, 1990; P.M. Churchland, 1988c, 1989c; disputed by O'Brien, 1991, 1993).

Clark has been at pains to maintain the importance of all these levels of explanation: Cluster analysis, the symbolic AI level and the common-sense psychological level (1989a, pp. 199-201). Surely some at least of these higher levels are going to count as explanatory, even, as Clark says, for the antisententialist unsatisfied with the propositional bias of classical AI (1990a, p. 218). But what principled account can be given of the status of these levels of explanation? It is not with the question of whether such higher level explanations may be justified, but with that of how and why they are justified, and of what would count as a justification, that my disagreements with Clark lie.

Clark's Causal Liberalism

Clark's defence of high-level explanations relies on the grouping of systems into equivalence classes defined according to the purpose of the explanation. "Each such grouping requires a special vocabulary, and the constructs of any given vocabulary are legitimate just insofar as the grouping is interesting and useful" (Clark 1989a, p. 187).

The interest or utility of a level of explanation is, for Clark, sufficient for its legitimacy. In particular, utility is sufficient for the legitimacy of the constructs of any equivalence class even when these constructs are not reducible to the constructs of a physical causal level of explanation. We should in psychological explanation expect no "neat mapping" between ascribed mental states and "scientific stories about the inner causes" of behavior (1989a, p. 57; p. 49, p. 94, p. 112, p. 196; 1988a, p. 267). Individual thoughts, Clark reiterates, "are perfectly real, but they are not the kind of entities that have neat, projectible, computational analogues in the brain" (p. 153).

Clark takes this position partly on the basis of a holistic ascriptivism about mental states: "ascription of a thought is ... ascription of a structured competence within a close-knit semantic domain" (1988a, p. 271; cf. 1988b, 1990b). Beliefs, for instance, are holistically ascribed on the basis of sufficiently rich and flexible bodies of behavior (p. 267). I don't want to quarrel about this ascriptivism: One could consistently accept it while still running the objections I am about to.

My queries are directed, rather, at the second strand of Clark's rejection of "in-the-head realism" (1988a, pp. 267-273). This is his set of views on explanation, causation, and reduction. It is most clearly set out in his rejection of what he calls the "condition of causal efficacy" on psychological explanation. The condition of causal efficacy is as follows: "A psychological ascription is only warranted if the items it posits have direct analogues in the production (or possible production) of behavior" (Clark 1989a, p. 196).

Clark's stated aim is to provide a picture of high-level explanation dissociated from this condition, one which will give "a more liberal, more plausible, and more useful picture of explanation in cognitive science and daily life" (p. 196). Such a "liberalism about causation" deliberately divorces (not just causal explanation but) causation from reduction (1988a, pp. 272-273).

This distinction between causation and reduction should result, suggests Clark, in a radical division within cognitive science. On the one hand would be an engineering project, seeking the in-the-head causes of behavior. On the other will be what he calls "descriptive cognitive science," which takes "sentential thought-ascriptions as its data and use[s] dynamic, computational models to chart the logical, epistemic or normative relations among thoughts so ascribed" (1988a, p. 274). It gives "a formal theory or model of the structure of the abstract domain of thoughts" (1989a, p. 153). Clark welcomes the prospect of a "rift" resulting from the lack of any "useful relation" between the two kinds of cognitive science (1988a, p. 273, 1989a, p. 159).

This leaves a puzzling lack of clarity concerning the relation between the two kinds of cognitive science, between formal description and engineering story, and more specifically between higher level psychological explanation and physical causal explanation. There are two ways to read Clark on these topics. He could be making what he calls this "distinction between description and cause" in order to deny the causal powers of the constructs of the descriptive project, in particular to reject the implication of mental states in the causation of action. But unless you're a hardened Wittgensteinian, denying mental causation just won't do. Explanation in terms of beliefs, desires, and the rest must be causal explanation of some sort if it is to be legitimate.

Mostly, Clark acknowledges this requirement. His liberalism is, after all, a causal liberalism, and such an extreme brand of neobehaviorism is not his. As he puts it, "the lack of in-head, engineering analogues to individual beliefs and desires need not deprive us of the right to treat beliefs and desires as real, causally active factors in the etiology of human action" (1988a, p. 273). He criticizes Fodor's view that the computational structure of the brain neatly mirrors the descriptive structure of propositional attitude ascriptions: Fodor, Clark says, is guilty of conflating the two kinds of cognitive science in that he adheres to an overstrict model of causation, buttressed by "a fear that beliefs and desires can only be causes if they turn up in formal guise as part of the physical story behind intelligent behavior" (1989a, p. 160; cf 1988a, p. 277, 1988b, p. 609). Clark thinks this fear is groundless:

> All that we need is that there should be some physical, causal story, and that talk of beliefs and desires should make sense of behavior. Such

making sense does involve a notion of cause, since beliefs do cause actions. But unless we believe that there is only one model of causation, the physical, this needn't cause any discomfort. (Clark 1989a, p. 160)

What kind of nonphysical model of causation, then, does Clark offer instead? How can truly causal explanation be exempted from the condition of causal efficacy? Abandoning an earlier discussion involving analogies to other allegedly nonphysical cases of causation (1988a; criticized by Tienson, 1990), Clark offers a principled defense of nonphysical causation drawn from Frank Jackson and Philip Pettit (1988; Clark, 1989a, pp. 196-198). Clark applies to connectionist explanation their defense of the view that "features that causally explain need not cause" (Jackson & Pettit, 1988, p. 392). This involves a distinction between "causal process explanations" and "causal programme explanations" (1988, pp. 388-399).

Briefly, a causal process explanation satisfies the condition of causal efficacy in that it cites the actual causally productive features that are efficacious in a particular or given range of cases. These process explanations will be those given by Clark's engineering project. A causal program explanation, on the other hand, cites a feature or property, common across a range of cases, which causally programs the result "without actually figuring in the causal chain leading to an individual action or instance" (Clark, 1989a, p. 198). In explaining a glass vessel's breaking either by its fragility or by an increase in the temperature of the gas inside it (to take two of Jackson and Pettit's examples), we are not citing the particular causes of the shattering, which might be, respectively, the categorical basis of the glass's structure or the impact of a number of molecules on the walls of the vessels (or indeed any of a multitude of ways that fragility or increase in temperature might have been realized) (Jackson & Pettit, 1988, p. 395). Although neither fragility nor increase in temperature causes the breaking, say Jackson and Pettit, they can be said to program the breaking, and thus explain it.

Clark's borrowing from Jackson and Pettit is intended to account for the value of high-level explanations of connectionist networks. The point for Clark is that such program explanations buy us an increase in generality "at the cost of sacrificing the citation of the actual entity implicated in the particular causal chain in question" (1989a, p. 197). It justifies the cluster analytic level of connectionist explanation, which cites global partitions in activation space as its constructs. Networks with distributed representations, when set running with different random distributions of hidden unit connection weights, may turn out to have identical cluster analyses even when embodying entirely different arrangements of individual connection weights (P.M. Churchland, 1989a, Section 5). One cluster analysis, in other words, is multiply realizable at the lower level of numerical specification of dynamic connectivity patterns. Churchland's point that the causal laws of cognitive evolution operate at the level of individual weights rather than at the level of the partitions in activation space (identified by cluster analysis) can be deflected, Clark thinks, by a good liberalism about causation. The cluster analysis "causally programmes the system's successful performance, but it is not part of any process explanation" (1989a, p. 199).

Clark goes on to give similar justifications for the explanation of connectionist networks at the yet higher levels of both symbolic AI and common sense psychological explanation. Equivalence class groupings at these higher levels may unite what would be otherwise apparently disparate cognitive mechanisms. They are not "mere approximations to the connectionist cognitive truth," but capture constructs which, though themselves causally inefficacious, highlight important facts about an important range of "cognitive constitutions" (1989a, p. 200-201). In other words, the interest or utility of a level of explanation is sufficient for its legitimacy.

Again, it is not the value of these explanations which I necessarily want to question, but rather the explanation of their value. I can agree with Clark that "explanation is a many-leveled thing," and that it is important in cognitive as in other sciences to subsume a single phenomenon "under a panoply of increasingly general explanatory schemas" (1990a, p. 196). In some cases, important higher level similarities between systems realized in different substructs might be invisible at the lower level. In connectionist explanation, in particular, explanations at the level of dynamic activation equations may obscure interesting cognitive similarities which are apparent at a higher level of generalization (Clark, 1989a, pp. 181-182, 197). But, I maintain, Clark's reliance on utility alone as a measure of the legitimacy of a high-level explanation leaves out important detail. The concomitant rejection of the condition of causal efficacy as a necessary condition on a level's legitimacy stems, I propose, from an overstrict idea of the kind of reductionism such a condition entails.

To carry this point, I need to step back for a moment from the specific problems of connectionist explanation, and give a positive account of the relations between explanation, reduction, and causation which will elucidate an acceptably weak constraint of reducibility on a level of explanation. This will then not only justify some high-level explanations, as Clark wants, but give an account of why they work, of the relations between levels of explanation in a way that his causal liberalism cannot. This is inevitably a sketchy treatment of controversial issues in the philosophy of science, detailed treatment of which I pursue elsewhere (Sutton, 1993). I can only plead that the sketchiness is justified by the urgent relevance of these debates to connectionism. They are inspired to some extent by the work on reduction in the psychological context of Richardson (1979), Hooker (1981), Enc (1983), and the Churchlands (P.M. Churchland 1979, 1985; P.S. Churchland 1986, 1988). Most notably, I am going to assume that the supervenience of one level on another entails the reducibility of the supervening level. A number of philosophers have recently argued for this (for example Rosenberg 1985,

Bacon 1986; both criticised by Kincaid, 1987). Not only does the case hold up, but the resulting conception of reducibility is attractively weaker than that accepted in the traditional positivists' arguments for the reductive unification of science. All that is important for my argument against Clark is that something like my picture of reduction and causal explanation both is plausible and promises a robust justification of the legitimacy of high-level explanations.

REDUCTION AND LEVELS OF EXPLANATION

Outline of a Theory of Reduction and Levels of Explanation

Theories and levels are open to reduction if their contents are. (From here, for convenience, I will talk of intertheoretic reduction, but the account applies equally to interlevel reduction). Reduction as an intertheoretic relation is dependent on an ontological relation between theory-contents, the actual things in the world that true theories quantify over, the actual entities, properties, and relations. I'll be talking about property reduction rather than event reduction or any other sort, but the metaphysics is adaptable to most preferred ontologies.

There are two methods of property reduction. First is plain identity. An identity theory simply identifies F-ness, for instance, with G-ness: There are not two properties, but one. Suppose that an identity theory is successful. Then the content of the theories involved, the properties cited in the theories' explanations, turn out to be literally identical. The theories reduce, the two theories are really one, and the two properties are really one.

Of course, the relationship between the properties in question might be more complex than plain identity. The other tool of reduction, besides identity, is supervenience. One difference between them is this: if one property supervenes on another, there remain two properties, whereas if one property is identical with another, to say there are two properties is strictly false.

Another, and perhaps the defining, difference, between identity and supervenience is that they bear different modalities. If F is identical with G, it is impossible that F be identical to H and not to G as well. Whereas, if F supervenes on G, it remains possible that F might supervene on H, and not on G as well. To put the same point differently, F can supervene on many properties, though it is identical with only one.

We can draw out the modality of this point by using a possible worlds analysis. If F is identical to G, it is so in all possible worlds. But if F supervenes on G, it does so in merely some world(s). In a world where F supervenes on G and on no other property, there would be no actual difference between the state of affairs in which F is identical with G, and that in which F supervenes on G.

The difference between these two cases is a matter not of actuality, but of accompanying modality. For practical purposes, this peculiarly metaphysical, transworld, difference might not be worth worrying about. If you restricted enough the domain of a theory — if, for instance, you restricted it to this world, or to a set of temporal or spatial parts of this world — it would turn out that the class of identical properties and the class of supervenient properties was co-extensive. Of course, the interesting cases are those in which, even within restricted domains, a property supervenes on a whole range of other properties. In these cases, restricting the domain to one particular realization of a supervenient property will often be a pointlessly tedious task: Here the difference between supervenience and identity remains, for practical purposes, marked.

But whatever the details of particular cases, it remains true that properties that supervene can be taxonomized separately, in virtue of the fact that they belong to different transworld classes. This metaphysical analysis gives us a clarification of the notion of levels. One level is different from another not in actuality, but merely in possibility. Levels are distinguished not by the properties they have intrinsically but by the relational properties they bear to other possible worlds. This fact partly serves to explain why levels are so odd.

Compare the case of property reduction by identity. Talk of levels, it seems, is particularly inappropriate. For, if the upper level is identical to the lower level, it is strictly a misnomer to talk of two levels. The only credence the notion of levels can be given in the identity case is a linguistic credence. Identical things can go by different names. For reduction by identity, then, levels are individuated merely linguistically; whereas, for reduction by supervenience, levels are related by their relational properties to other possible worlds.

How then does this metaphysical account of reduction and levels relate to specific problems of explanation in the philosophy of psychology? I suggest that it gives us the materials of a positive alternative to Clark's causal liberalism. His suggestion that the explanatory interest or utility of any equivalence class of systems is sufficient for its legitimacy left puzzles about how high-level explanations can explain, especially causally explain, without citing physical causes. We are owed an account of the relation, whether it is interesting and useful or not, between higher levels of explanation and lower levels.

I suggest, then, that the interest or utility of a level of explanation is neither necessary nor sufficient for the level's legitimacy. Instead, a level of explanation is legitimate if and only if it both:

1. cites real, causally active entities and properties, and
2. is reducible, in the ways specified, to another level of explanation.

Now, Clark's legitimate levels (on some readings at least) do meet the first criterion, since he claims that entities and properties don't have to be physically causally active to be causally active, but I have suggested that more detail needs to be added. That detail is to be found, I suggest, in the spelling out of the second criterion.

I expand first on my negative appraisal of pragmatics in psychological explanation, and discuss the kind of legitimacy that is at issue here, and secondly on how my kind of reductionism should be weak enough to deflate much traditional anti-reductionist criticism. It will then help to reinstate the condition of causal efficacy on explanation, and thus provide robust legitimation for genuine high level explanations.

Reduction, Legitimacy, and Explanatory Utility

The kind of legitimacy for which I have suggested criteria is ontological legitimacy. Explanation, the idea is, cannot just be free-floating: It is, among other things, ontologically committing. This is not intended to be anything like a full-scale theory of explanation. Explanation does a lot of things besides make ontological commitments. In particular, pragmatic considerations will often be of central importance: as van Fraassen suggests (1980), whatever reduces someone's puzzlement can count as an explanation. I am not denying the importance of utility, merely claiming that it isn't all there is to a theory of explanation, deliberately divorcing it from that part of the theory of explanation which arises from taking ontological commitments seriously.

Note first that what is excluded here is the purely epistemological point about what it is for an explanation to be interesting. Many levels of explanation which are legitimate on my criteria will be tedious in the extreme. These will most notably include cases where a higher level explanation cites entities or properties which are defined only functionally, or which are highly disjunctive. Such entities or properties will normally be reducible to a huge disjunction of entities or properties at a lower (micro)level. Examples of this kind would be watches (or the functional state of being a watch), airfoils, crumpled shirts, games, friendships, haircuts, and home runs. In these cases, no pragmatic benefit at all will come from focusing on the lower, reducing, level explanations: Indeed in these cases, as soon as you start to do any reducing at all, there is a likelihood of missing similarities, important to us, which can be understood at higher levels such as the level of description of gross behavior. These things just are realized too variously for the reductive stories to have any pragmatic value. But what you do get from knowledge of the low-level disjunct, or, more commonly, from knowledge that there is a low-level disjunct, is ontological sanction for the high-level construct cited in the explanation. I see no reason why this shouldn't be true even in the large number of cases where the lower level disjunct is open-endedly large (which has been suggested by Fodor (1986a, p. 19), and Kincaid (1987, pp. 344-347), as a problem for reductionism). Inductive confidence that there is a reduction possible in any particular realizing case is all that the reducibility criterion requires. There really are crumpled shirts, neurons, watches, molecules, haircuts and home runs in a way that there really aren't witches, Ptolemaic epicycles, animal spirits, sunrises, gods, and ghosts. But it seems an advantage of the present account that it leaves entirely open the question of which, of those things which there really are, will be reducible to an explanatorily interesting lower level.

All that this shows is that interest is not necessary for legitimacy: not very controversial. We are all too familiar with the fact that our limited epistemological horizons can't cope with the vast amount of genuine things in the world which could feature in (ontologically) legitimate explanations. To dispute Clark's claim that interest is sufficient for legitimacy, I have to show that the converse point holds, too, in other words, that a level of explanation can be interesting and useful without being legitimate.

Sincere theology and parapsychology, eighteenth century phlogiston theory and animal spirits theory, Cartesian dualism, and the like, are all fascinating discourses. But while the levels of explanation employed in such disciplines may be interesting and useful, they are not (ontologically) legitimate, for they posit entities, properties, and processes which are not reducible in my weak sense, do not exist, and have no causal powers. This is not just a cheap appeal to discredited ontologies: The possibility envisaged by eliminativists (error theorists) about any particular level is exactly that the constructs of that level are of the same status as the "denizens of [these] discredited ontologies" (Dennett, 1988, p. 538) were before they were discredited, that we are now on some critical cusp of conceptual change. The point is that it is impossible to know in advance whether any particular level of explanation is analogous to these eliminated levels or to levels, such as macroscopic levels of geological or meteorological explanation, which are reducible and thus legitimate. You can only find out which of these possibilities holds by looking for possible reductions in the particular case.

It can not, in other words, just be assumed that the psychological constructs cited in the higher levels of psychological explanation have the real causal powers they are thought to. Many of them, or things very like them, probably do exist, and probably do have causal powers pretty much like those which people think they do, but if this is so, it is because they are reducible in my sense to the constructs cited in lower level explanations. Only by way of this reducibility can we understand why such explanations work. If they are legitimate, they are so because of their reducibility, not in spite of their irreducibility. The interest of a level of explanation, then, has little or nothing to do with that level's legitimacy.

Varieties of Reductionism

A common challenge to this kind of reducibility constraint on explanation is that it is, or leads automatically to, a much stronger reductionism. This stronger reductionism is often described as a kind of a priori view that basic low-level physics is the only serious theory. Reduction, the complaint goes, would entail the elimination of the reduced levels and their replacement by the only legitimate level: Only the entities described in basic physics are "really real." On this view of reduction, there are no "flow" relations between levels — there is only one level. Clark seems to share this vision of what reductionism amounts to, for he claims that his causal liberalism will allay the fear of "the specter of reduction" (1989a, p. 181).

But this picture is misguided. Reduction in the sense outlined above does not entail elimination. This is impossible to stress too strongly, for the assumption that it does — that successful reduction spells the end of the legitimacy of the constructs of the reduced level or theory — still motivates much hostility toward what are actually weaker versions of a reducibility constraint (this misconstrual runs, for example, through the recent critique of physicalism by Crane & Mellor, 1990; see their criticism of Fodor & Field on p. 193 for one instance). But in fact reduction specifically rules out elimination: Successful, smooth reduction, on the contrary, actually guarantees the reality and the legitimacy of the higher reduced level. Finding out what the higher level constructs are identical with or supervenient on tells you what they are, not that they do not exist.

Of course some attempts to reduce may fail: Nothing like a smooth reduction may be possible. In these cases, reductionism may lead to complete displacement of the higher level, but this will be precisely because reduction has failed (P.M. Churchland, 1979, Section 11; P.S. Churchland, 1986, pp. 278-295; Duran, 1988, pp. 296-299). The reducibility constraint allows for a range of reductive possibilities ranging from smooth, retentive reductions, most notably identities, which "preserve ontology" (Hooker, 1981, p. 201) by guaranteeing the legitimacy of the reduced level or theory, to the opposite extreme where there is nothing to which the higher level reduces, and elimination becomes a live option.

So the reducibility constraint is intended to be sufficiently weak to escape criticism of the a priori scientism of that implausibly strong reductionism just sketched. All that it should include is what is naturalistically explicable within the constraints of physicalist monism. All that it should unproblematically exclude are theories which postulate gods, nonphysical minds, "queer" moral values (in Mackie's (1977) sense), phlogiston, animal spirits, and the like. But the ontological legitimizing of psychological explanation doesn't just mean drawing out the implications of materialism. It must also explain the success of psychological explanation. For understanding of how and why it works, there must be demonstrable confidence that the entities and properties it cites are reducible in the specified sense.

It may, however, still be thought that my reducibility constraint is too strong to do the job I want. I was looking for a principled defence of the condition of causal efficacy against Clark's causal liberalism (and other versions, like Dennett's, of "small-r" realism). My defense is meant to appeal at least to both Fodorian intentional big-R realists and to eliminativists, the two groups Clark sees as "united in [the] mutual error" of the condition of causal efficacy. But then, it may be objected, isn't Fodor in particular notorious for his view that psychology is irreducible to, say, neurophysiology (Fodor, 1981)? And don't functionalists in general support a thesis of the autonomy of psychology from lower level sciences? Haven't I, in other words, misclassified the relevant options on these questions of reduction, causation, and explanation?

I don't think so[2]. That the multiple realizability of psychological states is no bar to a sufficiently weakened reducibility constraint has been argued by a number of reductionists (P.M. Churchland, 1979, p. 112, 1988a; cf. Enc, 1983, Hooker, 1981, Richardson 1979). And here is Fodor in *Psychosemantics:* "It's hard to see ... how one can be a Realist about intentionality without also being, to some extent or other, a Reductionist" (Fodor, 1987, p. 97). The extent to which a Fodorian intentional realist might be a reductionist is captured, I claim, by something very like the weak requirement of reducibility on explanation which I have suggested.

That Fodor could be sympathetic to the kind of account I've sketched is confirmed by his immediately subsequent remarks:

> If the semantic and the intentional are real properties of things, it must
> be in virtue of their identity with (or maybe of their supervenience on?)
> properties that are themselves neither intentional nor semantic. If
> aboutness is real, it must be really something else. (Fodor, 1987, p. 97)

This is a pretty good statement of the reducibility requirement, and it fits neatly with Fodor's Representational Theory of Mind (RTM; see for example Fodor, 1986b). RTM's vindication of common sense psychology requires "a respectable science whose ontology explicitly acknowledges states that exhibit the sorts of properties that common sense attributes to the [propositional] attitudes" (1987, p. 10). This amounts to a commitment to finding "in-the-head reductive correlates of propositional attitudes," such that the correlates can be straightforwardly implicated in the physical causal chain (Clark, 1988a, p. 268; cf. 1988b).

Fodor, then, specifically accepts the condition of causal efficacy on explanation which Clark rejects[3]. For Clark, like Dennett and Wilkes but

---

2 See also Duran (1988, p. 298), discussing extremes of cognitive theories from Pylyshyn to Patricia Churchland: "Virtually no one, so far as I can see, is against the possibility of reduction."

3 For more on Fodor and Pylyshyn's (weak) reductionism (of classical symbol structures to physical structures in the brain) see Fodor and Pylyshyn (1988), pp. 13-14 and note 9. This is why Dennett has described an "imaginary vindication of the language of thought hypothesis" as "a triumphant cascade through Marr's three levels" (Dennett, 1987, p. 227; cf. Clark, 1990a, pp. 200-203)

unlike Fodor and the Churchlands, legitimate explanations don't have to cite properties which are identical with or supervenient on other properties, or which are directly implicated in the causal process leading to behaviour. What unusually unites the eliminativists with Fodor here is a parallel view about the factors relevant to explanatory legitimacy. They agree that legitimate explanation must cite real, causally active entities and properties, and that these must be reducible, in our weak sense, to another level. Of course the Churchlands make much of the radical consequences of reductionism, because their hunch, contrary to Fodor's, is that the search for reductive correlates of propositional attitudes will generally fail. But it is worth noting again that eliminativism will only be an option to the extent that the reductive enterprise fails.

THE VALUE OF HIGH LEVEL EXPLANATIONS

But what is persuasive about the condition of causal efficacy, even when it is spelled out in these weakly reductive fashions? Are there any considerations which make the requirement of reducibility attractive, other than the odd bedfellows it brings together in Fodor and the Churchlands? I think there are. I'll discuss them first in the specific context of cluster analyses of connectionist systems, then draw some general conclusions about Clark's liberalism, and finally look at the consequences of my approach for the debate over the status of common sense psychological explanation.

Cluster Analysis

Remember the way Clark defended the value of high-level explanations of connectionist networks. The partitions given in a cluster analysis, for instance, play no part in a genuine (low-level) causal process explanation (which would be in terms of connectivity weights alone). But this is no bar to, nor is it relevant to, the legitimacy of cluster analytic explanation, for which, says Clark, its utility is sufficient. In particular, it is a level of explanatory generalization at which are grouped only those systems capable of carrying out a particular task, of satisfying a function in extension. It brings together at a useful level of abstraction all and only the range of networks which can "negotiate that cognitive domain" (Clark, 1989a, p. 199).

Two responses to this are possible in the light of my metaphysical digression. The first is the radical one (originally by Paul Churchland), that genuinely causal explanation will be only at the numerical level, because only such an explanation will account for the specific characteristics of the actual network with respect to learning, generalization, performance on degraded input, and the like (P.M. Churchland, 1989a, Section 5; Clark, 1989a, pp. 193-194). The point would be that only a causal process explanation, and not a program explanation, will do justice to the phenomena.

But I don't find this eliminativist response satisfying, in the case of cluster analysis anyway.[4] My hunch is that cluster analysis can give us genuine causal process explanations of the results of processing. This second response accepts the value of cluster analytic explanation, but, in contrast to Clark, also has an account of why they are valuable, why they work. They are valuable because they are causal explanations in the strongest, process sense of causal explanation: because they both (a) cite real, causally active entities, properties, and processes; and (b) are (weakly) reducible, in fact supervene on, lower levels. "Causal program" explanations in general must be identical with or supervenient on lower level (process) explanations to be legitimate. The reducibility explains why they are valuable: because the partitions in state space which they cite, for instance, are really there in state space, constituted by, realized by, and supervenient on the (numerical level) connectivity weights in the particular case.

Causal Liberalism Revisited

This idea has already been applied more generally by Mark Rowlands to the examples given by Jackson and Pettit (Rowlands, 1989). While agreeing that functional and disjunctive properties can play a role in true causal explanations, Rowlands notes that this is because they bear some relation to properties which are causally productive (in the "process" sense). Such a property must be realized in an actual case by a lower level property which is causally productive (Rowlands, 1989, p. 272). "The explanatory capacity of the supervenient disjunctive or functional property rides on the causally productive capacity of the property which realizes it" (p. 273). Only the actual realization of an increase in temperature or of a glass's fragility is causally productive in a particular case. I would add to Rowlands' reading that it is only because of such causally active specific realizations that we say the increase in temperature or the fragility causes (and causally explains) the breaking. In each case, increase in temperature or fragility does cause, because both are supervenient on the particular realization in that case.

The point could be extended to bring into question the utility of the causal program/causal process distinction (on which Clark's causal liberalism is

---

[4] Indeed Churchland later accepts that whether we look to the specific point in weight-space or to partitions in activation space depends, centrally, on what we're doing. He thinks that "while the weights are of essential importance for understanding long-term learning and fundamental conceptual change, the partitions across the activation space, and the prototypical hot-spots they harbor, are much more useful in reckoning the cognitive and behavioral similarities across individuals in the short-term. People react to the world in similar ways not because their underlying weight configurations are closely similar on a synapse-by-synapse comparison, but because their activation spaces are similarly partitioned" (1989b, pp. 234). Utility comes in only here, after the reductive effort, when we already have sophisticated means of relating high level to low level.

based) itself. For antireductionists like Jackson, Pettit, and Clark, seeking to erode fear of "the specter of reduction," the "real" causal processes can surely only occur at the base level of microphysics. For even the numerical levels of connection weights or of synaptic biochemistry are multiply realizable in different configurations of constituent parts: The numerical level stands in the same kind of one – many relation to the subatomic level as does the cluster analytic level to the numerical level itself. To accept the views of causation and explanation espoused by reductionism as the antireductionists construe it would, it seems, lead necessarily to the denial of true causal process explanation at any level above subatomic physics. This, surely, is a *reductio ad absurdum* of their misconstrual of reductionism rather than an accurate picture of a serious view. According to the reductionism they attribute to reductionists, neurophysiological constructs like columnar processing and cell assemblies, or even neurons and their biochemical interactions could not figure in genuine causal process explanation. In Jackson and Pettit's examples, high-level explanation of the glass's breaking in terms of the increase in temperature of the gas inside, or of the glass's fragility, is not in principle any different in causal status to explanation in terms of the impact of molecules on the walls of the vessel (which realizes the increase in temperature), or of the categorical basis of the glass (which realizes its fragility)[5].

Rowlands makes similar observations on the program/process distinction. He thinks that "in itself, the distinction is fundamentally sound:" but this is odd, for he recognizes that "the use of program explanations in science is very widespread indeed ... natural science must deal almost exclusively in program explanations." If this is so, how can the distinction be sound, when one side of it is all but empty? "[A]lmost all the explanatory properties invoked by even a foundational science such as physics" are cited only in program explanations (Rowlands, 1989, p. 271). But apart from showing the emptiness of the distinction he claims to support, Rowlands also reiterates the traditional view that multiple realizability debars reduction: To deny the ubiquity of program explanations even in science is to fall victim to what Blackburn calls the Tractarian View of physical properties: The mistake of supposing that for any physical property there should be a story, in terms of the configuration of some constituent things, saying what it is. (Blackburn, 1991, pp. 206-208).

---

[5] One response here would be to refer to the view of David Braddon-Mitchell and John Fitzpatrick that true causation does occur only at the microstructural level. Only the actual microstructural instantiation of a high level does the causing, and high level regularities merely explain (Braddon-Mitchell and Fitzpatrick, 1990, section 4). I, in contrast, want to maintain true high level causation where suitable reductive relations between levels hold. Braddon-Mitchell and Fitzpatrick tend towards the neo-behaviourist position that the implication of mental states in the causation of action is an unnecessary requirement. Whatever the merits of their view, it won't help Clark, for he is committed to genuine causation at the higher levels of explanation.

The case is supported by the notorious example of the multiple realizability of temperature across different physical bases for solids, gases, plasma, and vacua. But the disjunctive nature of the physical bases is no objection to particular (domain-restricted) reductions. The Tractarian View can be usefully modified and, contra Blackburn, supported by adding the (later) Wittgensteinian point that a family resemblance is all that is required among reductive realizations. There are many possible but somehow related stories, in terms of configurations of constituents, to be told about your average high-level physical property (for weakly reductionist treatments of the temperature case, see Hooker, 1981, pp. 47-49; P.M. Churchland, 1988a, Ch. 2).

Common Sense Psychology and the Condition of Causal Efficacy

Folk-psychological explanation is, for Clark, "just one more layer in rings of ever-more explanatory virtue" (1989a, p. 200). Like other high-level explanations, it groups "apparently disparate physical mechanisms into classes that reflect our particular interests" (p. 201). But the utility of common sense ascriptions of mental states on the basis of behavior, for Clark, implies nothing about in-head processing, about the nature of the "engineering" account of the causes of that behavior (1988a, 1988b). Folk psychology works as a descriptive model which fixes on important regularities in behavior, not because there are any reductive correlates of its explanatory constructs in the head.

But such a defense of common sense psychology against the advance of neurophilosophy is unilluminating: it simply leaves unexplained the relation between the descriptive account and the engineering account. Clark does assert that his criterion of interest for the legitimacy of a level should not be taken to allow that "anything goes" (1989a, p. 201), but he still gives no principled grounds other than interest for distinguishing legitimate from illegitimate explanations. This defect is perhaps partly to be remedied by his commitment to mixed models of cognition, where connectionist and language of thought systems are working in tandem (1989a, Ch.7; 1989c, 1990b). In these cases some aspects of the descriptive project will, presumably, be backed by an engineering, in-the-head story which shares its form. But to the extent that Clark does support the connectionist rejection of causal processing descriptions which mirror the form of natural language semantics, his overview of causal explanation doesn't tell us why common sense explanation works as well as it does.

Even with functional concepts, defined in terms of a causal/functional role and not in terms of the occupant(s) of the role, we still need an account of how all the particular occupants come to fill the role, of what it is that makes them the sorts of things which can fill the role. If you're a functionalist about watches, or about beliefs, you still need a story of how specific physical configurations of lower level entities come to play the role watches or beliefs play. In the watch case, the reductive story will be very tediously disjunctive. Watches are so variously realized that, given our inductive confidence that reducibility could go through in any particular case, we won't tend to do it because it won't be very interesting. But we just don't know yet what reductive stories about mental states and processes would be like, where on the continuous spectrum of reductive possibilities they would fit. Would they reduce smoothly, to the retentive extreme (as suggested by both Fodor's Representational Theory of Mind and O'Brien's connectionist vindication of folk psychology)? Would they prove entirely irreducible, as forecast on the Churchlands' eliminative extreme? Or would they fall somewhere in between (as suggested, for example, by Smolensky's (1988, pp. 59-61) limitivism, which sees high-level cognitive explanation as approximately correct, as falling in the middle of the range of reductive possibilities for high-level explanation).

Tienson, criticizing Clark, has noted that even if mental states are individuated functionally or conceptually, the fact that something satisfies this conceptual demand on a kind of ascription is still an empirical, not a conceptual fact, and requires empirical explanation. The conceptual/functional demand does not, as Tienson puts it, explain its own satisfaction. "Quite the opposite. A satisfied a priori demand requires an empirical explanation. That it be to a considerable degree liquid is a conceptual demand on calling something soup. But its being liquid is an empirical fact, subject to empirical explanation" (Tienson, 1990, p. 160). Without a theory relating causal explanation at different levels to the reductive relations between those levels there seems little prospect of such empirical explanation.

Because Clark is wary of the ontological commitment of explanation, he cannot account for the way genuine true explanations latch onto the world. Explanations must, mostly at least, cite real entities, properties, and processes. If they did not, they wouldn't tend to work as often. But Clark, by exempting high-level constructs from the condition of causal efficacy and the need for (weak) reducibility, leaves them ontologically loose and free-floating. For him, the explanatory utility of high-level explanation is all that is required. But this is to close off a priori the discovery of error and of any possibility of revision of the high level. This attitude is perhaps clearest where Clark is discussing Fodor's attempt to find computational structure in the brain which reductively mirrors the structure of propositional attitudes:

> Fodor's approach is dangerous. By accepting the bogus challenge to produce syntactic brain analogues to linguistic ascriptions of belief contents, he opens the Pandora's box of eliminative materialism. For if such analogues are not found, he must conclude that there are no beliefs and desires. The mere possibility of such a conclusion is surely an effective *reductio ad absurdum* of any theory that gives it house space. (Clark, 1989a, p. 160)

This is a transcendental argument against eliminativism. If any theory allows the possibility that its own falsity would entail eliminativism's truth, that theory must be ruled out a priori as absurd. This is a strange argument, to say the least. Transcendental arguments against eliminativism are at best fairly pointless, since they have no prospect of ever convincing those against whom they are aimed, and at worst seriously misguided. Eliminativism may be implausible, but it is not incoherent (see Devitt's 1990 critique of Boghossian, 1990, for criticism of another such transcendental argument). The spectrum between "big-R" realism and eliminativism about the theoretical analogs of the concepts of common sense psychology is an exhaustive one. To refuse a position on it is to enshrine our present common sense as a priori true, and this could reasonably be considered not so much nicely liberal as dangerously conservative. The polemical point of early eliminativism was to erode the air of "a priori sanctity" (P.M. Churchland, 1982, p. 231) around folk psychology. The folk require a more robust defense than Clark can give them: The price of realism about common sense psychology is the requirement to produce empirical, not conceptual, refutations of eliminativism.

REFERENCES

Bacon, J. (1986). Supervenience, necessary coextension, and reducibility. *Philosophical Studies, 49,* 163-176.

Blackburn, S. (1991). Losing your mind: Physics, identity, and folk burglar prevention. In J. Greenwood (Ed.), *The Future of Folk Psychology.* Cambridge, UK: Cambridge University Press.

Boghossian, R. (1990). The status of content. *Philosophical Review, 99,* 153-184.

Braddon-Mitchell, D., & Fitzgerald, J. (1990). Explanation and the language of thought. *Synthese, 83,* 3-29.

Churchland, P.M. (1979). *Scientific realism and the plasticity of mind.* Cambridge, UK: Cambridge University Press.

Churchland, P.M. (1981). Eliminative materialism and the propositional attitudes. *Journal of Philosophy, 78,* 67-90.

Churchland, P.M. (1982). Is "thinker" a natural kind? *Dialogue, 21,* 223-238.

Churchland, P.M. (1985). Reduction, qualia, and the direct introspection of brain states. *Journal of Philosophy, 82,* 8-28.

Churchland, P.M. (1988a). *Matter and consciousness* (Second ed.). Cambridge, MA: MIT Press.

Churchland, P.M. (1988b). Folk psychology and the explanation of human behavior. *Proceedings of the Aristotelian Society, 62,* 209-221.

Churchland, P.M. (1988c). The ontological status of intentional states: Nailing folk psychology to its perch. *Behavioral and Brain Sciences, 11,* 507-508.

Churchland, P.M. (1989a). On the nature of theories: A neurocomputational perspective. In C.W. Savage (Ed.), *On the nature of theories* (Minnesota Studies in the Philosophy of Science, Vol. 14).

Churchland, P.M. (1989b). Learning and conceptual change. In P.M. Churchland, *A neurocomputational perspective: The nature of mind and the structure of science.* Cambridge, MA: MIT Press.

Churchland, P.M. (1989c). *A neurocomputational perspective: The nature of mind and the structure of science.* Cambridge, MA: MIT Press.

Churchland, P.S. (1986). *Neurophilosophy: Toward a unified science of the mind-brain.* Cambridge, MA: MIT Press.

Churchland, P.S. (1988). Reduction and the neurobiological basis of consciousness. In A.J. Marcel & E.J. Bisiach (Eds.), *Consciousness in contemporary science.* Oxford, UK: Clarendon Press.

Churchland, P.S., & Sejnowski, T.J. (1989). Neural representation and neural computation. In L. Nadel et al. (Eds.), *Neural connections, mental computation.* Cambridge, MA: MIT Press.

Clark, A. (1988a). Thoughts, sentences, and cognitive science. *Philosophical Psychology, 1,* 263-278.

Clark, A. (1988b). Critical notice: Psychosemantics. *Mind, 97,* 605-617.

Clark, A. (1989a). *Microcognition: Philosophy, cognitive science, and parallel distributed processing.* Cambridge, MA: MIT Press.

Clark, A. (1989b). Beyond eliminativism. *Mind and Language, 4,* 251-279.

Clark, A. (1989c). *Connectionism, non-conceptual content, and representational redescription* (Cog. Sci, Research paper CSRP 143). Sussex, UK: University of Sussex.

Clark, A. (1990a). Connectionism, competence, and explanation. *British Journal for the Philosophy of Science, 41,* 195-222.

Clark, A. (1990b). Belief, opinion, and consciousness. *Philosophical Psychology, 3,* 139-154.

Crane, T.M., & Mellor, D.H. (1990). There is no question of physicalism. *Mind, 99,* 185-206.

Dennett, D.C. (1978). *Brainstorms.* Montgomery, VT: Bradford Books.

Dennett, D.C. (1987). *The intentional stance.* Cambridge, MA: MIT Press.

Dennett, D.C. (1988). Precis of *The intentional stance. Behavioral and Brain Sciences, 11,* 495-546.

Devitt, M. (1990). *Transcendentalism about content.* Paper presented at the AAP Conference, Sydney, Australia, July 1990.

Duran, J. (1988). Reductionism and the naturalization of epistemology. *Dialectica, 42,* 295-306.

Elman, J. (1989). *Representation and structure in connectionist models* (Tech. Rep. CRL-8903). San Diego, CA: University of California, San Diego, Center for Research in Language.

Elman, J. (1990). Finding structure in time. *Cognitive Science, 14,* 179-211.

Enc, B. (1983). In defense of the identity theory. *Journal of Philosophy, 80,* 279-298.

Fodor, J.A. (1981). *Representations.* Cambridge, MA: MIT Press.

Fodor, J.A. (1986a). Why paramecia don't have mental representations. *Midwest Studies in Philosophy, 10,* 3-23.

Fodor, J.A. (1986b). Fodor's guide to mental representation: The intelligent auntie's vade-mecum. *Mind, 95,* 76-100.

Fodor, J.A. (1987). *Psychosemantics.* Cambridge, MA: MIT Press.

Fodor, J.A. & Pylyshyn, Z. (1988). Connectionism and cognitive architecture: A critical analysis. Cognition, 28, 3-71.

Hooker, C.A. (1981). Towards a general theory of reduction. *Dialogue, 20,* 38-59, 201-236, 496-529.

Jackson, F., & Pettit, P. (1988). Functionalism and broad content. *Mind, 97,* 381-400.

Kincaid, H. (1987). Supervenience doesn't entail reducibility. *Southern Journal of Philosophy, 25,* 343-356.

Mackie, J. (1977). *Ethics: Inventing right and wrong.* Harmondsworth, UK: Penguin.

Marr, D. (1977). Artificial intelligence: A personal view. In J. Haugeland (Ed.), *Mind design.* Cambridge, MA: MIT Press.

Marr, D. (1982). *Vision,* Cambridge, MA: MIT Press.

O'Brien, G. (1991). Is connectionism common sense? *Philosophical Psychology, 4,* 165-178.

O'Brien, G. (1993). The connectionist vindication of folk psychology. In S. Christensen & D. Turner (Eds.), *Folk psychology.* Hillsdale, NJ: Erlbaum.

Peacocke, C. (1986). Explanation in computational psychology: Language, perception and level. *Mind and Language, 1,* 101-123.

Price, H. (1988). *Facts and the function of truth.* Oxford, UK: Blackwell.

Ramsey, W., Stich, S.P., & Garon, J. (1990). Connectionism, eliminativism, and the future of folk psychology. In J. Tomberlin (Ed.), *Philosophical Perspectives,* Vol. 4, Atascadero, California: Ridgeview Press.

Richardson, R.C. (1979). Functionalism and Reductionism. *Philosophy of Science, 46,* 533-558.

Rorty, R. (1980). *Philosophy and the mirror of nature.* Princeton, NJ: Princeton University Press.

Rorty, R. (1983). Method and morality. In P. Rabinow et al. (Eds.), *Social science as moral inquiry.* New York: Columbia University Press.

Rosenberg, A. (1985). *The structure of biological science.* Cambridge, UK: Cambridge University Press.

Rosenberg, C.R., & Sejnowski, T.J. (1987). Parallel networks that learn to pronounce English text. *Complex Systems, 1,* 145-168.

Rowlands, M. (1989). Discussion of Jackson and Pettit, "Functionalism and broad content". *Mind, 98,* 269-275.

Smolensky, P. (1988). On the proper treatment of connectionism. *Behavioral and Brain Sciences, 11,* 1-73.

Stich, S.P. (1988a). From connectionism to eliminativism. *Behavioral and Brain Sciences, 11,* 53-54.

Stich, S.P. (1988b). Connectionism, Realism and realism. *Behavioral and Brain Sciences, 11,* 531-532.

Sutton, J. (1993). *Connecting memory traces: studies of neurophilosophical theories of memory, mental representation, and personal identity from descartes to new connectionism.* Doctoral dissertation, University of Sydney, Australia.

Tienson, J. (1990). Is this any way to be a realist? *Philosophical Psychology, 3,* 155-164.

van Fraassen, B. (1980). *The scientific image.* Oxford, UK: Oxford University Press.

Wilkes, K.V. (1984). Pragmatics in science and theory in common sense. *Inquiry, 27,* 339-361.

Wilkes, K.V. (1986). Nemo psychologicus nisi physiologicus. *Inquiry, 29,* 165-185.

Author Index

Page numbers in *italics* indicate figures

A

Abelson, H., 274, *282*
Abelson, R.P., 72, *76*
Adams, I.D., *179*
Addanki, S., 189, *210*
Alexander, J., 341, *346*
Alho, K., 107, *118*
Alkon, D.L., 59, *59*
Allen, J.F., 145, 149, 150, *156*
Amodei, N., 54, *61*
Anderson, C.W., 56, *59*
Anderson, J.R., 31, *43*, 56, *59*, 79, 80, 89, 90, 93, 96, *100*, *101*, 119, *125*, 239, *269*
Austin, J.L., 278, 279, *282*

B

Baars, B.J., vi, *vii*
Bacon, J., 355, *366*
Badler, N.I., 184, *186*
Bain, J.D., 20, 22, 28, *29*, 31, 39, 42, *43*
Bakiri, G., *179*
Balachandran, M., 200, *210*
Barlow, H., 227, *235*
Barnes, B., 344, *345*
Barrow, H., 229, *239*
Barsalou, L.W., 192, 194, 196, *210*
Bartlett, F.C., 238, 252, *269*
Barto, A.G., 49, 50, 52, 55, 56, *59*, *62*
Basar, E., 104, 116, *117*
Baxter, B., 168, *179*
Baylor, G.W., 20, *28*
Begg, I., 2, *16*
Bellingham, W.P., 55, *59*
Benyon, D., 72, *76*
Berbaum, K., 142, *144*
Berkeley, G., 268, *269*
Bever, T., 142, *144*
Biah, M.A., 170, *180*
Biederman, I., 227, *235*
Blackburn, S., 363, *366*
Blake, R., 120, 121, *125*
Block, N., 237, 254, *269*

Bloomfield, B.P., 345, *345*
Boakes, R., 45, *59*
Bobrow, D.G., 203, *210*
Boden, M.A., 345, *345*
Bodker, S., 67, *71*
Boghossian, P., 305, 308–310, *314*, 366, *366*
Boies, S.J., 5, *17*
Boring, E.G., 45, *59*
Bounds, D.G., 168, 169, *179*
Bower, G.H., 55, *59*
Braddon-Mitchell, D., 363n, *366*
Brady, M., 183, *186*
Bressler, S.L., 104, *117*
Brewer, W.F., 3, *16*
Broadbent, D.E., 158, 159, *165*
Brooks, D.N., 105, *118*
Brooks, L.R., 159, *165*
Brooks, M.J., 128, 129, 143, *144*
Brooks, R.A., 182, *186*
Brown, A., 64, *76*
Brown, J.S., 20, *29*, 203, *210*
Bruce, V., 121, 124, *125*
Bruner, J., vi, *vii*
Bullemer, P., 2, 4, *17*
Bullock, M., 22, *28*
Butterfield, H., 342, *346*

C

Capaldi, E.J., 53, *59*
Carberry, S., 145, 155, *156*
Carlson, R.A., 90, *101*
Carpenito, L.J., 219n, 220, *224*
Carpenter, P., 65, *76*
Chalmers, D.J., 158, 160, *165*
Chambers, D., 239, 240, 242, 243, 243, 251, 255–258, 261, 265, 266, 266n, *269–271*
Chan, M., 168, *179*
Chellappa, R., 129, *144*
Chesney, G.L., 103, *118*
Childers, D.G., 104, *117*
Chojnacki, W., 129, *144*
Chung, C.S., 142, *144*

369

Subject Index

Page numbers in *italics* indicate figures

A

abdominal pain, diagnosis of, 167-79
abduction, 205-6
abstract working memory, 159
abstraction
    functional level theory, 295
    levels of description, 297, 298
ACT* theory of skill acquisition, 79-80, 96
actions, 183-5
activation space, 354, 362n
activity-exercise pattern assessment, 219-22
activity theory, 66, 67
adaptive filters, 231
additive memory, 230
addresses, 327n
    see also memory address register
adverbial theory of sensory experience, 253
Against Method, 342
aggregation, 196, 198
algorithmic model of knowledge, 336, 339
alien processing, 280
ambiguity switching, 258
AMRs, *see* Autonomous Mobile Robots
analogical mapping, *23,* 24, 28
analytic processing, 158
anatomical functions, 290-2
animal conditioning, 58-9
ANN analysis, 104, 110-13, *112,* 114-17
anthropomorphism, in computing, 275, 276
anticipation, 47, *48,* 49
appendicitis, 167-8, 171, 178
approximation, 196
archetype, 189, 206, 209
articulation, of attributes, 195
artificial grammar, 1-2, 3-4
artificial intelligence
    algorithms, 228, 230
    Autonomous Mobile Robots, 183, 186
    classical symbol-systems, 347
    declarative representations, 228-30
    expert systems and social science, 335, 345

generality, 339-41
generalization, 189
knowledge typology, 336-8
logicist emphasis of paradigms, 344
methodologies, 343, 344
numerical representations, 226, 228-30
replication of basic skills, 339-40
symbolic representations, 228-9
artificial lesions, 349, 350
artificial neural network analysis, 104, 110-17, *112*
ascription, of thought, 351-2, 364, 365
associationist philosophy, 50, 163
associative learning, 4, 45-62
associative memory
    Anderson's model, 31
    extension of matrix model, 32-5
    Gregson's model, 35
    matrix model, 31-5, 42
    neural networks, 230
    nonlinear, 31-42
    TODAM model, 31, 42
associative strengths, classical conditioning, 50-2, 54
asymetry, levels of description, 289-92
asymptotes, 96, 100
attitudes, 306
attribute matching, 205-6
attributes, 190-1, 195-6, 201, 204, 205-6, 207, 209
attribution, beliefs and desires, 302
autoepistemic logic, 281
automatice information processing, 226
Autonomous Mobile Robots, 181-8
    analysis of motion, 183-5
    behavior, 185
    cognitive view, 183
    development methodology, 185-6
    function, 185
    trends in development, 182-3
autonomy, 183, 186
awareness, in learning, 3-16